Batsford Chess Library

John Nunn's Best Games 1985-1993

John Nunn

An Owl Book
Henry Holt and Company
New York

Henry Holt and Company, Inc.
Publishers since 1866
115 West 18th Street
New York, New York 10011

Henry Holt® is a registered
trademark of Henry Holt and Company, Inc.

First published in the United States in 1995 by
Henry Holt and Company, Inc.
Originally published in Great Britain in 1995 by
B. T. Batsford Ltd.

Library of Congress Catalog Card Number: 94-72762

ISBN 0-8050-3899-X (An Owl Book: pbk.)

First American Edition—1995

Printed in the United Kingdom
All first editions are printed on acid-free paper.∞

10 9 8 7 6 5 4 3 2 1

Editorial Panel: Mark Dvoretsky, John Nunn, Jon Speelman
General Adviser: Raymond Keene OBE
Managing Editor: Graham Burgess

Contents

Introduction

It is customary for the author of a *Best Games* book to write something about how the games were chosen and annotated, and I would not care to break with this tradition. Just as chess players are always relieved to hear the words 'My speech will be very short' at opening ceremonies, readers may be assured that this introduction is of absolutely minimal length, and that they will soon be on to the chess.

I have tried to adhere to the title of the book and choose games of the highest quality, regardless of the strength of the opposition or the sporting significance of the games. Readers searching for my win against Karpov at Rotterdam 1989, for example, will find it is not included, as the win resulted from a serious error by Karpov in time-trouble. Most of the games are against grandmasters. It is only too easy to produce a flashy combination against inferior opposition; although many famous games resulted from such circumstances, they are often false brilliancies produced by players who know they are going to win in any case. High-quality chess depends on having well-matched opponents.

There is inevitably a subjective element in the selection. However, it turns out that the games chosen offer a good cross-section of tournament play, from opening innovations through to tactical maelstroms, king-side attacks to positional squeezes. Long endgames are few and far between, but that is a true reflection of my chess style.

The book starts where *Secrets of Grandmaster Play* left off; indeed, the last game of that book was from round 2 of Wijk aan Zee 1985, and this book begins with my game from round 11 of the same event. The 40 games are arranged in chronological order, and represent my best efforts up to mid-1993.

Readers will find the style somewhat different from that of *Secrets of Grandmaster Play*, since this book is entirely my own effort and responsibility. I have included introductions to the games informing readers about the circumstances of each game, as external conditions can influence the moves played. The book is not all hard work since I have added some anecdotes and general commentary about the chess world to provide a break from the detailed analysis.

I would like to say a few words about the analysis itself. Readers may notice that some of the games have been previously annotated in magazines (this is not unusual in *Best Games* books). However, as these magazines were published in a number of different countries, it is unlikely that any individual reader will have seen more than a handful of the games annotated before. More importantly, I have thoroughly re-analysed each game for this book and added considerable general explanation, while removing outdated opening analysis. In many cases this has led to a fundamental reassessment of the whole game.

My quest for accuracy has been aided by recent technological developments. All the analysis was checked by computer, mainly by the *Mephisto Genius 2*, but a few of the later games were checked by an early version of *Fritz 3*. It turned out that the computer's help was only valuable in a certain range of tactical positions, but this type of position occurs relatively often in my games. The computer checking had two surprising results. First of all, an embarrassing number of analytical oversights were revealed and corrected. Secondly, the computer often suggested a move which I hadn't considered at all during the game. Usually the move was inferior, but sometimes the computer's suggestion was genuinely interesting and made me wonder how much human players limit themselves by operating with patterns. It is notoriously hard to see a move which does not fit any recognised pattern.

Finally, although the publishers allowed me a generous allocation of 320 pages I have, as usual, finished exactly on page 320, and then only by removing one game and all the indexes. However, the table of contents includes sufficient information for most purposes. The numbered items represent complete games, the others are game fragments. The tournament is given, followed by the *ECO* (*Encyclopedia of Chess Openings* – a standard method of classifying chess openings) code for the game.

Particular thanks go to Graham Burgess, who spent many long hours correcting the proofs of this book.

1985

It is common knowledge that Hastings is the oldest chess tournament in the world, but it is less well-known that the Hoogovens Chess Festival is the second oldest. In recent years it has been held in the tiny windswept town of Wijk aan Zee on the Dutch coast. The Hoogovens Festival has been held every year since 1938 with the exception of 1945. Chess players know it very well for its famous closing dinner, consisting entirely of pea soup, in memory of the war years when pea soap was the only food available. Many a famous grandmaster has sat waiting for the main course to arrive, only to be sadly disillusioned by his colleagues! The word 'Hoogovens' means 'high ovens' and is the name of the steel and aluminium company which sponsors the tournament, and has continued loyally to do so despite the difficult financial climate in the European steel industry.

While playing in such a small town is not to everybody's taste, I have always enjoyed participating at Wijk aan Zee and have made many friends there. The 1985 tournament was a success for me; Timman played very well to win with 9/13, but I was satisfied to share second place with Beliavsky on 8 points. My second round win against Beliavsky was given in *Secrets of Grandmaster Play*, but after a setback in the middle of the event when I lost badly to Romanishin, the following win, played in round 11, put me back on track for a good final result.

Game 1
J.Nunn – E.Lobron
Wijk aan Zee 1985
Caro-Kann

1	e4	c6
2	d4	d5
3	e5	♗f5
4	h4	

Round about 1985, I quite often played the line 4 ♘c3 e6 5 g4 ♗g6 6 ♘ge2, but for this game I decided to surprise Lobron by adopting an old variation played by Tal during the 1960s.

4 ...   c5?!

It is quite possible to play 3 e5 c5, so one might suppose that this represents an improved version, since White has spent a tempo on the apparently worthless move h4. But h4 turns out to be unexpectedly useful, because if Black plays ...e6, then the bishop at f5 can easily be trapped by g4, followed by f3 and h5 (if necessary). This makes it hard for Black to develop his kingside pieces.

Other lines are based on 4...h6 and 4...h5. Today, the latter move is thought to be soundest.

5 dxc5   ♘c6

5...♕c7 6 ♘c3 ♘c6 (6...♕xe5+ 7 ♗e3 is good for White, for example 7...♘f6 8 ♘f3 ♕c7 9 ♘xd5 ♘xd5 10 ♕xd5 e6 11 ♗b5+ keeping the extra pawn) 7 ♘f3 ♖d8 8 ♘b5 ♕c8 was played in Tal-Botvinnik, Moscow Wch (16) 1961 and now Smyslov's suggestion 9 c3 favours White.

After 5...♘c6 White's position certainly appears ugly; up to now he has only made pawn moves. His strategy is to try to keep the extra pawn on c5. The importance of this pawn lies partly in the material it represents, but mainly in the fact that while the pawn remains on c5, Black cannot develop his f8 bishop to a reasonable square. The e5 pawn is also weak, so White has to exchange the knight which attacks e5.

6 ♗b5   ♕a5+

Black is handicapped by the fact that 6...e6 loses a piece to 7 ♗xc6+ followed by 8 g4.

7 ♘c3   0-0-0

A provocative move since White has a dangerous pawn mass on the queenside. On the other hand Black is obliged to act quickly or else White keeps his pawn and gets a strong grip on the dark squares.

8 ♗xc6   bxc6

Not 8...d4 9 ♗xb7+! ♔c7 (the lines 9...♔xb7 10 ♕f3+ ♔c7 11 ♗d2 ♕xc5 12 ♕xf5 dxc3 13 ♗xc3 and 9...♔b8 10 b4! ♕xb4 11 ♖b1 ♕xc3+ 12 ♗d2 ♕xc2 13 ♗e4+! are winning for White) 10 e6! fxe6 (10...♕xc5 11 ♗a6 wins after 11...dxc3 12 ♗f4+ ♖d6 13 ♕f3 or 11...fxe6 12 ♕f3 transposing) 11 ♕f3 ♕xc5 12 ♗a6 and White wins.

9 ♕d4 *(1)*

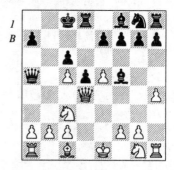

A practical decision; after 9 ♗e3 e6 White would be virtually forced to transpose to the game by 10 ♕d4

and he would have the additional headache of working out the consequences of 9 ♗e3 d4 10 ♗xd4 e6.

9 ...   e6

After 9...♗xc2 10 e6! fxe6 11 ♘f3 followed by ♘e5 Black has a horribly congested position. This line is interesting because White goes from being a pawn up to being a pawn down. Grabbing a pawn does not mean that you have to play defensively no matter what happens; you should still be on the lookout for attacking possibilities, even if this involves returning the extra material and more!

In a later game Yudasin-Sapis, Leningrad II 1989, Black played 9...h5, and after 10 b4 ♕a6 11 a4 ♕c4 12 ♕xc4 dxc4 13 ♖a2 e6 14 a5! (preventing ...a5 by Black, which would allow the f8 bishop to re-enter the game) ♘e7 15 ♘f3 ♘d5 16 ♘xd5 ♖xd5 17 0-0 ♗e7 18 ♗e3 ♖hd8 19 c3 White had consolidated his extra pawn and eventually won.

10 ♗e3

White has a choice of two different plans. The first is to castle queenside, defending all his pawns and hoping to exploit his material advantage. The problem is that Black can undermine White's centre by ...f6 and develop active piece play based on the two bishops and mobile central pawns. The second plan is to play for a queenside attack based on b4-b5 before Black can develop

counterplay. However, the immediate 10 b4 ♕a6 11 a4 is met by 11...♕c4 12 ♕xc4 dxc4, and because Black has played ...e6 instead of the less useful ...h5, White cannot both defend the c2 pawn and prevent ...a5.

10 ...   h5!

Black cannot play 10...♗xc2 11 ♖c1 ♗f5 (11...♗e4 12 b4 ♕a6 13 ♘xe4 dxe4 14 ♕xe4) 12 g4 ♘e7, when 13 gxf5 ♘xf5 14 ♕a4 wins a piece. After 10...h5!, however, Black threatens both ...♗xc2 and ...♘h6-g4, winning the c5 pawn by eliminating the e3 bishop.

11 0-0-0

It was also good to switch to Plan B by 11 ♘f3 ♘h6 (11...♗xc2 12 0-0 will very likely transpose) 12 0-0 ♗xc2 13 b4 ♕a6 14 ♕d2 ♗g6 15 b5 cxb5 16 ♘d4, with a very dangerous attack for White. This line again shows a reversal of material balance.

11 ...   ♘h6

12 f3

White cannot contemplate b4 with his king on the queenside, so he must prevent ...♘g4.

Judging this position is not easy. White has taken on a big responsibility by aiming to keep his extra pawn, and the many pawn moves he has made are an uncomfortable, if necessary, corollary. If White can maintain the *status quo* while he completes his development, then he will be well on his way to victory. But like a large mortgage, a small change in circumstances may mean that the burden proves too much for White's pieces, and then Black will be quick to repossess White's property.

12   ...   f6

This allows Black to develop a strong initiative, albeit at the cost of another pawn, but the complications eventually favour White. 12...♗e7 (12...♗xc2 13 ♔xc2 ♘f5 14 ♕f4 g6 15 ♘h3 followed by ♘g5 doesn't work, while after 12...♗g6 White can play 13 g4, keeping the knight out) 13 ♗g5! (13 ♘ge2 f6 14 exf6 ♗xf6 15 ♕d2 e5 is clearly good for Black) virtually forces Black to give up the exchange by 13...♗xc5 14 ♗xd8 ♖xd8 since the exchange of bishops would nullify Black's initiative. In the resulting position Black has some play for the sacrificed material, but after 15 ♕a4 ♕b6 16 ♘ge2 White holds the advantage.

13   exf6   gxf6

When you are already material up, it is often hard to judge whether to grab further material or to be content with the current material advantage. The advantage of greed is that it creates extra possibilities for fending off the attack by returning material later; the disadvantage is that you may overstep the mark and be unnecessarily mated. This case is quite clear; the pawn White takes is part of Black's dangerous central pawn mass, and if White didn't take it then Black would develop a similar initiative in any case.

14   ♕xf6   ♖h7

14...♖g8 15 ♗xh6 ♖g6 (15...♖xg2 16 ♘ge2 ♖g6 17 ♕xf8 ♖xf8 18 ♗xf8 is even better for White) 16 ♕xf8 ♖xf8 17 ♗xf8 ♖xg2 18 ♘ge2 is very good for White.

15   ♘ge2   ♗g7

16   ♕g5 *(2)*

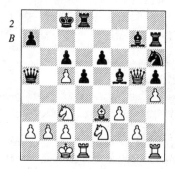

16   ...   ♘f7

Or: 1) **16...e5** 17 ♕xh5! d4 18 ♗xh6 ♗xh6+ 19 ♔b1 ♖f8 (19...♗e6 20 ♕g6) 20 ♘e4 ♗e3 21 ♘d6+ ♔b8 22 ♕xf5 ♖xf5 23 ♘xf5 ♕xc5 24 ♘xe3 dxe3 25 ♖d3 and White's two connected passed pawns start rolling before Black can develop any effective counterplay.

2) **16...♖g8** 17 ♕f4 ♗xc3 (or 17...e5 18 ♕a4 ♕xa4 19 ♘xa4 and the extra material is more important than Black's piece activity) 18 ♘xc3 ♖xg2 19 ♖h2 and White has nullified the attack by returning one of the two pawns.

17 ♕g3 e5

17...♘e5 18 ♘d4 ♘c4 19 ♘xc6 is good for White.

18 ♔b1! d4 *(3)*

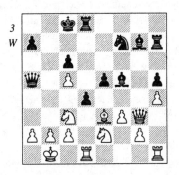

Black has given up too much material to play slowly.

19 ♗g5 dxc3

After 19...♖d7 20 ♘e4 White defends either by 21 ♘c1 followed by ♘b3, or by 21 ♖d3, while after 19...♘xg5 20 ♕xg5 ♗e6 21 ♕g6 Black loses more material.

20 ♗xd8 ♕a4

This loses by force but the alternative 20...♘xd8 21 ♘xc3 was also unpleasant, for example 21...♗f6 (21...♕xc5 22 ♖xd8+ ♔xd8 23 ♕g5+ and 21...♘e6 22 ♘e4 ♗xe4 23 fxe4 ♕xc5 24 ♕g6 are winning for White) 22 ♘e4 ♗xe4 23 fxe4 ♕xc5 24 ♕g6 ♕e7 25 ♖df1 ♗h8 and White has a material and positional advantage.

21 b3!

21 ♘xc3 ♕xc2+ 22 ♔a1 ♖xd8 is completely unclear.

21 ... ♗xc2+

21...♕a3 22 ♘xc3 wins because 22...♘xd8 is met by ♕g5.

22 ♔xc2 ♕xa2+

23 ♔xc3 e4+

23...♕xe2 (23...♘xd8 24 ♕h3+ ♔b7 25 ♕d7+ ♔a6 26 ♖a1 e4+ 27 ♘d4 wins the queen) 24 ♕h3+ ♔b8 25 ♗c7+ ♔b7 (Black's moves are forced in order to avoid mate) 26 ♕d7! gives White a decisive attack because 26...e4+ is met by the cross-check 27 ♗e5+.

24 ♔b4! *(4)*

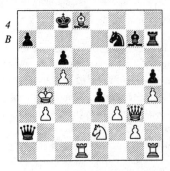

White's king is surprisingly safe on this square. The bishop on d8 prevents mate by ...a5+, and too many Black pieces stand between the rook on h7 and the juicy check on b7. Since 24...♘xd8 25 ♕h3+ ♔b7 26 ♕d7+ ♔a6 27 ♕c8+ mates next move and 24...♗e5 loses to 25 ♕g8, Black has to waste a tempo defending against the mate at c7.

24 ... ♘e5

25 ♘c3 ♕b2

Or 25...♘d3+ 26 ♖xd3 ♗xc3+ 27 ♔xc3 (27 ♖xc3 ♖b7+ 28 ♗b6 a5+ 29 ♔c4 ♕e2+ is less clear-cut) exd3 28 ♕g8 ♕c2+ 29 ♔b4 and White wins because 29...♖b7+ 30 ♗b6+ mates in three more moves.

26   fxe4

The simplest since Black cannot improve his position, for example 26...♗f8 27 ♕xe5 ♖b7+ 28 ♔c4 ♕xb3+ 29 ♔d3 ♖d7+ 30 ♔e3 or 26...♗f6 27 ♕g8 ♖g7 28 ♕e6+ ♔b8 29 ♗xf6 ♖b7+ 30 ♔a4. The move played is no better.

26	...	♗h8
27	♕g8	1-0

My next tournament was the Commonwealth Championship, which was held in the London Docklands during February 1985. This was at the tail end of the period during which the London Docklands Development Corporation (LDDC) sponsored chess. They had supported a number of chess events, in particular the USSR v Rest of the World match held in June 1984.

Unfortunately, the playing conditions for the Commonwealth Championship weren't very good. Most notably, a sunny day meant that it was almost impossible to play because the low angle of the sun in February meant that it was shining directly into one's eyes. The arbiters therefore arranged to stick paper over the offending windows, while leaving others exposed in order to avoid plunging the room into darkness. Owing to the rotation of the earth, these pieces of paper had to be gradually shifted from one window to another as the afternoon progressed. The sight of arbiters perched on chairs clutching paper and sticky tape gradually became commonplace, and the players turned their attention back to the chess.

The event was not a great success for me; I experimented with different openings, but learned the hard way that openings have to be thoroughly prepared before being used in tournament play. However, I did win two attractive games.

Game 2

J.Nunn – M.Chandler

London (Commonwealth Ch) 1985

Sicilian Najdorf

1	e4	c5	3	d4	cxd4
2	♘f3	d6	4	♘xd4	♘f6

5 ♘c3   a6
6 ♗g5

At the time I didn't use 6 ♗g5 very often, but for this game I turned to it because I knew Chandler favoured lines with an early ...♕c7. Kasparov used these double-edged lines in his youth, but he was always exceptionally well-prepared. I intended to try a very sharp idea against Chandler; the main problem with this idea was that if Black negotiated the complications correctly, the position would becomes very drawish. In some sense, therefore, the line was a bit of a bluff. In the end I decided the risk was justified. I would never recommend playing a line which is simply unsound, but in this case only half a point was at stake since best play led to a probable draw. It also makes little sense to use such a line against a significantly weaker opponent, because you can expect to outplay such an opponent in a normal position. A draw against Chandler would not be such a bad result, even with White, but first of all he had to find his way through the complications...

6 ...   e6
7 f4   ♕c7

In this line Black postpones natural developing moves such as ...♗e7 and ...♘bd7 in favour of immediate queenside play based on ...b5. Although 7...♕c7 has never been very popular, it came into prominence

during the early 1980s when Kasparov adopted it with success.

8 ♕f3   b5
9 f5!? (5)

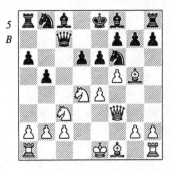

5
B

This was the new idea. The pressure against the pawn on e6 makes ...♗b7 impossible and normal development with 9...♗e7 fails to 10 fxe6 fxe6 11 e5 dxe5 (11...♗b7 12 ♘xe6) 12 ♘dxb5 and 13 ♕xa8. In fact, Black has only two playable moves, 9...♘c6 and 9...b4.

9 ...   ♘c6

After long thought Black decided to avoid the complications of 9...b4. Since 9...♘c6 seems good for White, 9...b4 represents the critical continuation. The following analysis is based on what I wrote at the time, updated to take into account more recent developments.

After 9...b4 10 ♘cb5! (10 fxe6 bxc3 11 ♗xf6 cxb2 12 ♖b1 gxf6 13 ♕xf6 ♕c3+ 14 ♔f2 fxe6 15 ♕xh8 ♘c6 wins for Black) axb5 there are two lines for White:

1) **11 fxe6** ♗e7 12 e5 dxe5 13 ♗xf6 (13 ♘xb5 ♕b7 14 ♕xb7 ♗xb7 favoured Black in the game Piaeren-Averkin, USSR 1969) gxf6 14 ♗xb5+ ♔f8 15 ♘f5 ♗xe6 (after 15...fxe6 16 ♘xe7 ♔xe7 17 ♕xa8 ♕b6 18 ♕a4 ♕d4 19 a3 ♗d7, Murei-Spraggett, Paris Ch 1991, White played 20 ♕xb4+? and lost; 20 ♗xd7! ♕e3+ 21 ♔f1 ♕f4+ 22 ♔e2 ♕e4+ 23 ♔d1 was better, with advantage to White) 16 ♘xe7 ♖a5 17 ♕xf6 ♖xb5 18 ♖f1 ♕xc2 19 ♕xe6 ♕e4+, Murei-Yudasin, Podolsk 1991, and the game ends in perpetual check.

2) **11 ♗xb5+** ♗d7 (11...♗e7 12 fxe6 followed by 0-0 or ♖f1 is very dangerous; if any other piece goes to d7, White takes on e6 in any case) 12 fxe6 ♗xb5 13 ♘xb5 and now we have a further branch:

2a) **13...♕b7** 14 ♗xf6 gxf6 was analysed in *New in Chess*. The continuations 15 0-0 ♕xb5 16 ♕xf6 ♕e5 and 15 ♕xf6 ♕xe4+ 16 ♔d1 ♕d5+ 17 ♔c1 ♕xb5 18 exf7+ ♔d7 19 ♕xh8 ♕g5+ 20 ♔b1 ♕xg2 were given as good for Black, while 15 exf7+ ♔xf7 16 0-0 ♘d7 17 ♕h5+ was recommended as being good for White. However, this latter line can be improved by 15 exf7+ ♕xf7! 16 e5 ♖a5! and White has little compensation for the piece. Fortunately the variation 15 0-0 ♕xb5 16 ♕xf6 ♕e5 can be continued by 17 ♕xf7+ ♔d8 18 ♕b7. If Black defends the

rook (e.g. by 18...♕c5+ 19 ♔h1 ♕c6) he loses to 20 ♖xf8+ ♖xf8 21 e7+ ♔e8 22 exf8♕+ ♔xf8 23 ♖f1+, while if he tries 18...d5, hoping for 19 ♕xa8 ♗d6 with counterplay, then 19 ♖f5 ♕d4+ 20 ♔h1 is crushing.

2b) **13...♕c5** 14 ♗xf6 and now there are two lines:

2b1) **14...fxe6** 15 ♘d4! (15 ♕h3 gxf6 16 ♕xe6+ ♗e7 17 0-0-0 ♕xb5 18 ♕c8+ ♔f7 19 ♕xh8 ♖xa2 20 ♕xh7+ ½-½, Monin-Kopylov, corr. 1988) gxf6 16 ♘xe6 (16 ♕xf6? ♕e5) ♕c4 17 ♕xf6 ♘d7 (17...♕xe4+ 18 ♔d1 only opens up fresh lines of attack against Black's king) 18 ♘c7+ ♕xc7 19 ♕xh8 ♘e5 20 0-0 ♕g7 21 ♖xf8+ ♕xf8 22 ♕xh7 and White has a slight advantage, according to Rashkovsky.

2b2) **14...♕xb5** 15 ♗xg7 (15 e5 fxe6 16 ♕xa8 gxf6 17 0-0-0 fxe5 18 ♕f3 ♗e7 was good for Black in the game Luther-Rashkovsky, Sverdlovsk 1989) ♗xg7 16 ♕xf7+ ♔d8 17 ♕xg7 ♖e8 *(6)* reaches the critical position:

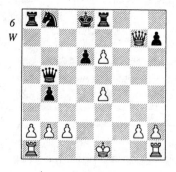

Here White may play 18 0-0-0 or 18 ♖f1. After **18 0-0-0** (given as slightly better for White by Gaprindashvili and Ubilava in *Informator*) ♖xe6 (18...♖xa2 19 ♖xd6+ ♔c8 20 b3 is very good for White) the analysis stops in both *Informator* and *New in Chess*. Although White has three pawns for the piece, Black's king will be well defended if he can play ...♘d7, while White's own king is in trouble because it is hard to defend a2. 19 ♕g8+ is one possibility (19 ♖hf1 ♘d7 is good for Black), when 19...♔d7 20 ♖hf1 is dangerous, so Black's best move is 19...♕e8, when he seems to have few problems. Perhaps White's best move is 19 ♖d5!, gaining a useful tempo to double rooks, with chances for both sides.

New in Chess awarded the alternative **18 ♖f1** an exclamation mark; Black must reply 18...b3! in order to expose White's king (18...♖xe6 19 ♖f8+ ♖e8 20 0-0-0 is very good for White). After 19 cxb3 Black has tried:

1) **19...♕b4+** 20 ♔f2 ♕c5+ and now the game Velimirović-Gaprindashvili, Bela Crkva 1984 continued 21 ♔g3 ♖a7 22 ♕f6+ ♖ae7 23 ♖ad1 and ended in a draw. However, *Informator* recommends 21 ♔e2 ♕b5+ (21...♖a7 22 ♕f6+ ♖ae7 23 ♖ac1 gives White an edge) 22 ♔e3 ♕c5+ 23 ♕d4 ♕xd4+ 24 ♔xd4 as being clearly better for White.

2) **19...♕a5+** 20 ♔d1 ♕h5+ 21 g4 ♕b5 22 ♖f3 ♖xe6 23 ♖f8+ ♖e8 24 ♕f6+ ♔c7 25 ♖f7+ ♔b6 26 ♕xd6+ ♘c6 27 ♖f5 ♖ad8 28 ♖xb5+ ♔xb5 was equal in Hector-Rashkovsky, Snekkersten 1992.

It may appear that 19 cxb3 is completely forced, but this is not so; in Hertzler-Ganesan, corr. 1991/2, White played the incredible 19 0-0-0!?, when 19...bxa2 loses to 20 ♖xd6+ ♔c8 21 ♕c3+ ♔b7 22 ♖f7+ with a mating attack. Black replied 19...♕c5 and won after 20 ♕f6+? ♔c7 21 axb3 ♘c6 22 ♕g7+ ♔b6 23 ♖f7? ♖g8 24 ♖b7+ ♔a6 25 ♕c7 ♖ac8 26 ♕d7 ♖gd8 0-1. Ganesan correctly points out that 20 axb3! would have been much more dangerous.

These lines have a certain drawish tendency, both because White's king is exposed to perpetual check and because many endings are drawn even if White has four or five pawns for the piece. The reason for the latter is that White is unable to defend his far-flung pawn islands against a concerted attack by Black's rook and knight.

Clearly more games are needed with 9...b4 before one can say whether 9 f5 is good or not.

The above analysis is a good example of a practical piece of home preparation. The available material was collected together, different annotations compared and a few fairly obvious errors noted. All this can be done in a fairly short time. Of course,

everybody would like to subject
lines to intense scrutiny, produce lots
of original ideas and so on, but few
players have the time for this in a
crowded tournament schedule. The
same applies to amateur players,
who have to fit chess in amongst
other responsibilities.

Nevertheless, you have an enormous advantage if you know such a
body of analysis, while your opponent has only a vague notion of what
to do. This applies particularly if you
have found mistakes in previously
published analysis. Then you have a
head start even if your opponent has
scanned all the available material.
Problems can arise only if he has
subjected the material to close personal scrutiny, and if you have chosen a slightly unusual line this would
be bad luck indeed, because nobody
has the time to carefully analyse
every possibility.

In this game Chandler decided not
to see what was in store, and headed
down a different variation. Scaring
your opponent away from critical
lines can in itself be a success. One
final point is that such analysis
should always be written down, even
if it is fairly superficial. A few weeks
later and it will all be forgotten, so a
permanent record is an excellent
idea. In this case the analysis wasn't
used, but it was down on paper in
case it needed to be dusted off and
used against another opponent.

10   ♘xc6

The various tactical tries all fail,
for example 10 e5 ♘xd4 11 ♕xa8
dxe5 or 10 ♘cxb5 axb5 11 ♗xb5
♗d7 12 fxe6 ♘xd4 13 ♗xd7+ ♚e7
with advantage to Black in both
cases. Therefore, White has to play
positionally. His main problem is
that the move f4-f5 has weakened
the key square e5; if a black knight
were to land there, White would be
in trouble, so I decided to exchange
both black knights.

10   ...   ♕xc6
11   ♗xf6   gxf6
12   ♗d3

12 fxe6 fxe6 13 ♕xf6 ♖g8 is an
alternative, but Black's two bishops
and good development offer adequate compensation for the pawn.
Yudasin-Ehlvest, Pamplona 1991/2
continued 14 ♗e2 ♗e7 15 ♕d4!
♖b8?! 16 ♗h5+ ♚d7 17 ♗f3 ♕b6
18 ♕d3 with advantage to White.
Yudasin gave '15...♖xg2! 16 0-0-0
♕c5 17 ♕h8+ ♚d7 18 ♗f3!' as the
critical line, but he didn't mention
18...♕e3+ winning a piece.

In general, White should only exchange on e6 if he has a forcing idea
in mind; otherwise he only makes
Black's life easier.

12   ...   ♗g7?

This leads to a tactical disaster,
but Black's position was uncomfortable because there is no safe place
for his king, whereas White intends
simply 0-0 and ♚h1. The possibility

of a4 will put Black off ...0-0-0, so he decides to head for the kingside. Even if he executes this plan correctly (by 12...♖a7 and only then ...♗g7, for example), White can still start an attack by ♘e2-g3-h5.

13 fxe6! fxe6
14 ♕h5+ ♔d8 *(7)*

14...♔e7 15 e5! is even worse than the game, e.g. 15...fxe5 16 0-0 or 15...♕c5 16 exd6+ ♕xd6 17 0-0-0 with a tremendous attack for White in both cases.

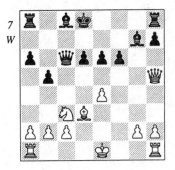

7
W

If Black had time to play ...♕c5 and ...♕e5, occupying the key central square e5, then he would probably have the advantage. But just at the moment Black's king is badly placed and he is behind in development, giving White the chance to start an attack.

15 e5!

This move exposes Black's king and brings White's minor pieces into the game. Hitherto, they were merely observing the pawn on e4,

but now that the e4 square is vacated they can spring into life.

15...dxe5 and 15...♕xg2 lose to 16 ♗e4, while 15...fxe5 sheds a piece to 16 ♕g5+, so Black decides to take the pawn with his queen. Declining the pawn is no help as White can continue with 0-0-0 or ♘e4 anyway. 15 0-0-0 was less accurate as Black could reply 15...b4.

15 ... ♕c5
16 0-0-0 ♕xe5

Her majesty reaches e5 in any case, but the situation is completely different when there is no pawn on e4. The queen on e5, far from being well placed, is simply a target for White's rooks.

17 ♕f3 ♖b8

17...♖a7 is no improvement as after 18 ♖he1 ♕xh2 19 ♕f2 the queen gains a tempo on its way to b6. The key point is that after 17...d5 18 ♗e4 White will sacrifice decisively at d5. It shouldn't be necessary to analyse variations, because it is obvious that Black cannot defend, but here is the grisly proof: 18...♗d7 19 ♗xd5 exd5 20 ♖xd5 ♗h6+ 21 ♔b1 ♕f4 22 ♖xd7+ ♔xd7 23 ♖d1+ ♔e6 24 ♕d5+ ♔e7 25 ♕b7+ and the rook falls with check.

18 ♖he1 ♕xh2

Moving to c5 or g5 is no better since White will subsequently gain a tempo by ♘e4. 18...♕g5+ 19 ♔b1 f5 tries to avoid this, but runs into 20 ♕c6.

19 ♔b1! *(8)*

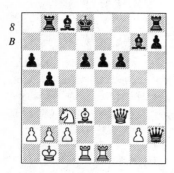

19 ♕c6 ♗d7 isn't at all clear, but this move preserves all White's options while cutting out any defensive possibilities based on ...♗h6+ and ...♕f4.

19 ...   ♗d7?!

Missing a threat to trap the queen, but Black's position was miserable in any case, for example 19...♕h6 20 ♕c6 ♗f8 21 ♗f5! ♗d7 22 ♕xa6 exf5 23 ♘d5 followed by ♕a5+, or 19...♗b7 20 ♕g4 ♗h6 21 ♕xe6. The best chance was 19...f5, but 20 ♗xf5! exf5 (20...♖f8 21 ♕c6 ♗e5 22 ♖xe5 ♕xe5 23 ♖xd6+ ♔e7 24 ♘d5+ ♕xd5 25 ♕c7+ ♔f6 26 ♖xd5 exd5 27 ♕d6+! wins easily, while 20...♗xc3 21 ♕xc3 and 20...♗b7 21 ♕e3 ♔c7 22 ♕xe6 are very good for White) 21 ♕c6 ♗e5 22 ♖xe5 ♕xe5 23 ♖xd6+ ♔e7 24 ♕c7+ ♗d7 25 ♘d5+ wins for White.

20	g3	♕h6
21	♖h1	♕g5
22	♖h5	1-0

The game J.Nunn-N.Murshed had a noteworthy finish, which gained it the brilliancy prize. What was this prize, you might ask? Well, it was a Novag chess computer, which was quite logical given that the Novag chess computer company sponsored the tournament. Nine months after the end of the tournament, following repeated complaints about the non-appearance of the prize, the computer finally arrived. It didn't work.

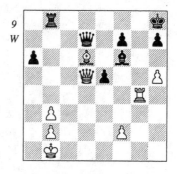

White was to play and the fun started with **32 ♕xe5!** (not 32 ♗xe5? ♕xg4 and after 33 ♗xb8 ♕e2 White cannot defend b2, so 33 ♗xf6+ ♔g8 is forced, with an unclear position) **♕d8** (the only move because 32...♕xg4 loses a piece after 33 ♕xf6+ ♔g8 34 ♗xb8) **33 ♕g3** (White's extra pawn provides cover for his king) **♖b5 34 h6** (setting up a permanent back rank mating net) **♖d5 35 ♗c7 ♕e8 36 ♔a2** (stopping annnoying checks and threatening both 37 ♕f3, forking d5 and f6, and 37 ♖b4 followed by ♖b8) ♖d2 (Black appears to have developed counterplay against b2)

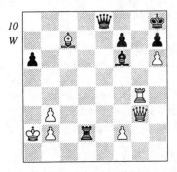

37 ♗e5! ♖xf2 (37...♗xe5 38 ♖g8+ ♕xg8 39 ♕xe5+ forces mate) 38 ♖e4 (this forces mate in six; in fact White can mate in five by 38 ♗xf6+ ♖xf6 39 ♖e4 ♕f8 40 ♖e8, but once you have found one forced win, there is little point in looking for another one) ♗xe5 (there is nothing better) 39 ♕g7+! 1-0 because White mates in two more moves.

My next tournament was the Lugano Open, a well-organised annual event in which I competed regularly, but which is now sadly defunct. Lake Lugano is a more obvious attraction than the sand dunes of Wijk aan Zee, and this tournament always enticed a strong entry to southern Switzerland. My score of 6½/9 was enough to be part of a large tie for second place, half a point behind the winner Tukmakov. In order to be successful

in a big open tournament, it is normally necessary to have at least one piece of luck. Mine arrived in round 7, when the following position arose in K.Rasmussen-J.Nunn:

White sealed his 41st move, and I had a feeling that Black's advantage was not going to be enough to win. Analysis confirmed my fears. After the obvious move 41 ♔xf4, Black can play 41...♖f8+ 42 ♔e3 ♖f1, but this only leads to a draw after 43 ♔d2 ♖f2 44 ♔e3. The alternative was 41...♔d5, but analysis showed that after 42 ♔e3 Black's winning chances were again minimal. When I returned to the tournament hall, I was stunned to discover that my opponent had sealed **41 ♘b1??**, and after **41...f3!** he had to **resign** because 42 gxf3 ♘c2 43 ♖xe2 ♖d4 is a midboard mate.

Holland has always been a centre of chess activity. Thanks to the legacy of Max Euwe, public interest is high and there is always good press coverage in newspapers and on radio and television. As mentioned above, the Hoogovens Festival has been going since before the Second World War; the summer tournament in Amsterdam was another enduring event. In the mid-1970s, this was sponsored by IBM, but then the insurance group OHRA took over the tournament, and it continued to be popular right up to its disappearance after the 1990 event. The format of the tournament was slightly unusual; there was a top event, called the 'Crown Group', which consisted of a six-player double-round tournament, together with a strong Swiss called the 'Grandmaster Group'. I played three times in the 'Crown Group', 1985 being the first of these. Despite losing both games to Karpov, I made a respectable score of 5½/10, sufficient for third place behind Karpov and Timman.

The following game was played in the last round, but before the game I received a surprising telephone call from Nigel Short. He had been playing in the Biel Interzonal, but had become involved in a play-off with Van der Wiel and Torre for the final Candidates qualifying place. Nigel had been seconded by Murray Chandler during the Interzonal, but now Murray had to return to Edinburgh for the British Championship. Nigel therefore asked if I could come to Biel after my tournament to help him out. I agreed to come the next day, and flew first to Heathrow, where Bob Wade handed me a file of preparation material and my mother handed me some clean clothes. An hour later I was in the air again heading for Zürich and then Biel. When I arrived in Biel, I found a disconsolate Nigel sitting in the bar; he had just lost the first game of the play-off to Van der Wiel. But in the end Nigel qualified by beating Torre 3-0, so that despite a 2½-½ loss to Van der Wiel, he finished level with Van der Wiel on 3½/6. A superior tie-break from the Interzonal took him to Montpellier for the Candidates.

Game 3
J.Sunye Neto – J.Nunn
Amsterdam (OHRA) 1985
English

1	c4	g6	3	g3	e5
2	♘c3	♗g7	4	♗g2	d6

5 e3   ♘c6
6 ♘ge2   h5

This move introduces some life into an otherwise unexciting variation, even if theory regards it as slightly doubtful.

7 h4

White sidesteps the challenge by simply preventing the advance of the h-pawn. The critical variation is 7 d4 h4 8 d5.

7 ...   ♗g4

It is also possible to play 7...♘ge7 8 d3 ♗e6 9 0-0 0-0, very much as if ...h5 and h4 had not been interpolated; in this case it isn't easy to say who benefits from the addition of ...h5 and h4. However, it seems more natural to exploit the weakness of g4 immediately.

8 d3   ♘ge7
9 b4

Now 9...♘xb4 10 ♖b1, followed by a3 if necessary, regains the pawn with advantage to White because the long diagonal has been weakened. 9...e4 is met by 10 d4 and Black's e-pawn is very weak.

9 ...   a6

This holds up b5 for some time, since 10 b5 axb5 11 cxb5 ♘a5 followed by ...d5 is good for Black. 10 a4 is met by 10...♘xb4 11 ♗xb7 ♖b8 followed by 12...0-0 with a secure outpost at b4.

10 ♖b1

Intending a4 followed by b5.

10 ...   ♖b8 *(12)*

This apparently irrelevant move is the key to Black's system, because it again holds up a4. The reason is that after 11 a4 a5 12 b5 ♘b4 13 ♗a3 c5 White cannot win a pawn by 14 bxc6 bxc6 15 ♗xb4 because the rook on b8 covers b4. In Pfleger-Nunn, Bundesliga 1986, White continued 14 ♗xb4 axb4 15 ♘d5 ♘xd5 16 ♗xd5 0-0 17 ♕c2 b6, but here Black has a slight advantage. The bishop on d5 can be exchanged or driven away by ...♗e6, and the excellent protected passed pawn on b4 prevents the knight on e2 from ever reaching d5. Meanwhile Black has active prospects on the kingside. Black eventually won by playing ...e4 to activate his g7 bishop and obtain two connected passed pawns on the queenside.

This is a good example of opening preparation which involves studying a whole system rather than individual moves. Playing a blockbuster novelty may be very satisfying, but you can only use it once and then it becomes common knowledge. By becoming fully familiar with all the do's and dont's of this particular set-up, I was able to gain more than one point.

The rook move also gives Black the option of countering on the queenside by playing ...b5 himself. This might seem to be contrary to the general principle of not weakening yourself on the side where you are being attacked, but is White really so much stronger than Black on the queenside? If Black can play ...b5 himself, then he can maintain the knight on c6 and prevent White gaining space on that side of the board. It is worth noting that Black's system is only possible when the knight on c6 is supported by its colleague from e7.

11 ♕c2   0-0

Both sides are fighting to prevent the opponent playing a pawn to b5. The immediate 11...b5 is bad as 12 cxb5 axb5 13 ♘xb5 ♖xb5 14 ♗xc6+ ♘xc6 15 ♕xc6+ ♗d7 16 ♕c2 ♕a8 17 e4 doesn't give Black enough compensation for the pawn. White can continue with ♘c3, ♗e3 and 0-0 followed by the advance of the queenside pawns. In contrast, Black has no obvious way to exploit the weak light squares on the kingside.

12 ♗d2?!

White wants to play ♘d5 at some stage, but achieving this is more difficult when the queen doesn't defend

e2. In Rechlis-Watson, Beersheba 1987 White played 12 a3, when 12...♕d7?! 13 ♘d5 ♖fc8 14 ♘ec3 b5 15 ♗d2 bxc4 16 dxc4 ♗f5 17 e4 ♘d4 18 ♕d3 ♗g4 19 f3 was slightly better for White. Black's problem was that he could not play 13...♘xd5 because 14 cxd5 followed by f3 would have trapped the bishop. Therefore the semi-waiting move 12...♖e8 was better, with an unclear position.

12 ...   ♕d7

White still doesn't have a major threat since 13 a4 is met by 13...a5, 13 ♘d5 is met by 13...♘xd5 14 cxd5 ♘e7 (this is one advantage of having the bishop on g4 rather than e6) and 13 b5 is met by 13...axb5 14 cxb5 ♘a7. So by the same logic as in the last note, 12...♖e8 is also possible. Then 13 b5 axb5 14 cxb5 ♘a7 (14...♘a5 15 ♘d5 ♘xd5 16 ♗xa5 is good for White) 15 a4 d5 leads to an unclear position, while 13 0-0 can be met by 13...♕d7.

13 ♘d5

White takes advantage of Black's last move to occupy d5; as before, 13...♘xd5 loses a piece to 14 cxd5 followed by 15 f3. Now 13...♗xe2 14 ♔xe2 is bad for Black; White's king is temporarily displaced, but Black gives up all his light-square control. On the other hand, White's ambitious move is rather risky, because he cannot castle while e2 is only defended by the king.

13	...	b5
14	a4 *(13)*	

14 ♘ec3 was the only real alternative, but then Black plays 14...bxc4 15 dxc4 e4! (15...♘xd5 is less energetic; 16 cxd5 ♘xb4 17 ♖xb4 ♖xb4 18 f3 ♖fb8 19 fxg4 ♕xg4 is fine for Black, but 16 ♘xd5 ♗f5 17 e4 ♘d4 18 ♕d3 ♗g4 looks slightly better for White) 16 ♘xe7+ (after 16 ♘xe4 ♘xd5 17 cxd5 ♘e5 18 0-0 Black can either grab the exchange by 18...♗e2, or play 18...♘f3+ 19 ♔h1 ♕f5, when the threats of ...♖fe8 and ...♕xd5 regain the pawn with a slight plus for Black) ♕xe7 17 ♕xe4 (17 ♘xe4 ♘e5 18 0-0 ♗e2 is good for Black, while 17 ♗xe4 ♘e5 is similar to 17 ♕xe4) ♘e5 18 ♘d5 ♕d7 19 ♕c2 (or else ...♗f5 is very strong) ♘f3+ 20 ♗xf3 (20 ♔f1? ♗f5 gains material) ♗xf3 with fantastic compensation for the pawn.

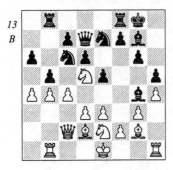

13
B

14	...	e4!

One of the most important chess skills is being able to recognise when

the position is turning against you strategically, and to spot this early enough to counter it. Here White intends ♘ec3 followed by 0-0, with a firm grip on the important central squares d5 and e4, so I decided that quick action was necessary. Black must take advantage of the fact that White's king is temporarily stuck in the centre. The only way to do this is to play ...e4, clearing the way for the c6 knight to jump into f3 via e5. The consequences are not at all clear-cut, but I played the move quickly because everything else allows White to consolidate his grip.

15	♘xe7+	

Or 15 dxe4 (15 cxb5 exd3 16 ♕xd3 ♘e5 is very good for Black, while 15 ♗xe4 ♘e5 will probably transpose into the game) ♘e5 (not 15...bxc4 16 f3!, sealing up the hole on f3, and only then ♕xc4) 16 cxb5 ♘xd5 17 exd5 ♘f3+ with good play for the pawn.

15	...	♕xe7
16	♗xe4	

Or: 1) 16 dxe4 ♘e5 17 cxb5 axb5 18 axb5 (18 ♘d4 bxa4 19 f3 c5 20 bxc5 ♖xb1+ 21 ♕xb1 dxc5 22 fxg4 cxd4 23 exd4 ♘xg4 is very good for Black) ♘f3+ 19 ♔f1 ♕xe4 20 ♕xe4 ♘xd2+ 21 ♔e1 ♘xe4 22 ♗xe4 ♖xb5 and Black has a clear plus in view of his two bishops and lead in development.

2) 16 d4 ♗f3 (Black can't let White take on e4 if his knight

doesn't gain access to e5) 17 ♗xf3 exf3 18 cxb5 ♘a7! 19 ♘f4 axb5 20 ♘d5 ♕e6 21 ♘xc7 ♕d7 (21...♕g4 22 a5! ♖fc8 23 ♖b3 followed by ♖c3 disentangles White's pieces) 22 ♘xb5 (22 ♘d5 bxa4 is fine for Black) ♘xb5 23 axb5 ♕xb5 24 ♕d1 ♕f5 gives Black good compensation for the pawn. White cannot castle, and the rook on b1 cannot defend both the a- and c-files.

16 ...   ♘e5
17 cxb5

Black threatened 17...bxc4 18 dxc4 ♘f3+ 19 ♔f1 ♕xe4.

17 ...   axb5
18 axb5

18 a5 is also possible, but after 18...c5 Black again has a very active position. 18 ♘d4 is a natural choice, freeing the king and covering the weak f3 square; Black continues 18...bxa4 19 f4 d5! 20 ♗xd5 ♖bd8 21 ♘c6 ♘xc6 22 ♕xc6 ♖d6 23 ♕c5 ♕d7 24 ♗c4 ♖xd3, regaining the pawn with a large advantage.

18 ...   d5! *(14)*

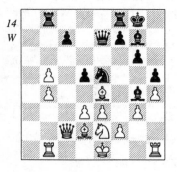

The only move to keep the attack going. The lines 18...♖xb5 19 ♘c3, 18...♗f3 19 ♗xf3 ♘xf3+ 20 ♔f1 and 18...♘f3+ 19 ♔f1 offer little.

19 ♗g2?

White unwisely balks at taking the third pawn. After 19 ♗xd5 ♖fd8 we have:

1) **20 ♗e4** (20 ♗c6 ♗f5 wins for Black) ♘f3+ 21 ♗xf3 (21 ♔f1 ♘xd2+ 22 ♕xd2 ♕xe4) ♗xf3 22 ♖g1 ♖xb5 with a dangerous attack for the two pawns. The immediate threat is to open more lines by 23...c5.

2) **20 ♗c4!** ♗f5 (20...♗f3 21 ♖g1 ♗e4 22 ♘f4 ♘f3+ 23 ♔f1 ♘xg1 24 dxe4 gives good compensation for the exchange) 21 ♘f4 (21 e4 ♗xe4 22 dxe4 ♘f3+ 23 ♔f1 ♖xd2 24 ♕b3 ♕xe4 25 ♗xf7+ ♔h8 26 ♘f4 ♗d4 and 21 0-0 ♘xc4 22 ♕xc4 ♗xd3 win for Black) ♗h6 22 ♖b3! (22 0-0 ♗xf4 23 exf4 ♘xc4 24 ♕xc4 ♗xd3 25 ♕c3 ♗xf1 26 ♔xf1 ♖xb5 is good for Black) ♗xf4 (22...♗e4 23 dxe4 ♘f3+ 24 ♔e2 ♖xd2+ 25 ♕xd2 ♘xd2 26 ♘d5, followed by ♔xd2, gives White ♖+♘+3♙ v ♕) 23 gxf4 ♗e4! 24 fxe5 ♗xh1 25 d4 with an unclear position; White is nominally ahead on material, but his king is still exposed.

The situation here is similar to that after Black's 13th move in Game 1. Grabbing the extra material gives White more chances to defuse the attack later, in this case by giving up the exchange or his queen. The leading exponent of the 'grab everything' method of defence is Viktor Korchnoi, who will take almost anything unless he can see a concrete refutation.

19 ...   ♘f3+
20 ♔f1

20 ♗xf3 is like line 1 above, but with Black having an extra pawn. The point of interpolating ...d5 is that White's bishop is buried at g2 rather than actively placed at e4.

20 ...   ♖xb5

Black has the advantage and White will have to defend accurately to hold on.

21 ♘g1

The best move; White must exchange the f3 knight or he will have to play without his h1 rook and g2 bishop. After 21 ♗c3 (21 ♘c3 ♖xb4) ♗xc3 22 ♘xc3 (22 ♕xc3 ♖fb8 is good for Black) ♖xb4 23 ♘xd5 ♖xb1+ 24 ♕xb1 ♕e5 25 ♕a2 ♖b8 Black has an enormous attack.

21 ...   ♘xd2+
22 ♕xd2   ♖fb8

22...c5 allows 23 ♗xd5.

23 d4! *(15)*

An excellent move to block out the ♗g7. After 23 ♘e2 ♖xb4 24 ♖xb4 ♕xb4! 25 ♕xb4 ♖xb4 26 f3 ♗f5 27 e4 (27 ♘f4 ♖b2) dxe4 28 fxe4 (28 dxe4 gives Black a dangerous passed pawn) ♗g4 the ending offers Black good winning chances.

23 ...   c5!?

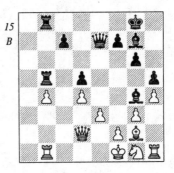

15
B

Trying to activate the ♗g7. The alternative 23...♗f5 (23...♖xb4 24 ♖xb4 ♖xb4 25 ♗xd5 and 23...c6 24 ♗f3 ♗f5 25 ♖b3 ♖xb4 26 ♖xb4 ♖xb4 27 ♔g2 are safe for White) 24 ♖b3 ♖xb4 25 ♖xb4 ♖xb4 26 ♗xd5 ♖b1+ 27 ♔g2 ♗e4+ 28 ♗xe4 ♕xe4+ 29 f3 ♕b7 30 ♕f2 (not 30 ♘e2? ♖xh1 31 ♖xh1 ♕xf3+, followed by ...♗h6) ♖b2 31 ♘e2 gives White more defensive chances, for example 31...c5 32 dxc5 ♕b5 33 ♖e1 ♗c3 34 ♘xc3 ♖xf2+ 35 ♔xf2 leads to a draw.

24 dxc5

Not 24 ♘e2 ♗f5 25 ♖b2 ♖xb4 26 ♖xb4 cxb4 and the b-pawn is too strong.

24 ...   ♕xc5

The point of the last move. 25 bxc5 ♖xb1+ 26 ♕e1 ♖xe1+ 27 ♔xe1 ♗c3+ 28 ♔f1 ♖b1 is mate, while after 25 ♖c1 ♕d6 followed by ...♖xb4 a black rook penetrates to b2.

25 ♗f3!

Another good move. After 25...♗xf3 26 ♘xf3 ♖xb4 27 ♖xb4

Xxb4 28 ♔g2 Xb2 29 Xc1 White escapes, so Black is forced to offer a pawn.

25	...	Xxb4
26	Xxb4	Xxb4
27	♕xd5	

Not 27 ♔g2 Xb2 28 ♕xd5 ♕xe3 and Black wins.

| 27 | ... | Xb1+ |
| 28 | ♔g2 | ♕c1 (16) |

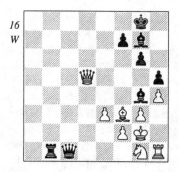

Despite the reduced material Black can still generate dangerous threats. White's main drawing hope rests in the fact that all the remaining pawns lie on one side.

29 ♔h2

29 ♕d3 is also possible, but does not lead to a clear-cut draw. The immediate 29...♗h6 fails to 30 ♗xg4 hxg4 31 h5 gxh5 32 ♕d8+ with a definite draw, and 29...♗xf3+ 30 ♔xf3 ♕c6+ 31 e4 (31 ♕e4 ♕b5 32 ♕a8+ ♗f8! is less accurate, since 33 ♔g2 is impossible, and so Black can play ...♕f1, aiming for ...Xb5-f5; note that 32...♔h7? is bad after 33

♘h3! Xxh1 34 ♘g5+ and White gives perpetual check) Xe1 (after 31...♕c1 32 ♔g2 White gradually escapes by ♕f3, ♔h2 and ♘e2) 32 ♔g2 Xxe4 33 ♘f3 is equal. However, if Black just improves the position of his king by 29...♗f6 and 30...♔g7 White has a serious problem finding any reasonable moves.

| 29 | ... | ♕f1 (17) |

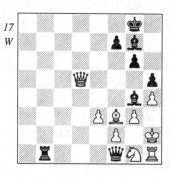

30 ♗g2?

This error was caused by serious time-pressure. White could see no good defence to the attack on f2, for example 30 ♗xg4 hxg4 (30...♕xf2+ 31 ♕g2 ♕xg2+ 32 ♔xg2 hxg4 33 ♘e2 Xb3 34 ♔f2 ♗h6 35 ♘f4 is a draw) 31 ♕g2 ♕d3 and White seems to have no moves, e.g. 32 ♕a8+ ♔h7 33 ♕g2 Xb2 and White is in zugzwang (34 e4 ♗d4). However White can defend by 32 ♘h3! gxh3 33 ♕a8+ ♔h7 34 Xxb1 ♕xb1 35 ♔xh3 and whether or not Black exchanges queens by ...♕f1+, the ending is completely drawn. With queens on the board White can put his king on g2, his queen on the long diagonal and just wait, while with queens off Black cannot prevent the exchange of his last two pawns.

31...♕a6!? is a better chance, but then White has two reasonable lines:

1) **32 ♘h3 gxh3 33 ♔xh3 ♖b2** and with rooks on the board Black has more chances to create threats along the second rank, but objectively the result should still be a draw.

2) **32 ♕e4 ♖b2 33 ♔g2 ♕a2 34 ♕xg4** (not 34 ♕f4? f5!, with total paralysis, nor 34 ♕e8+? ♔h7 and Black wins) ♖xf2+ 35 ♔h3 ♕a6 36 ♘f3 f5 37 ♕f4 and Black cannot do more than win the knight at the cost of his remaining pawns.

30 ...	**♕xf2**
31 ♘h3?	

Total collapse. 31 ♕e4 still offers resistance, although Black should win after 31...♗f6! 32 ♕f4 (32 ♕xb1? ♗e5 33 ♘e2 ♗xe2 34 ♖c1 ♗f3 forces mate in five more moves) ♕xf4 and now:

1) **33 exf4 ♖b2 34 f5** (34 ♘h3 ♗f3 35 ♖g1 ♗d4) ♗e5! 35 fxg6 fxg6 36 ♘h3 ♗f3 37 ♖g1 (37 ♘f4 is not possible thanks to Black's 34th move) ♗d4 38 ♔h1 ♗xg1 39 ♗xf3 ♗h2 40 ♘f4 (40 g4 ♗g3 wins) ♗xg3 41 ♘xg6 ♗d6 42 ♗xh5 ♔g7 followed by 43...♔h6 winning.

2) **33 gxf4 ♗xh4 34 ♘f3** (34 ♘h3 ♖b3) ♖xh1+ 35 ♗xh1 ♗f2 36

e4 (36 ♘e5 ♗e6 37 e4 h4 is very similar) h4 37 ♘e5 ♗g3+ 38 ♔g2 (38 ♔g1 ♗e2 39 ♘f3 ♗d3 wins) ♗e6 39 ♘d3 (39 ♘f3 ♗c8 40 ♔g1 ♗b7 wins) ♗c4 40 ♘b2 (40 ♘e5 ♗a6 41 ♘f3 ♗c8 transposes to the previous bracket) ♗e2 and wins.

31 ...	**♖xh1+**
32 ♔xh1	**♗xh3**
33 ♗xh3	**♕xg3**

0-1

White will lose all his remaining pawns in a few moves.

After Amsterdam, I played in the Lloyds Bank tournament at London, scoring a quite reasonable 7/9, enough to join a tie for second place behind Beliavsky, who scored 7½. The next major event was the Nimzowitsch Memorial tournament, held at Næstved in Denmark. It quite often happens that organisers are more enthusiastic about getting you to a tournament than in getting you home again. For Næstved, Chandler and I were picked up at Copenhagen airport and driven to Næstved, but when the time came to leave, the organisers provided a large hint by including a timetable for trains from Næstved to Copenhagen in the last round bulletin! The hotel was undergoing some major construction work during the tournament, another common feature of chess events. There is nothing like being woken up at half-past-seven every morning by assorted hammering, drilling, metal-bashing and so on.

The night life of Næstved turned out to be totally non-existent. If you were on the streets after nine in the evening, the only people you were likely to come across were other chess players wandering round the town. However, the discovery that the hotel possessed an internal video system offered a glimmer of hope. The three English players (Chandler, Short and myself) agreed to solve the only remaining problem, that the hotel had no videos, by visiting the local video shop. We each chose a film, and the entire hotel was subjected to *War Games, Midnight Express* and *The French Lieutenant's Woman.* Readers may guess who chose which film, but I can reveal that Nigel hid behind a chair during one gruesome scene from *Midnight Express.*

I started disastrously with two losses to Ftačnik and Chandler, but by the end of the event I had clawed my way back to 50%. The following encounter with the former world champion was my best effort.

Game 4

J.Nunn – M.Tal

Næstved 1985

Spanish

1	e4	e5
2	♘f3	♘c6
3	♗b5	a6
4	♗a4	♘f6
5	0-0	♘xe4
6	d4	b5
7	♗b3	d5
8	dxe5	♗e6
9	♘bd2	♘c5
10	c3	♗g4
11	♗c2	♕d7
12	h3	♗h5
13	♘b3	

A discussion of the opening would take us too far afield, and in any case the theory can be found in standard reference works. 9 ♘bd2 became popular after Karpov used it in his 1978 and 1981 world championship matches against Korchnoi. 10...d4 is an important alternative, as is 12 ♖e1 with the idea of ♘f1 followed by ♘e3 or ♘g3.

| 13 | ... | ♘e6 |

13...♘e4 14 ♖e1 is good for White.

| 14 | ♖e1 | ♗e7 |
| 15 | ♗f5 *(18)* | |

This position can also be reached via the move-order 11...♗e7 12 h3

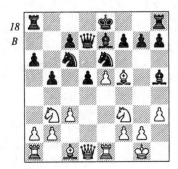

♗h5 13 ♖e1 ♕d7 14 ♘b3 ♘e6 15 ♗f5.

15 ...   ♗g6

I believe that this move was first played in Nunn-Tal. The alternatives are:

1) **15...♘cd8** 16 ♗e3 and now:

1a) **16...♘b7** 17 ♕e2 c5 18 ♖ad1 ♖d8 19 ♘bd2 ♕c6 20 g4 ♗g6 21 ♘f1 0-0 22 ♘g3 gave White a slight plus in Sigurjonsson-Stean, Munich 1979.

1b) **16...0-0** 17 ♕e2 a5 18 ♖ad1 ♗g6 19 g4 a4 20 ♘bd4 c6, Popović-Marin, Manila IZ 1990, and now 21 ♕d3 would have given White a small advantage.

1c) **16...a5** 17 ♗c5 (17 ♘c5 ♕c6 18 ♘d3 ♗xf3 19 ♕xf3 g6 20 ♗g4 h5 21 ♗xe6 ♘xe6 22 ♖ad1 ♖d8 23 ♖d2 0-0 24 ♖ed1 gave White an edge in Ehlvest-Hjartarson, Belfort World Cup 1988) a4 18 ♗xe7 ♕xe7 19 ♘bd4! (19 ♘bd2 c6 20 b4 ♘g5 21 ♕e2 g6 was played in the 1978 Karpov-Korchnoi match; according to Filip White could have obtained

an edge by 22 ♗d3 ♘de6 23 ♕e3) ♘xd4 20 cxd4 ♘e6 21 g4! ♗g6 22 ♖c1 0-0 23 ♕d2 ♖a6 24 ♖c2 ♖b8 25 ♖ec1 with a clear plus for White, Hamarat-Palmo, corr. 1990.

2) **15...0-0** 16 g4 (or 16 ♗xh7+ ♔xh7 17 ♘g5+ ♗xg5 18 ♕xh5+ ♗h6 19 ♗xh6 gxh6 20 ♕f5+ ♔h8 21 ♕f6+ ♔h7 22 ♕f5+ ½-½, Ilinčić-Lalić, Yugoslav Ch 1989) ♗g6 17 ♗e3 ♖ad8 18 ♕e2 (18 ♕d3 f6 19 ♗xg6 hxg6 20 exf6 ♖xf6 was unclear in Seibold-Beckemeyer, Bundesliga 1989) a5 19 ♖ad1 ♖fe8 20 ♔g2 a4 21 ♘c1 with equality in the game Bologan-Kotronias, Debrecen 1992.

16 ♘fd4

When Tal played 15...♗g6, I assumed that after the obvious 16 g4, Black would somehow make use of the fact that he has not castled. Therefore I chose an alternative which did not weaken my king position (usually a good idea against Tal!). However, in some later games White did play 16 g4 and Black just continued with normal development, for example: 16 g4 ♘cd8 17 ♗e3 0-0 18 ♕e2 ♘b7 (Marin recommends 18...a5, which might well transpose into Popović-Marin from line 1b of the previous note) 19 ♘bd4! (19 ♖ad1 c5 20 ♘bd2 c4 21 ♘e4 ♕c6 22 ♘g3 ♘bc5 23 h4 ♘d3 24 h5 ♘xe1 25 ♖xe1 was rather unconvincing in Renet-Kharitonov, Royan 1988, although White did win the game) c5 20 ♘xe6 fxe6 21 ♗xg6 hxg6 22 ♖ad1 ♘a5 23 h4 with a slight plus for White, Dimitrov-Marin, France 1991.

If Black cannot improve on this line, then 16 g4 appears stronger than 16 ♘fd4.

16   ...   0-0

Black has no time for 16...♖d8, because of 17 ♘xe6 fxe6 18 ♗xg6+ hxg6 19 ♕d3 ♔f7 20 ♘d4 with an awful position for Black. In general, Black will be reluctant to exchange on f5 himself, because the knight at f5 coupled with ♕g4 can give White a dangerous attack.

17   ♗g4!?

17 ♘xe6 fxe6 18 ♗xg6 hxg6 is not so good since ...♖f5 followed by ...♖af8 gives Black very active pieces, while 17 ♕g4 may be met by 17...♘cd8. The move played uses the omission of g4 to introduce a very serious threat of f4-f5; Black is obliged take immediate counter-action.

17   ...   ♘cxd4
18   cxd4

Certainly not 18 ♘xd4 c5.

18   ...   a5
19   f4   h5!

The best move. After 19...a4 20 ♘c5 ♗xc5 (20...♕c6 21 ♘xe6 fxe6 22 ♗e3, followed by ♖c1, is slightly better for White, but not 21 f5? ♘xd4!) 21 dxc5 h5 (21...f5 22 exf6 ♖xf6 23 ♖xe6 ♖xe6 24 f5) 22 ♗xh5 ♘xc5 (22...♗xh5 23 ♕xh5 ♘xc5 24

f5 gives White a decisive kingside attack) 23 ♗g4 ♗f5 24 ♗xf5 ♕xf5 25 ♕xd5 ♘d3 26 ♕e4 Black has insufficient compensation for the lost pawn.

20   ♗xh5   ♗xh5

This leads to a position in which Black's king is exposed, but if he follows it up accurately then Black should have enough counterplay. There was a second reasonable line in 20...a4 21 ♘c5 ♘xc5 22 dxc5 ♗xc5+ 23 ♗e3 ♗b4 (not 23...♗xe3+ 24 ♖xe3 d4 25 ♗g4, when the lines 25...♕d5 26 f5, 25...♕d8 26 ♖g3 and 25...♗f5 26 ♗xf5 ♕xf5 27 ♕xd4 ♖ad8 28 ♕b4 are all good for White) 24 ♖f1 ♗f5 with a double-edged position. It is curious that Black need not fear the exchange on g6, because transferring the pawn from f7 to g6 actually improves the security of his king.

21   ♕xh5   a4
22   ♘c5   ♘xc5
23   dxc5   ♗xc5+
24   ♗e3 *(19)*

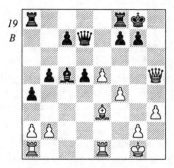

24 ...   ♗xe3+?

Transferring White's rook to the dangerous third rank with gain of tempo is too risky. Black should have preferred 24...d4 25 ♗f2 (25 ♖ad1 ♕d5 is similar, while 25 e6 ♕d6 gives White no advantage) ♕d5 26 f5 (otherwise Black plays ...♖fe8, and then the pressure on e5 prevents White's f5) d3 27 ♗xc5 ♕xc5+ 28 ♔h1 (avoiding a future capture on e5 with check) d2 29 ♖e4 and now 29...♕c1+ 30 ♔h2 is too dangerous, because 30...♕xa1 fails to 31 ♖h4. But there are two reasonable lines for Black, namely 29...♖fd8 30 ♖h4 (30 f6? ♕c1+ wins) d1♕+ 31 ♖xd1 ♖xd1+ 32 ♕xd1 ♕xe5 with equality, and 29...♖a6!?, preventing both 30 ♖h4 and 30 f6, with unclear complications.

25 ♖xe3   f5

White threatened to develop a crushing kingside attack by playing f5 himself, so this blocking move is best. Alternatives are very bad:

1) **25...d4** 26 ♖d1 (but not 26 ♖g3 f5!) ♖ad8 (26...c5 27 f5 or 26...f5 27 e6) 27 f5! dxe3 28 ♖xd7 ♖xd7 29 f6 and now Black has to start jettisoning pawns by 29...e2.

2) **25...g6** 26 ♕h6 (threat e6) ♖ae8 (26...♕f5 27 g4 ♕c2 28 f5) 27 ♖f1 ♖e6 (27...d4 28 f5) 28 ♖g3, followed by f5, with a decisive attack.

26 e6

26 exf6? ♖xf6 frees Black's position and exposes f4 to attack. Black's ...f5 has stopped White's kingside attack for the moment, but White has a new asset in the shape of his passed e-pawn. Black was threatening to play 26...♕e6, so the immediate advance is forced.

26 ...   ♕e7
27 ♖ae1   ♖ad8? *(20)*

This move loses by force, although White keeps a clear advantage however Black plays, for example 27...♖f6 (27...d4 28 ♖e5 exposes various pawns on the fifth rank to attack) 28 ♖e5 ♖a6 (28...♖d8 29 ♕g5! is also good for White) 29 ♕g5! and Black cannot avoid losing a pawn, for example **29...♔f8** 30 ♖xd5 ♖axe6 31 ♖xe6 ♕xe6 32 ♖xb5, **29...♖d6** 30 ♖xf5 ♖dxe6 31 ♖xe6 ♖xe6 32 ♕xe7 ♖xe7 33 ♖xd5, **29...d4** 30 ♖xb5 ♖axe6 31 ♖b8+ ♔f7 32 ♕h5+ ♔g6 33 ♕xf5+ or finally **29...g6** 30 ♖xf5.

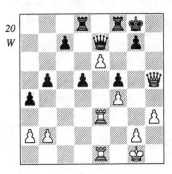

20
W

28 g4!

After the game Tal admitted overlooking this move. The threat is simply g5 followed by g6. The queen cannot budge because Black's last move set up a fork by e6-e7, so there is no way to clear an escape route for his king. If Black plays 28...fxg4, then 29 hxg4 followed by ♖h3 also leads to mate.

This oversight is easy to understand. By playing ...f5, Black blocked White's attack, but then he had to deal with the new problems associated with the e-pawn. In such a situation it is easy to forget that White can revert to Plan A.

| 28 | ... | | d4 |
| 29 | g5 | | g6 |

A sad necessity, but otherwise Black is mated.

30	♕xg6+		♔h8
31	♖e5		d3
32	♖xf5		♕b4

Or 32...d2 33 ♖d1; if Black's king were less exposed then the d-pawn would provide real counterplay, but as it is White need only be moderately careful.

33	♖xf8+		♖xf8
34	♕e4		♕c5+
35	♔h1!	

Not 35 ♔f1? ♕xg5, nor 35 ♔g2? ♕c2+ followed by 36...d2!.

| 35 | ... | | d2 |

35...♕f2 loses to 36 e7, just as in the game.

| 36 | ♖d1 | | ♕f2 |

Or 36...♖d8 (36...♕c1 37 ♕d4+) 37 ♕g6! ♕d5+ (37...♕f8 38 ♕f6+) 38 ♔h2 ♕d4 39 ♕f6+, when White

exchanges queens and wins with his four connected passed pawns.

37	e7		♖e8
38	♕e5+		♔g8
39	♕e6+		1-0

White mates in six more moves.

The game J.Nunn-C.Hansen had an attractive finish:

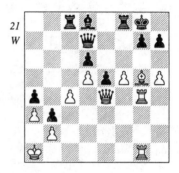

21
W

White was to play, and the game continued **34 h6** (the lines 34 ♗h6 ♗f6 35 ♗xg7 ♗xg7 36 h6 ♕xf5 37 ♖xg7+ ♔h8 and 34 ♗xd8 ♖cxd8 35 h6 ♕xf5 36 ♖xg7+ ♔h8 prove ineffective for the same reason – White cannot win Black's queen with ♖g8+ because of his weak back rank; after 34 h6, Tal wandered up and looked at the position for a few seconds, then gave me a broad grin – it hadn't taken him long to spot my next move!) ♕xf5 **35 ♗f6!!** ♕xg4 (35...♖xf6 36 ♖xg7+ ♔f8 37 ♖g8+ ♔e7 38 ♖1g7+ ♖f7 39 ♕xf5 mates Black next move, while 35...♕xe4 and 35...♕xf6 allow mate in two and three moves respectively) **36 ♕xg4 ♗xf6 37 hxg7 ♖fe8 38 ♕f5** (White not only wins material, but also retains his attack) **♗h4** (or 38...♗xg7 39 ♕d7) **39 ♖f1 1-0**

So far I have not given any games played in Britain. The reasons are historical. In the late 1970s there was a thriving weekend circuit, in which a number of top players participated. The tournaments were fun, and the prize money was sufficient to tempt players to trek to various parts of the country. I twice won the Cutty Sark Grand Prix during this period. But by the mid-1980s, the circuit had already gone into decline, with fewer and poorer events. By now the Cutty Sark Grand Prix had become the Leigh Grand Prix, and in 1985 I made an attempt to win it again. Because of international commitments, I had no chance to play in Britain during November and December, so I had to amass as many points as possible in October. This explains why I undertook a trip to South Wales for the Neath Open.

The following position arose in J.Nunn-A.H.Williams *(22)*:

A tactical explosion doesn't look likely, but just watch what happens! Black is to play, and although White's position is fairly solid, the two bishops are a potential long-term danger. Black would like to expel the knight from d5, but 26...c6 27

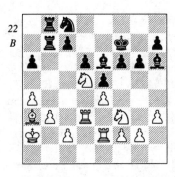

♘e3 ♖d7 28 c4 creates some pressure against d6; if then 28...f5, White can create tactical problems by 29 ♖ed2 threatening ♘xe5+. Perhaps 26...♔g7 is the most sensible, improving Black's king position in preparation for a later ...f5. In this case Black could claim a slight advantage, because he can hope to activate his bishops, while White's main hope is that Black will make a mistake!

26 ... f5?!
Too impatient. After this White is not worse.

27 exf5 gxf5?
And now White gains the advantage. 27...♗xf5 28 ♖c3 c5 was better, when White can reply tactically or positionally:

1) **29 ♗xc5?!** (interesting, but probably not completely sound) e4! (29...dxc5 30 ♘xe5+ ♔g8 31 ♘c6 ♖a8 32 g4 gives White sufficient compensation for the piece) 30 ♘d4 (30 ♗d4 exf3 31 ♖xf3 ♘e7 is good for Black) ♗g7! (30...dxc5 31 ♘c6

is fine for White) 31 ♘xf5 gxf5 and Black has a clear plus.

2) White should continue quietly, for example by **29 ♘e3 ♗e6 30 ♘g4** or **29 ♘d2 ♘e7 30 ♘xe7 ♚xe7 31 ♘e4**, with a roughly equal position in either case. The central pawns are dangerous, but White can restrain them by arranging to play c4.

26...f5 is obviously a positional mistake if Black cannot take back with the pawn, so by playing ...f5 Black 'announced' that he had overlooked White's next move.

28   ♖xe5!!

A mating attack erupts from nowhere.

28   ...   dxe5?!

Objectively, Black should have played 28...c6 (28...♘e7 29 ♘xe7 dxe5 30 ♘xe5+ ♚f6 31 ♘7c6 ♖e8 32 ♗b2 ♚g5 33 ♖d8! ♖xd8 34 ♘xd8 ♖b6 35 a5 is winning for White) 29 ♖xe6 ♚xe6 30 ♘d4+ ♚xd5 31 ♘xf5+ ♚e6 32 ♘xh6, but with two pawns for the exchange and very active pieces, White has a clear advantage.

29   ♘xe5+   ♚g7

After 29...♚g8 White forces mate in eight by 30 ♘f6+ ♚h8 31 ♖d8+ ♗f8 (31...♚g7 32 ♘h5 mate) 32 ♖xf8+ ♚g7 33 ♘e8+ ♚h6 34 ♗c1+ f4 35 ♗xf4+ ♚h5 36 ♘g7+ ♚h4 37 ♘f3 mate.

30   ♖g3+

Now it is mate in six instead!

30   ...   ♚h8 *(23)*

Or 30...♗g5 31 ♖xg5+ ♚h6 32 ♗c1 f4 33 ♗xf4, followed by 34 ♖g6+ and 35 ♖h6 mate.

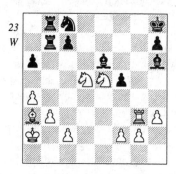

23
W

31   ♘f7+   ♗xf7
32   ♗b2+   ♗g7
33   ♗xg7+   ♚g8
34   ♘f6 mate.

Despite scoring 5/5 at Neath, my absence during the last two months of the competition proved too great a handicap and I was edged out by Peter Large. In the late 1980s the decline in the weekend circuit continued apace; at the time of writing, weekend tournaments offer much less prize money in numerical terms than they did in the late 1970s. As inflation over this period has been well above 100%, the prize money is effectively only a fraction of what was available 15 years ago. Only the entry fees and other expenses have kept up with inflation. After 1985, I never again made an effort to win the Grand Prix.

Readers will find a number of games from the German Bundesliga in this book. I have taken part in this competition every year since 1983, although I have changed clubs three times in the past eleven years. My first club was Hamburg, and fate eventually took me back there for the 1993-4 season. The format of the top division has been the same for the past decade; sixteen teams meet in a round-robin event played over eight weekends from (usually) October to May. During this decade, the strength of the teams has increased substantially, and playing on board one is now quite tough. The reason hasn't been so much increased sponsorship, but more the ready availability of ex-Soviet grandmasters who have high ratings and demand little cash.

British players are often curious as to where the money comes from for Bundesliga teams, but there is no single answer to this question. When I first played for Hamburg, the chess club formed part of the general Hamburg Sports Union, which provided money for a number of less popular sports. This Union was largely subsidised by the Hamburg football club, and my friends were baffled to find me closely studying the German football results, although I had never displayed any interest in the sport before. Alas, one year the Hamburg football team had a disastrous season, and several sports, including chess, lost their financial support.

Some other clubs are sponsored by a wealthy individual, sometimes local businesses are the main benefactors, and so on. The range of sponsorship sources seems to be much wider in Germany than in Britain, which is perhaps why they have so many more chess events.

British players have always been attracted to the Bundesliga, mainly because of the lack of a professional league in Britain. It is far from unusual to fly to Germany and then play an opponent who also lives in London, as in the following game.

Game 5
J.Nunn – C.Pritchett
Bundesliga 1985
Sicilian Sozin

1	e4	c5		3	d4	cxd4
2	♘f3	e6		4	♘xd4	♘c6

5 ♘c3   d6
6 ♗e3

Black's move-order is designed to reach a Scheveningen variation without allowing the Keres Attack. If White is prepared to play a Velimirović Attack, then he can cross this plan with 6 ♗e3 followed by ♗c4.

6 ...   ♘f6
7 ♗c4   a6
8 ♕e2   ♕c7
9 0-0-0   ♘a5
10 ♗d3

White's bishop normally retreats to b3 in the Velimirović Attack, but this position is an exception. Black has deliberately omitted ...♗e7 in order to save a tempo, the point being that after 10 ♗b3?! b5 White has no time for g4-g5, because his e-pawn is already threatened by ...♘xb3+ followed by ...b4. Black is very happy if he can force White to waste a tempo defending his e-pawn with the relatively useless move f3.

10 ...   b5

There are now three possibilities, namely 11 a3, 11 ♖hg1 and 11 g4. I have tried all three, but in this game I settled for the modest 11 a3. It has the advantage that White need not lose time with his knight after ...b4; the disadvantage is that Black can play ...♖b8 and ...b4, opening lines against White's king.

11 a3 (24)   ♗e7

The main line runs 11...♗b7, when 12 g4 d5 13 exd5 ♘xd5 14

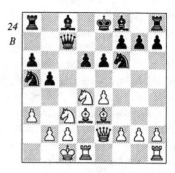

♘dxb5 ♕b8! (14...axb5? 15 ♗xb5+ ♔d8 16 ♘xd5 exd5 17 ♖d3 ♘c4 18 ♖c3 ♗b4?! 19 ♖xc4! dxc4 20 ♖d1+ ♔c8 21 ♖d4! gave White a decisive attack in Nunn-Sosonko, Thessaloniki OL 1984) 15 ♘xd5 ♗xd5 16 ♘c3 ♗xh1 17 ♖xh1 ♕c7 18 ♘d5! led to tremendous complications in Hawelko-Gaprindashvili, Polanica Zdroj 1986. White won this game, and nobody since has cared to repeat the line as Black.

Pritchett tries a different method of developing his queenside based on ...♖b8.

12 g4   ♖b8

This can introduce two possible plans. The first is to play ...♘c4 (but not the immediate 12...♘c4?, which loses to 13 ♘dxb5). The second is to exploit a3 by playing ...b4, but this normally requires preparation by ...♘d7-c5, or else it loses the pawn on a6.

13 ♖he1!?

An interesting move. The obvious plan is 13 g5 ♘d7 14 f4 intending f5, but this has the defect of driving Black's knight to the queenside, where it can help Black's counterplay. For example, after 14...♘c5 Black has defended the a6 pawn and is ready for ...b4.

Instead, I decided to try to restrain ...♘d7, by preparing to meet it with ♘f5; then g5 acquires extra force. The introduction of a non-standard idea is often a very effective weapon. Most chess players are creatures of habit, at least as far as the opening is concerned, and in most games the opening play is simply a combination of standard ideas. A novel plan, even if it differs only slightly from the norm, forces the opponent to think for himself and increases the possibility of error.

13   ...   ♘c4?!

A ♘f5 sacrifice against the centralised king is a standard idea in several lines of the Velimirović Attack, and in this particular position the build-up on the e-file lends it added power. It follows that Black should have played 13...0-0, removing his king from the dangerous file, and forcing White to decide whether or not to play ♘f5. However, after 13...0-0 14 g5 ♘d7 15 ♘f5 exf5 16 exf5 (16 ♘d5 ♕d8 17 exf5 ♗xg5 is safe for Black) ♗b7 (preventing ♘d5) 17 ♕h5 (17 f6 ♘xf6 18 gxf6 ♗xf6 defends) ♖fe8! (not 17...♘e5? 18 f6! ♘xd3+ 19 ♖xd3 gxf6 20 gxf6 ♗xf6 21 ♖g1+ ♔h8 22 ♗d4! ♗xd4

23 ♕xh7+ ♔xh7 24 ♖h3 mate), Black can meet 18 f6 by 18...g6 followed by ...♗f8, and so White's compensation appears insufficient. White would do better to answer 13...0-0 by 14 f4, improving his position while waiting for a better chance to play ♘f5.

13...0-0 would have exposed the dark side of committing the rook to e1 so soon, because against a king on g8 White might prefer to have his rook on g1.

If Black plays 13...♘d7, then 14 ♘f5 exf5 (14...♗f6 is met by 15 ♗f4!) 15 ♘d5 is similar to the game.

The move played precipitates a crisis, because White cannot afford to see his dark-squared bishop disappear, so he has to take immediate action.

14   g5   ♘d7 (25)

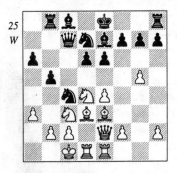

15   ♘f5!

Here the sacrifice is particularly effective because Black's 13th move allows White to clear the d-file with gain of tempo by exchanging pieces on c4.

15 ...   exf5

Black is more or less forced to accept the sacrifice because 15...♗f8 16 ♗d4 is very awkward (16...♖g8 17 ♕h5).

16 ♘d5   ♕d8

The alternative squares are worse:

1) **16...♕c6** 17 ♗xc4 ♕xc4 18 ♕xc4 (exchanging queens may appear surprising, but it is the best) bxc4 19 exf5 ♘e5 (or 19...♗b7 20 ♘xe7 ♔xe7 21 ♗a7+ ♔d8 22 ♗xb8 ♘xb8 23 ♖xd6+ with a won ending for White) 20 ♘xe7 ♔xe7 21 ♗c5! dxc5 22 ♖xe5+ ♗e6 23 fxe6 fxe6 24 ♖de1 ♖b6 25 ♖xc5 with a winning rook and pawn ending.

2) **16...♕b7** 17 ♘xe7 ♔xe7 (after 17...fxe4 18 ♘xc8 exd3 19 ♘xd6+ ♘xd6 20 ♕xd3 ♘e4 21 ♗d4 White regains the piece with a clear extra pawn) 18 ♗d4 f4 (the critical move, since if the e-file is opened then White has more than enough for the piece) 19 ♗xc4 bxc4 20 e5 d5 (or 20...dxe5 21 ♗xe5 ♘xe5 22 ♕xe5+ ♗e6 23 ♕xg7 and Black has no defence against the twin threats of 24 ♖xe6+ and 24 ♕f6+) 21 e6 ♘b6 (21...♘f8 22 ♗c5+ ♔e8 23 exf7++ ♔d7 24 ♕e7+ ♔d7 25 ♕d6+ ♔b5 26 ♖xd5 wins) 22 exf7+ ♔xf7 23 ♕h5+ g6 24 ♕h6 and White wins.

17 exf5   0-0

Leaving the king in the centre is asking to be mated:

1) **17...♗b7** 18 ♗xc4 bxc4 19 ♗f4 ♗xd5 20 ♖xd5 (20 ♗xd6 0-0 21 ♗xe7 ♕a5 is less clear) ♔f8 21 f6 gxf6 22 gxf6 ♘xf6 23 ♖xd6! ♕xd6 24 ♗xd6 ♗xd6 25 ♕d2 ♗e7 26 ♕h6+ ♔e8 27 ♕xf6 and wins.

2) **17...♘de5** 18 f4 ♘xd3+ 19 ♕xd3 0-0 20 f6 gxf6 21 ♗a7! ♖b7 22 ♖xe7 and wins.

3) **17...♘xe3** 18 ♕xe3 ♘e5 19 f4 wins.

18 ♕h5 *(26)*

White must be careful not to allow Black to return the material in favourable circumstances. After 18 f6? ♘xf6 19 ♗b6 (19 gxf6 ♗xf6 is also bad) ♘xd5! 20 ♗xd8 ♗xd8 21 ♗xc4 (if Black gets three pieces for the queen, then he is doing well; note that 21 ♕e4 fails to 21...♗xg5+ and 22...♘f6) ♗xg5+ 22 ♔b1 ♘f4! and Black keeps three pieces for the queen in any case.

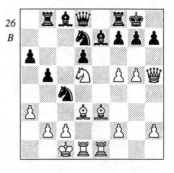

18 ...   ♘f6?

Black decides to return the piece immediately, but in this situation

White keeps both his f5 pawn and his attack. However, even with best play Black's position is dismal:

1) **18...♘xe3** fails to meet the threat of 19 f6.

2) **18...♘de5** 19 f6 ♘xd3+ 20 ♖xd3 gxf6 21 ♗a7 ♖b7 22 ♖xe7 wins.

3) **18...g6** 19 fxg6 fxg6 20 ♗xg6 hxg6 21 ♕xg6+ ♔h8 22 ♖d4 leads to mate.

4) **18...♘ce5!** (the only chance; the d7 knight must stay where it is to control f6) 19 ♗e4! (after 19 f6? ♘xd3+ 20 ♖xd3 ♗xf6! 21 gxf6 ♘xf6 the position is unclear, but not 20...♘xf6? 21 gxf6 ♗xf6 22 ♗d4 and White has a crushing attack) g6 (or else f6 again) 20 ♕h4 (threat f6) gxf5 (20...♖e8 21 f4 ♘c4 22 ♗d4 with the idea of ♖d3 and ♕xh7+ gives White a very strong attack) 21 ♗xf5 ♘g6 22 ♕h6 (22 ♗xg6 fxg6 23 ♘xe7+ ♕xe7 24 ♗a7 ♕f7 25 ♗xb8 ♘xb8 26 ♖xd6 is promising for White, but the text move appears even stronger) ♘de5 23 ♗xc8 ♖xc8 24 f4 ♘g4 25 ♕h3 ♘xe3 26 ♕xe3 ♖e8 27 h4! and there is no reasonable answer to the threat of 28 h5, for example 27...h5 28 gxh6 ♗xh4 29 ♕d4.

19	gxf6	♗xf6
20	♗xc4	bxc4
21	♗d4	

Removing the only defender standing between White's army and Black's king.

21	...	♗xd4
22	♖xd4	

Black was forced to exchange bishops, but now he has to deal with the threat of 23 ♘e7+ ♔h8 24 ♕xh7+. Both 22...♖b7 and 22...h6 lose to 23 f6, so again there is no choice.

22	...	♖e8 *(27)*

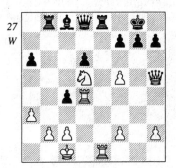

27
W

23 ♘f6+!

The quickest way to finish the game – the other knight also sacrifices itself on the f-file.

23	...	gxf6
24	♖g4+	

Not 24 ♖g1+? and the king can slip away after 24...♔f8.

24	...	♔h8
25	♖eg1	

Black can only delay the threat of ♕xh7+ by one move.

25	...	♗xf5
26	♕xf5	

Now White can mate in six more moves against any defence.

26	...	♖b5

Pritchett sportingly lets me sacrifice my queen as well.

27 ♕xh7+   1-0

In November, I had a relatively poor result in the World Team Championship at Lucerne, scoring 50% on board 2. Unfortunately I lost my last two games, which was to set a pattern for future team events – a good start, followed by a weak finish. I did play one attractive combination:

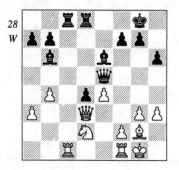

28
W

This position arose in H.Pfleger-J.Nunn. White is to play. Black has a promising position, and threatens to activate his passed pawn by playing ...♖c3. The game continued **22 f4?** (this only makes matters worse by opening the b6-g1 diagonal) **♖c3!** (almost a problem move; after 23

♖xc3 dxc3+, it is important that the lines b6-g1 and d8-d3 are opened simultaneously) **23 ♕b1** (the only move to avoid instant loss of material) **♕c7 24 ♔h2** (24 f5 ♗a2 25 ♕a1 ♖c8) **♖c8 25 ♖cd1 ♖xa3 26 e5 ♕c2** (returning the pawn to activate Black's rooks) **27 ♗xb7 ♕xb1 28 ♘xb1** (28 ♖xb1 ♖c2 29 ♖bd1 a5! 30 b5 a4 and the second passed pawn will prove too much) **♖c2+ 29 ♖d2 ♖aa2 30 ♖ff2** (30 ♖d1 d3 31 ♗e4 ♗c4! 32 ♔h1 ♖ab2 wins because 33 ♗xd3 ♗xd3 34 ♖xd3 ♖h2 is mate, while 33 ♖g2 ♖xg2 34 ♗xg2 ♗b3 35 ♖f1 d2 36 ♘c3 ♗d4 37 ♘d1 ♖b1 38 ♗f3 ♗c4 traps the rook) **d3 31 ♖g2 ♖ab2 32 ♖d1 ♖xg2+ 33 ♗xg2 ♗b3** (not the immediate 33...♗d5? 34 ♖d2, but now White has to move his rook along the rank, whereupon ...♗d5 does win) **0-1**.

I finished the year by playing a relatively weak Category 9 tournament, sponsored by OHRA and held in Brussels. My final total was a mediocre 8/13; although I only lost one game, to Sax (in 14 moves!), I scored too few wins to challenge for a leading position. Korchnoi won this event with the excellent score of 11/13.

1986

The new year started with a very strong open tournament in Vienna, sponsored by IBM. This event was notable for the fact that my hotel accommodation was the most luxurious I have ever experienced at a chess tournament – two rooms, two television sets, two bathrooms and three(!) telephones. When I rushed round to Murray Chandler's room to tell him, he invited me proudly into his own suite – two rooms (but smaller than mine) and two television sets, but only two telephones. I explained that I had to leave, as I was suffering from claustrophobia. He looked at me curiously, then suddenly caught on and demanded to see my rooms. Hitherto delighted, he was immediately disappointed at coming off second best!

The tournament was jointly won by Korchnoi and Beliavsky with 6½/9; I played quite well and ended in a tie for third place with 6/9, level with Karpov, Spassky and four other players.

By March it was once again time for the annual pilgrimage to Lugano, which this year ended in a quadruple tie for first place between Korchnoi, Gutman, Plaskett and Short. Again I was moderately successful, finishing with 7/9, the same score as in the previous year. A good tournament for British players!

Game 6

J.Nunn – V.Tukmakov

Lugano Open 1986

Sicilian

1	e4	c5
2	♘f3	d6
3	d4	cxd4
4	♘xd4	♘f6
5	♘c3	♘c6
6	♗c4	♕b6

This is a good way for Black to avoid the complexities of the Velimirović Attack (see page 35) and steer the game into more placid channels. White is more or less forced to retreat his knight, which reduces his prospects of a quick attack.

7	♘b3	e6

It may appear that White will gain time later by ♗e3, but after the reply ...♛c7 White has to lose a tempo himself, because the unprotected bishop on c4 is a tactical weakness and he will have to play ♗d3 or ♗e2. The net effect is that the knight on d4 will have been kicked back to b3 without loss of time for Black. In contrast to the Velimirović Attack, both sides usually castle kingside, and play proceeds along relatively quiet lines analogous to the Scheveningen variation.

8 0-0   ♗e7
9 ♗g5

This move is an attempt to exploit the position of the queen on b6. The theory is that Black's queen is blocking the b-pawn, so in order for Black to develop his normal queenside counterplay, he will have to play ...♛c7. If Black is going to retreat his queen voluntarily, there isn't much point in playing ♗e3; instead the more active deployment on g5 should be preferred. Well, that's the theory, but the reality is less clear-cut; the move ♗g5 has both positive and negative features.

9 ...   ♘e5

Although this reply has proved quite popular, I remain suspicious about its value. Sooner or later the knight will be pushed back by f4, and Black's idea is to support the kingside by retreating it to g6. 9...a6 and 9...0-0 are good alternatives,

both of which have accumulated substantial bodies of theory.

10 ♗e2   ♗d7

The main alternative runs 10...0-0 11 ♔h1 (after 11 ♗e3 ♛c7 12 f4 Black can reply 12...♘c4) a6 12 f4 (12 ♛e1 ♛c7 13 f4 ♘g6 14 ♛g3 ♔h8 15 ♖ad1 b5 16 a3 ♗b7 17 f5 exf5 18 exf5 is roughly equal, Ehlvest-Popović, Belgrade 1989) ♘g6 13 f5!? (or 13 ♗h5!? ♛c7 14 ♗xg6 hxg6 15 ♛e1 b5 16 e5 b4! 17 exf6 gxf6 with unclear complications, as in Neverov-Lukin, Blagoveshensk 1988) ♘e5 14 ♛d2 ♛c7 15 ♖ad1 ♔h8? (15...♖d8 would have been just slightly better for White) 16 ♗xf6 gxf6 17 ♘d4 with a clear plus for White, Galdunts-Serper, Kherson 1991.

11 ♔h1 (29)

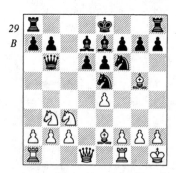

11 ...   ♘g6?!

This voluntary retreat is dubious. The point is that White would like to gain time by ♗e3 followed by f4, but at the moment this would be met by

...♕c7 followed by ...♘c4. If Black commits his knight to g6 before White plays f4, then the ♗e3 plan becomes viable.

The best line is the simple 11...0-0 12 f4 ♘g6, when White may play:

1) **13 e5** ♘e8 (not 13...dxe5 14 ♗xf6 ♗xf6 15 ♕xd7 ♖ad8 16 ♕b5 and Black doesn't have enough compensation for the piece) 14 ♗xe7 ♘xe7 15 ♗d3 ♗c6 16 ♕h5 (16 ♕e2 is level) g6 17 ♕h3 (17 ♕g5 ♘f5 was fine for Black in Minasian-Ruban, USSR Ch 1991) ♘f5 18 ♘e4 ♗xe4 19 ♗xe4 dxe5 20 fxe5 ♖c8 with an edge for Black, Semeniuk-Lagunov, Novosibirsk 1989.

2) **13 ♕d3** ♖ad8 14 f5 ♘e5 15 ♕g3 ♔h8 16 ♖f4 ♖c8 17 ♖af1 h6 18 ♕h3 with a very strong attack for White, Wahls-Wirthensohn, Hamburg SKA 1991, although in this example Black's play was feeble.

3) **13 ♗h5** ♘xh5 14 ♗xe7 ♘g3+ 15 hxg3 ♘xe7 16 g4 f5 17 exf5 exf5 18 g5 was equal in Rublevsky-Ruban, Smolensk 1991.

After the move played, 12 f4 is met by 12...h6 and White must part with his valuable bishop, so the alternative plan is both forced and strong.

12 ♗e3   ♕c7
13 f4   0-0

The position resembles a Scheveningen, the main difference being that Black's knight is on g6 instead of c6. This has certain advantages, namely that the kingside is better

defended and the c6 square is available for the d7 bishop. But these are outweighed by the disadvantages, that Black has lost time and that a later f5 will occur with gain of tempo. As in the Scheveningen, White can adopt a number of different plans, such as a piece attack by ♕e1-g3 and f5, a pawn attack based on g4 or central pressure by ♗f3, ♕e2 and ♖d1, perhaps followed by doubling rooks on the d-file. White's next few moves keep his options open while he completes his development.

14 ♕e1

In Rublevsky-Vekshenkov, USSR Ch semi-final, Voronezh 1991, White played on the queenside by 14 a4 ♖fe8 15 ♗d3 ♗f8 16 ♘b5 ♕b8 17 c4 ♗c6 18 ♘c3 b6 19 a5 ♖c8, which was adequate for a slight advantage. I didn't consider this plan at all, although it is quite logical to try exploiting the absence of the knight from the queenside.

14 ...   ♖fe8
15 ♖d1   ♗c6
16 ♗f3

Black's 15...♗c6 was his first really committal move, for if he doesn't follow up with a break in the centre White can play ♘d4. This would restrain any counterplay by Black, because ...b5 would be impossible, while ...e5 could be met by ♘f5.

16 ...   d5

17 e5

In the Scheveningen, it is very rarely a good idea to meet ...d5 by exd5. The reason is that the move f4 would be totally out of place in the resulting pawn structure, since it would serve only to weaken squares along the open e-file.

17 ...   ♘e4

The normal follow-up to ...d5. If Black has to retreat the knight in reply to White's e5, then he probably shouldn't have played ...d5 in the first place.

18 ♘d4

The queen on e1 defends c3, so White has time to strengthen his position. This move threatens 19 ♗xe4 dxe4 20 ♗g1, when Black cannot save the pawn on e4. Since 18...♗b4 loses to 19 ♘xd5, Black has to take on c3, which gives White a favourable type of French Defence in which he has undisputed control of d4.

18 ...   ♘xc3
19 ♕xc3 *(30)*

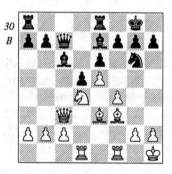

19 ...   ♖ac8

This pawn structure can arise from various lines in the French, although in many such lines White castles queenside. Control of d4 is the key factor, because Black would like to exchange minor pieces, reducing White's attacking chances, but this is normally only possible on d4. In this respect Black suffers from the position of his knight on g6. White's most obvious plan is to prepare f5, but the immediate 20 f5 exf5 21 ♘xf5 ♘xe5 leads to nothing. I therefore decided that the best way to strengthen the attack was to transfer the queen to the kingside.

20 ♕e1   ♗d7

Now that the pawn has advanced to d5, the bishop only blocks the c-file, so it moves to a square where it can restrain White's f5.

21 ♕g3   ♕b6?!

It is obviously very risky to put the queen opposite White's bishop, but if White cannot immediately exploit the position of Black's queen, then the attack on b2 is very awkward (22 b3 allows dangerous counterplay by 22...♖c3). Unfortunately for Tukmakov, White does have a strong reply.

Black should have defended passively, for example by 21...a6, when White would have to find a way of improving his position, for example by ♗e2-d3. In this case Black would have a lifeless but solid position.

22 f5!   **exf5**

Or 22...♗h4 23 ♕h3 exf5 24 ♗xd5 ♖xe5 (24...♕xb2 25 ♘xf5 forces 25...♖f8, or else ♗xf7+, but then 26 e6! fxe6 27 ♗b3! unexpectedly wins material by means of the double attack on h4 and d7) 25 ♗xf7+ ♔h8 (25...♔xf7 26 ♘xf5 wins) 26 ♗xg6 ♕xg6 27 ♗f4 and White gains material.

23 ♗xd5 *(31)*

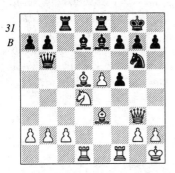

23 ...   **♗h4?!**

The obvious move is **23...♕xb2**, but White wins by 24 e6! fxe6 25 ♘xe6 ♗c6 26 ♗b3 ♗h4 (26...♔h8 27 ♗d4 wins) 27 ♗d4!! ♗xg3 (there is nothing better) 28 ♗xb2 and White finally reaps the harvest from the b3-g8 battery.

23...♗c5 is relatively the best defence, based on the surprising tactical point 24 ♘xf5 ♗xf5 25 ♗xc5 ♖xc5 26 ♖xf5 ♖xd5! 27 ♖xd5 ♕e6; White has nothing better than 28 ♕d3 ♘e7 29 ♖d8 ♘xf5 30 ♖xe8+ ♕xe8 31 ♕xf5, when although the

extra pawn gives White fair winning chances, Black can still hope for a draw.

Other Black 23rd moves do not meet the threats of 24 ♗xf7+ and 24 ♘xf5.

24 ♘xf5?!

Although White's advantage is considerable even after this move, it would have been even bigger after 24 ♕h3! transposing into the note to Black's 22nd.

24 ...   **♗xg3**
25 ♗xb6 *(32)*

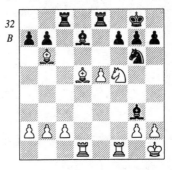

25 ...   **axb6?**

Tukmakov played this natural move with little thought, but it leads to an abrupt end. 25...♗xe5 was essential, when White has two possibilities:

1) **26 ♗xa7** gives White an extra pawn, although after 26...♗e6 Black's pieces are active and the win would be far from certain.

2) **26 ♘d6 ♗xd6 27 ♗xf7+ ♔h8 28 ♖xd6 ♗b5** (28...♖f8 29 ♖xd7

axb6 30 c3 is worse) 29 c4 (29 ♗xe8
♖xe8 is much less clear) ♗xc4 30
♗xc4 axb6 (30...♖xc4 31 ♗xa7 followed by ♗d4 with a material and
positional advantage) 31 ♗b5 and
White takes the b6 pawn, but there
will still be many technical problems
converting this into a win.

26   ♘d6!   1-0

This unexpectedly forces a decisive material advantage, for example
26...♗xe5 27 ♗xf7+ ♔h8 28 ♗xe8
♖xe8 29 ♘xe8 ♗xe8 30 ♖d8 or
26...♗h4 27 ♗xf7+ ♔h8 28 ♗xe8
♖xe8 29 ♘f7+ ♔g8 30 ♖xd7. After
thinking for 20 minutes, Tukmakov
resigned.

Last round games are always tense
when substantial prizes are at stake.
The effort invested during the whole
event can easily be thrown away by a
single slip at the eleventh hour. In
Open tournaments, it often happens
that both players need a win in order
to gain a significant prize; this can
make it easier, particularly when
playing Black, because you can rely
on your opponent not to steer the
game into drawish channels. My record in last rounds is not especially
good, but there have been occasions
when I produced a game I could be
proud of. The following game is an
example.

Game 7
J.Nunn – K.Bischoff
Lugano Open 1986
Sicilian

1	e4	c5
2	♘f3	e6
3	d4	cxd4
4	♘xd4	♘f6
5	♘c3	d6
6	g4	h6
7	h4	a6
8	♗g2	♘c6

Although Nunn-Bischoff was not
the first time 8...♘c6 had been
played, it had received practically
no attention before 1986 and was
certainly new to me. It experienced

a brief surge of popularity, but the
practical results were good for
White, and it wasn't long before it
disappeared again. During 1993, curiously, it reappeared in a couple of
games. The alternatives are 8...g6
and 8...d5.

9	g5	hxg5
10	hxg5	♖xh1+
11	♗xh1	♘d7 (33)

If Black attacks the g5 pawn by
11...♘xd4 12 ♕xd4 ♘h7, then White
continues 13 e5! ♘xg5 (13...dxe5 14

♕h4 traps the knight) 14 ♕a4+! (14 exd6 is also promising) ♗d7 15 ♕g4 ♗e7 (15...♘h7 16 ♕h5 loses a piece, while 15...f6 16 ♗xg5 fxg5 17 ♕h5+ is disastrous) 16 exd6 ♗f6 17 ♗xb7 with a clear advantage to White.

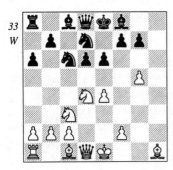

33
W

12 ♗g2?!

This move was the result of lengthy thought, but even so it wasn't the best. White has very few constructive moves apart from g6, and the immediate 12 g6 ♘xd4 13 gxf7+ ♔xf714 ♕xd4 ♕h4 15 ♗g2 ♘e5 is obscure. White might be able to claim a slight plus after 16 ♗e3 ♕g4 17 ♔f1, but both kings are unhappily placed and I wanted to find something safer. When confronted with an unexpected move in the opening, players usually react by steering clear of very sharp lines which may have been well prepared by the opponent.

12 ♗e3 is bad after 12...♘de5 threatening ...♘c4 (13 ♕e2 ♘xd4 loses a pawn).

Thus the only direct alternative to 12 g6 is 12 f4, but I was reluctant to create a huge empty space around my king. However, later analysis showed that Black has no way to exploit the temporary exposure of White's king, so in subsequent games White preferred the more accurate 12 f4!. Black has replied:

1) **12...♘xd4** 13 ♕xd4 ♕b6 14 ♕xb6 ♘xb6 15 a4!? ♗d7 16 a5 ♘c8 17 ♗e3 ♗c6 18 0-0-0 ♔d7 19 ♗f3 ♘e7 20 ♗g4 with a clear plus for White, Ghinda-Vogt, Halle 1987.

2) **12...g6** 13 ♗e3 ♕b6 14 a3 ♕c7 15 ♕e2 ♘a5 16 0-0-0 ♖b8 17 e5!? (not strictly necessary, but very dangerous) dxe5 18 ♘xe6 fxe6 19 ♕d3 with a strong attack for the piece, Nunn-Suba, London (Lloyds Bank) 1990.

3) **12...♕b6** 13 ♘de2 g6 14 b3 with a further branch:

3a) **14...♕c7** 15 ♗b2 b5 16 ♕d2 ♖b8 (16...♗b7 17 ♘d1 0-0-0 18 ♘e3 ♗e7 19 0-0-0 ♘b6 20 ♔b1 ♔b8 21 ♘c1 was also a little better for White in Grünfeld-Bischoff, Munich 1987) 17 ♗g2 (17 0-0-0 ♘b6 18 a3 ♗d7 19 ♗g2 b4 20 axb4 ♘xb4 was equal in Kir.Georgiev-Suba, Budapest Z 1993, but 18 ♖e1 b4 19 ♘d1 would have given White the edge, according to Stoica) a5?! 18 ♘d1! a4 19 ♘e3 b4 20 0-0-0 ♗a6 21 ♔b1 axb3 22 axb3 was good for White in Watson-Suba, Kuala Lumpur 1992.

3b) **14...♛c5** 15 ♛d2 b5 16 ♝b2 ♝b7 17 0-0-0 0-0-0 18 ♚b1 ♛f2!? (or 18...♝e7 19 ♞c1! f6 20 gxf6 ♞xf6 21 ♞d3 with an edge) 19 a4 (19 ♖e1 ♝e7 20 ♞d1 ♛c5 21 ♞e3 gave White a small but permanent advantage, Short-Kindermann, Dortmund 1986) ♛b6 20 axb5 axb5 21 ♞c1 ♞c5 22 ♛h2! with a distinct plus for White, Anand-J.Polgar, Madrid 1993.

The move played is inferior because White finds himself obliged to play f4 in any case, so it would have been better to play it at once.

12   ...   g6!

The idea behind 12 ♝g2 was that White improves the position of his bishop (particularly in the g6 line given above, because ...♛h4 no longer gains a tempo), while Black has trouble finding useful moves. 12...♞de5 allows 13 f4 with gain of tempo (13...♞c4 14 b3 ♛b6 15 ♞ce2), 12...♛c7 (or ♝e7) allows 13 g6 and 12...♛b6 13 ♞b3 loses time after a subsequent ♝e3. Black's reply is the best, cutting out g6 by White and again posing the question as to how White can improve his position.

13   f4

Now the defect of 12 ♝g2 is revealed. In the analysis of 12 f4 we saw that Black generally plays ...g6 in any case, while White's ♝g2 is often not necessary. Therefore Black may gain a tempo, although in this position the extra move is not especially valuable. Now that e5 is denied to Black's knights, White threatens simply ♝e3, so Black's reply is more or less forced.

13   ...   ♛b6
14   ♞de2

Now White can only complete his development by ♛d2 (or ♛d3), b3, ♝b2 and 0-0-0, so before playing f4 I had to make sure that Black couldn't use the four(!) free tempi to harass White's centralised king.

14   ...   ♛c5

Black settles for finishing his own development by ...b5 and ...♝b7. This is clearly best, because 14...♛c7 allows 15 ♝e3 and 14...♞c5 is met by 15 b3 in any case.

15   ♛d3

It would have been slightly better to play ♛d2 as the queen is exposed to possible knight attacks on d3. My idea was to leave open the possibility of ♝e3, but this is never feasible.

15   ...   b5
16   b3

16 ♝e3 is effectively countered by 16...♞b4!.

16   ...   ♝b7
17   ♝b2   ♖c8

A risky move; Black decides to leave his king in the centre in order to help his c-file counterplay. After 17...0-0-0 18 0-0-0 White has a small space advantage, just as in the above analysis of 12 f4.

18   0-0-0 *(34)*

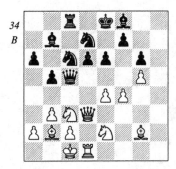

18 ...   ᐃb4

Thanks to Black's committal decision last move, he has to follow up with active play. If White is allowed to consolidate, then ᐃb1, ᐃf1 and ᐃd1-e3-g4 will inevitably give White a strong attack against the centralised Black king.

This is a very common situation in chess. Black, for example, makes a move which tips the long-term balance in White's favour; in return he acquires short-term benefits. Black then *has* to play aggressively, because if White is given the chance to neutralise Black's short-term assets, Black's future is bleak. The result of such situations often depends on whether or not Black's play can be justified tactically. In this case Black's idea is sound, but it needs to be followed up correctly.

19   ᐃd2   ᐃxc2
20   ᐃxc2   b4
21   ᐃb1   ᐃf2!

This is the point of Black's combination. The immediate 21...bxc3

22 ᐃxc3 leaves Black in a poor position, because his combination has failed to dent White's position, and the long-term prospects lie with White.

22   ᐃh1   bxc3

At this stage Black surprisingly offered a draw, but although White must adopt the much less satisfactory recapture with the bishop, thus leaving e4 weak, I decided to play on. It goes without saying that allowing the queens to be exchanged would give White no advantage, because his main asset is the vulnerable position of Black's king, and this can only be exploited in the middlegame.

23   ᐃxc3 *(35)*

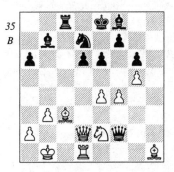

23   ...   ᐃa7?

A misjudgement. The main merit of Black's combination is that his queen has become a nuisance by taking up residence in the heart of White's position, the more so as White cannot contemplate a queen exchange. Bischoff retreats it to the passive square a8 in return for inconvenient but not really serious pressure against e4. He should have played 23...♘c5 24 ♗d4 ♕h2! (24...♘xe4 25 ♕d3! loses a piece, while 24...♕h4 25 ♘c3 e5 26 ♗e3 looks good for White) when White has problems with his e4 pawn. Then 25 ♕e3 e5 26 ♗b2 ♗g7 creates a very awkward threat of ...exf4, so White would have to play 25 ♘c3 ♕xd2 26 ♖xd2 with equality. The key to the position is the pin on the second rank, and Black should have preserved this.

24	♗b2	♕a8
25	♕e3	♘c5
26	♘c3	

26 ♘g3 with the idea of f5 is also promising.

26 ...   ♗g7

After 26...a5 the reply 27 ♕d4 ties Black up by preventing ...♗g7. Once again, Black's only chance is to create direct threats, because if White is allowed to play ♗f3 and ♖h1-h8, Black will be in serious trouble.

27 ♘d5! *(36)*

Before playing 26 ♘c3 I had to think very carefully about the tactics initiated by this move, since if White had been reduced to the passive 27 ♖e1 (27 ♖xd6 ♗xc3 is bad since Black wins after 28 ♗xc3 ♗xe4+ 29 ♗xe4 ♕xe4+ 30 ♕xe4 ♘xe4 or 28 ♕xc3 ♗xe4+ 29 ♗xe4 ♕xe4+ 30 ♔a1 ♕h1+ 31 ♗c1 ♘xb3+) then Black would be at least equal.

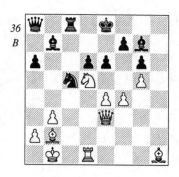

36
B

27 ...   ♗xb2

The most natural move. The alternatives are:

1) 27...♗xd5 28 exd5 ♗xb2 29 dxe6!? (29 ♔xb2 is slightly better for White) ♕a7 (preventing ♔xb2) 30 ♖xd6 ♔f8 (30...♗a3 31 exf7+ ♔f8 32 ♕c3 and 30...♗g7 31 ♗c6+ ♔f8 32 ♖d7 win for White) 31 ♖d7 ♕b6 32 e7+ ♔e8 33 ♖d8+ ♖xd8 34 exd8♕+ ♔xd8 35 ♕d2+ ♘d3 36 ♕xd3+ and the extra pawn gives White some winning chances in the ending.

2) 27...exd5 28 ♗xg7 ♘xe4 (28...dxe4 29 ♖xd6 is worse as the undefended ♘c5 prevents 29...♖d8, while 29...♘d3 allows ♖xd3) and now:

2a) 29 ♗xe4 dxe4 appears promising, as White has a strong attack on the dark squares, while Black's queen is buried on a8. However, it isn't easy to find a concrete way to proceed, for example 30 ♖xd6 ♖d8! 31 ♕d4 ♖xd6 32 ♕xd6 ♕d8 (or else ♗f6) 33 ♕f8+ ♔d7 34 ♕xf7+ ♔c8 wins a pawn, but in view of the opposite coloured bishops and Black's passed e-pawn this might not be enough to win.

2b) **29 ♗f3!** is better. The threat is simply ♖h1-h8, and the bishop can move to g4 to cut off the escape of Black's king.

28 ♘b6   ♗xe4+

After 28...♕a7 29 ♘xc8 ♗xc8 30 b4 (White can't take the bishop) ♕b7 (30...♕b6 31 bxc5 dxc5 32 ♕b3) 31 ♔xb2 ♕xb4+ 32 ♔a1 Black has insufficient compensation for the lost exchange.

29 ♔xb2   ♕a7

The only defence. Now 30 ♘c4 d5 31 ♗xe4 (31 ♘d6+ ♔d7 is good for Black, while 31 ♕d4 fails to 31...♘a4+! 32 bxa4 ♖b8+ followed by ...♕xd4 and ...♗xh1) is tempting, since 31...dxe4 loses to 32 ♕d4! ♖a8 (32...♖b8 33 ♘d6+ ♔f8 34 ♘xe4) 33 ♘d6+ ♔f8 34 ♕h8+ ♔e7 35 ♕f6+ ♔f8 36 ♖h1 ♘a4+ 37 ♔b1 followed by mate. However, Black has a better defence in 31...dxc4! 32 ♕d4 ♕c7, and it is doubtful if White has anything better than perpetual check.

30 ♖xd6   ♘d3+

Black's moves continue to be forced. 30...♗xh1 31 ♕d4! (attacking the rook on c8 and threatening 32 ♕h8+) ♖b8 (31...♖c7 32 ♕h8+ and mate at d8) 32 ♕xc5 (threat ♖d7) ♖d8 (32...♕e7 33 ♘c8 ♕b7 34 ♖xe6+ wins) 33 ♕e5 gives White a

decisive attack, e.g. 33...♖xd6/♕e7/ ♕b8 34 ♕h8+ or 33...♖b8 34 ♖xe6+ fxe6 35 ♕h8+.

31 ♔a3 *(37)*

31 ♖xd3 is met by 31...♗xd3.

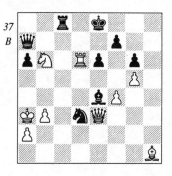

37
B

31 ...   ♖c6!

I had overlooked this ingenious defence when I played 26 ♘c3. Other moves lose quickly:

1) **31...♖c5** 32 ♖xd3 ♖a5+ (or 32...♕xb6 33 ♗xe4) 33 ♔b2 ♗xd3 (33...♗xh1 34 ♕d4) 34 ♗c6+ ♔d8 (or else a knight check wins the queen) 35 b4 ♖f5 36 ♕xd3+ ♔c7 37 ♕d7+ ♔xb6 38 ♕d4+ and Black loses his queen.

2) **31...♕c7** 32 ♖xd3 ♗xd3 33 ♘xc8 ♕xc8 34 ♕xd3 ♕c1+ 35 ♔b4 ♕xh1 36 ♕xa6 ♕e1+ 37 ♔b5 ♕e2+ 38 ♔b6 ♕f2+ 39 ♔b7 with a winning ending since 39...♕xf4 fails to 40 ♕a4+.

3) **31...♗xh1** 32 ♕h3 ♖b8 33 ♖xe6+ fxe6 34 ♕h8+ winning the queen.

32 ♖xc6

The best, as 32 ♘d5 ♕xe3 33 ♘f6+ is a draw by perpetual check and 32 ♖xd3 (32 ♕xd3 ♕xb6 is good for Black) ♗xh1 33 ♘c4 is roughly equal.

32   ...   ♕e7+ *(38)*

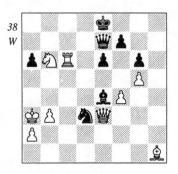

33   ♕c5!

33 ♖c5 ♗xh1 34 b4 ♘xc5 35 ♕xc5 is not so good since Black can avoid the exchange of queens by 35...♕d8, when White's exposed king means an almost inevitable perpetual check. After the game Bischoff admitted that he had not foreseen this move in time.

33   ...   ♕xc5+

Or 33...♘xc5 34 ♖c8+ ♕d8 35 ♖xd8+ ♔xd8 transposing into the game, except for an unimportant change in the position of Black's king.

34   ♖xc5   ♘xc5
35   b4!

White is aiming for a good knight v bad bishop ending. He can also head for a knight v knight ending by

35 ♗xe4 (35 ♔b4 ♘d3+ 36 ♔c3 ♘f2! leads to the same thing) ♘xe4 36 ♔b4, intending ♔a5, but although this is favourable for White, his advantage is less than in the game.

35   ...   ♗xh1
36   bxc5 *(39)*

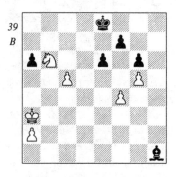

36   ...   ♗d5?

A blunder in severe time-trouble. He should have tried 36...♔e7 (36...f6 37 gxf6 ♔f7 38 ♘d7 is bad because 38...♗c6 is impossible, while even if Black's king were on d8, as in the note to Black's 33rd move, 36...♔c7 37 ♔b4 ♔c6 38 ♔c4 followed by ♔d4 and ♘c4-e5+ would win for White) 37 ♔b4 e5! (37...f6 38 ♔a5 ♗b7 39 ♘c4 followed by ♔b6 wins) 38 fxe5 ♔e6, but even here White wins: 39 ♘c4 ♗d5 40 a3! ♗xc4 (there is not much choice as a bishop move allows 41 ♔a5, and 40...♔e7 loses to 41 ♘e3 followed by 42 ♔a5) 41 ♔xc4 ♔xe5 42 ♔b4! (certainly not 42 a4? f5 43 gxf6 ♔xf6 44 ♔d5 ♔e7! 45 ♔c6 g5 46 ♔b7 g4 47 c6 g3 48 c7 g2 49 c8♕ g1♕ 50 ♕c7+ ♔e6 51 ♔xa6 reaching a position with ♕+a♙ v ♕, which the database confirms to be a draw; note that Black must avoid 44...g5? in this line, when 45 ♔d6 g4 46 c6 g3 47 c7 g2 48 c8♕ g1♕ 49 ♕f8+ wins his queen) ♔d5 (42...f5 43 gxf6 ♔xf6 44 ♔a5 g5 45 c6 wins) 43 a4 and Black is in a fatal zugzwang.

37 ♘xd5   exd5

White wins because Black's a-pawn has moved, while White's can still advance either one or two squares. This extra flexibility means that White can always arrange for the key reciprocal zugzwang position to arrive with Black to play.

38 ♔b4   ♔d7
39 ♔c3   1-0

Black lost on time, but in any case 39...♔c6 40 ♔d4 a5 41 a4 and 39...♔c7 40 ♔d4 ♔c6 41 a3 a5 42 a4 lead to the same position of reciprocal zugzwang.

In recent decades, London has not been a centre for top-class chess, but in 1980 there was a step forwards with the introduction of a new grandmaster tournament. This was a result of co-operation between the GLC (Greater London Council) and stockbrokers Phillips & Drew. It might be said that this was an early example of the type of collaboration between public and private bodies which has become very fashionable recently. The tournament was successfully repeated in 1982 and 1984, but by 1986 Phillips & Drew had pulled out, and the GLC, then in its death throes, was left to sponsor the final event in the series.

Very few sponsors have provided lasting support for chess. Sometimes the cause has been a change in the structure of the sponsor, for example Phillips & Drew were taken over by UBS (Union Bank of Switzerland), and the GLC was abolished. More often the critical factor has been the departure of a key person from the company. However, in many cases it may well be that the sponsors have felt that they were not getting value for money in publicity terms. I have considerable sympathy for chess organisers, because often it seems quite unclear exactly what the sponsors do want. Some sponsors seem to be quite happy with what seems to be very little publicity, while in other cases even the best press coverage is of no avail.

The 1986 GLC tournament, held in March, was remarkable because the reserve player, Glenn Flear, entered the tournament at 72 hours' notice and proceeded to win it outright, despite having the second-lowest rating. He must have been a busy man, because he had to take a day off during the tournament in order to get married. Glenn hasn't had a comparable success since, but then he hasn't got married since either.

Some other players were also busy, because there was a Bundesliga weekend in the middle of the tournament, and as this was near the end of the season they had to attend key matches. The tournament schedule had been arranged with this in mind, and after playing Murray Chandler on Friday morning, Murray and I flew to Frankfurt and then Nuremberg, where our captain picked us up and took us to Bamberg for the matches. I won on both Saturday and Sunday, and then we flew back to London on Sunday evening, ready to play again in the GLC tournament on Monday.

All in all an exhausting event, and I was happy to finish in joint fourth place with 7½/13. The tournament was a great success for the British players, who scooped the top four places (Flear made 8½ points, and Chandler and Short scored 8).

I had a slice of luck in round 3.

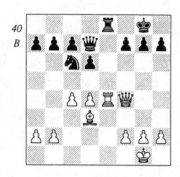

40
B

This position arose, with Black to play, in J.Nunn-J.Plaskett. The position is quite equal and after, for example, 20...♖xe4 21 ♕xe4 g6 a draw would be inevitable. Plaskett's play in this tournament was in some ways as remarkable as Flear's, because he went through the event without a single draw! Here Plaskett avoided the draw by 20...♘b4??, but after 21 ♕f5! he was dead lost. The game concluded 21...♖e6 (the only move, because 21...♕d8 allows mate in three by 22 ♖e7!, while 21...♕a4 is met by 22 b3) 22 d5 ♘xd3 23 dxe6 fxe6 24 ♕xe6+ ♕xe6 25 ♖xe6 ♔f7 26 ♖e2 1-0

Game 8

J.Nunn – M.Dlugy

London (GLC) 1986

Caro-Kann

How does a strong player like Dlugy (rated 2545 at the time) come to lose in just 18 moves? I should know, because I have lost several games just as quickly. If you want to lose a miniature, then here are three helpful tips. First of all, it is a big help if you are Black. Losing in under 20 moves with White requires a special talent which few possess. Secondly, choose a provocative opening, for example an opening in which you try to realise strategic ambitions, but at the cost of backward development and delayed castling. Thirdly, if something goes slightly wrong, don't reconcile yourself to defending a bad position – seek a tactical solution instead! Don't worry about the fact that tactics are bound to favour the better developed side; just go ahead anyway. Follow this advice and at least you will get home early.

1	e4	c6
2	d4	d5
3	e5	♗f5
4	♘c3	h5 *(41)*

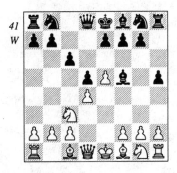

This odd-looking move was introduced by Seirawan. In contrast to the usual line 4...e6 5 g4 ♗g6 6 ♘ge2,

Black at once prevents White gaining space on the kingside. A further point is that Black envisages a French-type position arising after the exchange of his bishop on f5, and in this case the light-squared blockade with pawns on g6 and h5 is a standard idea. The defect of 4...h5 is that Black's king may have to remain in the centre until well into the middlegame.

5 ♗d3

I believe this move was first played in the game Glek-Vyzhmanavin, USSR 1985. The main alternative had proved less successful: 5 ♗e2 (if Black had to do something about his h-pawn this move would be very strong, e.g. 5...♗g6 6 ♘h3 and ♘f4, or 5...h4 6 h3 followed by ♘f3 and ♗g5, but Black can sacrifice it) e6 and now:

1) 6 ♗xh5?! c5 7 ♗e2 ♘c6! (7...cxd4? 8 ♘b5 ♗e4 9 f3 ♗g6 10 ♘xd4 ♗c5 11 ♗b5+ was good for White in Nunn-Seirawan, Toluca IZ 1982) 8 ♘f3 ♗g4 9 ♗e3 ♗xf3 (9...♕b6 is also good) 10 gxf3 (10 ♗xf3 cxd4 11 ♗xd4 ♘ge7 gives Black an edge) ♘ge7 11 ♗b5 cxd4 12 ♗xd4 ♘f5 and Black has excellent compensation for the pawn, Pandavos-Skembris, Athens 1983.

2) 6 ♘f3 ♗g4 (6...♗g6 7 0-0 ♘h6 8 ♗xh6 ♖xh6 9 ♕d2 a6 was unclear in Braga-Seirawan, Mar del Plata 1982; it seems more logical for Black to exchange the light-squared

bishop for a knight) 7 0-0 ♗xf3 8 ♗xf3 g6 9 ♗e3 ♗h6 10 ♕d3 ♔f8 11 ♘e2 ♘d7 12 c4 with equality, Nunn-Seirawan, Hamburg 1982. White's problem is that the theoretically good bishop on f3 is completely blocked out by Black's pawn chain.

Glek's move is designed to force the exchange of the f5 bishop and preserve White's king's knight, which will prove a more useful piece in a blocked position.

5   ...   ♗xd3
6   ♕xd3   e6

A superficial analysis would suggest that Black is doing well, because he has exchanged his 'bad' light-squared bishop. But this has been achieved at a price; Black's kingside has been permanently weakened by the move ...h5, and White has established a lead in development.

7   ♘f3   ♘h6

Black hastens to occupy the f5 square, which has been secured against g4 by the move ...h5. In a later game Short-Seirawan, Rotterdam World Cup 1989, Black continued 7...♕b6 8 0-0 ♕a6 9 ♕d1 ♘e7 10 ♘e2 ♘d7 11 c3 ♘f5 12 ♗g5 ♗e7 13 ♘g3 ♘xg3 14 fxg3, but White had a slight advantage here too.

8   0-0   ♘f5

It is probably premature to occupy f5 immediately since it only encourages White to challenge the knight by ♘e2-g3. 8...♘d7 would have been more flexible.

9   ♘e2   ♘d7

The Glek game mentioned above continued 9...♗e7 10 b3 (10 ♘g3 is also possible) ♘d7 11 c4 ♘f8 12 ♗d2 ♘g6 13 c5 and White's space advantage gave him a promising position. The game ended in a draw, but only after White missed a win.

10   ♘g3 *(42)*

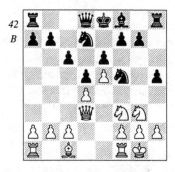

This is a slightly different plan. White still intends b3 and c4, but first of all he forces Black to decide what he is going to do about the f5 knight.

10   ...   ♘h4

After 10...♘xg3 11 fxg3 ♗e7 12 h4 followed by ♗g5 or ♘g5 White has a dangerous attack along the f-file, while 10...g6 11 ♘xf5 gxf5 (or 11...exf5 12 ♖e1 followed by e6) leaves Black with a weak h-pawn for the endgame (White could eventually swap dark-squared bishops and play h4, ♘g5, g3 and ♘h3-f4). After both 10...♘xg3 and 10...g6, the pawn structure is changed in White's favour, so Dlugy decides to adopt a line in which the pawn structure remains unchanged. The flaw is that Black has to waste more time with his queen.

| 11 | ♘xh4 | ♕xh4 |
| 12 | ♗e3 | ♕d8 |

The bishop on f8 can only be developed at e7, but to play 12...♗e7 immediately would leave the queen stranded on h4, so first of all the queen retreats.

13 ♖fd1

13 f4 is only good if it wins by force, since otherwise the f4 pawn only serves to obstruct White's bishop. Here 13 f4 g6 14 f5 gxf5 15 ♘xf5 exf5 16 ♕xf5 ♕e7 17 ♗g5 ♕e6 defends, so White switches to preparing b3 and c4. For this he needs to defend his queen, or else c4 will be met by ...dxc4 followed by ...♘xe5.

13 ... ♖c8?

The best idea was 13...♗e7, followed by ...g6 and ...♔f8-g7. White would play b3, c4 and ♖ac1 with a small but permanent plus based on two factors: his space advantage and Black's slightly weakened kingside which makes development of the h8 rook difficult. Note that White need never fear the advance of Black's h-pawn as ...h4 is met by ♘e2 and then ...h3 by g3. In either case the h-pawn would be disconnected from the rest

of Black's pawns and would be a liability in the endgame.

Seeing that this line condemns Black to a passive position, Dlugy decides to pre-empt White's c4 by playing ...c5 himself, but this plan is tactically unsound. The danger signals were all there to be seen; Black is opening the centre while well behind in development and with his king still two moves away from castling. White's tactics are no accident, but inherent in the position.

| 14 | b3 | c5 |
| 15 | c4 *(43)* | |

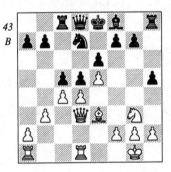

43
B

White aims to open lines, even at the cost of a piece.

15 ... cxd4

Or 15...h4 (15...♘b6 16 dxc5 ♗xc5 17 ♗xc5 ♖xc5 18 ♘e4 heads for d6) and now:

1) **16 cxd5** hxg3 17 dxe6 ♘xe5 (17...♘b8 18 ♕f5 ♖c7 19 ♗g5 wins for White) 18 dxe5 gxh2+ 19 ♔h1 ♕xd3 20 exf7+ ♔xf7 21 ♖xd3 is only slightly better for White. The

pawn on h2 may fall in the end, but it will require some effort to win it and in the meantime Black can activate his pieces.

2) **16 ♘e2!** dxc4 (16...cxd4 loses just as in the game, while 16...♘b6 is met by 17 ♖ac1, threatening cxd5, and after 17...dxc4 18 bxc4 cxd4 19 ♘xd4 ♗c5 20 ♕e4 ♕e7 21 ♕g4 Black has a very poor position) 17 ♕xc4 cxd4 (or else d5) 18 ♕xd4 ♗c5 19 ♕e4 ♗xe3 20 ♕xe3 and White has a large advantage. Black's a- and h-pawns are both very weak, he is in an unpleasant pin along the d-file and White can quickly double his rooks.

16   cxd5!   ♘xe5

After 16...dxe3 (16...exd5 17 ♗xd4

followed by e6 or ♘f5) 17 dxe6 exf2+ 18 ♔f1 Black has no defence:

1) **18...fxe6** (18...♘xe5 19 ♕b5+) 19 ♕g6+ ♔e7 20 ♖d6 and Black has to give up his queen by 20...♘c5 to avoid mate.

2) **18...♖c7** 19 exf7+ ♔xf7 20 e6+ ♔g8 (20...♔xe6 21 ♕f5+ ♔e7 22 ♖e1+ fxe1♕+ 23 ♖xe1+ mates in two more moves, while 20...♔e7 21 ♕e3 wins for White) 21 ♕d5! ♗e7 22 exd7+ ♔f8 23 ♖ac1 and the d-pawn is too strong.

17   ♕xd4   ♕xd5?

Losing a piece, but 17...♘g4 18 ♕xa7 is also hopeless.

18   ♕a4+   1-0

18...b5 19 ♖xd5 wins a piece, while 18...♕c6 19 ♖ac1 wins a rook.

Game 9
J.Nunn – J.Mestel
London (GLC) 1986
Sicilian Dragon

Some games do not appear to contain any strategy at all – they are just pure tactics from start to finish. This is one such.

1	e4	c5
2	♘f3	d6
3	d4	cxd4
4	♘xd4	♘f6
5	♘c3	g6

Some players have a very wide opening repertoire – Timman, for

example, can play almost any first move in reply to 1 e4. Others prefer to concentrate on just one or two openings, which they adopt consistently for several years. Mestel has played the Sicilian Dragon for virtually his entire career, and has only occasionally flirted with other openings. This approach has advantages and disadvantages; preparing for such an opponent is simpler, so he is in more danger of being caught out by a novelty. On the other hand, playing an opening for many years enables one to build up an excellent general understanding of the resulting positions. I feel that the increasing use of computers has shifted the balance in favour of a flexible approach. It is now just too easy to review what has been happening in a particular line and see if any dangerous weapons have appeared.

6	♗e3	♗g7
7	f3	0-0
8	♕d2	♘c6
9	♗c4	♗d7
10	0-0-0	♘e5
11	♗b3	♖c8
12	h4	h5
13	♗g5	♘c4

Mestel decides to avoid the main theoretical arguments surrounding 13...♖c5. The move 13...♘c4 was played in Geller-Miles, Linares 1983, and although White won that game, Mestel evidently found Geller's play unconvincing.

14 ♕e2 (44)

After 14 ♕d3 Black can reply 14...♘e5, since 15 ♕e2 would be an open invitation for Black to sacrifice on c3.

Curiously enough, approximately this position had arisen in a previous Nunn-Mestel game from 1976. The only difference was that h4 and ...h5 had not been played, but it was an important difference since the

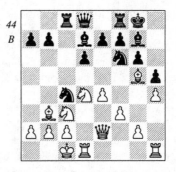

game continued 13 ♕e2 ♘xb2! 14 ♔xb2 ♖xc3 15 ♗xf6 (15 ♔xc3 ♕a5+) ♖xb3+ 16 axb3 ♗xf6 with advantage for Black. This time the bishop on g5 is defended, preventing 14...♘xb2. Evidently I had learned something in the intervening decade.

14	...	♘a5
15	♔b1	

For the moment Black has no threats because ...♖xc3 isn't dangerous when the knight prevents the queen moving to a5, so White takes the opportunity to make a useful consolidating move.

15	...	a6

This move represents the point of the manoeuvre ...♘c4-a5 – Black threatens to trap the knight on d4 by ...e5. If White were now forced to spend a tempo moving the queen, Black would play ...b5 with good counterplay. Everything depends on whether White can successfully ignore the threat of ...e5.

This is another example of risky play by Black. The knight on e5 is a cornerstone of Black's position in the Yugoslav Attack; many White kingside attacks have foundered because of the defensive influence of this knight. But here Black has played it away to the edge of the board, far from his king. Of course, he did it for a reason – to free e5 for the possible advance of the e-pawn – but nevertheless moving away a key defensive piece inevitably involves a large element of risk.

Now the onus is on White to come up with a concrete attacking plan that exploits the knight's absence.

16   g4 *(45)*

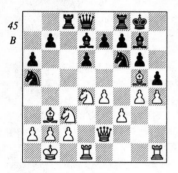

45
B

The most natural move. It is easier to play g4 when there is no knight on e5. On the other hand, the move does not counter Black's threat, so White must be prepared to sacrifice the knight on d4.

16   ...   e5

16...♘xb3 17 axb3 hxg4 is a possible alternative, when White has a choice:

1) **18 ♗xf6** (this was my intention during the game) ♗xf6 19 h5 g5 (opening the g-file by 19...gxf3 20 ♘xf3 is too risky) 20 fxg4 e6 (or else 21 ♘f5) 21 ♘f3 is slightly better for White. There are attacking chances based on e5 followed by ♘e4, or h6 followed by ♖h5, but Black's bishops are potentially dangerous, and 21...♗c6 creates counterplay against e4.

2) **18 h5!** gxf3 (18...♘xh5 19 fxg4 ♘g3 20 ♕h2 ♘xh1 21 ♖xh1 leads to inevitable mate) 19 ♘xf3 ♗g4 (19...♘xh5 20 ♖dg1 threatening ♖xh5 is very strong) 20 ♖dg1 gxh5 (20...♗xh5 21 ♗xf6 exf6 22 ♖xh5 gxh5 23 ♕g2 wins) 21 ♗xf6 exf6 22 ♖xg4! hxg4 23 ♘d4 and White's attack, based on ♘f5 and ♕xg4, is too strong.

A second alternative for Black is 16...♘xb3 17 axb3 e5, which we will discuss in the note to Black's 18th move.

17   gxh5!

The Geller-Miles game continued 17 ♘f5 gxf5 18 gxf5 ♘xb3 19 axb3 ♗c6 20 ♖hg1 ♔h7 21 ♖g2 ♖g8 and White went on to win, but at this stage White probably doesn't have enough compensation for the sacrificed piece.

17   ...   exd4
18   ♘d5! *(46)*

Geller's notes to the above game recommended 17 gxh5 exd4 18 h6 ♗h8 (18...dxc3 19 hxg7 ♔xg7 20

Ξxd6 wins) 19 h7+ ♔xh7 20 h5 and wins, but 18...♗xh6! 19 ♘xh6 ♘xb3 20 axb3 dxc3 is a big improvement, and the position is totally unclear. When conducting a sacrificial attack, it is very important to consider lines in which the defender returns material in order to exchange some attacking pieces. If the attacker has made positional as well as material concessions, then the defender may even be satisfied with a final material balance in his opponent's favour, as he may have a positional advantage or even a counterattack in compensation.

The move 18...♗xh6! is hard to see, because it is very unusual for Black to give up his 'Dragon' bishop voluntarily, least of all for a mere pawn.

18 ♘d5! was mentioned by Timman in the magazine *Schaakbulletin* (issue 184/185 from 1983). During the game I was unaware of this, and believed that 18 ♘d5! was a new move.

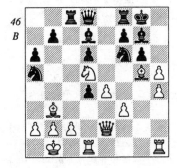

46
B

18 ...   ♘xb3 *(47)*

The only real defence to the threat of 19 h6 ♗h8 20 h7+ ♔xh7 21 h5 is to play ...gxh5. However, after 18...gxh5 White continues 19 Ξdg1 ♔h7 20 ♘xf6+ ♗xf6 21 f4 ♗g4 22 Ξxg4 hxg4 23 ♕xg4 ♘xb3 (after 23...♗xg5 24 hxg5+ ♔g7 25 ♕h5 White forces mate because the bishop on b3 is attacking f7) 24 ♕h5+ ♔g8 25 ♗xf6 ♕xf6 (interpolating 25...♘d2+ 26 ♔c1 doesn't help) 26 Ξg1+ ♕g7 27 Ξxg7+ ♔xg7 28 axb3 with a decisive advantage; the pawn on d4 is doomed, and capturing this will give White ♕+2♙ v 2Ξ in a position favouring the queen.

The above line only works because of the bishop on b3, and the move played in the game attempts to exchange on b3 before taking on h5, but in this position White doesn't need to recapture. If Black wanted to exchange on b3 he should have done so at move 16, with the continuation 16...♘xb3 17 axb3 e5 18 gxh5 exd4 19 ♘d5. I think that White can win, even in this case, but it is much more complex: 19...gxh5 20 Ξdg1 ♔h7 (20...♔h8 21 f4 ♗g4 22 Ξxg4! hxg4 23 h5 ♔h7 24 h6 ♗h8 25 ♕d3 ♔g8 26 h7+ wins) 21 f4 ♗g4 and now:

1) **22 Ξxg4** hxg4 23 ♗xf6 ♗xf6 24 ♕xg4 (this is very tempting, but Black has a surprising defence) ♔h6! (24...♗g7 25 Ξg1 loses after 25...♗h6 26 ♕f5+ ♔h8 27 ♘f6 or 25...Ξg8 26 ♕f5+ ♔h6 27 Ξg5) 25

♕f5 ♗h8! (25...♗g7 26 ♖g1 threatens 27 ♖g5 and after 26...♕xh4, White wins by 27 ♘e7! ♕h5 28 ♖g5 ♕h1+ 29 ♔a2 ♖c5 30 ♖g6+ ♔h7 31 ♖g1+ ♖xf5 32 ♖xh1+ ♗h6 33 ♘xf5) and now neither 26 ♖g1 ♖g8 nor 26 ♕g5+ ♕xg5 27 hxg5+ ♔g7 28 ♘f6 ♖g8! works.

2) **22 ♕d3!** ♔g8 (22...♔h8 23 ♖xg4 hxg4 24 h5 is worse) 23 ♖xg4 hxg4 24 h5 (this seems to be good even when White has a tempo less) ♘xd5 (24...♖e8 25 h6 ♗h8 26 h7+ ♔f8 27 ♗h6+ mates) 25 ♗xd8 ♘b4 (25...♘xf4 26 ♕f1) 26 ♕d2 d3 (26...♘xc2 27 h6) 27 cxd3 ♖c2 28 ♕xb4 ♖xb2+ 29 ♔c1 ♖xd8 30 d4 and White should win.

Black can also try deflecting White's rook by 18...d3 19 ♖xd3 gxh5, but now the d-file is open, so 20 ♖g1 ♔h7 21 ♘xf6+ ♗xf6 22 ♖xd6 ♗xg5 23 ♖xg5 wins easily.

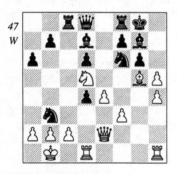

19 h6!

This move was the key point of Timman's analysis. It is even more clear-cut than transposing to the previous note by 19 axb3. The threats on the kingside are exceedingly strong, so White can afford to be calm even when he is two pieces down.

19 ...   ♗b5

Trying to generate counterplay, but there is no defence. The main line runs 19...♗h8 (after 19...♘xd5 20 hxg7 ♘d2+ 21 ♕xd2 ♘c3+ 22 ♔a1! White wins on material) 20 h7+ ♔xh7 21 h5 ♔g8 (21...♗g7 22 hxg6+ ♔g8 23 ♘xf6+ ♗xf6 24 ♕h2 and 21...gxh5 22 ♗xf6 ♗xf6 23 ♖xh5+ ♔g6 24 ♘f4+ both win easily) 22 ♕h2! (not 22 hxg6 fxg6 23 ♕h2 ♔f7) gxh5 (22...♘g4 23 fxg4 ♕xg5 24 hxg6 mates) 23 ♘xf6+ ♗xf6 24 ♕xh5 ♖e8 25 ♖dg1 ♔f8 26 ♕h6+ ♗g7 27 ♕xg7+ ♔xg7 28 ♗e7+ and mate next move.

20 ♕h2   d3
21 cxb3

Not 21 c3? d2! with dangerous counterthreats.

21 ...   ♘xd5

After 21...♖c2 22 hxg7 ♖xh2 23 gxf8♕+ ♔xf8 24 ♖xh2 Black loses the knight on f6.

22 hxg7

Not 22 ♗xd8? ♗e5.

22 ...   ♖c2

Black cannot avoid a fatal loss of material.

23 ♗xd8   ♖xd8
24 ♖d2   1-0

24...♘e3 is met by 25 ♕f2.

After the GLC tournament, 15 months were to pass before I played another game in Britain (except for quick-play games).

My next major event was in July, when I played at the annual Biel tournament in Switzerland. Although the playing conditions were rather cramped, I always enjoyed this event because the grandmaster tournament was just part of a large chess festival. This gave plenty of opportunities to meet old friends and make new ones. Twice previously I had finished joint first, but 1986 was less successful, and my final score of 6/11 was disappointing. Even more alarminglingly, my play lacked real imagination and, unusually for me, many of my games finished in quick draws.

The third Karpov-Kasparov world championship match started in London just before the end of Biel, and after I returned to London I started commentating on the games for Thames Television. Thames and the BBC both offered good coverage, and chess on television reached a pitch not seen again until the 1993 Kasparov-Short match. Unfortunately, I had already agreed to play a tournament in the middle of the world championship, but luckily this coincided with the interval when the match was transferred to Leningrad, so I only missed two games, neither of which was a thriller.

The tournament was the German Open championship, played in Krefeld. It took the form of an 11-round Swiss event, in which the German players faced two invited foreigners, Nigel Short and myself. This was the theory, anyway, but in fact not too many of the top German players took part. It was one of my most successful tournaments; I started with 8½/9, the only draw being with Short, and then coasted home with two draws, nevertheless finishing a full point ahead of the next players. The tournament was effectively decided by two games, the first being Short's loss to Sehner. The second was the following game.

Game 10
V.Hort – J.Nunn
Krefeld (German Open Ch) 1986
King's Indian

1	d4	♘f6		3	♘c3	♗g7
2	c4	g6		4	e4	d6

5 ♘f3   0-0
6 ♗e2   e5
7 ♗e3   h6!?

This move appears artificial, but if Black plays the usual 7...♘g4, then after 8 ♗g5 he has no really constructive reply. The idea of 7...h6 is to prepare ...♘g4 by cutting out ♗g5.

8 h3

In 1986, the move 7...h6 was a relatively new idea, and White players had not yet homed in on the most dangerous reply. As we shall see in Games 25 and 26, by 1989 the critical continuation had been discovered. This runs 8 0-0 (practice has shown that 8 dxe5 ♘g4 followed by ...♘xe5 leads to equality) ♘g4 9 ♗c1 ♘c6 10 d5 ♘e7 (10...♘d4 11 ♘xd4 exd4 12 ♘b5 ♘f6 13 f3 c5 14 dxc6 bxc6 15 ♘xd4 wins a pawn for inadequate compensation; 15...♕b6 is met by 16 ♗e3), followed by 11 ♘d2 or 11 ♘e1. The debate over this line has continued right up to the present day.

Hort's move is now considered inferior, because the interpolation of h3 and ...h6 helps Black.

8 ...   exd4
9 ♘xd4   ♖e8
10 ♕c2

This is the first problem for White; once he has played h3, he doesn't want to play f3 as well, since Black would have the awkward move ...♘h5 heading for g3.

10 ...   ♕e7!? (48)

10...♘bd7 11 0-0-0! ♕e7 12 ♖he1 ♘b6 (not 12...♘xe4? 13 ♘xe4 ♕xe4 14 ♕xe4 ♖xe4 15 ♘b5! and wins) 13 f3 d5 14 c5 ♘bd7 15 c6 ♘b6 16 ♗b5 was very complicated in Flear-Fedorowicz, Chicago 1983.

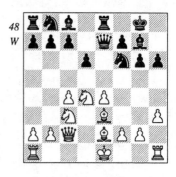

*48
W*

11 ♗f3

At the time, this was a new move. Hitherto White had tried:

1) **11 ♘d5 ♘xd5** 12 exd5 (12 cxd5 c5 13 dxc6 ♘xc6 is promising for Black) ♘a6 (12...c5!? is also possible) 13 0-0-0 ♘c5 14 g4 ♗d7 15 h4 ♕e5 16 ♗f3 b5 was unclear in Gross-Khalifman, Minsk 1986.

2) **11 f3** c6 12 0-0-0 d5 13 cxd5 ♘xd5! proved unpleasant for White in Szymczak-Thipsay, Czestochowa 1984.

3) **11 ♗d3** ♘a6 12 ♕d2 ♘c5 13 f3 ♘xd3+ 14 ♕xd3 c6 15 ♔f2 was equal in Portisch-Nunn, London (GLC) 1986.

11 ♗f3 seems to leave the bishop badly placed, but the queen on e7 is

also not very happy, being subject to attack by ♘d5. Moreover, the move ...h6 slightly weakens Black's kingside and this makes it hard for him to adopt any plan involving ...f5. Thus if White can castle and disentangle his pieces, he will have a typical favourable King's Indian position. Black must act quickly to exploit the temporary clumsiness of White's pieces.

11 ...   c5!?

This is a further example of the strategic concession versus temporary advantage debate. Positionally speaking, this move is a disaster for Black, because both the d5 square and the d6 pawn are seriously weakened. On the other hand Black gains time and may seize control of the square d4. Now, more than ever, Black is obliged to play actively. Quieter play by 11...♘bd7 (11...♗e6? 12 ♘xe6 ♕xe6 13 e5 and 11...♘c6? 12 ♘xc6 bxc6 13 e5 are very bad) 12 0-0 ♘c5 (12...♘e5 13 ♗e2 and a subsequent f4 will gain time) would only be good if there were a genuine chance of taking the pawn on e4, but after 13 ♖fe1 ♘cxe4 14 ♘xe4 ♘xe4 15 ♗xe4 ♕xe4 16 ♗d2 White wins material.

12 ♘de2

The most ambitious move, because if White has time this knight will move to f4 and then d5. However, in later games White has preferred 12 ♘b3 (so as to defend c4

and e4 by ♘d2 if necessary) ♘c6 13 0-0 ♗e6 14 ♗e2 (14 ♘d2 ♘d4 is fine for Black, while 14 ♘d5 ♗xd5 15 exd5 ♘e5 16 ♗e2 b5 17 ♖ad1 was equal in A.Sokolov-Shchekachev, Jurmala 1991) ♔h7 (one of many possible moves; 14...♖ad8 and the immediate 14...♘d7 are alternatives) 15 ♖fe1 ♘d7 16 ♖ad1 ♘b6 17 ♗f4 ♖ad8 and Black had a slight advantage in Bönsch-Vogt, Halle 1987. It seems that White has no route to an advantage after 8 h3.

12 ...   ♘c6
13 ♕d2

The defect of 12 ♘de2, as opposed to 12 ♘b3, is that White cannot play 13 0-0 on account of 13...♘e5. 13 ♘f4 ♗e6 followed by ...♘d4 is also fine for Black.

13 ...   ♗e6

13...♘e5 is tempting, but it loses a pawn after 14 b3 ♔h7 15 ♖d1 since 15...♖d8 allows 16 ♗xc5.

14 b3

White has to take time out to defend his pawn, because after 14 ♗xh6 ♗xh6 15 ♕xh6 ♗xc4 Black's more active bishop gives him the edge.

14 ...   ♔h7
15 ♖d1   ♖ad8 *(49)*

This is a critical moment, because Black has defended his d- and h-pawns, and now threatens 16...♘e5. One reply is 16 ♘g3, but after 16...♘d4 (16...♘e5 17 ♗e2 is good for White) 17 ♗e2 (17 ♗xd4 cxd4

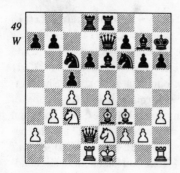

18 ♕xd4 ♘xe4 19 ♕xe4 ♗xc3+ 20 ♔f1 d5 is very good for Black) ♘d7 18 0-0 ♕h4 White is in an awkward position because the attack on g3 prevents him moving his f-pawn (19 f4 ♕xg3 20 ♗f2 ♕xc3), while the coming ...♘e5 will give Black attacking chances based on ...♗xh3.

16 ♘f4 is another idea, but after 16...♘d4 17 ♗e2 ♗d7 18 ♗d3 ♕e5 threatening ...♘xb3 or ...♗c6 Black again has a dangerous initiative.

Based on these lines, Hort concluded that it was too risky to move the e2 knight and thereby permit ...♘d4, so he adopts a plan in which the knight stays where it is.

16 g3

White's idea is kingside expansion by ♗g2, 0-0 and f4, while keeping e4 and d4 securely defended. If White succeeds in carrying out this plan he will have a winning position based on his big space advantage and Black's weaknesses on the d-file. The one bright spot for Black is the weak pawn at h3, which prevents

castling for one move. Black must make the most of this tempo.

16 ... a6

17 a4

This creates a slight weakness at b3, which is very important in the next few moves. After 17 ♗g2 b5 18 cxb5 axb5 19 0-0 (19 ♘xb5? d5 20 exd5 ♗xd5 wins for Black, for example 21 ♗xd5 ♘xd5 22 0-0 ♘xe3 23 ♕xe3 ♕f6 and the knight on e2 falls) b4 20 ♘d5 ♗xd5 21 exd5 ♘a7 22 ♕d3 ♕b7 followed by ...♘b5 Black is at least equal.

17 ... ♘d4! *(50)*

The tactics started by this move should lead to a draw with best play, but after any other move White has the advantage. The interpolation of ...a6 and a4 was necessary because otherwise ...♘d4 would have been met by the simple ♗g2.

18 ♗xd4?!

Now Black gains the advantage. The correct line was 18 ♘xd4 cxd4 19 ♗xd4 (19 ♕xd4? ♘d7! 20 ♕d2

♛f6 forks c3 and f3, thereby winning a piece) d5 20 cxd5 (20 ♗xf6 ♛xf6 attacks f3 and c3, 20 ♘xd5 ♗xd5 21 cxd5 ♘xe4 22 ♛e3 ♛b4+ wins for Black, and finally 20 e5 ♘e4 21 ♗xe4 dxe4 22 ♛c2 ♛c7 gives Black more than enough for the pawn) and now Black has two reasonable continuations:

1) **20...♘xd5** (20...♘xe4 21 ♗xe4 ♗xd5 fails to 22 ♗xg7 ♔xg7 23 ♛d4+ ♔g8 24 ♘xd5 with an extra piece) 21 ♗xg7 ♔xg7 22 ♘xd5 (22 0-0 ♘b4! 23 ♛b2 ♛f6 gives more than enough compensation for the pawn, for example 24 ♖xd8 ♖xd8 25 ♗g2 ♖c8 26 ♘d1 ♛xb2 27 ♘xb2 ♗xb3 is good for Black) ♗xd5 23 0-0 ♗xe4 24 ♛c3+ ♔g8 25 ♖xd8 ♛xd8 26 ♖d1 ♛b6 27 ♖e1 f5 with an edge for White.

2) **20...♗xd5!** and now:

2a) **21 0-0?!** ♘xe4 22 ♛b2 (22 ♗xe4 ♗xe4 23 ♛e3 ♗c2 and Black should win) ♗xd4 23 ♖xd4 ♛f6 24 ♖d3 ♗c6! with a clear advantage for Black.

2b) **21 ♗xf6?!** ♛xf6 22 ♘xd5 ♛xf3 23 0-0 ♖xe4 (after 23...♛xe4 24 ♖de1! Black has only a small advantage) 24 ♛d3 (not 24 ♛c2 ♗d4!, nor 24 ♛a5 ♖ee8! and White is in serious trouble) ♛f5 and Black has a significant advantage.

2c) **21 ♘xd5!** ♘xe4! (21...♖xd5 22 ♗xf6 ♖xd2 23 ♗xe7 ♖xd1+ 24 ♔xd1 ♖xe7 leaves White a pawn up, although ...♖c7-c3 will give Black

excellent drawing chances) 22 ♘xe7 ♘xd2 23 ♖xd2 (23 ♗xg7 ♖xe7+ 24 ♗e2 ♘f3+ 25 ♔f1 ♖xd1+ 26 ♗xd1 ♘d2+ 27 ♔g2 ♔xg7 is slightly better for Black – White can't get his rook out for the moment, 28 ♗c2 ♖c7 is unpleasant and in any case ...♖c7 followed by ...♖c1 or ...♖c3 is a threat) ♖xe7+ 24 ♖e2 (24 ♗e3? ♗c3 wins for Black, but 24 ♔d1 is also a draw) ♖ed7! (24...♖xe2+ 25 ♔xe2 allows White to win a pawn; 24...♖c7? loses to 25 ♗e3) 25 ♗xb7 (or else ...♗xd4 with an inevitable draw) ♖xb7 26 ♗xg7 ♔xg7 27 ♖e3 ♖db8 and the ending is a clear draw.

18 ...   cxd4
19 ♘xd4

Or 19 ♛xd4 d5 20 e5 (20 cxd5 ♘xd5 21 ♘xd5 ♗xd5 22 ♛e3 ♛b4+ wins after 23 ♛d2 ♛xb3 or 23 ♔f1 ♗xb3) dxc4 21 exf6 ♗xf6 22 ♛e3 ♖xd1+ 23 ♘xd1 ♛b4+ 24 ♛d2 (24 ♔f1 ♗xh3+ 25 ♖xh3 ♖xe3 followed by ...cxb3 wins, as does 24 ♘dc3 ♗d7) ♛xb3 25 ♘e3 (25 ♘dc3 ♗xc3 26 ♛xc3 ♛xc3+ 27 ♘xc3 ♗d5+ wins) ♛xa4, when the three connected passed pawns supported by the bishop pair are worth more than a knight. Note that 26 ♗xb7 is impossible, because of 26...♖d8 followed by 27...♛b4+.

19 ...   d5 (51)

The inevitable consequence of Black's play – the centre must be ripped open before White has a chance to castle.

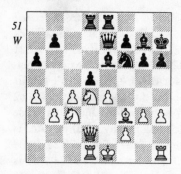

51
W

20   ♘xe6

Or 20 cxd5 and now:

1) **20...♘xe4** 21 ♗xe4 (21 ♘xe4 ♗xd5 is hopeless) ♗xd5 22 0-0 ♗xe4 23 ♕e3! (this seems very good for Black, but in fact White will exchange one of the bishops, when Black has only a small advantage) f5 (23...♗xd4 24 ♖xd4 ♖xd4 25 ♕xd4 ♗c6 26 ♘d5 forces a draw since 26...♕e5? 27 ♘f6+ ♔h8 28 ♕h4 would even lose, while 23...♕b4? 24 ♘xe4 ♗xd4 loses to 25 ♖xd4!) 24 ♘xe4 ♕xe4 25 ♕xe4 ♖xe4 26 ♘f3 with just an edge for Black.

2) **20...♗xd5** 21 ♘xd5 ♖xd5 22 0-0 ♘xe4 23 ♕e3 with a small plus for Black.

3) **20...♘xd5!** 21 ♘xd5 (21 0-0 ♘xc3 22 ♕xc3 ♗xh3 23 ♖fe1 ♕e5 wins and 21 ♘ce2 ♘b4! leaves White with no good reply to the threat of taking twice on d4) ♗xd5 22 0-0 ♗xe4 23 ♗xe4 (23 ♕e3 ♗xd4 24 ♖xd4 ♖xd4 wins) ♕xe4 24 ♖fe1 (24 ♖de1 ♕xd4) ♖xd4 and Black wins a piece.

20   ...   fxe6

The point of White's defence is that Black has to take with the f-pawn, blocking the e-file. The reason is that 20...♕xe6 21 cxd5 leaves Black with inadequate compensation for the pawns and the attempted brilliancy 20...♘xe4 21 ♘xe4 dxe4 22 ♘xd8 exf3+ 23 ♔f1 ♗c3 (23...♕e2+ 24 ♔g1 also fails), aiming for 24 ♕xc3 ♕e2+ 25 ♔g1 ♕xd1+ 26 ♔h2 ♕e2! or 24 ♕d3 ♕e1+!, loses to 24 ♕e3! ♖xd8 25 ♖xd8.

Unfortunately for White, Black retains a strong initiative even after the pawn capture. 21...dxe4 is a threat and 21 e5 dxc4 22 exf6 (22 ♕c2 ♘d7) ♕xf6 23 ♕e3 ♕xc3+ 24 ♕xc3 ♗xc3+ 25 ♔e2 cxb3 is a very good ending for Black, so White must move his queen.

21   ♕c2

Best. The knight must be defended (or else ...♕b4 wins a piece), but 21 ♕e3 is bad after 21...d4! 22 ♖xd4 ♖xd4 23 ♕xd4 ♘d7 24 ♕e3 (24 ♕d2 ♕f6 25 ♕xd7 ♕xc3+ 26 ♔e2 ♖f8 27 ♗g4 ♕c2+ wins) ♕b4 25 ♔d2 ♕xb3 and White's position collapses.

21   ...   ♘d7!

An important point of Black's combination. Thanks to the threat of 22...♕f6 23 ♖d3 ♘e5 White cannot castle, while the second threat of 22...♕b4 prevents 22 ♗g2. Thus White's knight must move.

22 ♘a2

The variation 22 ♘e2 ♘e5 23 ♗g2 ♕b4+ 24 ♕d2 ♕xb3 25 cxd5 exd5 is catastrophic for White, so Hort decides to stop the dangerous check on b4.

22 ... dxc4

23 0-0

After 23 bxc4 ♘e5 24 ♗e2 (24 ♗g2 ♖xd1+ 25 ♕xd1 ♖d8 followed by ...♘d3+ is worse) ♖xd1+ 25 ♗xd1 (25 ♕xd1 ♕a3 26 ♕c2 ♘c6 is similar) ♖c8 26 ♗e2 ♘xc4 27 ♗xc4 ♕c5 Black regains the sacrificed material and retains a big advantage in the endgame.

After the move played material is once again equal, but Black's minor pieces are much more active than their white counterparts.

23 ... ♕a3! (52)

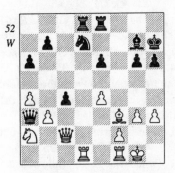

The final tactical point. Black's c-pawn cannot be taken thanks to the bad position of White's minor pieces, so b3 must be defended.

24 ♖b1?

Now Black's advantage becomes serious. The rook is relatively well placed on d1, so it would have been better to leave it there and instead defend the pawn by 24 ♘c1. Then 24...b5 (24...♘e5 25 ♗e2 is also rather unclear) 25 axb5 axb5 26 ♗e2 ♘c5 27 bxc4 b4 28 e5! isn't very clear, for example 28...b3 29 ♕c3 or 28...♗xe5? 29 ♗h5. Perhaps 24...c3 25 ♘d3 ♘e5 is best, when the protected passed pawn gives Black an indisputable advantage, but at the same time the opposite-coloured bishops limit his winning chances.

24 ... cxb3

24...c3 was also playable, but the endgame should be a win with correct play.

25 ♕xb3 ♕xb3

26 ♖xb3 ♘c5

Black's minor pieces are vastly more active than White's, while White has three weaknesses at f2, e4 and a4 (Black has only one, at b7). Moreover, Black can gain further time by attacking the badly placed pieces at f3 and a2. All this amounts to a decisive advantage.

27 ♖b4

Defending two of the weak pawns is best. 27 ♖a3 ♗b2 loses the a-pawn at once and 27 ♖b6 ♖e7 28 a5 ♖f7 (28...♖d2 29 ♘c1 ♗c3 is also not bad) 29 ♗g2 ♖d2 30 ♘c1 ♗d4 leads to the loss of a pawn.

27 ... ♖f8

The most accurate, since however

White meets the immediate threat to his bishop, Black can gain another tempo by attacking it with his other rook.

28   ♔g2

Or 28 ♗e2 ♖d2 29 ♘c1 ♗c3 30 ♖c4 (30 ♖b6 ♖f7) ♗d4 and there is no good defence to the attack on e4.

28   ...   ♖d3

29   ♗e2 *(53)*

53
B

29   ...   ♖d2?!

Very often, the side with a large positional advantage has to make a decision as to when to cash it in for some material (a pawn in this case). This is one of the most difficult areas of chess judgement. Too soon, and you will not have extracted the best value for the positional advantage. But it is also possible to manoeuvre too long; the optimum moment passes, and then the defender's chances start to increase again. Here I should have been satisfied with winning a pawn by 29...♖a3 30 ♗c4 ♘xe4 31 ♗xe6 (31 ♖xb7 ♘d6 wins)

♘c5 32 ♗c4 (32 ♗d5 ♖d8) ♖xa4 when Black should win; he has two connected passed pawns and White's minor pieces are still poorly placed. The move played is a misjudgement and makes Black's task harder.

30   ♘c1

Not 30 ♗c4 ♗d4 and wins.

30   ...   ♗d4

30...♗c3 31 ♖c4 ♗d4 is less effective when White's king is on g2 since White can reply 32 ♗f3 intending ♘e2. 30...♗b2 31 ♗f3 ♗xc1 32 ♖xc1 ♖xf2+ 33 ♔xf2 ♘d3+ 34 ♔e3 is completely wrong and may well be good for White.

31   ♗f3!

The only constructive move. If White does nothing, Black can improve his position by ...♖f7.

31   ...   ♖f7

32   ♘e2?!

32 ♘b3 ♘xb3 (32...♖b2 33 ♖xd4 ♖xb3 34 ♖c4! allows White to escape from all his troubles since 34...♘xa4 is met by 35 ♗d1!) 33 ♖xb3 e5 would have offered more drawing chances, even though the position remains bad for White. The a4 pawn is his main weakness, but after 34 ♖b4 ♖c7 (or else 35 ♖c4) 35 h4 (what else?) b6 followed by ...♖cc2 White loses his f2 pawn. In fact, White cannot avoid the loss of either his a-pawn or his f-pawn within a few moves, but even then the opposite-coloured bishops might offer some drawing chances.

32 ...   ♗e5
White is completely tied up and has no defence.

33 ♘c1
White prevents the dangerous ...♘d3 and threatens to free himself by ♖d1. The alternative was to play 33 ♖fb1, but 33...♔g7! (threatening 34...♘d3 35 ♖xb7 ♘e1+) 34 ♖c4 ♘d3 (threat 35...♖xe2) 35 ♖f1 ♗b2 (threats 36...♖xf3 and 36...♘e5) 36 ♖c8 ♖xf3 37 ♔xf3 ♘e5+ 38 ♔g2 (38 ♔e3 ♖d3+ 39 ♔f4 ♖f3 mate) ♖xe2 39 ♖c7+ ♔f6 40 ♖xb7 ♗d4 41 ♖b4 ♗c5 should be an eventual win for Black.

33 ...   ♖c2!
There is little to do about the unpleasant threat of 34...♗xg3! 35 ♔xg3 ♖c3 winning a vital pawn. 34 g4 ♖d7 leaves White with no decent moves, for example 35 ♘e2 ♖dd2 or 35 ♘b3 ♘d3 36 ♖b6 ♖b2. Now White's time trouble causes him to play a move which loses quickly, but the position was hopeless in any case.

34 ♘b3   ♘d3
34...♖xf3 35 ♔xf3 ♖c3+ also wins.

35 ♖b6   ♖b2
Threat 36...♘c5.

36 a5   ♗c3
With two threats: 37...♘e1+ and 37...♗xa5.

37 ♔g4   ♗xa5
38 ♗xe6   ♖bxf2+
                  0-1

My victory in the German Open Championship had an amusing aftermath. As mentioned prior to Game 5, the Hamburg Chess Club was part of the Hamburg Sports Union, and this body decided to present me with a special award. Three sportsmen were honoured at a ceremony in Hamburg, the other two being representatives of more physical sports. They probably wondered what the hell this weedy guy was doing on the platform with them. I didn't ask, but I suspected that I was the least fit person ever to receive the award.

My duties with Thames Television finished with the end of the Karpov-Kasparov world championship match, and in October I travelled to Utrecht for the CAP Gemini Theme Tournament, a very unusual event indeed. There were three round-robin groups of six players; each group consisted of two invited players plus four local players. The unique feature of the tournament was that the games would not start from the normal initial position, but from positions which had been circulated to the players in advance. These positions were mainly critical situations from sharp opening lines. The idea was that the local players would get together to analyse the positions, and this preparation would to some extent offset the greater playing strength of the invited players (whom, it seemed to be assumed, would be less diligent in their preparations).

I was in a group with Timman; the second group contained Miles and van der Wiel, and the third group included Hort and Zsuzsa Polgar. There was no play-off between the group winners. Drawing the same number as a player in another group meant that you had to play all the positions with the same colour, so Tony Miles, Zsuzsa Polgar and I immediately formed 'The No.2 Club', to pool our analysis before each round. Actually, these sessions consisted mainly of Tony and I listening attentively, while Zsuzsa showed us the analysis from her file. But Tony and I did have at least one good idea. One of the specified positions arose after the moves 1 d4 ♘f6 2 c4 e6 3 ♘f3 b6 4 ♘c3 ♗b4 5 ♗g5 ♗b7 6 e3 h6 7 ♗h4 g5 8 ♗g3 ♘e4 9 ♕c2 ♗xc3+ 10 bxc3. At the time, the line 10...d6 11 ♗d3 f5 12 d5 ♘c5 13 h4 g4 14 ♘d4 ♕f6 15 0-0 ♘xd3 16 ♕xd3 e5 17 ♘xf5 ♗c8 was considered critical. Tony and I had independently discovered the stunning innovation 18 f4!!, which immediately puts Black in a critical situation. Unfortunately, the No.2 Club didn't get a chance to use this idea in Utrecht, and as the opening wasn't part of my repertoire, the innovation wasn't much use to me. But it wasn't long before the trap was sprung; just a couple of weeks later, at Tilburg,

Tony Miles got the chance to play 18 f4!! against Beliavsky, gaining not only a point but also the prize for the best novelty in *Informator 42*. It received the astounding mark of 90/90, the only novelty ever to achieve a maximum score.

I won my group with 4/5, ahead of Timman on 3½. The other groups were won by Miles with 4½ and Hort with 4.

The Utrecht tournament was also notable for Tony Miles' stellar performance at a restaurant which had unwisely offered 'as many spare ribs as you can eat' on its menu.

I had a tight schedule after the event; the tournament finished late on Friday, but I had to be in Berlin on Saturday at 2 p.m. for my Bundesliga game. Why not fly from Amsterdam to Berlin? Well, I could have done that, but it turned out that the triangular trip would have been fabulously expensive. Thanks to the bizarre pricing policies of airlines, by travelling from Amsterdam to Berlin via London it was possible to save a couple of hundred pounds. So, early on Saturday morning, Tony Miles dropped me off at Schipol airport, where I caught a flight to London. Luckily, the departing flight for Berlin was from the same terminal at Heathrow, so I arrived in Berlin at about 1.30. The taxi-driver took me directly to the playing hall, and I strode in at 1.57, ready to whip out

1 e4 against Danny King. Suddenly, I became aware of a small problem – I was there, but the rest of my team wasn't! German Bundesliga rules are very strict – no member of a team is allowed to make a move until the full team list is handed in to the arbiter. So I had to sit there until the rest of the team ambled in from lunch, whereupon my e-pawn was released from its paralysis and we were off...

Game 11

J.Nunn – D.King

Bundesliga 1986

Sicilian Najdorf

1	e4	c5
2	♘f3	d6
3	d4	cxd4
4	♘xd4	♘f6
5	♘c3	a6
6	f4	e5
7	♘f3	♘bd7
8	a4	♗e7
9	♗d3	0-0
10	0-0	♘c5
11	♔h1	d5 *(54)*

54
W

This was the main line in 1986, but now 11...exf4 is preferred. For 11...♕c7, see game 14.

12 ♘xe5 *(55)*

It is hard to say which is the best capture on e5. After 12 fxe5 ♘fxe4 White may try:

1) **13 ♗xe4?** dxe4 14 ♕xd8 ♖xd8 15 ♘g5 h6 16 ♘gxe4 ♘xe4 17 ♘xe4 ♗f5 18 ♘d6 ♗xd6 19 exd6 ♖xd6 20 ♗f4 and now 20...♖e6 21 ♖f2 ♖ae8 22 ♔g1 ♖e2 23 c3 ♗d7 24 b3 ♖8e4, Kindermann-Chandler,

Vienna 1986 and 20...♖d5 21 c4 ♖d7 22 c5 ♖d5, Lesiège-Grünfeld, Philadelphia Open 1989, were both slightly better for Black.

2) **13 ♕e2?!** ♗f5 14 ♘d4 ♗g6 15 ♘f5 ♘xc3 16 bxc3 ♘xd3 17 cxd3 ♗xf5 18 ♖xf5 ♕c8 was good for Black in Mi.Tseitlin-Timoshchenko, Hastings Challengers 1990.

3) **13 ♗e3** ♗e6 14 ♘e2 ♖c8 15 ♘ed4 ♕d7 16 a5 ♗g4 17 ♗e2 ♘e6 with an edge for Black, Sznapik-Yrjölä, Pohja 1985.

4) **13 ♘d4 ♗g5?!** (this wastes too much time; 13...f6 14 exf6 ♗xf6 is better, but White may still have an edge after 15 ♗e3 as Black cannot easily develop the c8 bishop) 14 ♕h5 ♗xc1 15 ♖axc1 g6 16 ♕h6 ♘xc3 17 bxc3 f5 18 exf6 ♖xf6 19 ♖xf6 ♕xf6 20 ♖f1 with a dangerous attack, Sax-Grünfeld, Brussels 1985.

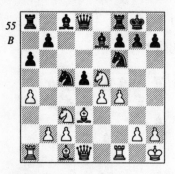

55
B

12 ...   ♘fxe4

All three captures on e4 are feasible. Here is a summary of the two alternatives:

1) **12...♘cxe4** 13 ♗xe4 dxe4 14 ♕e2 ♗f5 15 g4 (15 ♗e3 is too slow, and 15...h5 16 h3 ♕c8 17 ♗f2 ♕e6 18 ♗h4 ♖ac8 19 g4 hxg4 20 hxg4 ♗h7 was good for Black in Zso.Polgar-Loginov, Budapest 1993) ♗c8 16 ♖d1 ♕e8 17 g5 ♘d7 18 ♘c4 e3 and now there are two favourable lines for White, either 19 ♗xe3 b5 20 axb5 ♗b7+ 21 ♔g1 axb5, Kengis-Loginov, Pavlodar 1987, and now 22 ♖xa8 ♗xa8 23 ♘xb5 ♕c8 24 ♘cd6 ♕c6 25 ♔f2 gives Black inadequate

play for the two pawns, or the simple 19 ♕xe3.

2) **12...dxe4** 13 ♗e2 (Black gains time, but the pawn on e4 obstructs his pieces) ♕c7 (13...♕xd1 14 ♖xd1 ♗e6 15 ♗e3 ♖fd8 16 g4 g6 17 g5 ♘d5 18 ♘xd5 ♗xd5 19 b3 ♘e6 20 ♘c4 ♗xc4 21 ♗xc4 ♗c5 22 ♗xc5 ♘xc5 23 ♔g2 ♖ac8 24 ♔f2 was marginally better for White in Kindermann-de Firmian, Biel II 1986, but 19 b4 ♘e6 20 c4 ♗c6 21 ♘xc6 bc 22 ♖xd8 ♖xd8 23 c5 looks more dangerous) 14 ♗e3 (White may also play 14 ♕e1 first, so as to meet 14...♘e6 with 15 ♗d1 attacking e4) b6 15 ♕e1 ♗b7 16 ♕g3 ♖ad8 (16...♘e6?! 17 ♖ad1 ♗c5? 18 f5! ♗d6 19 ♖xd6 ♕xd6 20 fxe6 and White won, Beliavsky-Chandler, Vienna 1986) 17 ♖ad1 ♘cd7 (Black should have played for exchanges by 17...♖xd1 18 ♖xd1 ♖d8, but White is still slightly better) 18 ♗d4 ♘xe5 19 fxe5 ♘d7 and now 20 b3 followed by ♗c4 gave White a decisive attack in Psakhis-Balashov, Irkutsk 1986, but 20 ♗xa6! was even stronger.

13 ♗xe4   dxe4
14 ♘d5! *(56)*

White played 14 ♗e3 in Beliavsky-Portisch, Tilburg 1986 (a couple of weeks after the present game), but then 14...f6 15 ♗xc5 ♗xc5 16 ♘xe4 ♕xd1 17 ♖axd1 fxe5 18 ♘xc5 ♗g4 19 ♖de1 exf4 led to equality. The idea of 14 ♘d5 is to eliminate the e7 bishop; Black's remaining bishop will be obstructed by the e4 pawn, while White's can become active along the b2-g7 diagonal.

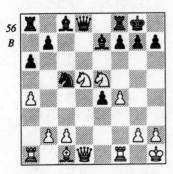

56
B

14 ...   ♗e6
Or:
1) **14...♗d6** 15 ♘c4! and Black has immediate difficulties since the natural developing move 15...♗e6 loses a piece to 16 ♘xd6. Otherwise White can proceed with ♘db6, or b4 followed by ♗b2.

2) **14...f5** 15 b4 ♘d7 was suggested by Busch and Olthof in *New in Chess*, but 16 ♗e3! is promising for White. Then both 16...♘f6 and 16...♘xe5 17 fxe5 ♗e6 lose material to ♘xe7+ and ♗c5.

3) **14...f6!** 15 ♘xe7+ ♕xe7 16 ♘c4 ♗e6 17 ♘e3 f5 leads to a structure similar to the game, except that Black has managed to play ...f5. White can continue with b3, ♗b2 and ♕e1, when his bishop is more effective than Black's. However, the opposite-coloured bishops will exert a drawish tendency, particularly if Black can exchange knights by ...♘d7-f6-d5.

15 ♘xe7+   ♕xe7
16 f5
This is the difference between 14...♗e6 and 14...f6!. The advance of the pawn to f5 benefits White in three ways. First of all, it increases the scope of his bishop; secondly, it prevents Black supporting the advanced pawn on e4 with another pawn, and thirdly it gives White attacking chances on the kingside.

16 ...   f6
16...♖ad8 (16...♗b3 is bad after 17 ♘g4, when both 17...♖ad8 18 ♕e2 ♗d5 19 f6 and 17...♗c4 18 f6 ♕e6 19 ♖f4 give White an enormous attack) 17 ♘g4 ♗c8 (17...f6 18 fxe6 fxe5 19 ♗g5 ♖xf1+ 20 ♖xf1 ♖f8 21 ♖xf8+ ♕xf8 22 h3 is very good for White) 18 ♕g3 (not 18 f6 ♕xf6!) f6 19 ♘g4 leads to a position much like the game, except that Black's bishop is on c8 instead of f7. From c8 it can exert pressure on f5, but in my view the bishop will be needed for defending the kingside and therefore the game continuation is better.

17 ♘g4
17 fxe6 fxe5 18 ♗e3 ♘xe6 19 ♕d5 may give White a minute advantage, but the move played is much more combative.

17 ...   ♗f7
The reply 17...♗c4 is ineffective

after 18 ♖f4, and the bishop will soon be driven away by b3.

18 ♕e1?!

I decided that it was time to start developing my queenside pieces, but I should have spent just one more tempo improving my position by 18 a5!. It looks strange to put a pawn on a dark square when White's plan is to block out Black's bishop using the pawns on c2, b3, a4, e4 and f5, but it is very useful to have the option of attacking the knight on c5. Not only may White push it away by b4 at a later stage, but by preventing ...b6 White can also set up an awkward pin by ♗a3. Moreover, the possible elimination of this knight gives White the option of playing for the win of the e4 pawn by ♕e1-h4, ♗a3 and ♖ae1.

This is a case in which it is worthwhile spending time to improve White's long-term prospects. Black has no way to exploit the loss of time tactically, so there would have been no risk involved.

18 ...   a5!

Black seizes on the mistake and permanently secures the c5 square for his knight.

19 b3   ♖fd8

This turns out to be a loss of time, since in a few moves Black decides that he needs a rook on f8 to support f6. Black could have set up the same position more quickly by 19...b6, followed by ...♖ad8-d6, but it is

doubtful if the extra tempo would have been much use.

20	♗b2	♖d6
21	♕g3	♔h8
22	♖ae1	b6
23	♕h4	♖f8 (57)

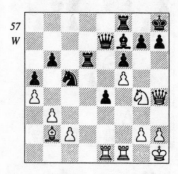

57
W

Now White has to decide on a plan. At first sight his position looks very promising, since f6 and h7 are weak, the knight on c5 cannot move without losing the e-pawn and Black has no real counterplay. However, it is hard to find a concrete way White can improve his position, since almost all his pieces are already on their best possible squares. Black's potential counterplay down the d-file limits the action of White's rooks, and although White can hope to win the e-pawn by a timely ♘f2xe4, the opposite-coloured bishops mean that this would probably not be enough to win the game. I could only conceive of two possible plans, namely ♘f2-h3-f4 coupled with ♖e3-h3 to aim at the weak g6 square, or g4-g5 to open up the long diagonal onto Black's king.

Unfortunately, neither plan can be forced through against accurate defence. White needs to cover d2 and d1 to prevent counterplay along the d-file, so it seems that the first step is to play ♗c3, covering the squares on the d-file, and then ♘f2-h3-f4. But this fails because of the undefended bishop on c3, for example Black can play ...♛c7 threatening ...♘d3.

I decided to make as much progress as I could without taking any risk, by trying to arrange a position with ♗c3, ♘f2 and ♖e3. This controls the d-file squares, and the bishop is defended so Black has no tricks. Of course, even if White reaches this position, it would still not be easy to make progress, because ♘h3 would allow ...♖d1. Still, one problem at a time.

Such situations are quite common in chess. One has a slight advantage, but no obvious way to proceed. The correct approach is based on the theory of probability. One should try to create a series of small problems for the opponent. He has to find a good reply each time, or his position will slip downhill. Failing all else, one can always hope that time-trouble will lend a helping hand.

24 ♖e3?!

White tries a little trick; perhaps Black won't notice the threat of 25 ♖h3 ♗g8 26 ♘e5.

24 ...   ♛d8

Unfortunately he does. Moreover, now it is hard to prevent a black rook invasion.

25 ♔g1

Avoiding immediate back rank problems and future long diagonal troubles after a possible g4. Note that Black cannot initiate counterplay by 25...♖d2 because of 26 ♘xf6 ♗g8 27 ♘h5!.

25 ...   ♗g8

Now, however, 26...♖d2 is a threat.

26 ♗c3

White must prevent ...♖d2, even if he thereby allows ...♖d1. If Black does nothing, White will be able to reach his target position by 27 ♘f2.

26 ...   ♖d1
27 ♖ee1   ♖d6?!

If correctly followed up, this is a perfectly reasonable defence, but the alternative 27...♖xe1 28 ♖xe1 ♛d6 29 ♘e3 ♛c6 (29...♖d8 30 ♖d1 ♛e7 31 ♖d4! ♖xd4 32 ♗xd4 is worse; if the black queen leaves the defence of the e-pawn ♗xc5 and ♛xe4 wins it, and otherwise White intends ♛f4-b8) is safer. Swapping a pair of rooks reduces White's attacking chances, and in this case Black would not have many problems drawing.

If White had played less carelessly at move 24 (e.g. by 24 ♗c3), then this possibility would not have existed.

28 ♘f2

Sometimes an oversight is the best chance to win! It seemed to me that this was the moment to set up the position with ♘f2 and ♖e3, but this move fails for tactical reasons. However, despite lengthy analysis, I can see no other way to make progress.

28 ...   ♛c8!

Since Black obviously cannot play ...♛xf5 because of ♘xe4, I decided to continue with my plan. There was nothing better in any case, since 29 ♛g3 ♖c6 is awkward.

29 ♖e3

After having made this move, I suddenly noticed that Black could play 29...♛xf5 30 ♘xe4 ♛e6! with a certain draw, but perhaps the confident way I had made the move led my opponent to believe that the pawn was invulnerable.

29 ...   ♖d5? (58)

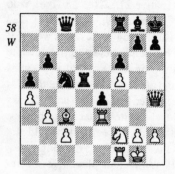

58
W

30 g4!

White not only achieves the position he has been aiming for, but in a

very favourable form, since the rooks on d5 and f8 are both vulnerable to the manoeuvre ♘h3-f4-g6.

30 ...   ♛c7

Perhaps Black could have offered more resistance, but the twin possibilities of ♘h3-f4 and g5 make his position very unpleasant.

31 ♘h3   ♘d3

New in Chess recommended 31...♗f7 32 ♘f4 ♖d6, but 33 ♘g6+ ♗xg6 34 fxg6 h6 35 g5 blows up Black's position. The move played involves an exchange sacrifice, but Black does not obtain sufficient compensation.

32 cxd3   ♛xc3
33 ♘f4   g5
34 ♘xd5

34 fxg6 is also promising, but this is simpler.

34 ...   ♗xd5
35 ♛e1

Thanks to the earlier ♔g1, Black has no real counterplay and he is soon forced to give up.

35 ...   ♛d4
36 dxe4   ♗xe4
37 ♛c3   ♛d5
38 ♛c4   1-0

After this it was time for the biennial Olympiad, which in 1986 was held in Dubai. Of the nine Olympiads I have attended, there is no doubt that Dubai offered the best conditions for competitors. The Hilton hotel was comfortable, the food was excellent and the playing conditions were very good. In addition, there were the extra touches which make the difference between a well-organised tournament and an outstanding one. For example, next to the playing hall was a second hall, which was given over to entertainments for the chess players. These included table tennis, dancing, and free video games. Unfortunately, Tony Miles came down with a severe case of 'Pengo finger' as a result of over-indulgence in one of the latter.

The Dubai Olympiad was the English team's best ever performance in an Olympiad. Three teams were in contention for first place, namely USSR, USA and England. Despite an unfortunate upset against Spain in round 10, we were just half-a-point behind the Soviet Union with one round to go. The last-round pairings were USSR v Poland and England v Brazil, so anything could happen. As usual, there was a free day before the last round, giving us plenty of time to prepare for the match. But, as any English team captain knows, the chances that members of the team will become incapacitated are far higher on a 'rest' day than on a playing day.

It all started innocently enough. Jon Speelman had transported a few books to someone at the British Embassy in Dubai, and later on some people from the Embassy suggested a trip on the free day before the last round. It sounded harmless enough, the weather was fine and, I was assured, I didn't even need to take my passport. Three of the Embassy staff came for the trip, together with assorted chess players, including Jon, Glenn and Christine Flear, and myself. The transport for this trip was a Land Rover plus a small four-wheel drive vehicle. After a picnic lunch on the beach, it was suggested that we go back via a different route avoiding the main roads and travelling instead over the mountains.

The first warning signal was a sign that cautioned drivers of hazardous conditions ahead, which was followed by another one asking if we were really sure that we wanted to continue down the road. But nothing untoward happened as we climbed a precipitous zigzag road to the summit of the mountain. This did indeed seem to be a wholly inhospitable place perched uneasily between the UAE (United Arab Emirates) and Oman. There were few signs of human life.

We stopped at the summit to admire the view and finish off the remnants of the picnic. By now the sun was starting to go down, and a chill wind blew over the rocky terrain. Nobody wanted to descend a dangerous road in poor light, so we decided to set off immediately. There was just one problem – the engine of the

Land Rover failed to start, and no amount of fiddling and cajoling could bring it back to life. The obvious plan was for some people to go in the smaller vehicle and try to find someone who would come and fix the Land Rover. This sounded a bit optimistic to me – I wouldn't have agreed to go up that vertiginous road in the dark – but there was no other course of action. But who should go with the driver? The most important thing, we decided, was to make sure that the players got back for tomorrow's crucial match, so Jon Speelman and I, with total lack of chivalry, abandoned the others on the top of the mountain.

After descending to sea level, the next problem manifested itself – rocky wastelands tend to be poorly signposted. We set off at random and soon came across an Omani border post. The two men with machine guns manning this post refused to let us into Oman; by now I was regretting my lack of a passport. So we turned round with the idea of finding a way back into the UAE, but after a couple of miles we were delighted to see the Land Rover descending the mountain. The engine had finally responded to the various admonitions and was no longer on strike. By now it was more or less dark, but curiously enough this made it easier to spot the lights of civilisation and we soon found our way out of the wilderness.

The unusual team preparation was obviously effective, because the next day we beat Brazil 4-0. Alas, the Soviet Union triumphed over Poland by exactly the same decisive margin, thus preserving their half-point lead. Nevertheless the Olympiad could be counted a great success for the English team. I was more than satisfied with my personal score of 7/11 on board 2.

Game 12

J.Nunn – A.Sokolov

Dubai OL 1986

Sicilian Defence

1	e4	c5
2	♘f3	e6
3	d4	cxd4
4	♘xd4	♘c6
5	♘c3	a6

6	♗e2	d6
7	♗e3	♕c7
8	f4	

I had anticipated playing Karpov, and only discovered shortly before the match that my opponent was actually Sokolov. I was therefore quite pleased when the game entered paths which were very familiar to me. Round about this time, I was meeting the Taimanov Sicilian with this set-up, the point of which is to retain the option of castling on either wing.

8 ... ♘a5?

One curious feature of this game is the similarity with a famous encounter from 50 years before: Lasker-Pirc, Moscow 1935. Of the pre-war champions, I have always had the greatest admiration for Lasker. His amorphous style is hard to define, and evidently his contemporaries also had problems getting to grips with it. I have always regretted that there is no really good book analysing Lasker's games throughout his career. One day, perhaps, I will write it myself.

The Lasker-Pirc game started with a completely different move-order, which is perhaps why Sokolov didn't realise the danger until too late. Pirc made the same basic mistake as Sokolov: the manoeuvre ...♘a5-c4, which more or less forces the exchange of one of White's bishops, is strategically very desirable, but it costs too much time. Black falls way behind in development and cannot bring his pieces out in a natural way. Once again, the game hinges on the relative merits of long-term and short-term advantages, but

in this game Black takes one risk too many. The natural 8...♘f6 was better.

9	**0-0**	**♘c4**
10	**♗xc4**	**♕xc4**
11	**f5** (59)	

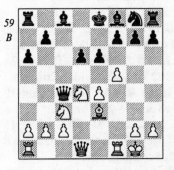

White must act quickly before Black develops his pieces. The immediate advance of the f-pawn is the only way to open avenues of attack into Black's position.

11 ... ♗e7

Sokolov thought for a long time before reconciling himself to this unnatural move. He must have intended to play 11...♘f6, but then realised that it wasn't possible for tactical reasons. In fact, after 11...♘f6 we have transposed exactly into Lasker-Pirc. During the game, I wasn't sure that the position was absolutely identical, but I knew the basic idea of Lasker's combination, and it didn't take long to check that it worked after 11...♘f6. Here is the conclusion of Lasker-Pirc: 12 fxe6 fxe6 (12...♗xe6 13 ♘xe6 ♕xe6 14 ♗g5 ♗e7 15 ♘d5 is very bad for Black) 13 ♖xf6! gxf6 14 ♕h5+ and now:

1) **14...♔d8** (the game continuation) 15 ♕f7 ♗d7 (after 15...♗e7 16 ♘f5 Black cannot play 16...♖e8 because of 17 ♘xd6 ♗xd6 18 ♗b6+ ♗c7 19 ♖d1+, so 16...♕c7 is forced, but then 17 ♘a4 ♖f8 18 ♕xh7 ♔e8 19 ♗b6 ♕d7 20 ♕h5+ ♖f7 21 ♘g7+ ♔f8 22 ♕h8 is mate) 16 ♕xf6+♔c7 17 ♕xh8 ♗h6 18 ♘xe6+! ♕xe6 19 ♕xa8 ♗xe3+ 20 ♔h1 1-0.

2) **14...♔d7** 15 ♕f7+ ♗e7 16 ♘f5 ♖e8 17 ♘xd6 ♔xd6 18 ♕xe8 with a crushing attack.

3) **14...♔e7** 15 ♘f5+! exf5 (15...♔d7 16 ♕f7+ ♔c6 17 ♘d4+ ♔b6 18 ♘b3+ wins) 16 ♘d5+ ♔d8 17 ♗b6+ ♔d7 18 ♕f7+ ♔c6 19 ♕c7+ ♔b5 20 a4+ ♕xa4 21 ♘c3+ ♔b4 22 ♖xa4 mate.

12   ♕g4?! *(60)*

This is the obvious way to exploit the omission of ...♘f6, but 12 fxe6 ♗xe6 (12...fxe6 13 e5! is very good for White) 13 ♘xe6 fxe6 (13...♕xe6 14 ♘d5) 14 e5! 0-0-0 15 ♖f4 ♕c6 16 ♕g4 is probably even stronger, for example 16...d5 17 ♕xg7 ♗c5 18 ♗xc5 ♕xc5+ 19 ♔h1 ♘e7 20 ♕f7 and Black's position collapses.

12   ...   h5?!

This forces the queen away from the powerful square g4, but now Black can forget about kingside castling. Alternatives are:

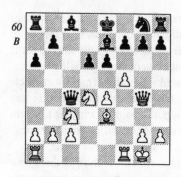

1) **12...e5** 13 ♘d5! (threatening 14 b3 or 14 ♕xg7) exd4 14 ♕xg7 dxe3 15 ♕xh8 ♔f8 16 f6 and White wins.

2) **12...♘f6** 13 ♕xg7 ♖g8 14 ♕h6 e5 15 ♖ad1! exd4 16 ♗xd4 ♘d7 (16...♘g4 17 ♕xh7 ♖f8 18 ♘d5 ♗d8 20 ♕g7 and White wins) 17 ♕xh7 ♖g4 18 ♕h8+ ♘f8 (or 18...♗f8 19 h3 ♖g5 20 ♘d5! ♕xc2 21 g4 and the threats of 22 ♖c1, 22 ♘f6+ and 22 ♗f6 are too much for Black) 19 f6 ♗d8 20 ♗e3, threatening ♗h6, and White has three pawns and a very strong attack for the piece.

3) **12...♗f6** is a safer idea. After 13 ♖ad1 ♘e7 14 fxe6 fxe6 15 ♘f3 White has a slight advantage, but nothing more.

4) **12...g6**, intending ...♘f6, also restricts White's advantage.

13   ♕f3   ♗f6?

Once again Black disregards his development, and this time the error is fatal. 13...♘f6 was compulsory, but after 14 ♖ad1 White has an ominous lead in development, while thanks to ...h5 Black's king is very insecure.

14 fxe6   fxe6 *(61)*

Or 14...♗xe6 15 ♘xe6 ♕xe6 (15...fxe6 16 e5 dxe5 17 ♕xb7 gives White a large advantage) 16 ♘d5 ♖c8 17 ♖ad1 and Black has a terrible position (17...♖xc2 18 ♖c1).

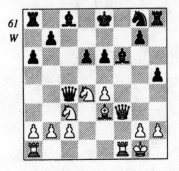

61
W

15 e5!

A typical sacrifice, rather reminiscent of the same move in Game 2 (Nunn-Chandler). Black is forced to take with the pawn, but this improves White's position in three ways; firstly, the d-file and the diagonal f3-a8 are opened, increasing White's attacking prospects; secondly, the bishop on f6 is hemmed in; thirdly, the square e4 is freed for the knight on c3. Of course these are only general points, indicating that 15 e5 is worth taking seriously; it is still necessary to calculate that the move actually works.

15 ...   dxe5
16 ♘e4   ♕c7

Other methods of avoiding the fork are no better, for example 16...♔e7 17 ♘b3, with ♗c5+ to come, or 16...♔d8 17 ♘d6 ♕c7 18 ♘b3, followed by ♖ad1.

17 ♕g3

A useful move, indirectly defending the knight on d4 and threatening either 18 ♕g6+ (see the next note), or to simply step up the pressure with 18 ♖ad1.

17 ...   ♘e7 *(62)*

After 17...h4 18 ♕g6+ ♔d8 (or 18...♔f8 19 ♘xe6+! ♗xe6 20 ♗c5+ ♘e7 21 ♖xf6+ gxf6 22 ♕xf6+ winning) 19 ♘xe6+! ♗xe6 20 ♖ad1+ ♗d7 21 ♘c5 White wins material.

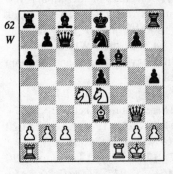

62
W

18 ♖ad1!

Conducting an attack often requires good judgement. Sometimes the attack demands quick action and there is no time to bring up reinforcements, but sometimes it is better to bring all the pieces into play before attempting a knock-out blow. Which of these holds true depends on whether or not the defender is threatening to consolidate quickly. If his weaknesses are structural, then the attacker may have time to bring all his reserves into action before the final onslaught. Here, for example, the impatient 18 ♘xf6+? gxf6 19 ♕g7 (not 19 ♖xf6? ♖g8, followed by ...exd4) ♖g8 20 ♕xf6 exd4 is insufficient, while 18 ♖xf6?! gxf6 19 ♕g7 (19 ♘xf6+ ♔f7 20 ♖f1 ♘f5 is also unclear) ♖f8 20 ♗h6 (20 ♘xf6+ ♖xf6 21 ♕xf6 exd4) ♖f7 21 ♕h8+ ♔d7 offers only nebulous compensation for White. It is clear that these lines would both be easy wins for White if he had a rook on d1, so 18 ♖ad1 deserves consideration. A few moments' thought shows that Black has nothing better than to play 18...h4, but then White can play ♘xf6+ having gained an important extra tempo.

18 ...   h4

There is nothing better:

1) 18...♖f8 19 ♘b5 axb5 20 ♘d6+ wins Black's queen.

2) 18...♗d7 19 ♖xf6! gxf6 20 ♘xf6+ ♔f7 21 ♘f3 ♔xf6 22 ♗g5+ ♔f7 23 ♘xe5+ ♔e8 24 ♗xe7 ♔xe7 25 ♕g7+ and mate in four more moves.

3) 18...♘f5 19 ♘xf5 exf5 20 ♘xf6+ gxf6 21 ♕g6+ ♕f7 22 ♖d8+ wins the queen.

4) 18...♘d5 19 ♕g6+ ♔f8 (or 19...♔d8 20 ♘b5! axb5 21 ♘xf6 gxf6 22 ♕xf6+ winning) 20 ♘xf6

gxf6 21 ♖xf6+ ♘xf6 22 ♘c6! and mates in four more moves, as readers may check for themselves.

19 ♘xf6+   gxf6
20 ♕g7 *(63)*

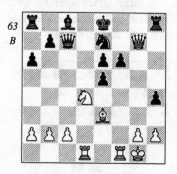

20 ...   ♖f8

Or 20...♖g8 21 ♕xf6 ♘d5 (after 21...exd4 White has an elegant win by 22 ♕f7+ ♔d8 23 ♖xd4+ ♗d7 24 ♕f8+! and mate next move) 22 ♘xe6 ♖xg2+ 23 ♔xg2 (23 ♔h1 ♖xh2+ 24 ♔xh2 ♕xc2+ 25 ♖d2 ♘xf6 26 ♖xf6! ♕xd2+! 27 ♗xd2 ♔e7 28 ♘c7 ♔xf6 29 ♘xa8 would be tricky to win) ♕xc2+ 24 ♖d2 ♕e4+ (24...♘xe3+ 25 ♔g1 forces mate) 25 ♕f3 ♕xf3+ (25...♘xe3+ 26 ♔g1 ♕xf3 27 ♘c7+ ♔e7 28 ♖xf3 wins) 26 ♔xf3 ♗xe6 27 ♗g5 with a winning ending for White.

21 ♖xf6

This is clearer than 21 ♗h6 ♖g8 22 ♕xf6 ♘d5, although even here White gains the advantage by 23 ♕xh4 (but not 23 ♘xe6? ♕b6+) exd4 24 ♕h5+ ♔d8 25 ♗g5+ and

Black is forced to take the opposing bishop.

21 ... ♖xf6
22 ♕xf6 ♕d6 *(64)*

Or 22...exd4 23 ♕h8+ ♔d7 24 ♖xd4+ ♘d5 25 ♕g7+ ♔e8 26 ♕g8+ ♔e7 (26...♔d7 27 ♕f7+ ♔c6 28 ♖c4+) 27 ♖xd5! exd5 28 ♕g7+ and Black loses his queen.

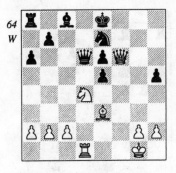

64
W

23 ♗g5!

The final point. Black has no defence against 24 ♕h8+ ♔d7 25 ♗xe7, for example 23...♕c5 24 b4!.

23 ... exd4
24 ♖xd4 ♘d5

24...♕c5 loses to 25 b4 ♕c7 26 ♕h8+ ♔f7 27 ♖f4+ ♘f5 28 ♕h7+.

25 ♖xd5 1-0

Black is mated in five more moves.

The Dubai Olympiad was also notable for developments off the chessboard. The collapse of the Keene/Lucena bid for the FIDE Presidency cemented Campomanes' power and,

perhaps in reaction to this, the GMA was founded. Kasparov and Bessel Kok were the motivating forces, with a number of other grandmasters offering support. However, this book is not about chess politics, so I will say little more about this aspect of the game.

Finally the excitement of Dubai came to an end, and soon I was back in Europe for the next event. This was a double-round tournament with six top players, held in Brussels and sponsored by OHRA, who were heavily involved in chess sponsorship (see also pages 20 and 40).

By 1986, Brussels had become quite a chess centre since, in addition to the OHRA events, SWIFT, under Bessel Kok, had started an annual tournament. With an average Elo rating of 2636, OHRA 1986 was the highest-rated tournament held since the inception of the Elo rating system. I believe the next two strongest were Johannesburg 1981 (average rating 2629) and Bugojno 1986 (average rating 2628). Since then these records have been broken several times, most notably by the series of tournaments at Linares, but in 1986 the record belonged to Brussels.

The six competitors were Kasparov, Portisch, Hübner, Short, Korchnoi and myself. I had the lowest rating and I started the tournament with a good deal of trepidation, which seemed justified when I was completely crushed by Kasparov in the first round. But it turned out that this was the worst moment, and later on I won two good games (and one very lucky one). The first was against Nigel Short in round 3.

Game 13

J.Nunn – N.Short

Brussels (OHRA) 1986

Spanish

1	e4	e5
2	♘f3	♘c6
3	♗b5	a6
4	♗a4	♘f6
5	0-0	♗e7
6	♖e1	b5
7	♗b3	d6
8	c3	0-0
9	h3	♘a5
10	♗c2	c5
11	d4	♕c7
12	♘bd2	♘c6

This is very much a sideline. The main variations involve taking on d4, either immediately or after 12...♗d7 13 ♘f1.

13 d5 *(65)*

Fischer used to play 13 dxc5, but this is no longer thought dangerous. White has tried virtually every other legal move (for example, 13 a3, 13 a4, 13 ♘f1, 13 ♘b3 and 13 ♗b1), but 13 d5 seems the most logical to me. Not only is Black forced to move his knight again, but a timely a4 will give White control of the a-file.

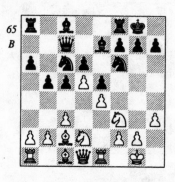

65
B

13	...	♘d8

13...♘a5, 13...♘a7 and 13...♘b8 have also been played. The idea behind 13...♘d8 is that the knight has two possibilities for redeployment. The first is to go to b7 and then, after a later ...c4, to c5. Of course 13...♘a5 also allows this option. The second plan arises if White attacks on the kingside; then Black can set up an effective defence based on ...♘e8, ...g6, ...f6, ...♘g7 and ...♘f7. In this case both knights would be participating in the defence, instead of one being stranded on the queenside. This plan was used in the game

R.Rodriguez-Kakageldiev, Manila OL 1992, which continued 14 b3 ♘e8 15 ♘f1 g6 16 a4 ♖b8 17 ♘3h2 f6 18 axb5 axb5 19 ♘g3 ♘g7 20 f4 exf4 21 ♗xf4 ♘f7 22 ♘f3 ♘e5 and Black had equalised.

14 ♘f1

14 a4 is normally played at once, but it makes little difference since ♘f1 will be essential sooner or later.

14 ...   ♘e8

The manoeuvre ...g6 and ...♘e8-g7 not only fortifies the kingside against White's attack, but also prepares counterplay with ...f5.

15 a4

If White wishes to play for a direct attack he can try 15 g4, but after 15...g6 16 ♘g3 ♘g7 17 ♔h2 (17 ♗h6 is a waste of time, since Black will play ...f6 and ...♘f7 in any case) f6 18 ♗e3 ♗d7 19 ♕d2 ♘f7 20 ♖g1 ♔h8 21 ♖af1 ♖g8 22 ♘e1 ♖af8 the position was equal in Robatsch-Padevsky, Amsterdam 1972. In olden times White would often attack by g4 and ♘g3 in the Closed Spanish; once in a while White would break through with a ♘f5 sacrifice, but now it is recognised that so long as all Black's pieces can reach the kingside, a direct attack should not work. Thus the emphasis has switched to diversionary queenside play, with a kingside attack being reserved for a favourable moment when Black's pieces have been lured away. Moreover, the kingside attack is usually

based on f4 rather than g4, since only f4 offers the chance of activating the light-squared bishop on c2.

White's preliminary a4 gives him control of the a-file; this may not appear relevant to the conduct of a kingside attack, but watch what happens later!

15 ...   ♖b8
16 axb5   axb5
17 b4 (66)

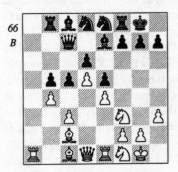

66
B

This prevents Black gaining space and counterplay by ...c4 and ...♘b7-c5, and thereby cuts out one of the two possible futures for the d8 knight. The move b4 is an important part of White's strategy; a consequence of this is that playing b3, as in R.Rodriguez-Kakageldiev above, is inaccurate.

17 ...   c4?!

Even though it has been played before, I believe this move is dubious. Black does not want to calculate the consequences of bxc5 in every variation, but by blocking the queenside he not only leaves White in possession of the a-file, but a later ♗e3 will introduce the possibility of ♖a7. Moreover, if White plays a later f4 and Black replies ...exf4, a white knight can come to d4, attacking the weak b5 pawn and the sensitive squares at c6 and e6. 17...g6 is more flexible.

18   ♘g3

The first new move of the game. Hitherto 18 ♘3h2 had been played and after 18...f6 (18...f5 19 exf5 ♗xf5 20 ♗xf5 ♖xf5 21 ♗e3 ♖f8 22 ♘f3 ♘f6 23 ♘g3 ♘f7 24 ♖a7 ♖b7 25 ♖a5 ♕f7 26 ♕d2 was thoroughly miserable for Black in Geller-Smyslov, Palma de Mallorca 1970; just as in the King's Indian, Black needs to be able to retake on f5 with a pawn) 19 f4 ♘f7 20 ♘f3 g6 21 f5 ♘g7 22 g4 White had a clear advantage in Karpov-Spassky, USSR Ch 1973. 18 ♘g3 may be slightly less accurate because the g3 knight can be a tactical weakness.

18   ...   g6
19   ♘h2   ♘g7
20   ♖f1

Necessary preparation, since the immediate 20 f4 is well met by 20...♗h4 21 ♕f3 f5 and White cannot cope with the tactics while his g3 knight is pinned.

20   ...   ♗d7?!

Black hopes to challenge the a-file one day, so he starts moving pieces off the back rank. However,

the bishop now blocks the second rank instead, preventing the queen crossing to support the kingside. The best defence was 20...f6 21 f4 exf4 (21...♘f7 22 f5 is very good for White, as in Karpov-Spassky above) 22 ♗xf4 ♘f7, when at least one black piece reaches a good square. White can continue by 23 ♘f3 ♘e5 24 ♘d4 or 23 ♘g4 ♘e5 24 ♘h6+ ♔h8 25 h4, with a slight advantage in either case, but Black has more counterchances than in the game. Other moves are not so good, e.g. 20...♗h4 (20...f5 21 exf5 gxf5 22 ♗h6 is also promising for White) 21 ♗h6 and now 21...f6 22 ♘f3 ♗xg3 23 fxg3 ♘f7 24 ♗e3 f5 (24...♘h5 25 ♘h4) 25 ♘h4 is good for White, while if Black does not play ...f6 he has no constructive plan.

21   f4   ♗h4
22   ♕f3

Now White has a clear advantage; he has taken the initiative on the kingside without losing time.

22   ...   f5

Black stops the threat of f5, but at the cost of exposing his king. 22...♗xg3 23 ♕xg3 ♘h5 24 ♕h4 ♘xf4 (24...exf4 25 ♗d1) 25 ♗xf4 exf4 26 ♖xf4 gives White a very strong attack without any sacrifice.

23   fxe5 *(67)*

It is important to make the exchanges in the right order since 23 exf5 allows 23...♗xg3 24 ♕xg3 ♗xf5 and Black defends.

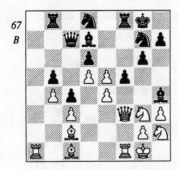

67
B

23 ... dxe5

The other critical line runs 23...f4 and now:

1) **24 ♘f5!?** (24 ♗xf4? ♕b6+ loses material after any of the five possible replies) gxf5 25 ♕xf4 ♗e7 26 e6 ♗xe6 (26...♗e8 27 exf5 gives excellent compensation for the piece) 27 dxe6 ♘dxe6 28 ♕h6 with advantage to White.

2) **24 ♘e2 dxe5 25 g3 ♗xg3** (otherwise Black loses a pawn for nothing) 26 ♘xg3 ♘f7 and White can have a better ending by 27 ♘e2 ♘g5 28 ♕g2 ♕b6+ 29 ♔h1 ♗xh3 30 ♕xg5 ♗xf1 31 ♘xf1 ♕f2 32 ♕g2 ♕xg2+ 33 ♔xg2 f3+ 34 ♔f2 fxe2+ 35 ♔xe2 or a better middle-game by 27 ♘g4 ♗xg4 28 hxg4 fxg3 29 ♕xg3 followed by ♗e3.

24 exf5 ♗xg3

24...gxf5 loses to 25 ♘xf5! ♖xf5 (25...♘xf5 26 ♕g4+ or 25...♗xf5 26 g4 winning an important pawn in both cases) 26 ♗xf5 ♗xf5 (26...♘xf5 still fails to 27 ♕g4+) 27 g4 e4 28 ♕f4 ♕xf4 29 ♗xf4 and Black has

two pieces attacked. Therefore Black has to exchange on g3 first, but without the dark-squared bishop his king is in danger.

25 ♕xg3 ♘xf5

Or 25...gxf5 (25...♗xf5 26 ♘g4) 26 ♘g4! fxg4 (e5 cannot be defended, and 26...f4 27 ♘h6+ ♔h8 28 ♕g5 is very unpleasant for Black) 27 ♗xh7+ ♔xh7 28 ♖xf8 ♕b6+ (or else ♕h4+ wins) 29 ♗e3 ♕g6 30 ♖a6! ♘f5 (there is nothing else) 31 ♕xe5 ♕xa6 32 hxg4! with a decisive attack.

26 ♕f2

26 ♕e1 gives White a clear positional advantage, but this move, based on an unusual tactical point, turns out to be even better. The threat is 27 g4.

26 ... ♘b7

With the threat of 27...♘d4. The alternative 26...♘f7 avoids an immediate disaster, but after 27 ♘g4 ♔h8 28 ♖a7 ♖b7 29 ♖a6 White has very strong pressure. 26...♕b6 is met by 27 ♕c5! followed by ♘g4.

27 ♘g4 h5 *(68)*

27...♕d6 was the alternative, but 28 ♕a7! followed by ♖a6 is very strong (28...♕xd5 29 ♕xb8!). If White were forced to move his knight after 27...h5, then Black could escape by 28...♘d4, but White can ignore the attack.

28 ♖a6!

The a-file which White opened at move 16 finally comes in useful.

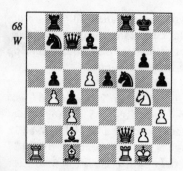

68
W

Black has no way to defend g6, for example 28...♔h7 (28...♔g7 29 ♗h6+ and 28...♘bd6 29 ♘xe5 are dead lost) 29 ♘f6+ ♔g7 30 ♘xh5+! gxh5 31 ♗h6+ ♘xh6 (31...♔h8 32 ♗xf8 ♖xf8 33 g4 wins) 32 ♖g6+ ♔h7 33 ♕e3! ♖xf1+ 34 ♔xf1 ♘f7 35 ♖c6+ and White wins.

| 28 | ... | hxg4 |
| 29 | ♖xg6+ | ♘g7 *(69)* |

The alternatives 29...♔h8 30

hxg4 and 29...♔h7 30 ♖xg4 are also hopeless.

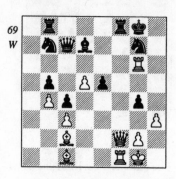

69
W

| 30 | ♖xg7+! | **1-0** |

30...♔xg7 31 ♗h6+ mates in two more moves.

In round 6 I lost again to Kasparov, even more quickly than in the first game, but in the following round my fortunes revived again.

Game 14
J.Nunn – L.Portisch
Brussels (OHRA) 1986
Sicilian Najdorf

1	e4	c5
2	♘f3	d6
3	d4	cxd4
4	♘xd4	♘f6
5	♘c3	a6
6	f4	e5
7	♘f3	♘bd7
8	a4	♗e7
9	♗d3	0-0
10	0-0	♘c5
11	♔h1	♕c7

For 11...d5, see Game 11.

| 12 | ♕e1 *(70)* |

Threatening 13 fxe5 dxe5 14 ♕g3 and Black has no natural way to defend the e5 pawn. Black can consider

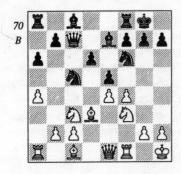

70
B

sacrificing it, for example by 12...♗d7 13 fxe5 dxe5 14 ♕g3 ♖ae8 15 ♕xe5 ♗d6 16 ♕d4, but his compensation looks inadequate in view of White's control of d5.

12 ...   ♗e6

A provocative move, since White can gain time to start a dangerous kingside attack. The main alternative is 12...exf4 (12...♖e8 is also possible, when 13 fxe5 dxe5 14 ♕g3 ♗d8 15 ♘h4 ♔h8 16 ♘f5 ♗xf5 17 ♖xf5 ♕c6 18 ♗e3 ♘xd3 19 cxd3 ♕d7 was level in Oll-Novikov, USSR 1986) 13 ♗xf4 ♖e8 (after 13...♗e6 14 ♘d4 ♕b6 15 ♗e3 ♘g4 16 ♗g1 ♘e5 17 ♘f5 ♗xf5 18 ♘d5 ♕d8 19 exf5 ♗f6 20 ♗e2 ♘ed7 White's two bishops gave him the advantage in Short-Gallagher, British Ch 1987) 14 ♘d4 ♗d7 15 ♗g5 ♕d8, Hazai-Novikov, Camaguey 1987, and now White should have activated his bishop by 16 ♗c4!, pointing it at the sensitive square f7.

In the years since 1986, nobody has cared to repeat Portisch's move.

While it is not definitely bad, tempting White to push his kingside pawns does involve a large element of risk.

13 f5   ♗d7
14 g4!?

14 ♗g5 ♗c6 15 ♗xf6 ♗xf6 16 g4 is an alternative method, which has the advantage of preventing the blockading idea used by Black in the game. On the other hand exchanging pieces frees Black's cramped position.

14 ...   ♗c6

14...♘xg4 loses to 15 ♘d5 ♕d8 16 ♖g1 ♘f6 17 ♗h6 ♘e8 18 ♖xg7+ ♘xg7 19 ♕g3 ♗f6 (19...♗g5 20 ♘xg5 is hopeless) 20 ♗xg7 ♗xg7 21 ♖g1 and White mates in a further three moves.

15 g5   ♘h5

The only move. Retreating to d7 gives White a completely free hand on the kingside, for example 15...♘fd7 16 f6 ♗d8 17 ♕h4 ♘e6 18 ♘d5 and White wins, while 15...♘fxe4 16 ♗xe4 doesn't work.

16 f6

16 ♕h4 just transposes, but anything else allows Black to move the f8 rook, allowing the bishop to retreat there rather than to d8.

16 ...   ♗d8 *(71)*

Not 16...gxf6? 17 ♕h4 winning.

17 ♕h4

White has certainly made a lot of progress on the kingside, but such pawn storms normally do not lead to

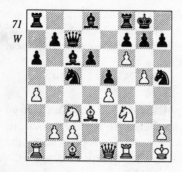

71
W

mate unless there are some pieces to back up the pawns. In this case, the pawns have run ahead of the rest of White's development, and now it is time for White to bring his queenside pieces into play. It is tempting to play 17 ♗c4, because if White could gain control of d5, then Black would have few, if any, possibilities for counterplay. However, this would be one non-developing move too far, and after 17...♘xe4! 18 ♘xe4 d5 Black has good counterplay, for example 19 fxg7 ♖e8 20 ♘f6+?! (20 ♗d3 dxe4 21 ♗xe4 ♘xg7 is better, with an unclear position) ♘xf6 21 gxf6 dxc4. This position is quite instructive, because it shows how such pawn advances can go wrong. The Space Invaders have landed on Black's position, but all White's pieces except his knight are on the first rank, and the knight is pinned. If White had better development he might be able to mate Black on h7, or get a knight to h6, but as it is White is just dead lost. His king is hopelessly

exposed to the fire of Black's bishops, and he will never have time to organise an attack on h7.

On the other hand, 17 ♗e3 is a promising alternative. This is based on the argument that Black is probably going to play ...g6 in any case, so spending a tempo on forcing it is counterproductive.

17   ...   g6
18   ♗e3

White's kingside attack has come to a temporary halt, so the time has come to bring the remaining pieces into play. There is a positional threat of 19 ♗xc5 dxc5 20 ♗c4, followed by the occupation of d5. Thus the c5 knight must move, but 18...♘e6 19 ♘d5 ♗xd5 20 exd5 ♘f4 21 ♗xf4 exf4 22 ♗f5! h6 (or else ♗g4 in any case) 23 ♗g4 hxg5 24 ♘xg5 ♘xf6 25 ♖xf4 gives White a decisive attack. So Black's move is more or less forced.

18   ...   ♘xd3
19   cxd3   ♔h8

A good defensive move. White can only revive his kingside attack by playing ♘e2-g3 to remove the blockading knight. When that happens Black cannot take on g3 (because the recapture hxg3 will give White a crushing attack down the h-file), so he must simply allow White to take on h5. Provided Black's king is safely on h8, this does not give rise to any dangerous threats to the king. Of course the capture on h5 wins a pawn, but White has expended three tempi to gain it; Black's task is to use that time to generate a pawn's worth of counterplay.

20 ♘e2 *(72)*

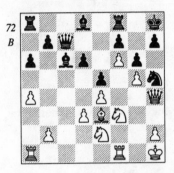

20 ... d5

A very natural move aiming to weaken e4 and activate the c6 bishop against White's king. However, it also weakens the important e5 pawn and this balances White's weak point at e4.

20...♗d7? (intending ...♛c2) is refuted by 21 ♖fc1 ♛b8 (21...♛a5 is bad after 22 ♖c4!, when Black has to go backwards with 22...♗c6 in order to meet the threat of 23 b4) 22 ♘g3 winning a pawn for nothing.

20...♛d7 is a good defence, attacking a4. After 21 b3 (21 a5 ♗b5) ♛e6 22 ♖ab1 ♖c8 23 ♘g3 ♗d7 Black gets counterplay by penetrating with his rook to c3 or c2, so White's best is 21 ♘g3 ♗xa4 22 ♘xh5 gxh5 23 ♛xh5 ♗b5 24 ♖a3 (intending ♖g1-g4-h4). However,

the attack down the h-file is unlikely to lead to mate since Black can defend by ...♖g8-g6 followed by ...h6, so the position must be judged unclear.

21 ♘g3 dxe4

Black cannot play 21...♛d6 because of 22 d4!, when both 22...dxe4 23 ♘xe5 and 22...exd4 23 e5 followed by ♗xd4 leave the c6-h1 diagonal blocked by a black pawn.

22 dxe4 ♛d6

Black aims to activate his queen by 23...♛d3 or 23...♛b4. After 22...♖g8 White can adopt a different plan: 23 ♖ac1 followed by ♖c5 and e5 is under fire.

23 ♖ad1 *(73)*

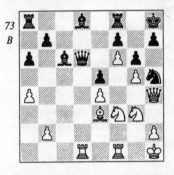

23 ... ♛b4?

Up to here Portisch has defended very well, but this move is a mistake. He intends exchanging queens on e4, but overlooks that once the e5 pawn falls, White's attack persists even without queens. The correct line was 23...♛e6 24 ♗c5 ♖g8, aiming to

maintain the pawn on e5 for as long
as possible. After 25 ♗d6 ♗xa4!
(not only grabbing a pawn, but also
enabling the bishop to defend the
weak square f7 by means of ...♗b3)
26 ♖d2 ♗a5 (not 26...♕c4 27 ♖a1
♗c6 28 ♘xe5 ♘xg3+ 29 hxg3
♕xe4+ 30 ♕xe4 ♗xe4+ 31 ♔h2 and
Black cannot defend f7) 27 b4 (27
♖d5 ♗b3!) ♖ad8 Black can defend,
since 28 ♘xe5 is well met by
28...♗c7!. The simple 25 ♘xh5
gxh5 26 b3 is White's best, with an
unclear position.

| 24 | ♘xe5 | ♘xg3+ |
| 25 | hxg3 | ♕xe4+ |

After 25...♗xe4+ 26 ♔g1 ♗b6
(or else ♖d4) 27 ♗xb6 ♕xb6+ 28
♖f2 Black cannot meet the threats of
♕xe4 and ♕h6, e.g. 28...♕b3 29
♖e1 ♗d5 30 ♖h2 h5 31 g4 ♕xa4 32
gxh5 ♕xh4 33 ♖xh4 gxh5 34 ♖xh5+
♔g8 35 ♖e3 mating.

| 26 | ♕xe4 | ♗xe4+ |
| 27 | ♔h2 | |

The exchange of queens does not
stop White's attack; the immediate
threat is 28 ♗c5.

| 27 | ... | ♗c7 (74) |

This meets with a tactical refutation, but even 27...♔g8 (27...♖c8 28
♖d7 ♔g8 29 ♘g4! followed by
♘h6+ wins because 29...♖c2+ is
met by 30 ♖f2) loses to 28 ♗c5 ♖e8
29 ♘xf7! ♔xf7 30 ♖d7+ ♔e6 31 f7
♖f8 (31...♔xd7 32 ♖d1+) 32 ♖d4
♖xf7 33 ♖d6+ and White wins the
exchange.

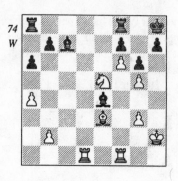

74
W

28 ♗c5!
Now White gains material by
force.

28	...	♗xe5
29	♗xf8	♖xf8
30	♖fe1	

Not 30 ♖de1 ♖e8!.

| 30 | ... | ♗c2 |

30...♖e8 31 ♖xe4 leads to a back-
rank mate, as does 30...♗f3 31 ♖d3
♖e8 32 ♖xe5. At last White's kingside pawn advance comes in useful!

| 31 | ♖d2 | ♗xa4 |

Black cannot get two pawns for
the exchange since 31...♗xg3+ 32
♔xg3 ♗xa4 33 ♖e7 threatens both
♖xb7 and ♖xf7.

| 32 | ♖xe5 | h6 |

After 32...♗c6 33 g4 Black's king
is permanently trapped on the back
rank and White wins by doubling
rooks on the d-file and playing ♖d8.
Black tries to release his king, but
only succeeds in getting mated.

33	gxh6	♔h7
34	g4	♔xh6
35	g5+	♔h7

After 35...♔h5 36 ♔g3, White mates by ♖h2.

| 36 | ♖e4 | ♗c6 |
| 37 | ♖h4+ | ♔g8 |

Provided White stops ...♗f3-h5, Black cannot prevent doubling on the h-file followed by mate.

| 38 | ♔g3 | 1-0 |

I was happy with my final score of 50% in view of the strength of the tournament. Kasparov took first place with 7½/10, two points ahead of Korchnoi.

1987

I started the new year with an Open tournament in Geneva. Although the tournament ended very successfully, it started inauspiciously. I already felt quite ill when I travelled to Switzerland and my condition rapidly deteriorated during the first two rounds. When the time for round three approached, I was in the throes of a major nosebleed, and was forced to telephone the organiser to say that I couldn't make it to the tournament hall. I considered withdrawing from the tournament, but the organiser suggested postponing the game for some hours. This sounded like a good idea to me, so he contacted Arlandi, my opponent, who generously accepted the plan. A few hours later my problems had temporarily abated and I succeeded in travelling to play the game. Arlandi achieved a winning position, only to fall into a back-rank swindle and lose. This was my lowest point in the tournament, and over the next few days both my health and my chess improved. After starting with 7½/8, I took a quick draw with Hort in the last round and won first prize outright; Tony Kosten was second with 7½ points. But I did learn one useful tip from this event – don't ever sneeze while you're having a nosebleed.

Soon after, Lugano time arrived again, but this time I played miserably, and finished on 6/9.

In April I competed in the annual tournament at Dortmund. I had played once before, in 1979, finishing in third place, so I was quite happy to participate again. Unfortunately, I had another bout of illness during this tournament. Of course, it is always a bit of a joke when a chess player says that he was ill during a tournament; everybody remembers the aphorism of one grandmaster who commented ironically that he had never beaten a healthy opponent.

When it comes to 'explaining' a poor result, illness is indeed one of the standard chess player's excuses. Despite this, it must be true sometimes, if only through pure chance. My own experience is that chess tournaments in winter are the ideal places to catch infectious diseases such as colds and influenza. Lots of people are cooped up together for hours each day and for several days in a row. With luck, you might just about escape the general miasma, but if you are unlucky enough to have an opponent who coughs, sneezes and splutters in your general direction, then you may as well reconcile yourself to coming down with a virus.

Once you have caught something, it is quite unusual to recover fully during the tournament. The best chance is if you are staying in the hotel housing the tournament itself and don't have to go outside. Dortmund was an example of the worst situation; there the journey from hotel to tournament hall involved a walk, a trip on the underground and then a second walk through a park. Pleasant in good weather, perhaps, but the weather was very cold that year. The stress of playing chess also delays recovery; it is doubly tiring to play when you are feeling ill, and there is no energy left to fight the infection itself.

At Dortmund I finished on 6½/11, which was not such a bad score, but my play was lacklustre. Balashov had one of his best results, winning outright with 8/11. The only noteworthy moment in my games was the following position from J.Nunn-K.Bischoff *(75)*. White is to play.

44 ♗a6

Now Black's bishop is doomed, but this doesn't guarantee a win because he will have two pawns for the piece and there will be few pawns remaining on the board. Moreover, White has a rook's pawn

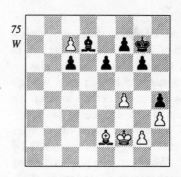

75
W

plus wrong bishop combination. Black's options are restricted because at any moment White can promote his pawn and capture Black's bishop. Black must take care to ensure that this doesn't lead to a win for White.

44 ... f5?

A natural move, because it keeps White's king out of the important squares e4 and g4, but it turns out that it loses because it is too committal. White's strategy is not to cash in his passed pawn immediately, but to retain two other lines of attack. The first is to support the advanced pawn with the king, starting with ♔e3-d4. In some lines White can drive Black's bishop away from control of c8 and promote the pawn; Black cannot ignore a threat to gain a whole queen. The other line of attack is to play ♔f3-g4 and win the h-pawn. In this case playing c8♕ too early is a mistake, because the tempo spent may be better employed advancing the king.

Black also has various lines of defence. His main defence against a plan of ♔e3-d4 is to play his king to d6, forcing c8♕. Then by playing ...c5 and ...f5 he can keep White's king out of the central squares. An eventual ...e5 will secure the draw.

On the other hand, his defence against ♔f3-g4 is to meet ♔f3 by ...f5; White can then play g4, forcing an exchange on g3, and try for ♘h4-g5. Whether or not this plan works depends on tactical considerations. We shall prove that 44...♔f6 and 44...f5 both lose, but 44...♔f8! draws. The reason is that 44...♔f8! is flexible. Black waits to see which way White's king is going; against ♔f3 he can still play ...f5, while against ♔e3 he can head for d6 without loss of time. 44...♔f6 fails because it blocks ...f5, making the ♔f3-g4 plan effective, while 44...f5 fails because Black's king is too slow to reach d6 after ♔e3-d4.

Here is the detailed analysis justifying these claims:

1) **44...♔f6** (44...g5 45 fxg5 ♔g6 46 ♔f3 ♔xg5 47 ♔e4!, followed by c8♕, is hopeless for Black) 45 ♔f3! (this is an important finesse; after the direct 45 ♔e3 ♔e7 46 ♔d4 ♔d6 47 c8♕ ♗xc8 48 ♗xc8 f5 49 ♗a6 c5+ 50 ♔e3, Black draws by 50...♔e7 followed by ...♔f6, ...e5 and ...g5 – in this line Black keeps White's king away from the central squares) and now:

1a) **45...♔f5** 46 c8♕ ♗xc8 47 ♗xc8 (now this wins, because Black cannot maintain his king on f5) c5 (47...g5 48 fxg5 ♔xg5 49 ♔e4! c5 50 ♗a6 ♔f6 51 ♔f4 wins the pawn on h4) 48 ♗a6 e5 (48...g5 49 ♗d3+ ♔f6 50 ♔g4) 49 ♗d3+ followed by 50 ♔g4 and the h-pawn is lost.

1b) **45...♔e7** 46 ♔g4 e5+ 47 ♔xh4 exf4 48 c8♕ ♗xc8 49 ♗xc8 ♔f6 50 ♔g4 ♔e5 51 ♔g5 c5 (or 51...♔e4 52 ♗b7) 52 ♗a6 ♔e4 53 ♗c4 f3 54 gxf3+ ♔xf3 55 ♗xf7 ♔g3 56 h4 wins.

2) **44...♔f8!** (the plan is again to head for d6, but this time Black avoids blocking his f-pawn) 45 ♔f3 (45 ♔e3 ♔e7 draws as in line 1, note to 45 ♔f3!) f5 (now Black can prevent ♔g4) 46 g4 and now:

2a) **46...♔e7** 47 g5 ♔d6 48 c8♕ ♗xc8 49 ♗xc8 e5 (49...♔d5 50 ♔e3) 50 ♗a6 (threat ♗c4-f7) ♔d5 51 ♗b7, followed by fxe5. In this line White wins because his g-pawn is much better placed on g5 than on g2.

2b) **46...hxg3!** 47 ♔xg3 ♔e7 48 ♔h4 ♔f6 49 c8♕ ♗xc8 50 ♗xc8 c5 51 ♗a6 (at first sight Black appears to be in a fatal zugzwang, but he can hold the draw by a single tempo) e5 52 fxe5+ ♔xe5 53 ♔g5 f4 54 ♔xg6 f3 55 h4 ♔d4! and now both 56 h5 c4 57 h6 f2 58 h7 f1♕ 59 h8♕+ and 56 ♗f1 c4 57 h5 c3 58 h6 c2 59 h7 c1♕ 60 h8♕+ lead to draws.

45 ♔e3   c5

This is a consequence of Black's previous move. White's king must be kept out of d4, because after 45...♔f6 46 ♔d4 Black is in immediate zugzwang.

46 ♔d3

White's king has to take a longer route, and this gives Black the chance to play ...e5.

46 ...   ♔f6

47 ♔c4   e5

After 47...g5 48 ♔xc5 White wins because the threat of 49 ♔d6 is too strong to ignore.

48 ♔xc5!

Not 48 fxe5+ ♔xe5 49 ♔xc5 g5 50 c8♕ ♗xc8 51 ♗xc8 ♔f4 52 ♔d6 (heading for f6, while avoiding the square e6, which would allow Black to draw by ...gxh3 followed by ...♔g3) g4 53 ♔e7 gxh3 54 gxh3, and now if we remove Black's f-pawn, we have a well-known theoretical ending. Black's king has to be in a 'drawing zone', which lies mainly in the upper half of the board. For our purposes, it is enough to note that e5 is in the drawing zone and so 54...♔e5 leads to a position which is drawn even without the f-pawn.

48 ...   exf4

After 48...e4 (48...♔e6 loses to 49 ♗c4+) 49 ♔d4 g5 (or else c8♕ wins easily) 50 fxg5+ ♔xg5 51 ♔e3 White can safely mop up the bishop, since his king will reach f4 whatever Black does.

49 ♔d6!

The only winning method. In *Informator*, I incorrectly claimed that 49 ♔d4 also leads to a win, but after 49...g5 50 c8♕ ♗xc8 51 ♗xc8 g4 52 hxg4 fxg4! (pointed out by Speelman; 52...f3 53 gxf3 wins after 53...f4 54 g5+ ♔xg5 55 ♔e4 or 53...h3 54 f4 h2 55 g5+ and 56 ♗b7) 53 ♗xg4 ♔g5 54 ♗h3 (54 ♗f3 h3) f3 55 gxf3 ♔f4 56 ♗g2 ♔g3 57 ♗h1 h3, followed by ...♔h2, Black draws.

49 ...   ♗e6

50 ♗b7! *(76)*

Now Black is in zugzwang. 50...♔f7 loses to 51 ♗d5, so he has no choice.

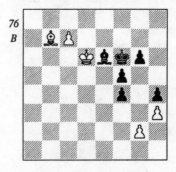

76
B

50 ...   g5

This weakens the pawn on f5, which introduces a new possibility for White.

51 ♗c6

After this White promotes his c-pawn by force; Black also promotes, but the resulting position is easily won. The threat is ♗d7, so Black's move is again forced.

51	...	♗c8
52	♗d7	♗a6

52...♗b7 53 ♔c5 followed by ♔b6 comes to the same thing.

53 ♔c6

If Black's pawn were still on g6, then he could play ...♔e7 here, which explains why White had to induce ...g5 before undertaking this manoeuvre.

53 ... g4

The only hope is to generate counterplay by advancing the kingside pawns, but White is too quick.

54	♔b6	f3
55	gxf3	gxh3

Or 55...♗c8 56 ♗xc8 g3 57 ♗xf5 g2 58 c8♕ g1♕+ 59 ♔b7 and Black has no checks.

56	♔xa6	h2
57	c8♕	h1♕ (77)

77
W

58 ♕f8+ ♔e5

White's material advantage is sufficient to win in any case, but it is interesting to note that he can either force mate or win Black's queen, for example 58...♔g5 (58...♔g6 59 ♗xf5+ transposes) 59 ♕xf5+ ♔h6 60 ♕f8+ ♔g6 (60...♔h5 61 ♕f6! ♕f1+ 62 ♗b5 ♕e1 63 ♗c4, or 60...♔g5 61 f4+ ♔h5 62 ♕f5+ ♔h6 63 ♕g5+ ♔h7 64 ♗f5+ ♔h8 65 ♕h6+ and mates) 61 ♗f5+ ♔g5 (after 61...♔h5 62 ♕h8+ ♔g5 63 ♕e5 White wins the queen or mates) 62 f4+! ♔xf4 63 ♗e4+! ♔xe4 64 ♕a8+ and wins.

59 ♕xf5+ ♔d4

Or 59...♔d6 60 ♕e6+ ♔c5 (60...♔c7 61 ♕e7! mates in four) 61 ♕e5+ transposing to the next note.

60 ♕e4+ (78)

78
B

60 ... ♔c3

After 60...♔c5 61 ♕e5+ there are two lines:

1) **61...♔c4** 62 ♗b5+ ♔b3 (we do not analyse every legal move by Black; other lines eventually lead to the same finish) 63 ♕e3+ ♔b2 64 ♕d4+ ♔b3 65 ♗c4+ ♔c2 66 ♕d3+ ♔c1 67 ♕c3+ ♔b1 68 ♗d3+ ♔a2 69 ♗c2! ♕f1+ 70 ♔a5 wins.

2) 61...♚b4 62 ♕d4+ ♔b3 63 ♗e6+ ♔c2 64 ♗f5+ ♔b3 65 ♕d3+ ♔b4 66 ♕b5+ ♔c3 67 ♕c5+ ♔b2 (67...♔d2 68 ♕d4+ ♔e2 69 ♗d3+ ♔d2 70 ♗b5+ ♔c2 71 ♗a4+ and White mates in seven more moves) 68 ♕c2+ ♔a3 69 ♕c3+ ♔a2 70 ♗c2!, as in line 1.

61 ♕e3+   ♔c2

Or 61...♔b2 (61...♔c4 62 ♗e6+ mates, while 61...♔b4 62 ♕d4+ is line 2 of the previous note) 62 ♕d2+ ♔a3 (62...♔b1 63 ♗f5+ ♔a1 64 ♕c3+ ♔a2 65 ♗c2, or 62...♔a1 63 ♗f5 ♕f1+ 64 ♗d3) 63 ♔a5 ♕b1 64 ♗e6 mates in four more moves.

62 ♗a4+   1-0

Readers may check that White mates in a further six moves.

After Dortmund, my next major event was the Interzonal tournament held in Szirák, Hungary. This was the second time I had participated in an Interzonal, the first being at Toluca, Mexico, during 1982. In 1987, the Interzonal stage of the FIDE World Championship cycle took the form of three round-robin tournaments. Twenty years earlier, at Sousse 1967, there had been one Interzonal tournament. The same held true at Palma 1970, but Palma was the last time there was just a single Interzonal; by 1973 the Interzonal had fissioned into two tournaments, held at Petropolis and Leningrad. The 1970 Interzonal had been an unwieldy event with 24 participants, but on the other hand it had included virtually all the world's top players, excepting Spassky and Petrosian, and was therefore an attractive event to stage. The 1973 Interzonals totalled 36 players, a 50% increase from three years earlier, and the first manifestation of a problem which has continued right up to the present day – the growing clumsiness of the FIDE World Championship cycle. Each time the cycle comes round, the number of participants at the Interzonal stage has steadily increased; from 36 in 1973, it was up to 52 by 1987.

This steady growth in numbers has had unfortunate consequences for the participants. Some top players were seeded directly into the Candidates, while the others were split between the three events, so each Interzonal contained just a handful of top players, making it unattractive to potential organisers and sponsors. The result was that with each new cycle, FIDE has had more and more difficulty finding venues satisfying even the minimal requirements for a top tournament. Of the three 1987 Interzonals, the one which ended up in Szirák caused FIDE the most trouble. The venue was undecided even at a very late stage, and the dates were changed a number of times, making it impossible for those taking part to guarantee participation in any other tournament for the whole period from June to September. FIDE ended up paying most of the prize money itself and, to be blunt, the conditions at the tournament were dreadful. This was not the fault of the Hungarian organisers, who were as helpful as they could be, but the venue was simply unsuitable for an Interzonal tournament.

In an attempt to solve this growing problem, the first Swiss system Interzonal was held in Manila in 1990. Of course the number of players had increased again, from 52 to 64. At Biel 1993, the ratchet had advanced another notch to 73. By switching to a single Swiss event, at least the participation of most of the top players could be guaranteed, making the event more attractive, but the expense of housing and feeding more than 60 players had also increased the cost of staging the Interzonal. If the bloating of numbers isn't somehow brought under control, then the problems of the 1980s will be repeated with the new Swiss-style Interzonal.

FIDE has never got to grips with this problem, and it is one of the manifestations of the main defect with the organisation – that it is too willing to give in to pressure from influential people within its own ranks, regardless of logic or fairness. Sometimes this has led to bizarre

rules; for example, in the 1990 FIDE Handbook, rule 8.2 deals with 'the right to participate' in the Interzonal. There is a list of possible qualification routes, after which we find the following clauses:

'8.25 Two players nominated by the Deputy President for the Americas

8.26 Two players nominated by the Deputy President for Africa

8.27 Two players nominated by the Deputy President for Asia

8.28 One player nominated by the Deputy President for Europe'

This rule has no place in a World Championship system supposedly based on merit, and I am very uncomfortable with the idea that miscellaneous FIDE officials should be given the power to dispense personal favours – perhaps this was only done so that they could keep their players in line!

By 1993, under the influence of the GMA-FIDE Experts Commission, these clauses had been abolished, but the problem of increasing numbers has not really been solved. It is so easy to dole out a few extra Interzonal places to this or that Zone, but an inflation rate of 15% per cycle is bound to lead to trouble in the end. A system for fairly allocating Interzonal places needs to be devised; at present some weak zones have too many Interzonal places, while some strong zones have too few. In 1987, for example, Canada had its own zone from which two players qualified for the Interzonal. These were Allan, rated 2310, who finished last at Szirák with 1½/17, and Baragar, rated 2320, who finished last at Zagreb with 1½/16. In the past, FIDE have been happy to bestow extra places in certain zones, but have been extremely reluctant to correct obvious anomalies such as the Canadian zone.

Szirák is a very small village about 100 miles from Budapest. Its main attraction is a hotel housed in what was once a royal retreat in the country; this was the venue for the tournament. Communication with the outside world was practically nonexistent. The one and only telephone was erratic, letters failed to arrive and newspapers were things which might have existed in another continuum, but were certainly not to be found in Szirák. The event lasted 17 rounds, and the organisers had generously allocated seven rest days. So for nearly a month the 18 players and their seconds were cut off from the world.

The tournament quickly settled into a routine. Each day William Watson and I debated the crucial question – should we walk round the village clockwise or anticlockwise? The fusspot vegetarians complained about the daily quota of dead flies in their food. But my most vivid memory of Szirák resulted from a severe stomach ailment. Most of the players and seconds fell ill with stomach problems at some time during the tournament, and I was no exception. I asked for a doctor, who duly came to examine me. He ordered me to drop my trousers and closely inspected my stomach. Then he asked me to lie face down on the bed. Thinking this was to be a continuation of the examination, I complied. My error became obvious after a few seconds, because the doctor had decided to deliver a massive injection in my bum. Perhaps the injection worked, or maybe it was just fear that further treatment might be necessary, but my stomach rapidly improved.

There was plenty of time for chess in Szirák; despite the ups and downs I played well in the Interzonal. The following game is typical of tournament chess. Published games are often 'clean kills', in which the defender puts up little resistance, but in reality most games aren't like this. Annotations, particularly those by third parties, often promote the concept of the game in which the winner does everything right, while the loser does everything wrong. This is rare in practice, except when one player is much stronger than the other. This game is more representative; stretches of accurate play are interspersed with mistakes and the defender doesn't go down without a fight, but puts up a fierce and determined resistance right into the endgame.

Game 15

J.Nunn – J.de la Villa Garcia
Szirák IZ 1987
Spanish

1 e4	e5
2 ♘f3	♘c6
3 ♗b5	f5
4 ♘c3	♘d4

For many years Inkiov was virtually the only practitioner of this unusual line; 4...fxe4 is far more common.

5 exf5   c6 *(79)*

6 ♘xe5!? *(80)*

I had been waiting for over four years to play this move, but one doesn't often meet the Schliemann Defence in present-day grandmaster play! Hitherto, the critical line was believed to be the piece sacrifice 6

♘xd4 exd4 7 ♕h5+ ♔e7 8 0-0, but recent games had not given White any advantage:

1) **8...dxc3** 9 dxc3 ♘f6 10 ♖e1+ ♔d6 11 ♗f4+ ♔c5 12 ♗e3+ ♔d6 13 ♗f4+ ♔c5 ½-½, Marjanović-Inkiov, Bor 1983.

2) **8...d5** 9 ♖e1+ (9 b3 dxc3 10 ♗a3+ ♔d7 11 ♕f7+ ♘e7 12 f6 gxf6 was winning for Black in Fernandez Garcia-Tatai, Torremolinos 1983) ♔d6 10 ♖e8 ♕f6 11 d3 ♘e7 12 ♗f4+ ♔c5 13 ♘e4+!? dxe4 14 dxe4, G.Johansson-G.Andersson,Sweden 1985, with a complete mess.

Perhaps it is not surprising that top players, when faced by the Schliemann, have preferred to avoid running into prepared analysis and have chosen quieter continuations. When Sax faced the Schliemann against Romero Holmes at Rome 1986, he played the modest 6 ♗e2 ♘f6 (6...d6 7 ♘xd4 exd4 8 ♘e4 ♗xf5 9 ♘g3 is just slightly better for White) 7 ♘xe5 ♕e7 8 ♘d3 d5 9 0-0 ♗xf5 10 ♘e1 0-0-0 11 d3 ♕c7 12 ♗e3 ♘xe2+ 13 ♘xe2 ♗d6 14 ♘g3 and gained a clear advantage. Later Black improved with 6...♕f6 7 ♘xd4 exd4 8 ♘e4 ♕xf5 9 ♘g3 ♕f7 10 0-0 d5 11 ♖e1 ♔d8 12 ♗g4 ♗c5, which was unclear in Aseev-Bräuning, Kecskemet 1992.

White found yet another plan in the game Wedberg-de la Villa Garcia, Lugano 1988, which continued 6 ♗d3 ♗xf3+ 7 ♕xf3 ♘f6 8 ♕e2 ♕e7 9 b3 d5 10 f3 (by maintaining the pawn on f5, White prevents the c8 bishop being developed to an active square) ♗d7 11 ♗b2 0-0-0 12 0-0-0 ♖e8 13 ♕f2 ♔b8 14 g4 and White had definitely kept his extra pawn.

White's best sixth move is far from clear, since he seems to have a number of promising lines; in any case, Schliemann players seem to have abandoned this variation.

80
B

6 ... ♘f6

It is hard to believe that Black can afford to simply develop when he is two pawns down. The alternatives are:

1) **6...♘xb5** 7 ♕h5+ ♔e7 8 ♕xb5 cxb5 9 ♕f7+ ♔d6 10 d4 gives White a massive attack in return for the piece.

2) **6...cxb5** 7 ♕h5+ g6 8 fxg6 ♘f6 9 g7+ ♘xh5 10 gxh8♕ ♘xc2+ 11 ♔d1 ♘xa1 12 ♕xh7 wins for White.

3) **6...♕e7** 7 0-0 ♔d8 8 ♖e1 ♘xb5 (8...cxb5 9 ♘d5 is clearly bad) 9 ♘xb5 cxb5 is old theory; I had prepared the innovation 10 d4!, when White has two pawns and a strong attack for the piece. The position is still unclear, but I believe that White cannot be worse, and in practice Black's defensive task is formidable.

4) **6...♕g5!?** (perhaps the critical continuation) 7 ♗d3 ♕xg2 8 ♗e4 ♕h3 9 ♘e2 (9 ♘f3!? is also possible) ♘xe2 10 ♕xe2 ♗e7 11 ♖g1 d5 12 ♗f3 ♗xf5 13 ♖xg7 0-0-0 14 ♘f7 ♘f6 15 ♘xh8 ♗b4 16 ♖g3 ♕xh2 17 ♔d1 ♗d6 18 ♖g5 ♖e8 19 ♕f1 ♘e4 20 ♖g2 ♕h3 21 ♗e2 ♖xh8 22 d3 ♘c5 23 ♖g5 ♕xf1+ 24 ♗xf1 ♖f8 (a blunder, but Black had little to show for the exchange in any case) 25 ♖xf5 1-0, J.Polgar-de la Villa Garcia, Pamplona 1990.

7 ♗d3!

This is the key move. By defending c2 White prepares to retreat the e5 knight to g4. Although the c1 bishop is blocked in for a few moves, this should not matter if White plays accurately.

7 ... d6?!

Black plays to win back the f5 pawn as quickly as possible, but it proves insufficient for equality. The best line is probably 7...d5 (7...♗c5 8 0-0 d6 9 ♘f3 and 7...♕e7 8 0-0 are very bad for Black) 8 0-0 ♗d6 9 ♘g4 (9 ♘f3 should be slightly better for White) 0-0 10 ♘e3 ♘d7 11 ♘e2 ♘xe2+ 12 ♗xe2 d4 13 ♘c4 ♗c7 14 d3 ♘c5, Maus-Hermann, Bundesliga 1990/1. Now White played 15 b4? and Black soon gained the advantage. After the sensible 15 ♗f3 Black has some compensation for the pawn, but I would assess the position as slightly better for White.

8   ♘g4

Not 8 ♘f3 ♕e7+ and White must either move his king or allow his f-pawns to be doubled.

8   ...   ♘xf5

After 8...♕e7+ 9 ♘e3 White can safely castle whilst Black has hemmed in his bishop.

9   0-0   ♗e7

10   ♘xf6+

The opening has gone badly for Black, and White has more than one route to an advantage. 10 ♘e3 was also good; after 10...♘d4 (10...♘xe3 11 dxe3) 11 ♘e2 ♘e6 (11...♘xe2+ 12 ♗xe2, followed by d4) 12 c3 followed by ♗c2 and d4 Black would have had almost nothing for the pawn, but it was just too tempting to force Black to move his king!

10   ...   ♗xf6

11   ♖e1+   ♔f7

White's problem is that Black's pieces are controlling d4, so the plan of ♗f1 and d4 isn't possible. Of course, White can always play 12 ♗xf5 ♗xf5 13 d4, but in this case the two bishops would provide some compensation for the pawn. The solution is to move the knight, whereupon White can support d4 by playing c2-c3.

12   ♘e4   ♖f8

13   c3   ♔g8

14   ♗c2

It may appear logical to use the bishop to defend the kingside, but after 14 ♗f1 d5 15 ♘xf6+ ♕xf6 16 d4 ♘h4 Black has a dangerous initiative, for example 17 ♗e3 ♕g6 18 ♔h1 ♗h3! 19 gxh3 ♕e4+ 20 f3 ♖xf3 21 ♗f2 ♖e3+ 22 ♔g1 ♖xe1 23 ♗xe1 ♘f3+ and Black wins.

14   ...   d5

15   ♘g3!

The alternative was 15 ♘xf6+ ♕xf6 16 d4 ♘h4 17 ♗e3. During the game I rejected this line because 17...♗h3 looked dangerous, but some sober analysis would have convinced me that 18 gxh3 ♘f3+ 19 ♔g2 (19 ♔h1? ♕d6) ♖ae8 (White wins after 19...♕d6 20 ♕xf3!) 20 ♖g1 followed by ♔h1 is very good for White. In fact, Black would do better to play more slowly by 17...♗f5 18 ♗xf5 ♕xf5 and after 19 h3 (threat ♕g4) h5 20 ♕b1 ♕f6 he has fair compensation for the pawn because it isn't easy for White to

complete his development. The move
played is better.

15 ...   ♘xg3
16 hxg3

If White had time to play d4 and
♗f4 then Black would be lost, but it
is Black's turn and he can cut across
White's plan. The struggle now revolves around the development (or
otherwise) of the c1 bishop.

16 ...   d4!
17 ♗e4!

White must not allow Black to
drive a wedge into his position by
...d3; this can now be met by ♖e3.
On the other hand White has his own
threat of d3, since taking twice on c3
would allow ♕b3+.

17 ...   ♕b6

This is the most natural move, because it sets up a potential threat
against the weak point at f2.

18 ♕c2!

White can force a draw by 18
♕h5 g6 19 ♗xg6 hxg6 20 ♕xg6+
♔h8 (20...♗g7? 21 ♖e7 wins) 21
♕h6+, but it is quite wrong to play
18 ♕b3+ ♔h8 19 ♕xb6 axb6 since
20 c4 (intending d3) d3! 21 ♗xd3
♗d4 22 ♖f1 ♗g4! is better for Black
despite the two minus pawns.

18 ...   d3 *(81)*

18...♗g4 19 d3 dxc3 (White can
meet 19...♖ae8 with simple development by 20 ♗f4) 20 bxc3 ♗xc3 21
♕xc3 ♕xf2+ 22 ♔h2 should win for
White.

19 ♕xd3?

81
W

Mistakes are very often made for
purely psychological reasons. Here
White misses 19 ♕b3+! ♕xb3 20
axb3 ♗e6 (20...♖d8 21 ♖e3 is no
better) 21 ♗xd3 (there is no need for
White to be greedy with 21 ♗xh7+
♔xh7 22 ♖xe6 ♖ae8 23 ♖xe8 ♖xe8
24 ♔f1 ♖e5, when Black threatens
to force a draw by 25...♖h5 26 ♔f1
♖e5) ♗xb3 22 ♗e4 ♖fe8 23 d3 (23
d4 ♗c2 24 f3 is also good) and
White is a clear pawn up in the ending.

The mental block was that having
rejected ♕b3+ a move earlier, the
idea of playing it a tempo down
didn't even occur to me. It doesn't
take long to see that Black's 'extra
tempo' weakens the d-pawn and is
actually very helpful to White.

Note that White should certainly
avoid 19 ♗xd3?? ♕xf2+! 20 ♔xf2
♗d4++ 21 ♔e2 ♗g4 mate.

19 ...   ♗xc3

Forced, or else ♕c4+ followed by
d4 wins.

20 bxc3!

I was torn between two lines. The other idea was 20 ♗xh7+ ♔h8 21 ♖e4! ♕xf2+ 22 ♔h2 (threat ♖h4) ♗f6 23 ♖f4 ♕c5 24 ♗g6. At first sight Black's king is in much more danger than White's, for example 24...♗e6 25 ♕e4 (threat ♖h4+) ♗d5 26 ♕f5, or 24...♕d5 25 ♕xd5 cxd5 26 d4 with a clear plus for White. At the time I felt vaguely uneasy about this line, and home analysis revealed the accurate defence 25...♕d5! (instead of ...♗d5) 26 ♖h4+ ♔g8, when White can give perpetual check but no more. If the queens are exchanged then White's damaged pawn structure and poor development give Black more than enough compensation for the pawn.

20 ...   ♕xf2+

I had always wanted to play a double rook sacrifice, but one can hardly expect a contemporary player to fall into the sort of naïve traps which were common in the 19th century. By now de la Villa Garcia undoubtedly realised the danger he was in, but his moves have been more or less forced since 17...♕b6. The soundness of the sacrifice depends on some long tactical lines.

21 ♔h2   ♕xe1

He has to accept because 21...♖f6 22 ♕d8+ ♔f7 (22...♖f8 23 ♕h4 h6 24 ♗a3 wins) 23 ♗d5+ ♔g6 (or 23...♗e6 24 ♗xe6+ ♖xe6 25 ♕d7+) 24 ♕e8+ followed by d4+ wins for White.

22 ♗a3   ♕xa1
23 ♗xh7+   ♔h8
24 ♗xf8 (82)

82
B

24 ...   ♗e6!
We may dispense with 24...♕xa2/♕d1 25 ♕g6 and 24...♕e1 25 ♕d4 at once, but the other two bishop moves require more careful analysis.

24...♗g4 is very good for White after 25 ♗xg7+ ♔xg7 26 ♕g6+ ♔f8 (26...♔h8 is met not by 27 ♗g8? ♗f5!, but by 27 ♕h6! and Black cannot meet the twin threats of 28 ♗g6+ ♔g8 29 ♕h7+ ♔f8 30 ♕f7 mate and 28 ♗c2+ ♔g8 29 ♗b3+ – note that 27...♕xa2 fails to 28 ♗b1+) 27 ♕g8+ (not 27 ♕xg4? ♕xa2) ♔e7 28 ♕xa8, since he has two extra pawns.

However, **24...♗f5** 25 ♕xf5 ♖xf8 puts up more resistance since 26 ♕xf8+ ♔xh7 27 ♕f5+ ♔h8 28 ♕c8+ ♔h7 29 ♕xb7 ♕xa2 only leads to a draw. The reason is that Black has a passed a-pawn which can advance just as rapidly as the c- or d-pawns. Instead White must play

26 ♕h3! (26 ♕h5 ♖f6 27 ♗g6+ ♔g8 is less clear-cut) g6 (if now 26...♖f6, then White forces mate by 27 ♗g6+ ♔g8 28 ♕c8+ ♖f8 29 ♕e6+) 27 ♗xg6+ (and not 27 ♕h6? ♖f1! 28 ♗xg6+ ♔g8 29 ♕h7+ ♔f8 30 ♕h8+ ♔e7 31 ♕e5+, when White cannot do better than a draw) ♔g7 28 ♕h7+ ♔f6 29 ♕h6! and now there are only three moves to avoid an immediate loss:

1) 29...♖d8 30 ♗h5+ (White has to be precise; 30 ♕h4+ ♔xg6 31 ♕xd8 ♕xa2 is only slightly better for White because of the troublesome a-pawn, while 30 g4 ♕e1! leads to nothing clear) ♔e7 (or else the rook drops at once) 31 ♕g5+ ♔d7 32 ♗g4+ ♔e8 33 ♕g8+ ♔e7 34 ♕g7+ ♔d6 35 ♕f6+ ♔c7 36 ♕e7+ and wins.

2) 29...♖b8 30 ♗d3+ ♔e7 (or 30...♔f7 31 ♗c4+) 31 ♕g7+ ♔e6 (31...♔d6 32 ♕f6+) 32 ♗c4+ ♔d6 33 ♕f6+ ♔c7 34 ♕e5+ and wins the rook.

3) 29...♖a8 30 ♗h7+ ♔f7 (after 30...♔e5 31 d4+ ♔d5 32 ♕e3 White has a decisive attack) 31 ♕g6+ ♔e7 32 ♕g7+ ♔e6 (32...♔d6 33 ♗f5! ♕xa2 34 d4 completes the mating net around Black's king) 33 ♕xb7 ♖f8 34 ♕xc6+ and White has four pawns and a continuing attack for the exchange.

Therefore the move played in the game was Black's best defence.

25 ♗xg7+ ♔xg7

26 ♕g6+ ♔h8
After 26...♔f8 27 ♕xe6 White can force a win, but the process is quite lengthy: 27...♕d1 (27...♖d8 28 ♕f6+ ♔e8 29 ♗g6+ ♔d7 30 ♗f5+ ♔e8 31 ♕h8+ ♔e7 32 ♕g7+ ♔d6 33 ♕f6+ ♔c7 34 ♕e7+ wins the rook) 28 ♕f6+ ♔e8 29 ♗g6+ ♔d7 (White can only take the rook when the bishop is on g6 or f5, preventing a perpetual check) 30 ♕f7+ ♔d6 31 ♕f4+ (those of you who have read *Secrets of Pawnless Endings* will recognise the manoeuvre I called a 'two-step') ♔d7/e6 (31...♔c5 32 ♕d4+ ♔b5 33 ♗d3+ or 31...♔e7 32 ♕e5+ ♔d7 33 ♗f5+) 32 ♗f5+ ♔e7/e8 (32...♔d8 33 ♕d6+) 33 ♕e5+ ♔f7 34 ♕e6+ ♔f8 (34...♔g7 35 ♕g6+ transposes) 35 ♕h6+ (a second 'two-step') ♔f7 36 ♕h7+ ♔f6 37 ♕g6+ ♔e7 38 ♕g7+ ♔d6 39 ♕d7+ ♔c5 40 ♕d4+ ♔b5 41 ♗d3+ ♔a5 42 ♕b4 mate.

27 ♕h6 ♗d5
After 27...♗xa2 28 ♗g6+ ♔g8 29 ♕h7+ ♔f8 30 ♕h8+ ♔e7 31 ♕xa8 ♕b2 32 ♕xa7 ♔f6 (32...♕xd2 33 ♕xb7+ is hopeless) 33 ♗d3 ♕xd2 34 ♕d4+ ♔e7 35 c4! White also has very good winning chances, since Black's bishop is shut out of the game (35...♕h6+ 36 ♕h4+).

The move chosen by Black is designed to force White to exchange bishops, which removes the danger to Black's king and thereby increases his drawing chances.

28 ♗e4+

Better than 28 ♗g6+ ♔g8 29 ♕h7+ ♔f8 30 ♕h8+ ♔e7 31 ♕xa8 ♕xa2 32 ♕xb7+ ♔f6 followed by ...♕xd2 attacking g2, when Black draws without difficulty.

28	...	♔g8
29	♕h7+	♔f8
30	♗xd5	cxd5
31	♕h8+	♔e7
32	♕xa8	♕xa2
33	♕xb7+	♔d6

A century ago, such a sacrificial attack would probably have been met by a feeble defence allowing mate, but times are harder now. Although White has two extra pawns, this ending is not at all easy to win. In a queen ending a lone passed pawn can outweigh any number of extra pawns, because there is only time for the materially superior side to push one of his many pawns. Here Black's a-pawn provides a ready source of counterplay. It is true that White's g-pawns are also passed, but it is not easy to advance them without exposing White's king to awkward checks. I regard White's task in this ending to be harder than in any of the endings arising above, so Black's plan of defence was well thought out.

34	♕b8+	♔c6 (83)
35	♕f4?!	

Almost immediately White plays a weak move. He should have continued checking, choosing his plan

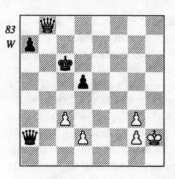

depending on Black's king moves, e.g. 35 ♕c8+ ♔d6 36 ♕f8+ ♔c6 37 ♕f6+ ♔b7 (after 37...♔d7, the reply 38 ♕f4! really is good, since 38...♕c4 39 ♕f7+ wins the a-pawn) 38 d3!? a5 (or 38...♕e2 39 ♕f5) 39 g4 with a better position for White than in the game, as Black's queen blocks the a-pawn.

35 ...   ♕c4!

Black moves his queen to a more active position with gain of tempo. This was another case of a psychological blind spot; it simply hadn't occurred to me that Black could offer the exchange of queens while two pawns down.

36 ♕f5

The queen must move, and this is the best available square. From f5 she can cover the advance of the g-pawn, while also preparing d3 to dislodge Black's queen from the excellent square c4.

36	...	a5
37	g4	a4
38	d3	♕c5

Or 38...♕b3 39 ♕c8+ ♔d6
(39...♔b6 40 g5 and Black cannot
play ...a3) 40 g5 ♕d1 (not 40...a3 41
g6 a2 42 g7 a1♕ 43 g8♕ and Black
has no checks) 41 ♕f8+ ♔c6 42
♕f6+ ♔b5 43 ♕f5! (after 43 g6 ♕g4
Black can put up more of a fight)
♕h5+ (43...a3 44 ♕xd5+ ♔b6 45 g6
wins after 45...♕g4 46 ♕d4+ or
45...a2 46 ♕xa2 ♕h5+ 47 ♔g1
♕d1+ 48 ♔f2) 44 ♔g3 ♔c6 (44...a3
45 ♕xd5+ ♔b6 46 d4 wins) 45
♕f6+ ♔b5 46 g6 ♕h6 47 ♕f5 ♔c6
(47...♕e3+ 48 ♔g4 ♕e2+ 49 ♔h3
♕e3+ 50 g3 ♕h6+ 51 ♔g4 doesn't
help) 48 ♕e6+ ♔c5 49 ♕e7+ ♔c6
50 g7 ♕g6+ 51 ♔f2 and White wins.
This line is typical; Black needs to
push his a-pawn, restrain the g-pawn
and defend d5, all at the same time,
but it is just too much to ask from his
limited force. Note that White's extra pawns are useful mainly because
they provide shelter for his king.

39   ♕c8+   ♔b5

39...♔b6 40 ♕b8+ followed by
41 ♕a8+ and 42 ♕b7+ transposes.

40   ♕b7+   ♔a5

41   g5 (84)   ♕d6+?

Strangely enough Black made
this mistake after long thought. The
continuation **41...d4** 42 ♕b4+ ♕xb4
43 cxb4+ ♔xb4 44 g6 a3 45 g7 a2 46
g8♕ a1♕ 47 ♕c4+ ♔a5 48 ♕c5+
♔a6 49 ♕c6+ ♔a7 50 g4 ♕c3 51
♕e4 is winning for White, because
Black will never have a perpetual
check while White's queen is on e4,

and Black cannot both defend d4 and
restrain the g-pawn.

Therefore, the critical line is
41...♕xc3 (41...a3 42 g6 leads to line
2 below after 42...♕xc3) 42 ♕xd5+
♔b4 and now:

1) **43 ♕c4+** ♕xc4 44 dxc4 a3 45
g6 a2 46 g7 a1♕ 47 g8♕ ♕e5+ 48
♔h3 (48 ♕g3 ♕h5+ 49 ♔g1 ♔xc4
looks like a draw, an impression
which is confirmed by the database)
♕h5+ 49 ♔g3 ♕e5+ 50 ♔g4 ♕e2+
51 ♔h4 ♕e1+ 52 g3 (White's queen
must remain on g8, because if Black
takes the pawn on c4 the result will
be a draw – White's g-pawn is too far
back to win) ♕h1+ 53 ♔g5 ♕c1+ 54
♔f5 ♕b1+ 55 ♔f6 ♕a1+ 56 ♔e7
(the database confirms that 56 ♔f7
♔xc4 is a draw) ♕a7+ and I don't
see how White can escape the checks
without losing the pawn on c4.

2) **43 g6!** a3 44 ♕b7+! (White
has a number of promising lines, but
this appears strongest; his aim is to
transfer the queen to d7, e7 or f7 with
gain of tempo, and then play g7)

Ka4 (44...Ka5 45 Qa7+ is no better after 45...Kb4 46 Qe7+ and 47 g7, or 45...Kb5 46 Qd7+ as in the main line) 45 Qd7+ and now:

2a) **45...Kb3** 46 Qf7+ Kb2 47 g7 a2 (47...Qe5+ 48 g3 Qe2+ 49 Kh3 is the end of the checks) 48 g8Q a1Q 49 Qb8+ wins easily.

2b) **45...Kb4** 46 Qe7+ Ka4 47 g7 and Black has no checks at all.

2c) **45...Ka5** 46 g7 Qe5+ 47 Kh3 Qh5+ 48 Kg3 Qg5+ 49 Kf3 Qh5+ (49...Qf6+ 50 Ke4 Qh4+ 51 g4 Qh1+ transposes) 50 g4 Qh3+ 51 Ke4 Qh1+ 52 Ke5 Qh2+ 53 Kf6 and Black's checks run out after 53...Qh6+ 54 Kf7 or 53...Qf4+ 54 Kg6.

42 g3

Now White is clearly winning; Black's king is confined to the edge of the board, and perpetual check is unlikely when there are two g-pawns to shelter White's king.

42	...	a3
43	g6	Ka4

The lines 43...a2 44 Qa7+ Qa6 45 Qc5+ Qb5 46 Qxb5+ Kxb5 47 g7 a1Q 48 g8Q and 43...Qxg6 44 Qb4+ Ka6 45 Qxa3+ Kb6 46 Qb4+, followed by 47 Qd4, are hopeless, so Black has to waste time.

44 g7

Black has no perpetual check, so this is the simplest way to win, but 44 Kg2 a2 45 g7 would also have been effective.

| 44 | ... | Qh6+ |

45	Kg2	Qd2+
46	Kh3	Qh6+
47	Kg4	Qg6+
48	Kf4	Qf6+
49	Ke3	d4+

Or 49...Qh6+ (49...Qe5/e6+ 50 Kf2 Qf5+ 51 Kg2 loses at once, while 49...Qg5+ 50 Kf3 Qh5+ 51 g4 transposes) 50 Kf3 (not 50 Kd4 Qf6+ and White has to go back) Qh5+ (50...Qh1+ 51 Kg4 Qd1+ 52 Kh4 Qh1+ 53 Kg5 Qc1+ 54 Kg6) 51 g4 Qh1+ 52 Kf4 Qh2+ 53 Kf5 Qf2+ 54 Kg6 and White wins.

50	Ke4	Qe6+
51	Kxd4	Qg4+
52	Kc5	1-0

After 52...Qf5+ 53 Qd5 or 52...Qg5+ 53 Qd5 Qe7+ 54 Kb6 the checks come to an end.

The following game received the brilliancy prize for the Szirák Interzonal. This prize turned out to be an enormous painting, much too large to take back on the plane. I had absolutely no idea how I could get it home, but I didn't like to offend the organisers by refusing to accept the prize. Then I noticed Glenn Flear coveting the painting, so a solution immediately presented itself – I offered it to Glenn on condition that he arrange to get it to England himself. After many vicissitudes, including being impounded at Customs, the painting did finally arrive to grace the Flear household.

Nunn-Marin was later given third prize in the FIDE 'Best Game of 1987' award (no painting was involved, fortunately).

Game 16

J.Nunn – M.Marin

Szirák IZ 1987

Sicilian Najdorf

1	e4	c5
2	♘f3	d6
3	d4	cxd4
4	♘xd4	♘f6
5	♘c3	a6
6	♗e3	e6
7	♕d2	b5
8	f3	♘bd7

These were the early days of the so-called 'English Attack'. At first the plan of ♕d2, f3 and g4-g5 proved devastatingly effective. White's e4 pawn is solidly defended, making it hard for Black to develop counterplay in the centre, and in a straight race between the two attacks, White usually struck first on the kingside. In many ways White's strategy is similar to that in the Sämisch King's Indian and the Yugoslav Attack against the Dragon. In all three cases White combines a flank attack with a solid central pawn structure.

Black players gradually refined their strategy, learning to time their central counterplay to hit White with ...d5 at the most inconvenient moment. The English Attack is still playable, but it has lost its uniqueness and become just one more opening variation, no better or worse than many others.

9	g4	h6
10	0-0-0	♗b7
11	♗d3	

At the time this was the most fashionable line, but in recent years it has fallen out of favour. 11 h4 is the current 'main line'.

11	...	♘e5
12	♖he1	

This move was first played in Short-Kasparov, Brussels (OHRA) 1986; hitherto White had preferred either 12 h4 or 12 ♔b1. The idea of 12 ♖he1 occurred to me during 1986; the idea is that Black's main source of counterplay is to play ...b4 and then ...d5. By putting the rook opposite Black's king, White hopes to hold up Black's ...d5 long enough to allow White to consolidate by ♔b1 and h4. I suggested 12 ♖he1 to Nigel before his game with Kasparov and he used it to good effect. I was sufficiently confident about this idea to try it a second time, even though the surprise element had already been lost.

12   ...   ♘fd7!? (85)

The position on the board could hardly have been a surprise to Marin, and this innovation was his reaction. Short-Kasparov had continued 12...♖c8 13 ♔b1 ♗e7 14 h4 b4 15 ♘a4 (15 ♘ce2 d5! is good, since 16 g5 hxg5 17 hxg5 may be met by 17...♘xe4!) ♕a5 (15...d5 16 g5 is now good for White since the d3 bishop is not trapped) 16 b3 ♘fd7 17 g5 g6 18 f4 ♘xd3 19 cxd3 with a slight advantage for White. Later it was discovered that Black can call White's bluff by playing 12...b4 13 ♘a4 d5 in any case, and it was this that caused White players to switch to 11 h4.

I had never analysed 12...♘fd7, so I was on my own now.

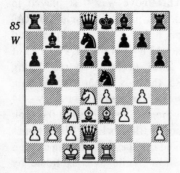

13   f4!? (86)

The only challenging move, for otherwise Black secures his position

by 13...♘c5, followed by ...♗e7 and ...0-0; a sample line is 13 ♕e2 ♘c5 14 f4 ♘exd3+ 15 cxd3 b4, forcing the knight back to the dreadful square b1. White needs to play f4 to make progress, but spending a tempo defending g4 is too slow. Therefore, the best chance is to sacrifice the g-pawn before Black consolidates, hoping to break through by a direct attack.

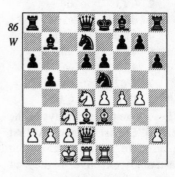

13   ...   b4?

Black declines the first sacrifice, only to be offered a larger one next move. The problem with declining such sacrifices is that the attack may gather strength anyway, and you may be forced to accept material later under less favourable circumstances.

After 13...♘xg4 (13...♘xd3+ 14 cxd3 followed by ♔b1 is good for White as his centre is secure and he has a ready-made kingside pawn storm if Black plays ...0-0) 14 e5 Black may play:

1) **14...♘xe3 15 ♘xe6!** (not 15
♕xe3 ♕b6! 16 f5 ♗e7 17 ♔b1 ♗g5,
and after 18 ♕h3 dxe5 19 fxe6 0-0 or
18 ♕g1 ♘xe5 19 fxe6 0-0 White has
insufficient compensation for the
sacrificed pawn) ♕b6 (forced since
taking the knight allows mate in two,
while 15...♕c8 16 ♕xe3 fxe6 17
exd6 ♘c5 18 ♗g6+ ♔d8 19 f5 gives
White a crushing attack) 16 ♖xe3
fxe6 17 ♗g6+ ♔d8 18 exd6 ♘c5 (or
18...♗xd6 19 ♖xe6 ♗xf4 20 ♖xb6
♗xd2+ 21 ♖xd2 with equal material
and a decisive White attack; the alternatives 18...♕xd6 19 ♖d3 and
18...b4 19 ♖xe6 ♘f6 20 ♘a4 ♕b5
21 ♕d4!, threatening 22 ♖xf6, are
no better) 19 f5 and now the lines
19...b4 20 fxe6, 19...e5 20 ♖xe5 and
19...exf5 20 ♘d5 ♕xd6 21 ♕a5+ are
all very good for White.

2) **14...dxe5 15 ♘xe6 fxe6 16
♗g6+ ♔e7 17 fxe5 ♘gxe5** (the line
17...♘dxe5 18 ♗g5+ transposes) 18
♗g5+ ♘f6 (18...hxg5 19 ♕xg5+
wins easily) 19 ♕e3 ♕c7 20 ♗f4
(with the idea 20...♘fg4 21 ♕g3)
and White regains the piece while retaining a ferocious attack against
Black's king.

3) **14...♘c5 15 ♘xe6!?** (the line
15 ♘dxb5 ♘xd3+ 16 ♕xd3 axb5 17
exd6 ♕d7 is unsound) ♘xe6 16 f5
♘xe3 17 ♖xe3 ♗e7 (17...♘c5 18
exd6+ ♔d7 19 ♘xb5!? is also dangerous for Black) 18 fxe6 ♗g5 19
exd6 ♕b6 and after 20 ♖de1, for example, the position is very unclear.

4) **14...b4! 15 ♘xe6** (15 ♘e4!? is
possible) bxc3 (the lines 15...♕c8 16
♘xg7+ ♗xg7 17 ♘e4 ♗xe4 18
♗xe4 ♘xe3 19 ♕xe3 ♖b8 20 ♖xd6
and 15...♕a5 16 ♘e4 fxe6 17
♘xd6+ ♗xd6 18 ♗g6+ ♔d8 19
♕xd6 ♗d5 20 ♖xd5 exd5 21 ♗f5
are very good for White) 16 ♕xc3
♕c8 and White can continue in two
different ways:

4a) **17 ♘c7+ ♔d8 18 ♘xa8**
♕xc3 19 bxc3 ♗xa8! (not 19...♘xe3
20 ♖xe3 ♗xa8 21 exd6 ♗xd6 22
♗f5 ♔c7 23 ♖xd6! ♔xd6 24 ♖d3+,
which is good for White) 20 exd6
♗xd6 21 ♗f5 ♗a3+ 22 ♔b1 ♘gf6
and Black escapes.

4b) **17 ♕b3!? ♘xe3** (17...fxe6
18 ♕xe6+ ♔d8 19 ♕xg4 is clearly
good for White) 18 ♖xe3 fxe6 19
♕xe6+ ♔d8 20 exd6 (20 ♗f5 d5! 21
♖c3 ♗c5 defends) ♘f6 21 ♕e5! (not
21 d7? ♕c6!) ♗d5! (the only move,
for example 21...a5 22 ♗b5 ♗c6 23
♖c3 ♘d7 24 ♕e2 or 21...♕c6 22
♕a5+ ♔c8 23 d7+! and White wins
in both cases) 22 ♗g6 ♕c6 23 ♖xd5
♕xd5 24 ♕xd5 ♘xd5 25 ♖e8+ ♔d7
26 ♖xa8 ♘xf4 and Black has an advantageous ending.

In the cold light of day, White's
attack may not be completely sound,
although in such a complex position
it is hard to say anything for sure. In
any case, with so many plausible
continuations the odds were certainly against Black finding the best
defence over the board.

After the move played White gains the advantage by force.

14 ♘d5!

An easy decision to make since 14 ♘a4 (14 fxe5 bxc3 15 ♕xc3 ♘xe5 is slightly better for Black, while 14 ♘ce2 ♘xg4 is a safe extra pawn) ♘xg4 15 ♕xb4 ♘xe3 16 ♖xe3 ♖b8 17 ♕e1 gives Black a pleasant position after 17...e5 or 17...♗e7. In such a position, it is quite easy to decide on moves like 14 ♘d5!, because if the knight cannot go to d5 then White must have already gone wrong.

14 ...   ♘xd3+

14...♘xg4 (14...exd5 15 fxe5 dxe4 16 exd6 ♗xd6 17 ♘f5 ♗e5 18 ♕xb4 is bad for Black) 15 ♕xb4 ♖b8 (15...♘xe3 16 ♕xb7 ♘xd1 17 ♘c7+ ♔e7 18 ♘c6+ wins) 16 ♕a4 is also dangerous for Black, for example 16...exd5 17 exd5 ♗xd5 18 ♗g1+ ♗e7 19 ♘f5 ♗e6 20 ♘xg7+ ♔f8 21 ♘xe6+ fxe6 22 h3 ♘gf6 23 ♖xe6 and White, with two pawns and an enduring attack for the piece, has the advantage.

15 ♕xd3 *(87)* **exd5**

The d5 knight doesn't threaten anything immediately, but Black cannot complete his development while it remains on the board. Six months after this game was played, Sax stumbled into the same bad position in game 5 of his Candidates' match against Nigel Short (St.John, 1988). From the amount of time Sax

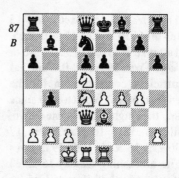

consumed, it was obvious that he did not know the precedent, which is remarkable given that this game was widely published and that I was Short's second in St.John! Short-Sax continued 15...♘c5 16 ♕c4 ♖c8 (16...exd5 17 exd5 leads into the next note) 17 ♕xb4 exd5 18 exd5 ♗xd5 19 ♘f3 ♗e6 20 f5 ♗e7 21 ♗xc5 ♖xc5 22 fxe6 0-0 23 ♕xc5 (the preliminary 23 exf7+ is even stronger) dxc5 24 ♖xd8 ♖xd8 with a clear extra pawn for White.

16 exd5 *(88)*

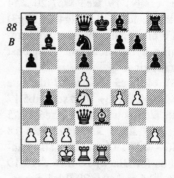

16 ...   ♗e7

Or 16...♘c5 17 ♕c4 ♔d7 (White wins after 17...♗e7 18 ♘f5) 18 ♕xb4 (18 ♘c6? ♕b6) ♕c7 (and not 18...♗e7? losing to 19 ♘c6) and White has two pawns and an attack for the piece. If he could mobilise the queenside pawns and drive the knight from c5 then Black's position would collapse, but it is not easy to execute this plan. Therefore White has to use his pieces to eliminate the knight, which suggests 19 ♘b3, threatening 20 ♗xc5 dxc5 21 ♕a4+. Black should reply 19...♔d8 (after 19...♘xb3+ 20 axb3 ♖c8 21 ♖e2 Black has no defence to the threat of 22 ♗b6 followed by ♕a4+) but after 20 ♘a5, for example, White has two pawns and a continuing attack for the piece. I would judge this position to be favourable for White.

17 ♘c6!

It is hard to refute 17 ♘f5 0-0 18 h4 with a slow attack, but as the move played gives White a clear plus it deserves preference. In this game we see all the typical characteristics of a ♘d5 sacrifice in the Sicilian – the pressure down the e-file traps Black's king in the centre, and White can make use of the outpost at c6.

17 ...   ♗xc6
18 dxc6   ♘f6? *(89)*

Now White wins by force. The alternatives were:

1) **18...♘f8** 19 f5! (threat 20 ♗b6 ♕xb6 21 ♖xe7+ ♔xe7 22 ♕xd6+ ♔e8 23 ♖e1+ ♘e6 24 fxe6) ♖b8

(19...♘h7 20 ♗b6 ♕xb6 21 ♖xe7+ ♔f8 22 ♕xd6 is devastating) 20 ♗f4! and Black is murdered down the central files.

2) **18...0-0** 19 cxd7 ♕xd7 is relatively best, but White has a clear advantage in any case. Black has problems not only because of his isolated pawn, but also because White's kingside attack persists.

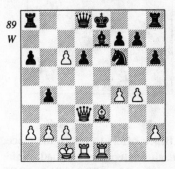

89
W

19 ♗b6!

This is not a standard idea after a ♘d5 sacrifice, but chess does not consist solely of stock patterns. If White did not have this follow-up, his play would be impossible to justify.

19 ...   ♕xb6

19...♕b8 defends d6, thereby preventing ♖xe7+, but 20 ♕d4! is decisive, since Black has no way to stop the threat of c7 followed by ♖xe7+.

20 ♖xe7+   ♔f8
21 ♕xd6   ♔g8
22 g5

White has far more than enough compensation for the piece. If the knight moves, then White's attack switches to the weak pawn on f7.

22 ... hxg5
23 fxg5 *(90)*

23 ... ♖c8

Black offers to return the piece. The alternatives are also bad: White wins after 23...♕f2 24 c7! ♖xh2 25 ♕d8+ ♔h7 26 ♕d3+ ♔g8 27 ♕c4, 23...♘e8 24 ♕d5 ♕f2 25 g6 or 23...♘g4 24 ♕f4.

24 c7!

After 24 gxf6 ♕xc6 25 ♕xc6 ♖xc6 26 ♖d8+ ♔h7 27 ♖xh8+ ♔xh8 28 ♖xf7 gxf6 it is likely that White should still win, but there would be plenty of fight left.

24 ... ♕xd6
25 ♖xd6 ♘g4

25...♘h5 is met by the game continuation, while 25...♔f8 26 gxf6 gxf6 27 ♖dd7 ♖h7 28 ♖e3 ♔g7 (28...♖h8 29 ♖d8+ followed by ♖g3+ and ♖h3+) 29 ♖g3+ ♔h6 30

♖d4 ♔h5 31 ♖d8 ♖xc7 32 ♖h3+ ♔g6 33 ♖g8+ costs Black a rook.

26 ♖d8+

Not 26 ♖e8+? ♖xe8 27 ♖d8 ♔h7! 28 c8♕ ♖xd8 29 ♕xg4 with an unclear position.

26 ... ♔h7
27 ♖ed7! 1-0

The final point is that Black has no defence to the threat of 28 ♖xh8+ followed by 29 ♖d8.

Ljubomir Ljubojević, usually called Ljubo for short, is one of the more colourful characters on the international circuit. He is fluent in several languages and is capable of talking at an amazing speed in all of them, so much so that he has acquired the nickname 'Motormouth'. Having a post-mortem with Ljubo is usually great fun; he will try to defend any position, no matter how bad, saying over and over 'It's not so simple'. If you find a nice tactic, he will remark 'You're very trickful'.

He is also famous for his erratic results. In 1989, he finished joint first with Kasparov in the Barcelona World Cup, an amazing result given that his rating at the time was only 2580. But just two months later, he finished in joint 14th place in the Rotterdam World Cup. He only won one game in the latter event but, true to his reputation, this win was against Karpov and was instrumental in deciding the result of the tournament! At one time Ljubo participated in all the top events, but at the time of writing his rating is 2580, and these days that isn't enough to secure invitations to major tournaments. So the chess world sees less of Ljubo, which is a pity in view of his entertaining style both on and off the board.

Late news: Ljubo no longer says 'trickful'. The other players had carefully avoided correcting him for years, but some spoilsport must have told Ljubo that the word is 'tricky'.

Game 17
L.Ljubojević – J.Nunn
Szirák IZ 1987
Spanish

1	e4	e5
2	♘f3	♘c6
3	♗b5	a6
4	♗a4	♘f6
5	0-0	♗e7
6	♖e1	b5
7	♗b3	0-0
8	c3	d5
9	exd5	♘xd5
10	♘xe5	♘xe5
11	♖xe5	c6
12	d4	♗d6
13	♖e2	

The main line has always been 13 ♖e1, but there is an enormous amount of theory on this move and many players are reluctant to spend a long time studying all this analysis just for the few occasions when they meet the Marshall. In 1987, 13 ♖e2 was considered a bit of a sideline, but now it has acquired its own body of analysis. The current verdict is that Black should have few problems.

The idea behind the move is clear enough; the rook defends the second rank, while at the same time leaving the first rank clear for White's queen to move to f1 (normally White has to play ♕d1-d3-f1). On the other hand, the rook is clumsily placed on e2 and is vulnerable to attack by ...♘f4 or ...♗g4.

13	...	♕h4

13...♗g4 14 f3 ♗h5 is an alternative approach.

14	g3	♕h3

White had some initial success with 13 ♖e2, but this was mainly because Black adopted the inferior move 14...♕h5. One example was 14...♕h5 15 ♘d2 ♗h3 16 f3 ♗c7 17 a4 b4 18 c4 ♘f6 19 ♘e4! ♕g6 (19...♕xf3 20 ♘g5 ♕h5 21 ♘xh3 ♕xh3 22 ♗g5 is very good for

White) 20 ♘f2! ♗f5 21 ♗c2 and Black had little compensation for the pawn in Short-Nunn, Brussels (OHRA) 1986, although I later swindled a win.

15   ♘d2   ♗f5
16   ♗c2

The tactical justification for 15...♗f5 lies in the line 16 ♘e4? ♗g4 17 ♘xd6 ♕h5 18 ♔f1 ♕xh2 19 f3 ♗h3+ 20 ♔e1 ♕xg3+ picking up the knight. 16 ♕f1 is a reasonable alternative, but in this case the move ...♗f5 gains point because after 16...♕h5 White must spend a tempo dealing with the threat of ...♗d3. These days the main line is 16 a4; I can't resist quoting the continuation 16...♖ae8 17 ♖xe8 ♖xe8 18 axb5?? (18 ♘f1) ♘f4! 19 gxf4 ♗xf4 20 ♘f3 ♕g4+ 21 ♔f1 (now Black mates in seven) ♗d3+ 0-1, Kotronias-Adams, Chalkidiki 1992.

16   ...   ♗xc2

16...♖ae8 17 ♗xf5 ♕xf5 18 ♖xe8 ♖xe8 19 ♘f1 ♘f6 eventually turned out well for Black in the 1985 correspondence game Sklarczyk-Müller, but at this stage Black's compensation looks inadequate.

17   ♕xc2   f5

White's queen and rook are badly placed to deal with ...f4-f3, so quick action by White is necessary.

18   c4

18 f4 ♕g4 19 ♘f1 ♗xf4 20 ♖f2 ♗d6 21 c4 was highly unclear in A.Sokolov-Khalifman, Sochi 1982.

18   ...   ♕g4 (91)

The sacrifice 18...♘f4 19 gxf4 ♕g4+ 20 ♔f1 ♖ae8 is refuted by 21 ♕d3.

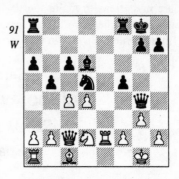

91
W

19   ♖e6?

The first new move of the game. I have only been able to trace one earlier game reaching this point, namely Mokry-Panczyk, Polanica Zdroj 1984, which continued 19 ♖e1 f4 20 f3 ♕h3 21 cxd5 fxg3 22 ♘f1 gxh2+ 23 ♔h1 ♖f6 with a double-edged position.

Later Ljubojević suggested 19 ♘f1; since the game continuation is promising for Black, this is probably White's best option. The main line runs 19...bxc4 (19...♘b4? 20 ♕d2 bxc4 21 ♖e6! is good for White) 20 ♕xc4 f4 21 ♕xc6 fxg3 22 ♕d5+ ♔h8 23 ♘xg3 ♗xg3 24 f3! ♕h3 (24...♖xf3 25 ♕xa8+ ♗b8+ 26 ♖g2 ♕xd4+ 27 ♗e3 wins for White) and despite White's slightly exposed king, I doubt that Black has enough compensation for two pawns.

19 ...   ②f4? *(92)*

This should lead to a draw by perpetual check, which is a satisfactory outcome as Black, but in fact 19...f4! is even better, when White may continue:

1) **20 cxd5** fxg3 21 hxg3 (21 fxg3 is also blown up by 21...♗xg3) ♗xg3 22 f3 ♕xd4+ mating in four more moves.

2) **20 ♖xd6** fxg3 21 hxg3 (21 fxg3 ②e3 22 ♕b3 ♕e2) ♖xf2 22 ♔xf2 ♖f8+ 23 ♔g1 ♕xg3+ mating in a further five moves.

3) **20 ♕e4** (both players rejected 19...f4 because of this move, overlooking the surprising reply) ②e3! (threat ...♕d1+) and now:

3a) **21 fxe3** ♕d1+ 22 ♔g2 (22 ②f1 fxg3) fxg3! (Black need not be satisfied with a draw by 22...♕e2+) 23 hxg3 (23 ♖xd6 ♖f2+ 24 ♔h3 ♕h5+ 25 ♔xg3 ♕xh2+ 26 ♔g4 h5+ leads to mate) ♕e2+ 24 ♔h3 ♖f2 and I cannot see a defence for White, for example after 25 ②f3 ♖xf3 26 ♖xd6 Black simply plays 26...♖f2.

3b) **21 ②f1** ②xf1 22 ♔xf1 (22 ♖xd6 ♖ae8 also wins for Black) ♕h3+ 23 ♔e1 (23 ♔g1 f3) ♕xh2 24 ♖xd6 fxg3 25 fxg3 ♖f2 wins.

3c) **21 ②f3** (the only way to continue) fxg3 (21...②xc4? 22 b3) 22 ♕xg4 (not 22 hxg3 ♕xe4 23 ♖xe4 ②c2 nor 22 ♗xe3 gxf2++ 23 ♔xf2 ♖xf3+ 24 ♕xf3 ♕xe6 with a winning position for Black in both cases) gxh2+ (after 22...gxf2+ 23

♔xf2 ②xg4+ 24 ♔g2 ♖f6 Black has a very slight advantage, but of course the result should be a draw) 23 ②xh2 ♗xh2+ 24 ♔xh2 ②xg4+ 25 ♔g3 ②xf2 26 ♖xc6 bxc4 and Black's more active pieces, coupled with the two connected passed pawns, give him the advantage.

I cannot see how White can equalise after 19...f4!, which reinforces the view that 19 ②f1 was correct.

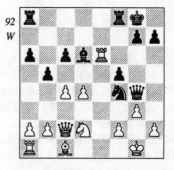

92
W

20 ♖xd6?

This move loses. The right continuation was 20 f3 ②h3+ 21 ♔g2 ②f4+ (there is no clear refutation of 21...♕h5; 22 ②f1 ♖ae8 23 ♖xe8 ♖xe8 24 ♗e3 f4 25 g4 ♕h6 gives Black some play for the pawn, while 22 ♖xd6 ♖ae8 23 ②f1 ♖e1 is double-edged) and now 22 ♔g1 leads to a draw by perpetual check. Indeed, two months after Ljubojević-Nunn was played, the game Hübner-Timman, Tilburg 1987 finished this way.

The crucial question is whether White can play for a win by 22 ♔h1

♕h3 23 gxf4 ♗xf4 (23...♖ae8? 24 ♖e5! wins) 24 ♖e2 ♖ae8 25 ♕d1 (25 ♕d3 ♗xh2). Black can try *(93)*:

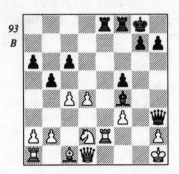

93
B

1) **25...♖e6** 26 d5! (forcing the rook away from e6) ♖e5 (26...♖h6 27 ♕g1) 27 ♖g2 ♖fe8 28 ♘e4! fxe4 29 ♗xf4 exf3 30 ♖f2 (30 ♖g3 ♖e1+! 31 ♕xe1 ♖xe1+ 32 ♖xe1 f2 wins) ♖e2 31 ♕f1 ♕h4 (31...♖xf1+ 32 ♖fxf1 wins for White) 32 ♗g3 ♕xc4 33 d6 and White should win.

2) **25...♖e3** 26 ♖f2! is good for White after 26...♖fe8 (26...♗g3 27 ♘f1!) 27 ♘e4! fxe4 28 ♗xe3 ♗xe3 29 ♖f1 ♗f4 30 ♕e2.

3) **25...♖e7** and now:

3a) **26 ♖g2 ♕h4!** (not 26...♖fe8 because of the tactical point 27 ♘e4! ♗xc1 28 ♘f6+ and wins) with a promising position for Black.

3b) **26 ♖f2 ♖fe8 27 ♘f1 ♗g3!** (27...♖e1? 28 ♗xf4 wins) 28 ♘xg3 ♖e1+ 29 ♖f1 ♕xf1+! (29...♖8e2 30 ♕xe2 ♖xe2 31 ♘xe2 ♕xf1+ 32 ♘g1 bxc4 33 b3 is unclear) 30 ♘xf1 ♖xd1 and Black wins.

3c) **26 ♕f1!** ♕xf1+ 27 ♘xf1 ♖xe2 28 ♗xf4 ♖xb2 (28...bxc4 29 ♖c1 is somewhat better for White) and White may have an edge, but a draw is much the most likely result.

4) **25...♕h5** (this attempts to reach the same type of position as in line 3a above, but without allowing White to liquidate to an ending as in line 3c) 26 ♖f2! (the threat was 26...♖xe2 27 ♕xe2 ♖e8 28 ♕f2 ♖e1+, and 26 ♖g2 ♕h4! is similar to line 3a) and now:

4a) **26...♕h4** 27 ♕f1 (27 ♕g1 ♗e3) ♖f6 28 ♘b3! ♗g3 29 ♖g2 f4 (29...♖e1 loses to 30 ♕xe1! ♗xe1 31 ♗g5) 30 ♗d2 ♖h6 31 ♕g1 ♗xh2 32 ♕xh2! (certainly not 32 ♖xh2? ♖e2! with advantage to Black) ♕f6 and White will have more than enough for the queen.

4b) **26...♗g3!** 27 ♕g1 ♗xf2 28 ♕xf2 f4 29 cxb5 axb5 30 ♘f1 (30 ♘e4 ♖xe4 is a draw) ♕g6, with the idea of 31 ♗d2 ♕d3. White is slightly up on material, but his minor pieces have no scope and Black's rooks are active.

So the verdict on 20 f3 is unclear; what is clear, however, is that it would have been much better than the move played.

20   ...   ♖ae8 *(94)*

In return for the piece Black has a substantial lead in development, and all his pieces are participating in the attack on White's exposed king. Moreover, White's forces are poorly coordinated; his rooks, in particular, are mere spectators. Such general arguments never guarantee success, but they do indicate where one's analytical effort should be directed. In the end there is no substitute for concrete analysis, even with the limited time available in tournament play.

The immediate threat is 21...♖e1+ 22 ♘f1 ♕h3 and mate next move.

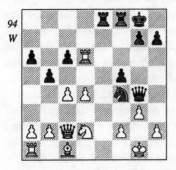

94
W

21 cxb5

The alternatives are also bad:

1) **21 ♘f1 ♘h3+ 22 ♔g2 ♖e2 23 ♕xe2** (the best chance; 23 ♕d3 ♖xf2+ 24 ♔h1 ♖xf1+ 25 ♕xf1 ♕e4+ 26 ♔g2 ♕e1+ and 23 ♘e3 ♘f4+ 24 ♔f1 ♕f3 both lead to forced mate) **♕xe2 24 ♗d2 f4 25 ♖e1** (25 ♔xh3 fxg3 26 hxg3 ♖xf2 wins for Black) **♕h5** with a clear advantage for Black.

2) **21 ♘f3 ♖e2 22 ♕b3** (22 ♕xe2 ♘xe2+ 23 ♔g2 f4 is winning for Black) **♕xf3!** and mates in four more moves.

3) **21 ♘e4** (desperation!) fails to 21...♘h3+ 22 ♔g2 fxe4 23 ♗e3 ♕f3+ 24 ♔xh3 ♖f5.

21 cxb5 looks suicidal, but it is not so easy for Black to win because White has acquired a useful check on c4. The variations 21...♖e1+ 22 ♘f1 ♕h3 23 ♕c4+ ♔h8 24 ♗xf4 and 21...♕h3 22 ♕c4+ ♔h8 23 ♕f1! ♖e1 24 gxf4 are winning for White, while the obvious 21...♘h3+ 22 ♔g2 ♘f4+ is only a draw.

21 ... ♖e2!

Ljubojević had overlooked this move. Although the main threat is the relatively slow 22...♘h3+, White has no defence.

22 ♕c4+

22 ♕xc6 ♖e1+ 23 ♘f1 ♖xf1+ 24 ♔xf1 ♕d1 mate and 22 ♕b3+ ♔h8 23 ♘f3 ♕xf3 lose more quickly.

22 ... ♔h8

23 ♕xe2

White is helpless against the threat of 23...♘h3+ 24 ♔f1 (or 24 ♔g2 ♖xf2+ 25 ♔h1 ♕d1+) ♖fe8 followed by mate. The only alternative was 23 d5 ♖e1+ (not 23...♘h3+ 24 ♔f1 ♖fe8 25 ♖e6!) 24 ♕f1 (24 ♘f1 ♘e2+), but this also wins for Black after 24...♖xf1+ 25 ♘xf1 ♘e2+ 26 ♔g2 ♕e4+ 27 f3 ♕d4 28 ♗d2 ♕g1+ 29 ♔h3 ♕f2.

23 ... ♘xe2+

24 ♔g2

Or 24 ♔h1 (24 ♔f1 ♖e8 followed by ...♕h3+ wins easily) f4 25 f3 ♕h3 26 g4 ♖e8, when there is no defence to the threat of ...♘g3+, so Black wins.

24   ...   f4! *(95)*

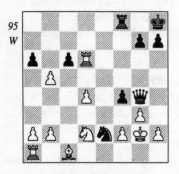

Trickful. 25 f3 and 25 h3 are both met by the queen sacrifice 25...fxg3! 26 fxg4 (26 ♖d8 ♘f4+) ♖(x)f2+ leading to mate next move.

25 bxc6   fxg3

This forces mate in a further five moves.

26 hxg3   ♘f4+

0-1

It is mate after 27 ♔g1 ♘h3+ 28 ♔h1 ♕d1+ 29 ♔g2 ♖xf2+ 30 ♔xh3 ♕h5.

The Interzonal ended in a disappointment for me. Salov and Hjartarson shared first place with 12½/17, and I finished in a tie with Portisch on 12 points. Since there were three qualifying places for the Candidates, this meant that I was involved in a play-off match with Portisch. Of course this was a good result for me, and had I been offered it at the start of the tournament I would have happily taken it. But I felt that it should not have been necessary; I had been in or near the lead throughout, but then I missed a more or less forced mate against Beliavsky in round 15 and a clear win against Portisch in round 16. In the last round I drew with Christiansen; Portisch needed to win with Black against Velimirović to draw level with me. My heart sank when I saw the Yugoslav grandmaster make a totally unsound piece sacrifice as early as move 12.

The rules for the Interzonal stated that a play-off match should occur immediately after the tournament, but I was understandably reluctant to have my stay in Szirák prolonged. Portisch did not press the point, and we agreed to have the match in Budapest at the end of September.

The Lloyds Bank tournament started just two weeks after I returned from Szirák. I had underestimated how tired I would feel after playing 17 games in the Interzonal, and I found the event a bit of a struggle, especially after I lost a very long game to Benjamin. In the end I crawled up to 7/10, a point behind the joint winners Chandler and Wilder.

At the start of September, I arranged to travel with Murray Chandler to the British Isles Open, a weekend tournament held in Swansea. We stayed in the same small hotel. At breakfast on Saturday morning, I was surprised by Murray's absence. Thinking that perhaps he had overslept, I went to his room and banged on the door. Murray shouted 'Thank God you've come, I can't get out of my room'. I summoned the owner, who admitted that guests being unable to leave their rooms was a common problem; after fiddling with the lock on the door he released the grandmaster from his confinement. When asked why the locks had this unusual feature, he replied 'Well, it's because of the fire regulations...'.

Murray and I both scored 5/6, sharing first place with Rogers, Kudrin and Adams.

Then it was back to Hungary for the Portisch match. From the outset I knew that this match was not going to be easy; I was on my opponent's home ground, and the tie-break from Szirák favoured Portisch, so a 3-3 draw would not be good enough. The organisation and conditions for the match were excellent, and the whole event was thoroughly enjoyable except, that is, for the result. Portisch's match experience and thorough preparation were too much for me, and I went down by 4-2. This was only the second match I had played in my life, and I had learned the hard way that preparing for a match is not the same as preparing for a tournament.

After the shock of throwing away what had seemed near-certain qualification for the Candidates, I felt no enthusiasm for playing and I decided to take some time away from chess to recover. Indeed, for the next three months I played only a few Bundesliga games. My next event was not until the end of the year, at Hastings.

1988

Perhaps it was not surprising, given my lack of practice, that Hastings was unsuccessful. The conditions at Hastings were an additional factor. At this time the tournament was played in the Queen's Hotel, a relic from the early part of the century. I had fallen ill almost every time I had played at Hastings, partly due to the fact that in earlier years the players had stayed at the Yelton Hotel, famous mainly for its lack of central (or, indeed, any other type of) heating. When I was invited to the 1987/8 tournament, I made only one condition, namely that I would be given a room with central heating. Every couple of months I would phone to confirm that this wish would be satisfied. On 28th December I arrived and – guess what? – found a freezing cold room without any form of heating. Unfortunately, I had arrived rather late in the day, and no heated room was available. This might seem surprising given the size of the hotel, but during the famous 1987 'hurricane', one of the large chimneys at the top of hotel had collapsed right through the building, killing one person. The wrecked part of the building was still sealed off.

In due course I moved to a heated room, but this was one of the most depressing hotel rooms I have ever stayed in. It was small and dark, the only window being almost completely obscured by the lattice of a fire escape. The general conditions in the hotel weren't too much fun either; it was a red-letter day when hot water was available. The players took their meals in the hotel restaurant, which was notable for being situated in a very exposed position, having no double glazing and, yes, you guessed it again, no heating. Some players took to dining in their overcoats, but eventually the hotel procured a device resembling a jet engine, which partially warmed the restaurant at the cost of drowning out any possible conversation.

Many years ago there was a great deal of controversy when Tony Miles attacked the conditions at Hastings in print. At the time Tony was writing, the tournament was played in the White Rock Pavilion rather than the Queen's Hotel, but basically Tony was dead right – the conditions at Hastings were a disgrace. Moreover, the tournament seemed to do its best to avoid any kind of publicity. The lack of tournaments and difficulties in attracting sponsors are perennial problems in British chess. The reasons are too complex to go into here, but I can tell one story which sheds some light on the subject. At one time William Ritson-Morry, who died in January 1994, was the main organiser. Now 'Ritson', as he was universally known, did a great deal for British chess, but his organisational style was rather idiosyncratic. Once, in the early eighties, I wasn't playing at Hastings myself, but I decided to go down for the day. At the time I had a monthly column in *The Illustrated London News* and I intended to devote one column to Hastings. Of course, I needed to choose a game to publish. Having asked a couple of players to recommend games, I went over to Ritson to see if I could get copies. There was no photocopy machine, but I was prepared to write them out by hand. Unfortunately, Ritson couldn't find the game scores in question. Finally I asked if I could be sent the bulletin at the end of the event. Ritson said that he would send me one, but I would have to pay for it. I agreed to pay and handed over the money. At the end of the tournament I eagerly awaited the arrival of the bulletin, but the wait was to be a long one. It finally turned up 357 days after the end of the tournament, in fact just after round seven of the following year's event. Perhaps Woodward and Bernstein would have succeeded in uncovering the secret game scores of Hastings, but it was evidently beyond me.

During the 1987/8 event I won but a single game during the 14 rounds; in the middle of the tournament I came down with food poisoning and lost two games in a row. All my other games were drawn. The whole experience was thoroughly depressing and I was delighted to agree an early draw against Short in the last round, which gave him first prize and me the delightful knowledge that the event was at an end. On my way out of the tournament hall I was verbally mugged by a woman who complained that my quick draw was a disgrace, I should be ashamed of myself and so on. For some reason she didn't feel it necessary to attack Nigel the same way, even though he was White in the game in question. Of course she did have some kind of point, but perhaps she wouldn't have been full of fighting spirit herself after two and half weeks in the Queen's Hotel and an attack of food poisoning. It seemed an appropriate end to the event, somehow, but I didn't really mind – Hastings was over!

Murray Chandler had offered to give me a lift back to London. When I asked him if he was leaving after the closing dinner or the following morning, he looked at me strangely and said 'After the dinner, of course'. I could understand his desire not to stay one night more than necessary in the Queen's Hotel. I dubbed the journey back 'Escape From Hastings'. The dinner finished just before midnight and a thick mist had sprung up as we left the hotel. I began to imagine that at any moment I would be mercilessly exposed in a sudden searchlight beam and hotel staff would grab me by the arms and drag me back for another two and a half weeks in the hotel. As it happens, we made it undetected to the car park and drove slowly (so as not to arouse suspicion) out of Hastings.

I resolved never to play again at Hastings if it involved staying in the Queen's Hotel.

This rather gloomy saga has a happy ending. In the past few years Hastings has been transformed from the laughing stock of the international chess community into a desirable event. The tournament is now in the comfortable Cinque Ports Hotel, which offers much better facilities for both players and spectators. The Challengers event has also moved from the traditional venue of the Falaise Hall to a ballroom (this usually means 'disco') at the end of the pier. Playing chess suspended over the waves sounds rather alarming, but the new venue is far more spacious than the Falaise Hall and the noise from the waves is only distracting during really bad weather.

What of the Queen's Hotel? The last time I saw the hotel, it had already been shut for some time and the building was gradually falling into even more disrepair. Only the old restaurant was being used, having been turned into a pub. I didn't go in to see if the jet engine was still functioning.

My next tournament was at Linares. These days Linares has been built up into far and away the world's strongest traditional tournament, but in 1988 it hadn't quite achieved the same stature, although it was a very respectable category 15 (i.e. average Elo 2601-2625). I had an up-and-down time there; I started with a good win against Hjartarson, but lost to Timman in round three. In round 5 I was White against Kiril Georgiev. The game started 1 e4 c6 2 d4 d5 3 ♘d2 dxe4 4 ♘xe4 ♘d7 5 ♘g5 h6 6 ♘e6 ♕a5+ 7 ♗d2 ♕b6 8 ♗d3 *(96)*.

96
B

I had previously analysed this position and come to the conclusion that 8...♘gf6 was the main line, so I was astonished when Georgiev quickly played 8...fxe6??. After 9 ♕h5+ ♔d8 10 ♗a5 it was obvious that he had overlooked something important. He could have resigned immediately, but in fact he struggled on until move 42. If his motive was to make the game less publishable, then his strategy didn't work, because several magazines printed the game as ending on move 10.

Game 18

M.Chiburdanidze – J.Nunn

Linares 1988

King's Indian

1	d4	♘f6
2	c4	g6
3	♘c3	♗g7
4	e4	d6
5	♘f3	0-0
6	♗e2	e5
7	d5	

This move introduces the Petrosian System. By closing the centre immediately, White gains greater freedom of action. The usual idea is to play ♗g5, tempting Black to drive the bishop away by ...h6 and ...g5. This weakens the light squares on the kingside and makes an eventual ...f5 less effective. The Petrosian System has never been one of the most popular anti-King's Indian systems, but it remains dangerous; even Kasparov has encountered problems when facing it.

7	...	a5 (97)
8	h3?!	

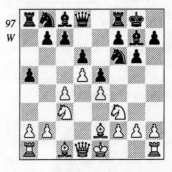

The normal line is 8 ♗g5 h6 9 ♗h4 ♘a6, with White castling kingside at some stage. Chiburdanidze envisages a different idea based on playing g4 to inhibit ...f5. This is a common enough plan against the King's Indian, but the problem is that there is no safe spot for White's king, rendering the idea distinctly double-edged.

White's plan in this game should be compared with the theoretical variation 1 d4 ♘f6 2 c4 g6 3 ♘c3 ♗g7 4 e4 d6 5 ♘f3 0-0 6 h3 e5 7 d5 ♘bd7 8 ♗e3 ♘c5 9 ♘d2 a5. The tempi are the same, but in Chiburdanidze-Nunn White is already committed to playing ♗e2. Since White doesn't normally play ♗e2 in the above line (the bishop is sometimes developed to h3 later), we may conclude that if White simply develops normally, then Black will have a favourable version of a line which isn't particularly dangerous in any case.

8 ...   ♘a6

8...♘h5 has also been tried; after 9 g3 (9 ♘d2 ♘f4 10 ♗f1 is another idea) f5 10 exf5 gxf5 11 ♘g5 ♘f6 12 g4 ♕e7 13 ♕c2 ♘e8 14 ♗d2 ♘a6 15 0-0-0 the position was unclear in Koen-V.Johansson, Debrecen European Team Ch (wom) 1992.

9 ♗g5

Aiming to induce the weakening ...h6, so as to enhance a possible kingside attack by White. If White plays 9 ♗e3 ♘c5 10 ♘d2 ♘e8 11 g4, the argument given above suggests that Black should have easy equality.

9 ...   ♘c5

It is tempting to play 9...h6 10 ♗e3 ♘h5, but the pawn sacrifice 11 ♕d2 ♔h7 12 g4 ♘f4 13 ♗xf4 exf4 14 ♕xf4 isn't necessarily correct because White can castle queenside, while the simple 11 g3 followed by ♘d2, forcing the knight to retreat, is also good.

10 ♘d2   h6
11 ♗e3 (98)

11 ♗h4 ♗d7 followed by ...♕e8 and ...♘h7 leads to a standard position from the Petrosian system, except that White has played h3, which here is just a waste of time.

After 11 ♗e3, we have arrived at a familiar position, except that White has played ♗e2 at the cost of a tempo, and Black has played ...h6 free of charge. It isn't clear whether ...h6 benefits Black, but the ♗e2 tempo could certainly have been better spent on a different move.

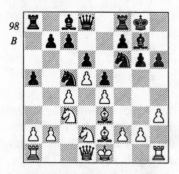

98
B

11 ...   ♗d7

This isn't bad, but Black could have exploited White's play most effectively by 11...♘h7 (making use of ...h6) 12 g4 f5 13 gxf5 gxf5 14 ♖g1 ♔h8 15 exf5 ♗xf5. The only danger in this type of position is that White will set up a firm piece blockade on e4, but here Black can play ...♕h4 and ...♘f6 (or ...♘g5) to destroy any such blockade. For example, 16

♗xc5 dxc5 17 ♗g4 is met by
17...♕h4 and now White has to
worry about f2 (if 18 ♘f3, then
18...♕f6). White's position is simply
not strong enough to support such an
ambitious strategic plan, and in fact
she should be most concerned about
the fact that her king is still two
moves away from castling.

The move played is really a waiting move. Black develops another
piece, while keeping open the twin
options of ...♘h7 (or ...♘e8), followed by ...f5, or queenside play by
...c6, ...a4 and ...♕a5.

12 g4   c6 *(99)*
Now Black commits himself to
queenside play; this is reasonable
enough, given that White's g2-g4
renders kingside castling impossible. Black's queenside activity will
make 0-0-0 far too risky, so White's
king is destined to stay in the centre
indefinitely. This means that White
will be unable to connect her rooks,
greatly reducing the force of the
kingside attack.

13 h4?
Never reticent when it comes to
launching an attack, Chiburdanidze
has spotted the slight weakness created by ...h6 and decides to go for the
king. Now the game takes on a clear-
cut form: White's kingside attack
against Black's queenside counterplay.

There are two common errors
when faced by such a direct attack.
The first is to be terrified by the attack, resulting in unnecessary and
time-wasting defensive moves. The
second error is made by players who
know perfectly well that such flank
attacks shouldn't really succeed and
believe that any old plan will be
enough to show the opponent the error of his (or her) ways. Both errors
can prove fatal.

King's Indian (and Dragon) players have learnt to treat this type of
flank attack with contempt, possibly
because there isn't much they can do
to stop it! The attack usually takes
quite a long time to generate serious
threats, but this is no excuse for delaying counterplay, since when the
threats finally materialise they are
usually quite powerful.

As the subsequent play shows, accurate play by Black should serve to
refute the attack, but Chiburdanidze
was probably under few illusions
about the objective merit of her plan.
The motivation for such moves is
often psychological; an attacking

player prefers (and plays better in) an attacking position, and heads for one regardless of the objective assessment.

13 b3 would be more solid, preparing to meet ...a4 by b4, and thereby restricting Black's queenside counterplay.

13   ...   a4

The plan is 14...♕a5, when the threat of 15...♘fxe4 will force White to make a defensive move. The move played involves a pawn sacrifice, but I didn't spend long on the consequences of acceptance because giving up the initiative is not in Chiburdanidze's style.

14   g5

Not 14 h5 (14 a3 ♕a5 15 ♔f1 ♘h7 preparing ...f5 is good for Black because 16 h5 ♘g5 brings the attack to a dead stop) ♕a5 15 hxg6 fxg6 16 ♗xh6 ♗xh6 17 ♖xh6 ♔g7 18 ♖h1 ♘fxe4 and White's king is the more exposed.

The main alternative is 14 ♗xc5 dxc5 15 ♘xa4 cxd5! (15...♕a5 16 ♘c3 b5 17 g5! is good for White) 16 ♘xc5 dxe4 and now:

1) 17 ♘dxe4 ♗c6 18 ♕xd8 ♖fxd8 19 f3 ♘xe4 20 ♘xe4 ♗xe4 21 fxe4 ♖d4 regains the pawn with advantage to Black.

2) 17 ♘cxe4 ♗a4 18 b3 ♘xe4 19 ♘xe4 ♕a5+ prevents 20 ♕d2 on account of 20...♗xb3, while 20 ♔f1 ♗c6 gives Black more than enough for the pawn.

3) **17 g5 hxg5** 18 hxg5 ♘h7 19 ♘xd7 (after 19 ♘dxe4 ♗c6 20 ♕xd8 ♖fxd8 21 ♗f3 ♖ac8 Black will regain the pawn with a slight advantage) ♕xd7 20 ♘xe4 ♕f5 with a promising position for Black. White will have difficulty maintaining the extra pawn and, as the position is opened up, the exposed position of White's king becomes more and more significant.

White decides, quite reasonably, to carry on with the attack.

14   ...   hxg5

15   ♗xg5

15 hxg5 ♘h7 16 ♘f3 ♕a5 threatening ...♘xe4 and ...a3 gives Black excellent counterplay. White's queen is several moves away from arriving on the h-file and even then ...♖fc8 and ...♘f8 sets up a defence. The problem with hxg5 is that the pawn structure on the kingside becomes static; White can only attack down the h-file, and if that comes to nothing it is hard to suggest an alternative plan. After the move played, White has the option of h4-h5, stripping away the defences from Black's king.

15   ...   ♕a5

Now White must take time out to deal with the threats of 16...♘fxe4 (this would be the reply to 16 h5) and 16...a3. 16 ♕c2 is bad in view of 16...cxd5 17 cxd5 ♖fc8, when the line-up on the c-file gives Black extra tactical chances.

16 ♛b1

White avoids the c-file pin and at the same time arranges to meet ...a3 by b4. This move was more or less forced, but White's kingside attack isn't likely to be dangerous unless the pieces on a1 and b1 are able to join in.

16 ... cxd5

Now is the time to make this exchange, because Black can prevent ♘c4 by White.

17 cxd5

17 ♗xf6 ♗xf6 18 ♘xd5 ♗d8 doesn't help; White cannot play h5 because of ...♗g5, whilst otherwise ...♔g7 and ...♖h8 lines up against the weak h-pawn.

17 ... b5 (100)

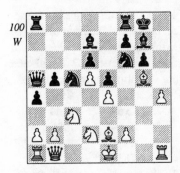

18 a3

White still cannot proceed with the attack because 18 h5 b4 19 ♘d1 (19 h6 ♗h8 certainly doesn't help) ♘xh5 20 ♗e7 (after 20 ♗xh5 gxh5 21 ♖g1 f6 22 ♗h6 ♖f7 White's pressure is only temporary) ♗b5! 21

♗xf8 (21 ♗c4 ♖fc8! is good for Black because 22 ♗xd6 fails to 22...♘b7) ♗xe2 22 ♔xe2 (22 ♗xg7 ♛b5! gives Black an enormous attack) ♛b5+ 23 ♔f3 ♖xf8, followed by ...f5, gives Black fantastic compensation for his small sacrifice.

After 18 a3 Black cannot play 18...b4 because of 19 ♘c4 followed by 20 axb4, so a preparatory move is necessary.

18 ... ♖fb8
19 h5 b4

This move was motivated by my desire to get on with the attack and not waste time capturing the h-pawn, but it is probably not best. The defect is that it allows ♘c4 with gain of tempo and this in turn opens up a route for White's queen to reach the kingside via c1.

Both captures on h5 are very promising. After **19...♘xh5** 20 ♗xh5 gxh5 21 ♛d1 ♘d3+ (21...b4 22 axb4 ♛xb4 23 ♛xh5 ♛xb2 24 ♖d1 ♛xc3 is also good for Black: 25 ♗e7 may be met by 25...f5, while after 25 ♛h7+ ♔f8 26 ♗h6 ♗xh6 27 ♛xh6+ ♔e7 28 ♛g5+ f6 29 ♖h7+ ♔d8 the king runs away) 22 ♔f1 ♗g4 (the greedy 22...♘xb2 is also possible) 23 f3 ♗d7 Black is ready for ...b4, and White's queen cannot move to the h-file. **19...gxh5!?** could be best of all: 20 ♖g1 ♔f8 is not dangerous, while 20 ♛d1 is ruled out because Black can take on e4.

20 ♘c4 ♛c7

21	axb4	Xxb4
22	hxg6	

22 h6? &h8 followed by ...⒪h7 or
...⚔h7 stops the attack.

| 22 | ... | fxg6 |
| 23 | &xf6? | |

White stakes everything on the
immediate attack, but Black can take
the material and survive. 23 Xa3
might have been a better chance, but
after 23...⒪b3 24 ⒪e3 ⒪d4 followed by ...Xab8 Black has a clear
advantage in any case. Objectively,
White's move deserves its question
mark, but a wild attack is perhaps
more likely to induce an error than
simply accepting a rancid position.

| 23 | ... | &xf6 |
| 24 | ♛c1 | ⒪b3! (101) |

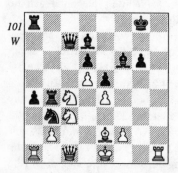

Precise calculation was necessary
before playing this move; letting the
queen in to h6 appears dangerous,
but the King's Indian bishop holds
Black's position together.

| 25 | ♛h6 | &e8 |

25...Xxc4 (25...⒪xa1? 26 ♛xg6+

&g7 27 ⒪xd6 is bad for Black) 26
&xc4 ⒪xa1 26 Xg1 &e8 27 ♛e6+ is
less clear-cut than the game.

| 26 | Xd1 | |

26 &g4 ♛g7 27 &e6+ ⚔f8 defends the king and leaves a1 and c4
hanging, while 26 ⒪xd6 is met by
the simple 26...♛xd6 27 ♛h7+ ⚔f8.

| 26 | ... | ⒪d4 |

Black could also have won with
the greedy continuation 26...Xxc4
27 &xc4 ♛xc4 28 ♛h7+ ⚔f8 29
Xh3 &f7! (during the game I saw
only 29...⒪d4? 30 Xxd4! followed
by 31 Xf3, when White wins) 30 Xf3
⚔e7. White cannot create any immediate threats and Black's counterattack by ...Xh8 or ...⒪d4 will be
devastating.

| 27 | &g4 | |

White has little choice but to sacrifice; both 27...Xxe2 and 27...Xxc4
were threatened, while 27 ⒪e3 and
27 ⒪d2 are met by 27...Xxb2 and
White's position starts to collapse.

27	...	Xxc4!
28	Xxd4	exd4
29	&e6+	&f7
30	♛xg6+	&g7
31	Xh3	

Black also wins after 31 Xh8+ (31
Xg1 &xe6) ⚔xh8 32 &xf7 ♛xf7 33
♛xf7 dxc3 and White has no perpetual check.

| 31 | ... | dxc3 |
| 32 | Xf3 (102) | Xf8 |

After the game I wrote that
32...Xa7 is a mistake, allowing 33

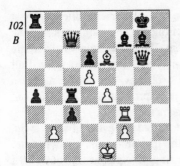

102
B

♖g3 ♗xe6 34 ♕e8+ with perpetual check. Now I can see that even 32...♖a7 wins, because 33 ♖g3 may be met by 33...♖xe4+! 34 ♕xe4 (34 ♔f1 ♕c4+ and 35...♕d4) cxb2.

33 ♖h3   ♗xe6

Avoiding the last trap 33...♖e8? 34 ♖g3 ♖xe4+ 35 ♔f1 ♖e1+ 36 ♔g2, when Black has nothing better than 36...♗xe6 37 ♕xe8+ with a draw.

34 dxe6

Or 34 ♕h7+ ♔f7 35 dxe6+ ♔e8 and Black's king slips away.

34	...	♖f6
35	♕e8+	♗f8
36	♖g3+	♔h7
37	♕h5+	♗h6
38	♕g4	♕g7
39	♕e2	

39 ♕h4 is also met by 39...♕xg3.

| 39 | ... | ♕xg3 |

0-1

My next event was the first GMA World Cup tournament, held in Brussels. Although I was one of the lower rated players in the cycle, I was excited by the prospect of competing in a series of tournaments with the best players in the world. Although I had previously played occasional events with top players, **all** the leading players were involved in the World Cup and I had the chance to play in four tournaments. The World Cup was a major innovation in a chess world which had become rather stale. Hitherto, the same events occurred year after year with clockwork regularity; occasionally there would be a new event, or one might disappear, but there was no real sign that chess was becoming more popular. The World Cup was a genuine innovation and, for me, it was a sign that chess was making progress.

The first event in the cycle was missing Kasparov (each player participated in four of the six events), but the field was nevertheless extremely strong. The tournament was sponsored by SWIFT (Society for Worldwide Interbank Financial Telecommunications) and set new standards for the organisation of chess tournaments. The players used special boards, which appeared normal, but which had sensors under the squares to feed the positions to an electronic display system. The result was that spectators could easily follow the games both in the tournament hall and outside, since screens were located at several strategic spots in the hotel. Just six years later this type of system appears commonplace, but at the time it was a revolution. One of the great problems with presenting chess as a spectator sport is that very often the spectators can't follow the action. Manually operated demonstration boards have the flaw that the operators tend to make mistakes, or lose track of the game during the time scramble, which is the often the most exciting and entertaining part of the game. The introduction of electronic display systems has not solved all the problems, but it is certainly a huge improvement over what had gone before.

I started the event in solid style, with eight draws and one win from my first nine games. In round 10 I had to face the ex-world champion Mikhail Tal.

Game 19
J.Nunn – M.Tal
Brussels World Cup 1988
Caro-Kann

1	e4	c6
2	d4	d5
3	♘d2	dxe4
4	♘xe4	♘d7

The most solid variation of the Caro-Kann, intending to challenge the e4 knight by 5...♘gf6. Normally, White continues with 5 ♘f3 or 5 ♗c4, but in the mid-1980s a new idea based on ♗d3 and ♘g5 started to score well. It quickly became clear that 5 ♗d3 ♘df6! causes few problems for Black, so White players adopted the move-order with 5 ♘g5. After a few successful years, Black players gradually fought back; now the line is considered relatively harmless and is rarely seen.

5	♘g5	♘df6 (103)

An unusual move; it looks very odd to take away the most natural square from the king's knight, but Anatoly Karpov has played it a number of times, so it can't be so bad. 5...♘gf6 is the standard continuation.

6	♘1f3	

The alternative, which has been more popular in practice, is 6 ♗c4 and now:

1) **6...e6** 7 ♘1f3 (7 ♘e2 c5 8 0-0 h6 9 ♘f3 a6 10 a4 cxd4 11 ♘exd4 ♗d6 12 ♕e2 ♘e7 was roughly equal in de Firmian-Karpov, Biel 1990) h6 8 ♘h3 ♗d6 9 ♕e2 ♘e7 (9...b5 10 ♗b3 ♘e7 11 ♘e5 ♕b6 12 ♗f4 c5 13

103
W

dxc5 ♗xc5 14 a4 ♗b7 15 0-0 g5 is
unclear; Arnason-Thorsteins, Reykjavik 1988) 10 ♗d2 ♕c7 11 0-0-0 b5
12 ♗d3 a6 13 ♖he1 ♗b7 14 g3 c5 15
dxc5 ♕xc5 with an edge for White;
Hübner-Karpov, Belfort World Cup
1988.

2) 6...♘d5 7 ♘1f3 g6 8 0-0 ♗g7
9 ♖e1 h6 10 ♘e4 ♗g4 11 c3 (11 a4
♘gf6 12 ♘xf6+ ♗xf6 13 ♖a3 ♔f8
14 h3 is also better for White;
Spassky-Karpov, Belfort World Cup
1988) ♘gf6 12 ♘c5! ♕c7 13 h3
♗xf3 14 ♕xf3 0-0 15 ♗b3 b6 16
♘d3 b5 17 a4 a6 18 ♗f4! with a
clear advantage for White; Psakhis-
Am.Rodriguez, Sochi 1988.

It seems to me that 6 ♘1f3 is more
natural than 6 ♗c4, since White can
choose later whether to develop his
bishop at d3 or c4. Unfortunately,
nobody has ever played this move
against Karpov, so we don't know
what he had prepared in reply.

6 ... e6

Black cannot expel the knight
since 6...h6 7 ♘xf7 ♔xf7 8 ♘e5+

♔e8 (8...♔e6 9 ♗c4+ ♘d5 10 ♕g4+
♔d6 11 ♘f7+ ♔c7 12 ♕g3+ wins
the queen) 9 ♗d3 is very good for
White.

The alternative 6...♘h6 is also not
very tempting; after 7 c3 g6 8 ♗c4
♗g7 9 0-0 0-0 10 ♖e1 ♘f5 11 ♘e5
♘d5 12 ♘gf3 ♕c7 13 ♗b3 e6?! 14
c4 ♘f6 15 g4 ♘e7 16 ♗f4 ♕a5 17
♖c1 White had a clear advantage in
Smirin-Smyslov, USSR Ch 1988.

7 ♘e5

Technically an innovation, although the move is perfectly obvious. White would like to play 7 ♗d3
♗d6 8 ♘e5, but it loses a pawn after
8...♗xe5 9 dxe5 ♕a5+. In game 8 of
the 1988 Candidates Match between
A.Sokolov and Spraggett, White
tried the line 7 ♕d3 ♗d6 8 ♘e5, so
as to meet 8...♗xe5 9 dxe5 ♕a5+ by
10 ♕c3 (10 ♔d1 is another idea, to
meet 10...♕xe5 by 11 ♕d8+!, but
10...♘g4! is much better) ♕xc3+ 11
bxc3 with advantage to White. The
game continued 8...♘h6 9 ♗d2 a5
and now, instead of 10 a3 ♕c7 11
♘c4 ♗e7 12 g3 ♘f5 13 ♗g2 h6 with
equality, Yurkov evaluates 10 ♘e4
♘xe4 11 ♕xe4 ♘f5 12 0-0-0 0-0 13
♗d3 as clearly better for White.
Moving the queen to d3 seemed artificial to me, and I preferred an alternative solution to White's dilemma:
simply invert the moves ♘e5 and
♗d3.

7 ... ♘h6
8 ♗d3 (104)

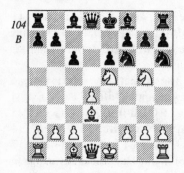

104
B

8 ...   &d6?

Tal uncharacteristically declines the challenge. The only way to test White's idea is by 8...♕xd4; after 9 ♘gxf7 ♘xf7 10 ♘xf7 &b4+ (both 10...♘e4 and 10...&c5 fail to 11 &e3, while 10...♘g4 11 0-0 &c5 12 ♘xh8 ♘xf2 13 &g6+ hxg6 14 ♕xd4 &xd4 15 ♖xf2 rescues the knight and wins) 11 c3 &xc3+ (11...♖f8 12 0-0 ♕d5 13 cxb4 ♖xf7 14 ♕e2 gives White a clear positional advantage) 12 bxc3 ♕xc3+ 13 &d2 ♕xd3 14 ♘xh8 ♕e4+ we arrive at the critical position. One idea is to play 15 ♕e2 ♕xe2+! (but not 15...&d7 16 ♕xe4 ♘xe4 17 &e3 and Black has problems rounding up the h8 knight, for example 17...♔e7 18 f3 ♘c3 19 &d4 and 20 &xg7) 16 ♔xe2 &f8 17 ♖hc1 ♔g8 18 ♘g6 hxg6 19 ♖ab1 when Black has two pawns for the exchange, but his kingside pawns are broken and he has some problems developing his remaining pieces. On the other hand, d5 is a wonderful square for his knight and,

in the absence of open files, White's rooks are not particularly effective. The alternative is 15 ♔f1, which makes it harder for Black to round up the knight on h8, but seriously obstructs White's own development. Whatever the verdict, Black should certainly have tried this, because in the game he falls into a position with few prospects of counterplay.

9 c3

Not only stopping the threat of 9...&xe5 10 dxe5 ♕a5+, but also preparing ♕c2 and defending d4 in anticipation of ...♘f5.

9 ...   ♕c7?!

Now Black's position becomes critical. At first sight 9...0-0 isn't possible, because of 10 ♕c2 ♘f5 11 g4 &xe5 12 gxf5, but Black can continue 12...♕d5! 13 f3 h6 14 fxe6 hxg5 15 exf7+ ♖xf7 16 dxe5 ♕xe5+ 17 ♕e2 ♖e7, with perhaps just an edge for White. In fact White would do better to continue quietly with 10 0-0, but if there is no direct refutation, then castling must be the right move.

10 ♕e2   c5

This is a desperate move, but after the more natural 10...0-0 11 ♘gf3 ♘f5 (11...♘hg4 12 h3) 12 g4 ♘e7 13 h4 White has an automatic kingside attack while Black's counterplay hasn't started.

11 &b5+

After the game, Tal said that he was more frightened of 11 &d2,

but I preferred to fix his king in the centre.

11 ...   ♔e7

Not 11...♗d7? 12 ♗xd7+ ♘xd7 13 ♘exf7! 0-0 14 ♘xe6 and Black's position collapses.

12 0-0

Tal is aiming for a counterattack against d4. 12...a6 13 ♗d3 b6 is most directly met by 14 f4 with an immense attack.

13 cxd4   ♘f5

14 ♗e3!

The simplest. There is no need to enter the murky complications of 14 ♘exf7 ♗xh2+ 15 ♔h1 ♖f8 16 ♗d3, although this may also be good for White. The move played aims to develop White's remaining pieces before continuing with the attack.

14 ...   ♘xe3 *(105)*

If 14...♗xe5 15 dxe5 ♕xe5, then 16 ♗xa7 ♕xe2 17 ♗c5+ ♘d6 18 ♗xe2, followed by ♖fd1, and the pin is almost unbreakable.

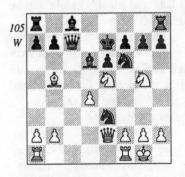

15 fxe3?

This attempt to force an immediate decision gives Black drawing chances. The correct continuation is 15 ♕xe3 ♘d5 16 ♕g3 (16 ♕h3 ♗xe5 17 dxe5 ♕xe5 18 ♕a3+ ♔f6 19 ♘f3 ♕f4 is unclear) f6 and now:

1) **17 ♖ac1 ♕b6!** (17...♗xe5 18 dxe5 ♕xe5 19 ♕a3+ ♕d6 20 ♕xd6+ ♔xd6 21 ♘f7+ ♔e7 22 ♘xh8 ♗d7 23 ♗xd7 ♔xd7 24 ♘f7 ♖f8 and now 25 ♘e5+ or 25 ♘h6 gives White good winning chances) 18 ♘xe6 g6! (18...fxe5 19 ♕xg7+ ♔xe6 20 ♖xc8 ♕xb5 21 ♕xh8 ♖xc8 22 ♕xc8+ should win for White) and, with three pieces under attack, it isn't clear what White's next move should be.

2) **17 ♘e4! ♖g8** 18 ♕h4 ♗xe5 (18...♔f8 19 ♖ac1 ♕e7 20 f4! gives White a decisive attack) 19 dxe5 ♕xe5 20 ♕xh7 and material equality is restored with White still having a very strong attack. In particular, 20...♗d7 loses to 21 ♗xd7 ♔xd7 22 ♘c5+ followed by ♖ae1.

15 ...   ♗xe5

The only chance is to accept.

16 dxe5   ♕xe5

17 ♕d3 *(106)*

The point of 15 fxe3: the threat of ♕a3+ is very hard to meet.

17 ...   ♕xg5?

A blunder leading to immediate defeat. The alternatives are:

1) 17...♖d8? 18 ♕xd8+.

2) 17...b6 18 ♖ac1 only makes matters worse.

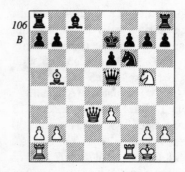

106
B

3) **17...♗d7** 18 ♕a3+ ♕d6 (or
18...♔e8 19 ♗xd7+ and f7 falls) 19
♕xd6+ ♔xd6 20 ♖ad1+ ♔e7 21
♖xd7+! (not 21 ♗xd7 h6!) ♘xd7 22
♖xf7+ wins.

4) **17...♖f8** 18 ♖ad1 ♘d5 (or
18...♕c5 19 ♖c1) 19 e4! and Black's
position collapses.

5) **17...a6!** (the only move) and
now:

5a) **18 ♗a4** b5 19 ♖ad1 (19
♕a3+ ♔e8!) ♗b7! (not 19...bxa4 20
♕a3+ ♔e8 21 ♖d8+) and there is
nothing clear for White, for example
20 ♕a3+ ♔e8 21 ♘xf7 ♔xf7 22
♖d7+ ♔g6 23 ♗c2+ ♗e4 24 ♖xg7+
(what else?) ♔xg7 25 ♕e7+ ♔h6 26
♖xf6+ ♗g6 and Black defends.

5b) **18 ♕a3+!** ♕d6 19 ♕xd6+
♔xd6 20 ♘xf7+ ♔e7 21 ♘xh8 axb5
22 g4 (22 e4? e5 and Black is better)
♗d7 (22...♖a4? 23 h3 and 22...g5?!
23 ♖f3! ♗d7 24 ♖af1 are very good
for White) 23 g5 ♖xh8 24 gxf6+
gxf6. This position represents best
play for both sides after 15 fxe3.
White has a material advantage but

Black's bishop has a good stable
square at c6. If White could exchange rooks he should win, so the
best plan is ♔f2, followed by ♖g1,
hoping to attack the weak h-pawn or
double rooks on the g-file. I would
evaluate this position as being
evenly balanced between a draw and
a win.

18   ♕a3+   ♔d8
19   ♖ad1+   ♗d7
20   ♗xd7   1-0

Black has no reasonable defence
to the threat of mate in five by 21
♗a4+ ♘d5 (or 21...♔c8 22 ♖c1+)
22 ♕d6+ ♔c8 23 ♖c1+, for example:

1) **20...a6** is destroyed by 21
♖xf6 gxf6 (21...♕xf6 22 ♕a5+) 22
♗e6+ ♔e8 23 ♗d7+ ♔d8 24 ♗f5+
♔e8 25 ♖d7.

2) **20...♘xd7** 21 ♖xf7 ♕b5 22
♕d6 leads to a forced mate.

3) **20...♘d5** 21 ♖xf7 ♕xe3+ (or
21...♕h5 22 ♖xd5!) 22 ♕xe3 ♘xe3
23 ♖d3 and Black's knight will be
lost to a discovered check.

4) **20...a5** is relatively best, but
even here White wins by 21 ♗xe6+
♔e8 22 ♖xf6 ♕xf6 23 ♗d7+ ♔d8
24 ♕c5, closing the net around
Black's king, and forcing mate in a
further five moves.

Whatever the result, I always enjoyed playing Mikhail Tal. During
the post-mortem he would enthusi-
astically demonstrate variation after

fantastic variation, proving time and again that he had a wonderfully inventive chess mind and an amazingly quick tactical vision. Not all of the lines were sound, as he himself was well aware, but he was fascinated by the beauty and depth of chess, indeed his passion for chess was one of the dominant features of his life. Misha, as he was known to his friends, had suffered from illness so often in his life that at times he seemed indestructible. Finally, and very sadly, his body could take no more and he died on 28th June 1992. I visited him a number of times in the last months of his life, when he was living with his wife and daughter in Germany. Although he was physically very weak, he enjoyed talking about chess and on one occasion, when I claimed that a certain queen ending was drawn, he quickly and convincingly proved me wrong. Misha continued to play chess right up to the end; he loved chess and would not give it up. I am proud to have known Misha and to have played against him.

The Brussels World Cup was one of my most successful tournaments. After fifteen games I had scored four wins and eleven draws, but in the last round disaster struck and I lost to Ljubojević. Nevertheless, my joint third place behind Karpov and Salov was an unexpected and therefore particularly pleasurable success.

My next major event was another visit to the OHRA Amsterdam tournament in August. Once again my tendency towards self-destruction in the face of imminent success struck. After eight of the ten rounds I had scored five points, and one point out of the last two would almost certainly be enough for a tied first place. Moreover, in round nine I was due to play White against Ljubojević, who had just lost four games in a row. Beating Ljubojević would have given me excellent chances of outright first place. In fact I played horribly, and a resurgent Ljubo polished me off with ease. A draw in the last round left me in outright second place, half a point behind the winner Korchnoi. Not a bad result, of course, but, just as in Szirak and Brussels, I had failed to make the most of a spell of good form because of simple nervousness.

The next major event was the Reykjavik World Cup in October. Between OHRA and Reykjavik, I played just six games of chess, winning the Barbican Open with a 100% score. The World Cup event was my first visit to Iceland, which I found a fascinating country, although a little on the chilly side. The organisation was very good and there was extensive television coverage. I had never before played in a tournament in which, walking down the street, people would come up to me and ask me about my game from the day before!

Once again, I played in my most solid style, drawing the first seven games. In round eight I faced Lajos Portisch.

Game 20
J.Nunn – L.Portisch
Reykjavik World Cup 1988
Spanish

1	e4	e5
2	♘f3	♘c6
3	♗b5	a6
4	♗a4	d6
5	♗xc6+	bxc6
6	d4	exd4
7	♕xd4	

7 ♘xd4 is often played, but current theory suggests that the reply 7...c5 gives Black good equalising chances.

| 7 | ... | ♘f6 |

It seems to me that 7...c5 is dubious after 8 ♕d3, since White has effectively gained the useful move ♕d3 over the 7 ♘xd4 line. Nevertheless, this line has occurred several times in practice. One example is Kotronias-Tisdall, European Team Ch, Haifa 1989, which continued 8...g6 9 ♘c3 ♗g7 10 ♗g5 f6 11 ♗f4 ♗e6 12 h4 ♘h6 13 ♘d5 0-0 14 0-0-0 ♘f7 15 ♗d2 a5 16 h5 g5 17 h6!? ♘xh6 18 ♖xh6 ♗xh6 19 ♖h1 ♗g7 20 e5 with tremendous complications; White eventually won.

| 8 | 0-0 | |

The most natural move. Timman-Portisch, Tilburg 1988 continued 8 b3?! c5 9 ♕d3 ♗b7 10 ♘c3?! ♘xe4! 11 ♘xe4 ♕e7 with advantage for Black.

| 8 | ... | ♗e7 |
| 9 | ♘c3 | |

The only real alternative is 9 e5 c5 10 ♕d3 dxe5 11 ♕xd8+ ♗xd8 12 ♘xe5 ♗e7 13 ♖e1 (13 ♘c3 ♗f5 14 ♖e1 0-0 15 ♘c6 ♗d6 16 ♘e7+ ♗xe7 17 ♖xe7 ♖fe8 ½-½, Van der Wiel-Portisch, Wijk aan Zee 1990) 0-0 14 ♗g5 ♗e6 15 ♘d2 ♖fe8 16 h3 h6 17 ♗h4 with a slight edge for White, Kasparov-Short, PCA World Ch (19), London 1993.

| 9 | ... | 0-0 *(107)* |
| 10 | ♖e1 | |

This rather mechanical move is not the most accurate. The reason is that Black will continue with ...♗g4 and ...♗xf3 in any case, so as to gain control of e5, and then enhance his grip with ...♘d7 and ...♗f6. Against this, White has no chance of forcing through e4-e5 directly, so playing

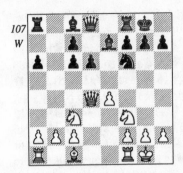

107
W

♖e1 is redundant. Ultimately, White may aspire to f4 and then e5, possibly as a pawn sacrifice, but in this case the f-file will become open and the rook will probably be just as useful on f1 as on e1. At any rate, White should certainly not commit himself to ♖e1 so soon. In a later game against Portisch, at Wijk aan Zee 1990, I played the more accurate 10 b3; the continuation was 10...♗g4 (10...♘d7 11 ♗a3 ♗f6 12 ♕d2 is favourable for White, because Black is stuck with his light-squared bishop) 11 ♕d3 ♗xf3 12 ♕xf3 ♘d7 13 ♗b2 (in retrospect, 13 ♗a3 ♗f6 14 ♖ad1 is probably better, much as in Tal-Portisch below, because then the c3 knight is not pinned) ♗f6 14 ♕e3 (clearing the way for f2-f4) ♖e8 15 f4 c5 16 e5 (this tactical sequence breaks the rather awkward pin on the f6-b2 diagonal) dxe5 17 ♘e4 exf4 18 ♘xf6+ ♘xf6 19 ♕xf4 ♖e6 20 ♖ae1 ♖xe1+ 21 ♖xe1 ♖b8 22 ♕g5 ♖b6 23 ♕xc5, with just a slight edge for White.

10 ...   ♗g4

The traditional method of assessing such positions is to say that Black has an inferior pawn structure, but in compensation he has the two bishops. Looked at this way, Portisch's plan appears strange. However, a static evaluation takes no account of the potential activity of Black's pieces. His main problem is the future of the c8 bishop; he doesn't want to play ...♗d7, because that would prevent the manoeuvre ...♘d7 and ...♗f6, which is his best chance of activating the other minor pieces. After ...♗e6, the bishop would be a target for a later ♘f3-d4 or f2-f4-f5, and it would block the e-file, making it impossible to develop pressure against the e4 pawn by ...♖e8. The only real solution is to get rid of the bishop by ...♗g4 followed by ...♗xf3. This plan has to be executed immediately, or else White plays ♕d3, preparing to meet ...♗g4 by ♘d4. Perhaps there is even an argument for 10 ♕d3!?, although this might tempt Black to develop his bishop another way – by 10...a5 followed by ...♗a6.

The exchange on f3 not only relieves Black's slightly cramped position, it also gives him a grip on e5.

11   ♕d3   ♗xf3
12   ♕xf3   ♘d7
13   b3

Curiously enough, White's main problem is also his queen's bishop.

13 b3 appears strange, because it invites Black to pin the knight, but there is no really good square for the bishop. On d2 or e3 it would block a rook, while on f4 it obstructs the advance f4 which will be needed sooner or later to regain control of e5.

13   ...   ♗f6 (108)

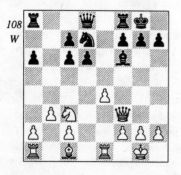

The game Tal-Portisch, from an earlier round of the same Reykjavik tournament, reached this position with the minor difference that Black's pawn was on a7 instead of a6. That game continued 14 ♗a3 ♖e8 15 ♖ad1 ♖e6 16 ♘e2 ♗e5 17 ♕d3 c5 18 f4 ♗f6 19 e5 ♗h4 20 ♖f1 ♗e7 21 ♗b2 ♗f8 22 ♘g3 ♕b8 23 ♘e4 ♕b6 24 c4 with a clear plus for White, who went on to win the game. After this heavy defeat, I had expected Portisch to switch to another opening entirely and I was surprised that he had adopted the same line. I knew very well that he would have an improvement prepared and I

was trying to guess what it might be. Suddenly, I became worried about 14 ♗a3 ♘e5!?, when 15 ♕h3 ♕c8 16 ♕g3 ♕g4 is equal, while 15 ♕e3 ♘g4 16 ♕h3 (16 ♕g3 ♗e5) ♗e5 17 ♗b2 (17 g3 ♘xf2) ♕g5 is very good for Black. However 14 ♗a3 ♘e5 15 ♕g3 is playable, although 15...♘g6 16 ♖ad1 ♗e5 followed by ...♕f6 or ...♕h4 is roughly equal. I decided to choose a different move, although it would have been interesting to see what Portisch had prepared.

14   ♗b2

This is safer than 14 ♗a3, but the knight is uncomfortably pinned and White cannot hope for more than equality.

14   ...   ♖e8

Tactical ideas are harmless now that the c3 knight is well defended, so Black switches to the simple but dangerous plan of attacking e4.

15   ♖ad1

The simplest way to relieve the pin is to play 15 ♘a4, although White has no advantage after this. Chandler-Motwani, London (Watson, Farley and Williams) 1990 continued 15...♗xb2 16 ♘xb2 ♖e6 (16...♕g5 is the safest; then Black can meet 17 ♕c3 by 17...♘c5) 17 ♕c3 c5 18 ♘d3 ♕e7 19 f3 ♘b6 20 a4 a5 21 ♖ad1 c4 22 ♘f4 ♖e5 23 ♘d5 ♘xd5 24 ♖xd5 cxb3 25 cxb3 and by now White does have the advantage.

15   ...   ♖e6

Already White has to be careful not to lose his e-pawn after some combination of ...♕e7, ...♖ae8 and ...♘c5. Note that playing f3 doesn't help White, since the pin on the e-file will allow Black to step up the pressure by ...d5.

16 ♕h3? *(139)*

This is the right idea, but poorly executed. The plan is to clear the way for f4, but h3 isn't the best square for the queen; White should have preferred 16 ♕e3. It may seem odd to put the queen opposite Black's rook, but sooner or later the e-pawn will prove indefensible, when White will have to play the pawn sacrifice e5 dxe5 f5. This will block the e-file, so the opposition of queen and rook is less dangerous than it appears. After 16 ♕e3 ♕e7 17 f4 ♖e8, for example, White can play 18 ♕a7 (not 18 e5? ♘xe5!) with the point that 18...♘c5 19 e5! is good for White.

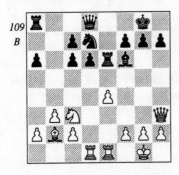

16 ...   ♕e8!

It was also possible to play 16...♕e7. During the game, I intended to reply 17 f4 ♘c5 18 e5 dxe5 19 f5 ♖d6 20 ♗a3 ♖xd1 21 ♖xd1 and now I could see no way for Black to meet the threats of 22 ♘a4 and 22 ♕e3. Surprisingly, Black can defend by 21...e4! 22 ♘a4 (22 ♕e3 ♕e5!) ♖d8! 23 ♖xd8+ (23 ♕g4 ♖xd1+ 24 ♕xd1 ♕d6! is fine for Black, since after 25 ♕xd6 cxd6 26 ♘xc5 Black has a check on d4) ♕xd8 24 ♗xc5 ♕d1+ 25 ♔f2 ♕d2+ with a draw by perpetual check.

The move played has the same intention of increasing the pressure on e4, but it sidesteps a possible pin along the a3-e7 diagonal. If Portisch had followed up this move correctly, then he would have obtained an advantage.

17 f4   ♖d8?

White's imminent e4-e5 pawn sacrifice will open the d-file, so Black spends a tempo improving the position of his rook. However, this tempo gives White the chance to prevent ...♘c5. Black should have played the immediate 17...♘c5, when White can try:

1) **18 e5** dxe5 19 f5 (19 ♗a3? exf4) ♖d6 (not 19...♖e7 20 ♗a3) 20 ♗a3 ♖xd1 21 ♖xd1 ♗e7 (21...♘d7 22 ♕f3 is unclear) 22 ♕e3 ♘d7 23 ♗xe7 ♕xe7 24 ♘e4 ♘f6 is slightly better for Black.

2) **18 ♕g4** ♘xe4! 19 ♘xe4 ♗xb2 20 f5 h5! (not 20...♖e7? 21 f6)

21 ♕f4 (21 ♕h4 ♕e7!) ♖e5 22 f6 ♕e6 and the pin on the e-file is far more important than White's meagre threats on the kingside.

18 ♕e3!

Correcting the mistake at move 16. Now 18...♘c5 may be safely met by 19 e5 and, moreover, Black must worry about the possibility of 19 ♕a7. White is effectively a tempo down over 16 ♕e3, but Black cannot make much use of his extra move.

18 ...   ♘b6 *(110)*

Portisch is one of those players who write down moves before playing them, in order to make a final check. Here he wrote 18...c5 on his score sheet, but in this case 19 e5 dxe5 20 f5 ♖d6 21 ♘d5! is good for White.

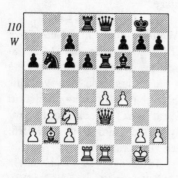

110
W

19 e5?!

This sacrifice is only good enough for equality, so White should have played 19 ♕e2! a5 (19...♘d5 20 ♘xd5 cxd5 21 ♗xf6 is very good for White after 21...♖xe4 22 ♕xe4 dxe4

23 ♗xd8 or 21...♖xf6 22 exd5) and only now 20 e5 dxe5 (20...♗h4 21 g3 ♗e7 22 ♘e4 is also good for White) 21 ♘e4!. All the forcing lines are good for White, for example 21...exf4 22 ♘xf6+ gxf6 23 ♕g4+ ♔f8 (23...♔h8 24 ♕xe6! fxe6 25 ♗xf6+ is a neat win) 24 ♗a3+ wins, or 21...♖xd1 22 ♕xd1 ♘d5 (playing 22...exf4 loses as before) 23 f5 ♖e7 24 c4 ♘b4 (24...♘f4 25 g3 ♘h3+ 26 ♔g2 ♘g5 27 ♘xf6+ gxf6 28 h4) 25 ♘xf6+ gxf6 26 ♕g4+ ♔h8 27 ♕h4 ♔g7 28 ♗c1 h5 29 ♗g5! (29 ♕xh5 ♕h8 is less clear) fxg5 (29...♘d5 30 c4) 30 ♕xg5+, followed by f6, and White wins. Therefore Black would have to return the pawn at e5, when White's superior pawn structure gives him a clear advantage.

19 ...   dxe5

Black must accept or else 20 ♘e4 is strong.

20 f5   ♖xd1

Not 20...♖ed6? 21 ♖xd6 ♖xd6 22 ♘e4 ♖d7 23 ♘xf6+ gxf6 when White is a tempo up over the game and wins by 24 ♕g3+ ♔h8 25 ♖xe5! ♖d1+ (25...♕d8 26 ♖e8+) 26 ♔f2 ♖d2+ 27 ♔f3.

The alternative 20...♖e7 21 ♘e4 should transpose into the game.

21 ♖xd1   ♖e7
22 ♘e4   ♖d7

Better than 22...♘d5 23 ♕a7! ♕c8 24 c4 ♘b6 25 ♕xa6 and White has a large advantage.

23 ♘xf6+

White must play this before Black defends the bishop by ...♘d5.

23 ...   gxf6
24 ♖e1

In return for the pawn, White has attacking chances against Black's exposed king. Indeed, if he can regain the pawn his better pawn structure will give him an advantage. However, Black's control of the d-file is a major asset and should enable him to hold the balance.

24 ...   ♕d8!

Not 24...♘d5 25 ♕g3+ ♔h8 26 ♗c1 with dangerous threats. The move played defends f6 and forces White to waste time meeting the threat of 25...♖d1.

25 ♕e4   ♘d5

Portisch seizes the chance to bring his knight back into the game and at the same time shield his c6 pawn. The other option 25...♔h8 26 ♕g4 (26 ♕xc6 ♖d1 is safe for Black) ♖d2 (26...♕g8 27 ♕h4 ♕g7 28 ♗c1 is good for White) leads to a perpetual check by 27 ♗c1 ♖xc2 28 ♗h6 ♕g8 29 ♖e4 ♕xg4 30 ♖xg4 ♖xa2 31 ♗g7+ ♔h8 32 ♗h6+. After the game Portisch made it clear that at this stage he was playing for a win.

26 ♕g4+

The immediate 26 ♗c1 is bad after 26...♘f4 (threats 27...♖d1 and 27...♖d4) 27 ♗xf4 ♖d4 28 ♕xc6 ♖xf4 with advantage to Black, e.g. 29 ♕xa6 ♕d4+ 30 ♔h1 ♕d2 31 ♖g1 ♕xc2 and the f5 pawn falls.

If White's dark-squared bishop disappears, Black's king is often quite safe at g7.

26 ...   ♔h8
27 ♗c1 (111)

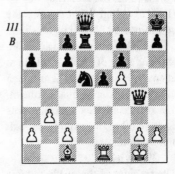

After the game I wrote that this move prevents 27...♘f4 because of 28 g3, but it turns out that Black has the stunning reply 28...♖d2!, forcing a draw after 29 gxf4 (29 ♗xd2 ♕xd2 is very bad for White) ♕d4+ 30 ♔h1 ♕d5+. However, 27...♘f4 can be met by the simple 28 ♗xf4, because 28...♖d4 fails to 29 ♖xe5! ♖d1+ 30 ♔f2 fxe5 31 ♗xe5+ f6 32 ♗xf6+ ♕xf6 33 ♕xd1 ♕xf5+ 34 ♔g1 with a extra pawn for White. Therefore, Black would have to reply to 28 ♗xf4 by 28...exf4, when 29 ♕xf4 gives White some positional advantage because of Black's many weak pawns.

27 ♗c1 threatens 28 ♗h6 ♕g8 29 ♕h4 ♖d6 (or else c4) 30 ♖e4 followed by ♖g4.

27 ...   ♕f8

Another good defensive move, preventing ♗h6 and preparing to activate the queen with gain of tempo by ...♕c5+ or ...♕b4.

28   c4   ♘b4

28...♕c5+? 29 ♔f1 (but not 29 ♔h1 ♕f2) is bad because once the knight moves, ♗h6 will be crushing. 28...♘e7 29 ♕h4 ♘g8 is a solid defence, but after 30 ♗e3 White is at least equal. He intends ♕f2 and ♗c5 with complete dark-square control, and in any case Black's weak pawns and passive knight provide enough compensation.

29   ♕h4

The transfer of the queen to h6 is the best way to meet the threat of 29...♘d3.

29   ...   ♕d6

30   ♕h6

Now White may answer 30...♘d3 31 ♖d1 ♕d4+ by 32 ♗e3; moreover, he has his own threat of 31 ♗g5! fxg5 32 f6.

30   ...   ♖d8

Frees the queen from the defence of f8 and prepares to meet 31 ♗g5 fxg5 32 f6 by 32...♖g8.

31   h3

By giving the king a flight square, this little move carries the deadly threat of ♖e4. Portisch didn't appreciate how lethal this threat is and concluded that he could afford the luxury of a further consolidating move.

31   ...   c5??

Up to this point both sides have played well, but here Black should have continued 31...♖g8 32 ♖e4 ♖g7 33 ♗d2 (33 ♕h4 ♕d1+ 34 ♔h2 ♕xc1 35 ♕xf6 ♕g5 wins for Black) and now not 33...♘xa2? (33...♕d3 34 ♖g4 and 33...c5 34 ♗e1 are also promising for White) 34 ♗e1 (intending ♗h4) ♕d3 35 ♖g4 ♖xg4 36 hxg4 ♕d4+ (36...♔g8 37 ♕xf6 is also better for White) 37 ♗f2 ♕xg4 38 ♕xf6+ ♔g8 39 ♕d8+ ♔g7 40 f6+ ♔g6 41 ♕g8+ ♔f5 42 ♕xf7 and White is better since 42...♕g6 loses to 43 ♕d7+. The correct move is 33...♘d3!, preventing ♗e1, with a roughly level position in which White's pressure balances Black's extra pawn.

32   ♖e4   ♖g8 *(112)*

The only defence to the threat of ♖h4, but by blocking g8 it allows a combination forcing mate in four.

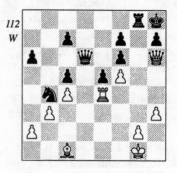

112
W

33   ♕xh7+!   1-0

33...♔xh7 34 ♖h4+ ♔g7 35 ♗h6+ ♔h7 36 ♗f8 is mate.

As I played this move, Portisch looked bemused for a moment, then he shook his head and held out his hand in resignation. It was a premature end to a hard-fought game, but the full point was very welcome.

After the Portisch game, I scored four more draws, including one with Black against Kasparov. Then I faced Viktor Korchnoi.

Game 21

V.Korchnoi – J.Nunn

Reykjavik World Cup 1988

King's Indian

1	d4	♘f6
2	c4	g6
3	♘c3	♗g7
4	e4	d6
5	♗g5	

Quite a shock for me. So far as I was aware, Korchnoi had never played this variation before and I knew next to nothing about it.

5	...	♘bd7!? *(113)*

I did know that the main line was thought to be 5...h6 6 ♗h4 c5 7 d5 0-0, and that a few recent (i.e. from

1987 and 1988) games had followed this path. Clearly, Korchnoi would have carefully studied these games before venturing 5 ♗g5 over the board, so my instinct was to steer the game into original paths as soon as possible. The move played seemed to fit the bill. White can reply 6 ♗e2 0-0 transposing into a line of the Averbakh Variation, while 6 f3 would be a kind of Sämisch, but Korchnoi does not normally play either of these variations. 6 ♕d2 is inaccurate, because Black may hunt the bishop down by 6...h6 (this is the advantage of delayed castling) 7 ♗h4 (or 7 ♗e3 ♘g4) g5 8 ♗g3 ♘h5. One may raise a similar objection to 6 ♘f3. The remaining possibilities seemed to be 6 h3, so as to play ♕d2 and meet ...h6 by ♗e3, and the ultra-aggressive 6 f4. Korchnoi doesn't normally play for mate from the first move, so I expected 6 h3.

6	**f4**

Korchnoi proved me wrong by playing this ambitious move almost instantly.

6 ...   0-0

Black may also be able to play 6...c5, for example 7 e5 ♘h5 8 exd6 f6 9 ♗h4 exd6 10 ♘d5 ♘b6! with a promising position for Black. White should reply 7 d5, when Black may transpose into the game by 7...0-0 8 ♘f3, or try the provocative and risky 7...♘h5.

7 ♘f3

7 e5 is not dangerous, since both 7...♘e8 (intending ...f6 or ...c5) and 7...♘h5 (with the idea 8 g4 f6) are satisfactory for Black.

7 ...   c5

Black cannot play ...e5 because White's bishop is on g5, so this is the only way to challenge White's centre.

8 d5

Not 8 e5 cxd4 (8...♘h5 is also possible) 9 ♕xd4 (9 exf6 exf6) ♘g4 with an advantage for Black.

After 8 d5, White must not be allowed to complete his development by ♗e2 and 0-0, because the general structure of the position favours White. Compared with the Four Pawns Attack, White's bishop is actively developed on g5, and the position of the knight on d7 means that Black will be unable to challenge the centre by ...e6 (because of dxe6 followed by ♕xd6).

8 ...   b5

It follows that this is the only move. In Tukmakov-Sirkia, Örebro 1966, Black played 8...♕a5 9 ♕d2 a6 10 ♗d3 b5 11 0-0 bxc4 12 ♗xc4 ♕b4 13 b3 and now White had a clear advantage.

9 cxb5

9 e5 (9 ♗d3 ♘h5!? is unclear) b4 causes Black no problems after 10 exf6 exf6 or 10 ♘b5 a6.

9 ...   a6 (114)

This type of pawn sacrifice occurs in the Benko Gambit and in many lines of the King's Indian. In comparison with these standard lines, here White's development is better than normal, but the bishop on g5 is badly placed, being exposed to attack and leaving the queenside poorly defended.

Once Black has set out on the sacrificial path, there is no turning back; he has to fight for the initiative at every move. It is worth noting that this type of pawn sacrifice very often gives Black purely positional compensation for the pawn, based on pressure along the half-open a- and b-files. This theme is not a significant factor in the present game, but even here it is important that the rook on a8 can capture on a2.

10 ♘d2?!

After this Black has at least equality. As usual in this type of position, White delays moving the bishop on f1 because Black would counter with ...axb5, and after the forced reply

114
W

♗xb5, White would have given Black a free tempo. For the same reason, Black will avoid ...axb5 while the bishop is on f1. However, other useful moves are not easy to find for White:

1) **10 e5 ♘g4!** (not 10...♘h5 11 g4! f6 12 gxh5 fxg5 13 ♘xg5 with the awkward threat of 14 ♘e6) 11 exd6 (11 h3 ♘e3 12 ♕e2 ♘xf1, followed by 13...f6) f6 12 ♗h4 exd6 and the e3 square is a serious weakness.

2) **10 bxa6 ♕a5** 11 ♕d2 ♗xa6 12 ♗xa6 ♕xa6 and White has problems castling because 13 ♕e2 ♖fb8 14 ♕xa6 ♖xa6 15 ♖b1 (15 0-0-0 ♘xe4! 16 ♘xe4 ♖xa2 is promising for Black) ♘h5, threatening both 16...h6 and 16...♗xc3+, is good for Black.

3) **10 ♕d2!** (this position can also arise from the Sämisch via the sequence 1 d4 ♘f6 2 c4 g6 3 ♘c3 ♗g7 4 e4 d6 5 f3 0-0 6 ♗e3 ♘bd7 7 ♕d2 c5 8 d5 ♘e5 9 ♗g5 a6 10 f4 ♘ed7 11 ♘f3 b5 12 cxb5, although

this move-order takes two extra moves) and now:

3a) **10...axb5?!** (breaking the rule about ...axb5) 11 ♗xb5 ♕a5 12 0-0 ♘xe4 13 ♘xe4 ♕xb5 14 ♗xe7 ♕xb2 15 ♕xb2 ♗xb2 16 ♖ae1 ♗a6 17 ♖f2 ♖fe8 18 ♘xd6 ♖eb8 and White had a favourable ending in Timman-Nunn, Wijk aan Zee 1985, although Black managed to draw.

3b) **10...♕a5!** 11 e5 (Black is threatening to take on b5 and then on e4, so this is the only dangerous move) dxe5 12 fxe5 ♘g4 13 ♗xe7 ♖e8 14 d6 ♗h6 (Black must displace the queen or else White plays ♘d5) 15 ♘g5 (15 ♗g5 ♘dxe5 is impossible, 15 ♕e2 ♘e3 ties White up, while after 15 ♕d5 Karpov recommends 15...♕b4!? as best) ♘gxe5 16 ♗e2 (16 ♘d5 ♕xd2+ 17 ♔xd2 ♗b7 18 ♘c7 f6 is good for Black) axb5 17 0-0 (not 17 ♗xb5? ♖b8 18 ♗xd7 ♖xb2 19 ♕xb2 ♘d3+ 20 ♔d2 ♘xb2 with advantage to Black; Krinichny-Sirota, corr 1988) c4 18 ♗f3 with a totally unclear position, Karpov-Nunn, Wijk aan Zee 1993.

10 ...   ♘h5!

Not 10...h6 11 ♗h4 ♘h5 12 ♕f3; Black cannot play 12...♘xf4, as 13 ♕xf4 g5 14 ♗xg5 would involve the loss of his g- and h-pawns.

11 ♕f3

The alternative defences to the threat of ...h6 are:

1) **11 g4 f6** 12 gxh5 fxg5 13 fxg5 (13 hxg6 ♖xf4 14 gxh7+ ♔h8) ♘e5

(during the game I intended to play 13...♗d4 14 ♘f3 ♘e5, since 15 ♘xd4 cxd4 wins for Black, but after 15 ♘xe5 the position is unclear) 14 ♖g1 (14 ♗e2 axb5) axb5 15 ♗xb5 c4! 16 ♘xc4 (16 ♗xc4 ♕b6 is similar) ♘xc4 17 ♗xc4 ♕b6 18 ♖g2 ♗xc3+ 19 bxc3 ♕e3+ followed by 20...♕xc3+ wins for Black.

2) **11 g3 h6 12 ♗h4 axb5 13 ♗xb5 ♗a6 14 ♗xa6 ♖xa6 15 0-0 ♖b6 16 ♖b1** (16 ♘c4 ♖b4 17 ♕e2 ♘b6 18 ♘xb6 ♕xb6 is similar) **♖b4** and Black has better chances than in the Benko Gambit because the bishop on h4 is very badly placed. In particular, White cannot play 17 g4 because of the reply 17...♘xf4 and 18...g5.

3) **11 f5 ♘e5** and again we have a Benko Gambit type of position, but with Black having the advantage of free access to e5.

11   ...   f6
12   ♗h4   ♘xf4

Not 12...f5 13 e5! dxe5 14 d6 winning material, e.g. 14...e4 15 dxe7 exf3 (15...♕xe7 16 ♗c4+ ♔h8 17 ♕xh5 wins for White) 16 exd8♕ ♖xd8 17 ♗xd8 ♗b7 and now the simplest win is by 18 ♘xf3 ♖xd8 19 bxa6.

13   ♕xf4   g5
14   ♕f2

White could win two pawns instead of one by 14 ♗xg5 fxg5 15 ♕xg5 ♘e5, but the open f-file permanently prevents castling and 16

♘c4? loses to 16...♖xf1+. In this case too Black has more than enough compensation.

14   ...   gxh4
15   ♕xh4   ♘e5
16   ♗e2

White finally concedes the battle over the ...axb5 tempo, but he has little choice since Black threatens to prevent castling by ...f5 and ...fxe4, as after 16 ♘c4 ♘g6 17 ♕g3 axb5 18 ♘xb5 f5, for example.

The next few moves revolve around White's attempts to castle kingside. If he can achieve this, then Black's compensation will be inadequate, but if he fails, Black will have ample initiative for the pawn.

16   ...   axb5
17   ♗xb5   ♕a5! *(155)*

Only this move interferes with White's intended 0-0.

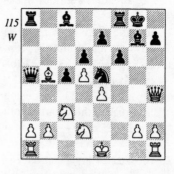

115
W

18   ♕g3

After 18 0-0 ♕b4 19 ♖ab1 ♕d4+ 20 ♕f2 ♘g4 (20...♗h6 21 ♘b3 ♕xf2+ 22 ♔xf2 f5 is also promising, for example after 23 ♔g1 fxe4 24 ♖xf8+ ♔xf8 Black has regained the pawn – in this line the pressure on the half-open a-file suddenly became useful) 21 ♕xd4 cxd4 22 ♘e2 f5, with the threats of ...♖xa2 and ...♗h6, Black has excellent play for the pawn.

18 ...   ♕b4
19 ♖b1

White intends 20 a3, when 20...♕d4 would fail to 21 ♘b3. Moreover, the immediate 19...♕d4 is well met by 20 ♘b3. It follows that Black must employ drastic measures to prevent castling. At each stage Black has to find a way to keep his initiative going, even at the cost of further sacrifices.

19 ...   ♖xa2!
20 ♘xa2   ♕xb5 *(116)*

Now White is unlikely to castle.

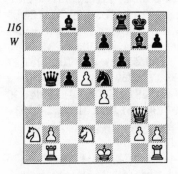

116
W

21 ♘c3?!

After this, Black gains a clear advantage. The best defence was 21 ♘c1, covering d3 and preparing 22 ♕b3 offering the exchange of queens. Then White can meet ...♕a6 by ♕a3, so Black would have to acquiesce to an exchange of queens, allow a draw by repetition, or permit White to castle. After 21 ♘c1, Black should reply 21...f5 and now:

1) **22 ♕b3 ♕xb3!** 23 ♘cxb3 (after 23 ♘dxb3 fxe4, Black's extremely active pieces are far more important than White's minute material advantage, for example 24 ♖f1 ♗b7 grabs another pawn) ♘d3+ 24 ♔e2 fxe4 25 ♘xe4 ♘xb2 with a clear advantage for Black.

2) **22 ♖f1!**. This move, again intending ♕b3 and ♕a3, is the best defence. After 22...♔h8 (22...c4 is well met by 23 b3) 23 ♕b3 ♕xb3 24 ♘cxb3 (24 ♘dxb3 fxe4 25 ♖xf8+ ♗xf8 26 ♘e2 ♘d3+ 27 ♔d2 ♗b7 28 ♘c3 ♘b4 is somewhat better for Black) ♘d3+ 25 ♔e2 ♘xb2 26 ♖f4 ♘a4! Black has a slight advantage, but the odds would probably be on a draw.

21 ...   ♕a6

White's last move gained a tempo, but now there is no way to drive Black's queen off the a6-f1 diagonal. White's problem is that Black has an obvious plan to improve his position, by ...♔h8 followed by ...♗h6, possibly coupled with ...f5, whereas White's exposed king and inactive pieces are defects which are not easily remedied.

22 ♔d1

White gives up any ideas of castling and heads for c2 with his king. The alternative was 22 ♘f3 (22 ♖f1 ♘d3+ 23 ♔d1 f5 is good for Black) ♘d3+ 23 ♔d2 ♔h8 and now:

1) **24 ♖a1** ♗h6+ 25 ♔c2 (25 ♘g5 ♗xg5+ 26 ♕xg5 fxg5 wins for Black) ♘b4+ 26 ♔b3 ♕b6 and Black has a crushing attack.

2) **24 ♕h4** (to prevent ...♗h6) ♘b4 25 ♘e1 ♕c4! (threat 26...f5) 26 g3 f5 27 exf5 ♗xc3+ 28 bxc3 ♕xd5+ 29 ♔e3 ♖xf5 with a decisive attack for Black.

22 ... f5

Black finally opens the long diagonal for his dark-squared bishop. It remains only to unpin the bishop, and White's weak dark squares will start to suffer.

23 ♖f1

Or 23 ♔c2 f4 24 ♕f2 (24 ♕h4 ♕d3+ 25 ♔c1 ♘g4 followed by ...♘e3 is crushing) ♕d3+ 25 ♔c1 (25 ♔d1 ♗g4+ or 25 ♔b3 ♗a6) ♕xc3+ winning material.

The move played aims to prevent Black opening up the position further by ...fxe4, because this would mean the exchange of rooks and a consequent dilution of Black's attack.

23 ... ♖f6! (117)

A surprising but strong move, which shows that Black has a second way of unpinning the g7 bishop. After ...♖g6 White's queen will have no good square; on ♕f2 or ♕e1 she can be hit by ...♘d3, while ♕e3 permits ...♗h6.

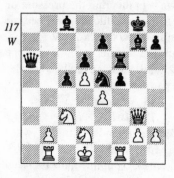

24 exf5

White decides to return the exchange. If he tries to hang on to the material by 24 ♔c2, then Black replies 24...♖g6 and now:

1) **25 ♖a1** loses material after 25...♖xg3 26 ♖xa6 ♖xc3+.

2) **25 ♕e3** ♖xg2 (25...♗h6 26 ♕e2 ♕xe2 27 ♘xe2 ♗a6 is unclear after 28 exf5! ♖xg2 29 ♖g1) 26 b3 (or else ...♘c4) c4 27 b4 ♕a3 with a winning attack for Black.

3) **25 ♕h3** fxe4 26 ♖a1 ♕b7 27 ♕e3 (27 ♖a7 ♕b8) ♖xg2 (threat ...♘c4) 28 b3 ♘f3 29 ♖f2 ♘d4+ 30 ♔b2 (30 ♔c1 ♖xf2 31 ♕xf2 ♘xb3+ 32 ♘xb3 ♕xb3 wins for Black) ♘f5 and Black wins.

4) **25 ♕f2** ♕d3+ 26 ♔b3 (26 ♔c1 ♗h6) fxe4 27 ♘dxe4 ♗b7 with a decisive advantage for Black.

Therefore the move played was the best chance.

24 ... ♗xf5

25 ♖xf5

White cannot contemplate 25 ♖c1 ♘d3, when all Black's pieces are aimed at White's endangered king.

25 ... ♖xf5
26 ♔c2

Material is equal and Black has no immediate threats, but White is in serious trouble. All the black pieces are more active than their white counterparts and White's king is permanently exposed. Currently the knights provide some defence, but if Black could exchange them, White would be helpless. On top of his bad position, Korchnoi was running short of time.

26 ... ♔h8 *(118)*

27 ♘b3?

It turns out that the intended ♖a1 may be prevented by tactical means, so this move is just a waste of time. The alternatives were:

1) **27 ♖e1 ♖f8!** (on f5 the rook is a tactical weakness, for example 27...♗h6? 28 ♕h3; the retreat to f8

not only safeguards the rook, but also allows it to switch to the b-file) 28 ♕e3 ♖b8 (threat 29...♘d3) 29 ♖b1 and after 29...c4 followed by ...♘d3 or 29...♕a5 followed by ...♕b4 Black has a clear advantage.

2) **27 b4 ♘c4** 28 ♘xc4 (28 b5 ♘a3+ 29 ♔c1 ♕a5 30 ♖b3 c4 wins) ♕xc4 29 bxc5 ♖f8 30 cxd6 (30 c6 ♗e5 31 ♕e1 ♗d4 followed by 32...♖f2+ wins for Black) exd6 (note that ...♗xc3 is met by ♕xc3 with check) 31 ♖b6 (White must try to meet the threats of 31...♖c8 32 ♖b3 ♕e2+, 31...♗d4 followed by ...♖f2+ and 31...♗e5 32 ♕e3 ♗d4) ♖f2+! 32 ♕xf2 ♕xc3+ 33 ♔d1 ♕a1+, followed by 34...♕a2+, 35...♕xf2+ and 36...♗d4+.

27 ... ♗h6 *(119)*

Creating the deadly threat of ...♖f2+.

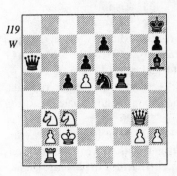

28 ♖a1?

Korchnoi misses Black's threat, but even after 28 ♖d1 ♕b6! (and not 28...♖f8 29 ♘xc5) 29 ♖a1 (White

cannot wait since Black threatened
29...c4 30 ♘d4 ♘d3!) ♖f8, threatening both 30...c4 and 30...♖b8, Black
has a favourable version of line 1
above and should be winning.

| 28 | ... | ♖f2+ |
| 29 | ♔b1 | ♖f1+ |

Winning a piece. Black doesn't
finish the game off in the most effi-
cient manner, but the moves played
were good enough in the end.

30	♔c2	♖xa1
31	♘xa1	♕xa1
32	♕h3	♕c1+
33	♔b3	c4+
34	♔a2	♘d3
35	♕c8+	♔g7
36	♕b7	♗g5
37	♘e4	♗f6

37...♕e1 was also effective, since
38 ♘xg5 allows mate in three by
38...♘c1+ 39 ♔b1 ♘b3+.

| 38 | ♘xd6 | ♔g6 |
| 39 | ♘c8 | c3 |

Black should have played
39...♗xb2! 40 ♘xe7+ ♔g5 41 h4+
♔f4 and after 42 g3+ ♔e3 or 42
♕c7+ ♔e4 the checks run out,
whereupon White is mated.

| 40 | d6 | ♕xb2+ |

I didn't want to throw away the
win on the last move of the time control, so I decided to play safe. In fact
40...cxb2 41 ♘xe7+ ♗xe7 42 ♕e4+
♔h6 43 ♕e6+ ♔g5 44 ♕xe7+ ♔f4
45 ♕f6+ ♔e3 wins easily, since
Black can hide from the checks on
h1.

41	♕xb2	cxb2
42	d7	♘b4+
43	♔b1	♘c6
44	g4	♔g5
45	h3	♔h4
46	♘b6	h6
47	♘d5	♔xh3

0-1

The Reykjavik World Cup was a
modest success for me. I did lose to
the local player, Petursson, but
games against local players didn't
count for the overall World Cup. In
the rest of the tournament I made
8½/16, but as usual it could have
been better. In the last round I had a
winning position against Timman,
but I felt completely exhausted and
failed to wrap up what should have
been a simple knight ending.

After returning to London, I still
felt drained of energy, which led to a
somewhat embarrassing experience.
I had played for Hamburg in the
Bundesliga for five years, but in
1987-8 the Hamburg football club
had a disastrous season, which had
severe financial repercussions for
the chess club. I had therefore
changed clubs and was playing for
Solingen in the 1988-9 season. The
Reykjavik tournament had caused
me to miss the first weekend of the
season, but I was scheduled to play
in the second weekend ten days after
returning from Iceland. Unfortunately, I had still not recovered and

lost both games, one to a relatively weak player. Although I scored well for Solingen in subsequent years, this first season was a struggle and I ended up with a distinctly mediocre 6/11.

A few days after this disastrous weekend, the English team left for the Olympiad in Thessaloniki. After our success at Dubai, the team was feeling confident, while recognising that the Dubai result was based on having a number of players on good form simultaneously, a coincidence which cannot happen every time.

Unfortunately, the build-up in the chess press was less than helpful. One good result, whether by an individual or a team, tends to send the chess journalists into a frenzy of anticipation. Before the 1988 Olympiad, the only subject discussed in the newspaper columns was whether or not the English team could win the Olympiad. Realistically, the chances of this happening were small, at most 1 chance in 20. In order to win, not only did our team have to play well above our ratings but, as in Dubai, the Soviet team also had to play below their usual strength. After the fright in 1986, it was clear that the Soviets would not take success for granted and would be exerting themselves to the utmost. Columnists who wrote that the English team had good chances to win the Olympiad, and then had to report

that we finished six points behind the Soviet Union, seemed reluctant to admit that it was their original assessment which was in error. The only other explanation for this 'disappointment', as they described finishing second in the Olympiad, was that we played badly. Thus one columnist gave great prominence to the team's losses, publishing Short's loss to Kasparov and Speelman's loss to Karpov.

It doesn't help with the team's sponsors if they read about disappointments, bad play and so on. Sponsors don't mind if the team tries hard and comes home with a creditable result, even if the gold medals go elsewhere, but it is very damaging if they gain the impression that the team wasn't taking the event seriously. In fact, Olympiads and other team events are very exhausting; not only do you have to worry about preparing for your own game, but you often have to help other members of the team if they have opening problems.

I am not suggesting that the chess press should censor bad news, but at times they seem to take a great delight in knocking British players, even when they have made a good result. When, at Lugano 1984, I scored 7/9 to finish joint second, one columnist published two games from the tournament – the two games I lost. The seven wins, which included one game with an attractive sacrificial attack, disappeared into a black hole.

The following encounter was my best game from the Thessaloniki Olympiad.

Game 22
J.Pinter – J.Nunn
Thessaloniki OL 1988
King's Indian

1	d4	♘f6
2	c4	g6
3	♘c3	♗g7
4	e4	d6
5	♗e2	0-0
6	♘f3	e5
7	0-0	♘c6
8	d5	♘e7
9	♘e1	♘d7
10	f3	f5
11	g4 *(119)*	

This line, called the Benko System, appears to contradict one of the basic precepts of chess, namely that one shouldn't advance pawns where one is being attacked. This rule applies particularly in the case of an attack on the king, such as Black usually develops in this variation of the King's Indian. Nevertheless, in this special situation there is logic behind White's plan. He intends to block the kingside completely, whereupon play can only take place on the other wing, where the pawn structure favours White. For example, if Black plays 11...f4, then

White will reply 12 h4, meeting ...g5 by h5 and ...h5 by g5. Similarly 11...h5 by Black is met by 12 g5. If Black exchanges on e4 or g4, then his attacking chances are reduced and White may even play g5 and ♗g4 later, blocking in the g7 bishop and exchanging off his own bad bishop. Normally Black shouldn't resolve the tension on the kingside unless he has a concrete idea in mind.

Nevertheless, the move 11 g4 is risky, since if Black can avoid the blockade and open the position up then White will have cause to regret his pawn advance. A second point is that White's pieces tend to become tied down to the defence of e4 and g4, which often impedes normal development.

| 11 | ... | ♚h8!? |

In my view this is a logical move. At the time it was regarded as slightly dubious, but now it has been promoted to the exalted status of 'main line'. Black's worst placed

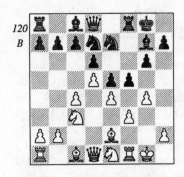

120
B

piece is his knight on e7 and by playing it to g8, Black prepares both ...♗h6 and an assault on the weak e4 pawn by ...♘c5 and ...♘g8-f6. The main theoretical recommendation used to be 11...♘f6, but Pinter specialised in demolishing this move, for example 12 ♘d3 ♔h8 13 ♗e3 c6 14 h3 b5 15 ♘b4! bxc4 (15...cxd5 16 ♘bxd5 ♘exd5 17 ♘xd5 ♗b7 18 ♘xf6 ♕xf6 19 cxb5 is clearly better for White, Pinter-Sznapik, Prague 1985) 16 ♘xc6 ♘xc6 17 dxc6 ♗e6 18 ♕a4 fxe4 19 fxe4 d5 20 ♗c5 with a slight plus for White, Pinter-Mortensen, Copenhagen 1985.

12 ♘g2

One of many possible moves; 12 ♘d3, 12 h4 and 12 ♗e3 are the alternatives, with the last currently being thought critical. The main line runs 12 ♗e3 ♘g8 13 ♕d2 f4 (after 13...a6 14 ♘g2 f4 15 ♗f2 h5 16 gxh5? g5! Black was slightly better in Pinter-Nunn, Dubai OL 1986, but 16 h3 ♗f6 17 ♔h2 ♖f7 18 ♖h1 ♖h7 19 ♔g1 a5 20 b3 would have given

White an edge) 14 ♗f2 h5 15 h3 (the point is that 15 h4 doesn't block the kingside because of 15...g5) ♖f7 16 ♔g2 ♗f6 17 ♘d3 ♖h7 18 ♖h1 ♗h4! 19 ♗d1 ♘f8 20 c5 ♗xf2 21 ♕xf2 g5 and with dark-squared bishops exchanged Black is not worse, Jaćimović-Vukić, Kaštel Stari 1988.

12 ... a5

The problem with 12 ♘g2 is that while the knight is on e1 White has the option of ♘d3, but now Black's d7 knight is given free access to c5. This, coupled with ...♘g8-f6, will exert uncomfortable pressure on e4 and g4. Other plans have turned out well for White, for example 12...♘g8 13 h4 ♘df6 14 exf5 gxf5 15 g5 ♘h5 16 f4 ♘xf4 17 ♘xf4 exf4 18 ♗xf4 ♗d7 19 ♕d2 ♕e7 20 ♗f3, Vasilchuk-Gipslis, Alma-Ata 1963, or 12...♘f6 13 ♗d2 c5 14 ♖b1 ♗d7 15 ♔h1 ♕c7 16 a3 ♖f7 17 exf5 gxf5 18 g5 ♘h5 19 f4 ♘xf4 20 ♗xf4 exf4 21 ♗h5 ♖ff8 22 ♘xf4, Bilek-Stein, Stockholm 1962, with the same type of advantage for White in both cases.

In these early games, Black made the mistake of playing only on the kingside. The defensive knight on g2 means that this is unlikely to succeed. Instead, Black should maintain a fluid position, keeping open the option of play on either wing. White's pieces already have a heavy duty in maintaining control of e4 and g4; further responsibilities may well prove to be too much.

13 h4

White cannot manage without this move indefinitely, for example after 13 ♗e3 ♘g8 Black threatens 14...f4 15 ♗f2 h5, and White cannot block the kingside with 16 g5. So White would have to play 14 h4, transposing into the game.

13 ...   ♘c5
14 ♗e3   ♘g8 (121)

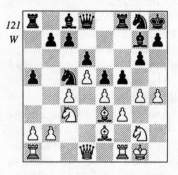

121
W

Black should not disturb the kingside pawns, since any change he might make will favour White by either releasing the tension or blocking the position. Nor can White improve his own kingside set-up, for example 15 g5 is met by 15...f4 16 ♗f2 h6, strong here because a White rook cannot reach the h-file quickly. In Zilbershtein-Petrushin, USSR 1979 White released the tension himself by 15 exf5 gxf5 16 g5 but after 16...f4 17 ♗xc5 dxc5 18 ♘e4 ♘e7 19 ♘xc5 ♘f5 20 ♘e4 ♖a6 21 ♗d3 ♖g6 22 ♖f2 h6 Black had a very strong attack for the pawn.

15 ♖b1

Since there is a deadlock on the kingside, White decides to start a queenside pawn advance.

15 ♖c1 was played in Markowski-Dolmatov, Polanica Zdroj 1993 and after 15...♕e7 16 a3 fxg4 17 fxg4 ♖xf1+ 18 ♔xf1 ♘f6 19 ♗f3 ♗d7 20 b4 axb4 21 axb4 ♘a4 Black had a comfortable position. Black could also have played 15...♗d7, as in Pinter-Nunn.

15 ...   ♗d7

The alternative was 15...♘f6, based on the idea 16 exf5 gxf5 17 h5 ♖g8 (not 17...h6 18 ♘h4) 18 h6 ♗f8 19 g5 f4! (19...♘h5? 20 f4 is dangerous for Black because the d4-h8 diagonal is so weak) 20 ♗xc5 ♖xg5! 21 ♗a3 (21 ♗f2 ♕d7 22 ♘e4 ♘xe4 23 fxe4 ♕h3 24 ♗f3 ♗xh6 followed by 25...♗d7 and 26...♖ag8 is also winning for Black; note that 21...♗h3 22 ♔h2 ♗xg2 23 ♖g1 is less clear-cut) ♕d7 22 ♖f2 ♕h3 23 ♗d3 (to meet the threat of ...♖h5) ♗xh6 followed by ...♗d7 and ...♖ag8 with a decisive attack for Black. However, White has a better reply in 16 exf5 gxf5 17 g5! ♘h5 18 f4 and Black's light-squared bishop is blocked in. Therefore, I decided to improve my position on the queenside and wait for a better moment before playing ...♘f6.

16 b3

One of the points of Black's previous move is that White cannot play the immediate 16 a3 because of 16...a4, not only blocking the queenside but also preparing ...♘b3-d4. Other moves are also bad, e.g. 16 ♕d2 fxg4 17 fxg4 ♘f6 forks e4 and g4, forcing White to play the horrible ♗xc5.

16 ...   b6

Anticipating White's next move, which might result in a half-open b-file. 16...♕c8 was one reasonable alternative, and 16...fxg4 was another; after 17 fxg4 ♖xf1+ 18 ♔xf1 ♘f6 19 ♗f3 ♕c8 (19...h5 20 gxh5 gxh5 21 ♗g5 is good for White) 20 g5 ♘g4 21 ♗g1 h5 the position is unclear.

17 a3   a4!

It is unusual for Black to take the initiative on the queenside in the King's Indian. Here he is justified because White has heavily committed himself on the other side of the board, so if Black can open up the position or deflect some of White's pieces from the kingside, then White's king will become exposed. The move ...b6 was useful because the b7 pawn cannot become *en prise* to the rook on b1, and White cannot easily play b4 and c5. White is already worse, but it is hard to pinpoint a definite error; perhaps the whole idea of g4 and ♘g2 is doubtful.

18 b4

Otherwise White is left with a weak isolated a-pawn.

18 ...   ♘b3

If White allows ...♘d4 he won't be able to keep his kingside pawn structure intact, for example 19 ♖b2 ♘d4 20 ♖d2 ♕c8 and now White must capture on f5.

19 ♘b5

Keeping the knight out of d4, but leaving the e4 pawn vulnerable.

19 ...   ♘f6

White cannot defend both e4 and g4, so he must resolve the tension on the kingside.

20 exf5

20 g5 (20 gxf5 gxf5 opening the g-file is a disaster) ♘h5 threatens 21...f4 followed by ...h6, or 21...♘g3 followed by ...fxe4.

20 ...   gxf5 *(122)*

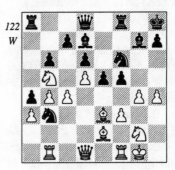

122
W

21 ♘c3

An unfortunate necessity. There was a threat of 21...f4 22 ♗f2 e4 (this is the answer to 21 h5, for example), whilst 21 g5 f4! (21...♘h5 22 f4 is unclear) 22 gxf6 (22 ♗f2 ♘h5) ♗xf6 23 ♗f2 (23 ♗d2 ♘xd2 24 ♕xd2 ♗xh4 followed by ...♖g8

is crushing) ♖g8 24 ♔h2 (24 ♖e1
♗h3 25 ♗f1 ♖xg2+ 26 ♗xg2 ♕g8
27 ♔f1 ♕xg2+ 28 ♔e2 e4 wins)
♖xg2+ 25 ♔xg2 ♗xh4 26 ♖h1 (26
♖g1 ♕g5+ 27 ♔f1 ♗h3+ and 26
♔h1 ♕f6 27 ♕e1 ♕f5! are both winning for Black) ♕g5+ 27 ♔f1 ♗xf2
28 ♔xf2 ♕g3+ 29 ♔f1 ♖g8 wins for
Black.

21 ...   e4!

21...f4 22 ♗f2 is much less clear
(22...e4 is impossible with the knight
on c3).

22 g5

After 22 fxe4 ♘xg4 23 ♗xg4
fxg4 the pawn on e4 is very weak,
while 22 gxf5 ♗xf5 23 fxe4 ♘xe4
24 ♘xe4 ♗xe4 results in a weak h4
pawn and an exposed white king.

22 ...   ♘h5

Attacks c3, threatens 23...f4 and
prevents 23 f4 because of 23...♘g3
winning the exchange. 22...exf3 23
gxf6 ♕xf6 24 ♖xf3 ♕xc3 25 ♗xb6
is less promising.

23 fxe4   f4

This pawn sacrifice gives Black
the advantage, but other players
might have preferred 23...♘g3 24
♖f3 ♘xe2+ 25 ♘xe2 fxe4, when the
two active bishops give Black a positional plus.

24 ♗d2

Taking on f4 loses a piece, whilst
24 ♗xh5 fxe3 25 ♕d3 (25 ♖xf8+
♕xf8 26 ♕c2 ♕f2+ wins a piece)
♘d2 26 ♖xf8+ ♕xf8 27 ♖d1 ♕f2+
28 ♔h1 ♗h3 29 ♘xe3 ♘f1! 30 ♖xf1

♗xf1 31 ♘xf1 ♗d4 is a win for
Black.

24 ...   ♘xd2
25 ♕xd2   ♕e8

This simple continuation gives
Black an unopposed dark-squared
bishop and an outpost on g3; more
than enough for a pawn.

26 ♗f3

Not 26 ♗xh5 ♕xh5 27 ♖xf4 (or
else ...f3) ♖xf4 28 ♘xf4 ♕xh4 and
White's kingside falls apart.

26 ...   ♘g3
27 ♖fe1   ♗e5
28 ♘e2 (123)

Trying to remove the powerful
knight. If White plays passively,
Black can improve his position by
...♕g6-g7 and ...♖ae8, with ...h6 to
follow later.

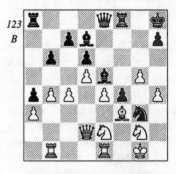

123
B

28 ...   ♘xe4!

28...♕f7 was tempting, with the
idea 29 ♘xg3 (29 ♘d4 ♕g7 30
♖bd1 is also possible, when the
well-placed knight on d4 gives
White good defensive chances) fxg3

30 ♖f1 ♕xf3!? 31 ♖xf3 ♖xf3. At first sight Black has an enormous attack, but the lines 32 ♘e3 (32 ♖f1 ♖xf1+ 33 ♔xf1 ♖f8+ 34 ♔g1 ♖f2 35 ♕d1 ♖a2 36 ♘e1 ♗h3 is genuinely good for Black) ♖f2 33 ♕d3 ♗h3 34 ♘f5 ♖g2+ 35 ♔h1 ♖h2+ 36 ♔g1 ♖f8 37 ♖d1 g2 38 ♔f2 and 32 g6 ♖af8 33 h5 are unclear.

The move played doesn't change the material balance, but it does open more lines for Black's bishops.

29 ♗xe4   f3
30 ♘ef4

After 30 ♖f1 (or 30 ♗xf3 ♖xf3, and if the a3 pawn falls Black's passed a-pawn will decide the game) ♕h5! 31 ♘ef4 ♖xf4 32 ♘xf4 ♕g4+ 33 ♘g2 (33 ♔h1 ♗xf4 34 ♕c3+ ♗e5 35 ♕xf3 ♕xh4+ mates) ♕xe4 34 ♖be1 ♕g4 Black is heading for a decisive material advantage.

30 ...   fxg2
31 ♘xg2   ♕h5

The queen probably belongs on g7, but there is no harm in this move since White cannot do anything constructive. The threat is 32...♗h3 followed by taking on g2 and h4, when White's dark squares will collapse.

32 ♕d3

Swapping rooks by 32 ♖f1 ♗h3 33 ♖xf8+ ♖xf8 34 ♖f1 ♖xf1+ 35 ♔xf1 ♕xh4 is very bad for White, who cannot even hope for the exchange of queens because in an ending the weak pawns at a3 and g5 would be fatal.

32 ...   ♗g4

Intending 33...♗f3, if appropriate, and preventing 33 ♖f1 because of 33...♗e2 34 ♖xf8+ ♖xf8 35 ♕c2 ♗d4+ 36 ♔h2 ♖f2, with a decisive attack for Black.

33 ♖e3   ♕f7

Black gains a tempo to reach g7.

34 ♕d2

Not 34 ♖f1?, when 34...♕xf1+ and 35...♗h2+ wins material.

34 ...   ♕g7

Black's dark-squared pressure and attacking propsects against White's exposed king offer very good compensation for the pawn, but it is not at all clear if Black can win against accurate defence.

35 ♖d3   ♖f7
36 ♖e1   ♖af8

White now has very few moves which do not lose at once. In fact there are only four: 37 ♕e3, 37 ♖b1, 37 ♘e3 and 37 b5 (not 37 ♖de3? ♗d4, nor 37 ♖c1? ♖f2 38 ♕xf2 ♗h2+ 39 ♔f1 ♖xf2+ 40 ♔xf2 ♕b2+). Which one White chooses makes little difference, for example after 37 ♕e3 ♗h5 White has nothing better than 38 ♕d2.

37 ♘e3   ♖f4

Time-trouble.

38 ♘g2   ♖4f7
39 ♘e3   ♗h5 *(124)*
40 ♖f1?

This blunder on the last move of the time-control loses by force. The best way to meet the threat of

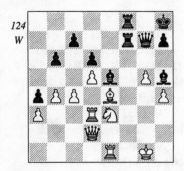

124
W

40...♗g3 is by 40 ♘g2 (40 ♕g2? ♖f4 wins for Black). The question then is whether Black can avoid the draw. The answer is that there is no forced win, but Black can step up the pressure at no risk to himself.

The position after 40 ♘g2 is very unusual; White has only three moves not to lose immediately (♕e3, ♖b1 and b5), but Black cannot easily improve his position. After 40 ♘g2 Black may try:

1) **40...♖f2** (the move I was considering during the game, but it is a mistake) 41 ♕xf2 ♖xf2 42 ♔xf2 ♗d4+ and now:

1a) **43 ♘e3 ♕e5** 44 ♗f3 (44 ♗g2 ♕f5+ is worse) ♕f4 45 ♖xd4 ♕xd4 46 ♗xh5 ♕xh4+ and Black wins.

1b) **43 ♔g3 ♗c3!** and now the lines 44 ♖b1/h1 ♕e5+ 45 ♘f4 ♕xe4, 44 ♖f1 ♗e2, 44 ♖ee3 ♗e5+ 45 ♔f2 ♗d4 and 44 ♖g1 ♗e5+ 45 ♔f2 ♗d4+ 46 ♘e3 ♕f7+ 47 ♔e1 ♕f4 lose material at once. 44 ♖c1 is more resilient, but 44...♗e5+ 45 ♔f2 (45 ♘f4 ♕d7 46 ♗f3 ♕f5) ♗d4+ 46

♔f1 (46 ♘e3 ♕e5 as in line 1a, 46 ♔e1 ♕e5, or 46 ♔g3 ♕e5+) ♕f7+ 47 ♗f3 ♗b2 wins.

1c) **43 ♔f1!** (at first sight this is a blunder, but it actually gives White the advantage) ♕f7+ 44 ♗f3 and now Black cannot equalise, for example 44...♗xf3 45 ♖xd4 ♗xd5+ 46 ♔g1 ♗xc4 47 ♖f4 and 44...♗b2 45 ♔g1! ♗xf3 (45...♕f5 46 ♗e4) 46 ♖f1 are clearly favourable for White. Perhaps the best chance is 44...♗g6 45 ♖xd4 ♕xf3+ 46 ♔g1 ♕xa3 47 ♖f4 ♕xb4 48 ♖e7, but even here Black can only hope for a draw.

2) **40...h6!** 41 b5 (White is practically in zugzwang; 41 gxh6 ♕f6! leaves White helpless against the threat of 42...♕f1+) ♖g8 42 ♖h3 ♗g4! 43 gxh6 ♕f6 44 ♖d3 ♗e2! 45 ♕xe2 ♕xh4 and Black wins. This is only a sample line, but in view of White's virtual paralysis, the extra threats introduced by playing 40...h6 (i.e. 41...♖g8 and perhaps even 41...♗f4) are hard to meet.

40 ...	**♖xf1+**
41 ♘xf1	**♖f4**
42 ♕e1	

Or 42 ♘g3 (42 ♗g2 ♖xh4, with either ...♗d4+ or ...♗f4 to come) ♖g4 43 ♕g2 ♗xg3 44 ♖xg3 ♕d4+ and wins, but the move played only lasts slightly longer.

42 ...	**♗d4+**
43 ♔g2	

43 ♔h1 ♕e5 44 ♘g3 ♗f3+ is even worse.

43 ...   ♕e5

The erroneous exchange of rooks has allowed Black's pieces to occupy commanding positions with gain of tempo. Material loss is inevitable.

44 ♘g3   ♗g4! *(125)*

Black can win the queen at any time by ...♗f2 or ...♖f2+, but it turns out that he can win the queen for two minor pieces instead of a rook and a minor piece.

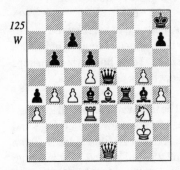

45 b5

White cannot escape the coming blow. The queen, bishop and knight cannot move, 45 ♖d2 and 45 ♔h1 both lose to 45...♗f3+ and 45 ♔h2 ♖f2+ 46 ♔h1 ♗f3+ is the same.

45 ...   ♗f2

46 ♕xf2   ♗h3+

0-1

This is the point of the preliminary ...♗g4; after 47 ♔g1 ♕a1+ White loses too much material.

We were paired against Holland in the last round of the Olympiad and the Dutch offered us a 2-2 draw before the match. This would have given England good chances of second place, but it would also have given the USA or Hungary the chance to take the silver medals with a big win. Rightly or wrongly, the English team declined the offer and the match went ahead. Things didn't go well; Murray Chandler lost to Jeroen Piket, while Short and Speelman could only draw. The final game was my own battle with Paul van der Sterren, which had reached an ending in which I was a pawn down with an inferior position. Had Van der Sterren won, then the Dutch would have finished clear second and Paul would have made a grandmaster norm. The pressure proved too much and I succeeded in swindling a draw.

This left England and Holland level on 34½ game points, so the silver medals hung on the tie-break, which was based on the sum of opponents' scores. This system leads to a slightly bizarre situation in which top places are decided by games taking place way down on the lower boards. A long wait eventually led to the good news – England had won the tie-break by 457 points to 455. This hat-trick of Olympic silver medals was by far the best set of results ever made by an English team, but sadly these exceptional performances had no effect on the British chess scene. Chess was one of the few activities in which the national team was an unqualified success, but publicity was not forthcoming. Good publicity for the national team might have led to more sponsors and increased chess activity, but in many quarters there seems to be an inbuilt resistance to the idea that people might be interested in chess.

My personal score in the Olympiad was a very successful 8½/12, consisting of five wins and seven draws.

Just at the end of the Olympiad I came down with a viral infection. In due course I recovered, but there were strange after-effects. I felt weak and curiously unable to concentrate for months afterwards. Whether this had something to do with the virus, or was perhaps the result of a seriously overloaded playing schedule in October-December 1988 I cannot say. In any case, the next few months were a nightmare; I could hardly play chess at all and I started making blunders left, right and centre (and on other parts of the board).

My final event of the year was at the chess festival in Groningen, but it was a calamity. I lost badly to Rogers and Lautier and before the last round I had only 50%. My one good effort was in this final game. White against A.Greenfeld, I sprung some home opening analysis and the position was soon ripe for a tactical execution.

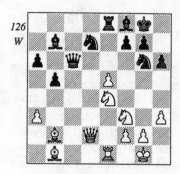

126
W

The game continued:
25 e6!
An attractive sacrifice on one of the best-defended squares in Black's position. Now both white bishops are operating against Black's king.
25 ... ♘b6
The three captures are all impossible. 25...♕xe6 loses to 26 ♘g3 and 25...♖xe6 to 26 ♘d4 ♖d6 27 ♘xc6 ♖xd2 28 ♘xd2 ♗xc6 29 ♗xg6 fxg6 30 ♖e6, followed by ♖xg6. 25...fxe6 is slightly less straightforward, but after 26 ♘g3 (26 ♘eg5 is also strong) ♘e7 (26...e5 27 ♗e4 wins) 27 ♕d3 g6 (27...♖c8 28 ♕h7+ ♔f7 29 ♘h5 is hopeless) 28 ♗a2! ♘f5 (28...♘c5 29 ♕c3) 29 ♘xf5 gxf5 30 ♕xf5 Black's position collapses.
26 ♗xg7!
A second blow on an apparently well-defended square.
26 ... ♘c4
After 26...♗xg7 (or 26...♔xg7 27 ♕d4+) 27 exf7+ ♔xf7 28 ♘d6+ White has a decisive material plus.
27 ♕xh6

There was a beautiful forced win by 27 exf7+ ♔xf7 28 ♕xh6 ♗xg7 29 ♘fg5+ ♔f8 30 ♘h7+ ♔g8 31 ♘ef6+ ♔h8 (31...♗xf6 32 ♕xg6+) 32 ♘f8+!! ♗xh6 33 ♘xg6+ ♔g7 34 ♘xe8+ ♔f7 (other moves lose the queen immediately) 35 ♖e7+ ♔g8 36 ♗e4! ♕b6 (the queen must retain control of f6) 37 ♖xb7 ♕e6 38 ♗d5!. Of course, you have to be very sure of your calculations before embarking on such a line, but most of Black's moves are absolutely forced, so it wouldn't have been too difficult. In fact, I simply overlooked the move 32 ♘f8+.

The move played also wins, though by comparison rather prosaically.

| 27 | ... | ♖xe6 |

Now 27...♗xg7 is totally out of the question, because of 28 ♘f6+ ♔f8 (28...♗xf6 29 exf7+ ♔xf7 30 ♗xg6+ ♔g8 31 ♕h7+ ♔f8 32 ♕f7 mate) 29 ♘d7+ ♔g8 (29...♔e7 30 exf7+) 30 exf7+ ♔xf7 31 ♘g5+ ♔g8 32 ♕h7 mate.

28	♗xf8	♘xf8
29	♕g5+	♖g6
30	♕f4	

Black is a pawn down with a hopelessly exposed king. The immediate threat is 31 ♘eg5.

| 30 | ... | ♘e6?! |
| 31 | ♘f6+ | 1-0 |

Since 31...♔g7 (31...♔h8 32 ♖xe6 ♕xe6 33 ♗xg6) 32 ♘h5+ ♔g8 33 ♕b8+ loses a further exchange.

1989

After the disaster at Groningen, I didn't play a tournament during the first two months of 1989. When I did return to the chessboard, at Lugano in March, the result was not a success. After a very erratic start, I had scored 5½/8, which meant that a last-round win would be sufficient for a reasonable result. I thought it was my lucky day when I was paired against Marinelli of Italy, Elo 2260,

just about the lowest-rated opponent I could have met. In the event I lost rather convincingly, leaving Marinelli with an IM norm and my Elo rating in free fall. In just a couple of months I had plummeted from 2620 to 2575, a drop sufficient to ensure that I would not be invited to any top tournaments.

The only consolation was that I won an attractive game at Lugano.

Game 23

J.Nunn – K.Thorsteins

Lugano 1989

Sicilian Scheveningen

1	e4	c5
2	♘f3	e6
3	d4	cxd4
4	♘xd4	♘f6
5	♘c3	d6
6	g4	♗e7
7	g5	♘fd7
8	h4	0-0
9	♗e3	♘c6
10	♗c4!? *(127)*	

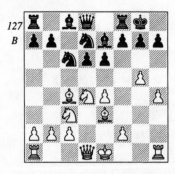

Although this was not a novelty, it would certainly be new to anyone except the most diligent worker. I am forced to admit that I have no great faith in 10 ♗c4, which has the obvious defect of exposing the bishop to attack by ...♘b6 or ...♘de5. The move does have some positive points, of course, and to appreciate these points you have to be familiar with the theory of the Velimirović Attack. This runs 1 e4 c5 2 ♘f3 ♘c6 3 d4 cxd4 4 ♘xd4 ♘f6 5 ♘c3 d6 6 ♗c4 e6 7 ♗e3 ♗e7 8 ♕e2 a6 9 0-0-0 0-0 10 ♗b3 ♕c7. Now White would like to play 11 g4, but this has the slight tactical defect that 11...♘xd4 has to be met by 12 ♖xd4, since the more natural reply 12 ♗xd4 allows 12...e5. In fact, White often plays 11 ♖hg1 to prepare g4, but this costs a tempo. In the Velimirović Attack, White can count himself lucky if he can play g4-g5 without wasting a tempo on ♖hg1 or making some other concession. If we return to the position after 10 ♗c4!? in Nunn-Thorsteins, it follows that if Black continues slowly with ...a6 and ...♕c7, White will be able to play ♕e2, 0-0-0 and ♗b3, arriving at a favourable type of Velimirović Attack.

The usual moves after 9...♘c6 are 10 ♕d2, 10 ♕e2 and 10 ♕h5, which have been played roughly equally often. All these moves have slight drawbacks; 10 ♕h5 blocks the further advance of the h-pawn, while d2 is not the most active square for the queen. e2 appears the most natural destination, but the immediate 10 ♕e2 blocks in the bishop on f1. Playing ♗c4 first solves this problem.

Thus far the positive side of the move ♗c4. There is a darker side. As already mentioned, it exposes the bishop to attack, but it also delays queenside castling by one move, increasing the risk that White's king will be caught in the centre. Moreover, it is very committal; it is far from clear that the bishop will be best posted on the b3-g8 diagonal, and alternatives preserve more flexibility. These factors make it impossible for me to recommend the move as being objectively best and I have never played it again. Nevertheless, such moves often succeed in practice; Black is confronted by a new and unfamiliar plan, and unless he is also acquainted with the Velimirović Attack it is unlikely that he will fully appreciate the poison contained in the move.

10 ...   ♘xd4

I could only find one earlier reference to 10 ♗c4; tracking this down provides a typical example of the difficulties facing chess researchers. *The Sicilian Scheveningen* by Kasparov and Nikitin gives '10...♘b6 11 ♗b3 d5 12 exd5 exd5 13 ♕e2 ♗b4 =, Ivkov-Gligorić, 1966'. Unfortunately they do not quote a tournament reference. This note goes back unchanged through all editions of Kasparov and Nikitin's book (at some stages it was called *Sicilian: ...e6 and ...d6 Systems*) right back to Nikitin's work in the late 1960s.

However, Pritchett, in *The Sicilian Scheveningen* (chess books have such original titles), gives a more precise reference to what is presumably the same game, namely the 1966 Yugoslav Championship. There is one important difference in that Pritchett claims that White played not h4, but f4. Finally, *Svetozar Gligorić: Collected Games* by Colin Leach gives the score of the whole game, supports Kasparov and Nikitin's sequence of moves, but claims that the game was played in the 1965 Yugoslav Championship.

After tracking down the bulletins of the event, I can confirm that Leach is the only 100% correct source. In any case, Gligorić's response looks perfectly reasonable and should be sufficient for equality.

10...♘de5 is another natural reply; after 11 ♗b3 ♘xd4 12 ♗xd4 ♗d7 13 ♕e2 ♘c6 White played the slightly odd 14 0-0-0 in Sznapik-Cvitan, Manila OL 1992 and after 14...♘xd4 15 ♖xd4 b5 16 ♖hd1 a5 17 ♘xb5 ♗xg5+ 18 hxg5 ♕xg5+ 19 f4 ♕xb5 Black was slightly better. Even the more natural 14 ♗e3 gives White no advantage after 14...♘a5. Compared to the Velimirović Attack, Black has gained time by missing out the moves ...a6 and ...♕c7. Alternatively, after 10...♘de5 11 ♗e2 ♘xd4 (11...d5!? and 11...♘a5 are also playable) 12 ♕xd4 ♘c6 13 ♕d2 a6 14 f4 (14 0-0-0 b5 is less accurate,

since White doesn't have a good square for the knight after ...b4) b5 15 ♗f3 the position is unclear.

The immediate exchange on d4 is not an error, but it does give White an extra option.

11 ♕xd4 *(128)*

After 11 ♗xd4, Black can play 11...♘e5 12 ♗b3 ♗d7 transposing into Sznapik-Cvitan above.

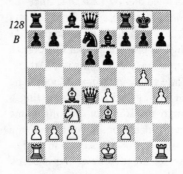

11 ...   a6?

This is definitely wrong. The analogy with the Velimirović Attack has rather broken down, because White's queen has gone to d4 instead of e2, but the basic argument is still valid. If Black plays slowly, then White achieves a favourable type of Sicilian in which his kingside attack is already well-advanced. Therefore, it would have been better to play 11...♘e5 12 ♗e2 ♘c6 13 ♕d2 a6, transposing into the previous note.

12 0-0-0

Now there is no fork on f3, so White can meet 12...♘e5 by 13

♗b3, keeping the bishop actively placed on the b3-g8 diagonal.

12	...	b5
13	♗b3	♘c5

For the moment Black cannot play ...b4, and 13...♕a5 would be met by 14 h5. White's attacking possibilities are demonstrated by the continuation if Black plays the natural 13...♖b8, namely 14 h5 ♗xg5 15 h6 gxh6 (15...♗f6 16 ♕xd6 ♗e5 17 ♕c6 is also unpleasant) 16 ♖dg1 e5 17 ♖xh6! exd4 18 ♗xg5 ♕xg5+ 19 ♖xg5+ ♔h8 20 ♘d5 with a miserable ending for Black.

In such a double-edged situation, one error is often enough to put Black in a critical condition. Although the general Sicilian structure is a familiar one, two factors make White's initiative more dangerous than normal. Firstly, White has not spent a move playing f3; similar positions arise in the English Attack, but here White has a clear extra tempo. Secondly, the bishop is much more dangerous on b3 than on f1, since a breakthrough by h5 and g6 will undermine the e6 pawn and the b3-g8 diagonal. Therefore, Black decides to exchange the dangerous bishop, but this costs him yet more time.

After the move played, White cannot continue with the immediate 14 h5 because then Black really can take on g5.

14	f4	♕a5

After 14...♖b8 15 h5 b4 16 h6 gxh6 17 gxh6 ♘xb3+ 18 axb3 ♗f6 19 e5! bxc3 (19...dxe5 20 ♕a7 ♕a5 21 ♘e4 wins) 20 exf6 Black won't survive very long. The move played also prepares ...b4 and provides a tactical defence to h5-h6. Unfortunately for Thorsteins, White can refute this defence with a queen sacrifice.

15	h5	b4
16	h6	e5 *(129)*

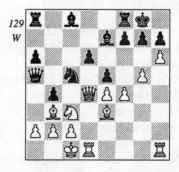

129
W

This is Black's idea. The diagonal from d4 to g7 is blocked, and if White plays 17 fxe5 dxe5 18 ♕xe5, Black can win the queen by 18...♘xb3+.

17 ♘d5!!

Completely refuting Black's idea and leading to a forced win for White.

17	...	♘xb3+

If Black captures the queen immediately, then White forces mate in nine by 17...exd4 18 ♘xe7+ ♔h8 19 hxg7+ ♔xg7 20 ♗xd4+ f6 21 gxf6+

♖xf6 22 ♖dg1+ ♗g4 23 ♖xg4+ ♔f8 24 ♖g8+ ♔xe7 25 ♖xh7+ ♖f7 26 ♖xf7.

18 axb3   ♗xg5

Equivalent to resignation, since material remains balanced while White retains a devastating attack. The main line runs 18...exd4 19 ♘xe7+ ♔h8 20 ♗xd4 f6 (20...♖g8 21 hxg7+ ♖xg7 22 ♖xh7+ forces mate) 21 g6! (threatening mate in two by 22 hxg7+ ♔xg7 23 ♖xh7) ♖g8 (21...gxh6 22 ♖xh6 and 21...hxg6 22 ♘xg6+ ♔g8 23 h7+ ♔f7 24 ♘xf8 lose immediately) 22 hxg7+ ♔xg7 (22...♖xg7 23 ♖xh7+ ♖xh7 24 ♗xf6+ ♖g7 25 ♖h1+ mates) 23 ♖xh7+ ♔f8 24 ♖f7+ ♔e8 25 ♘xg8 followed by ♘xf6+ and Black will have to give away at least another rook in order to avoid mate.

19 fxe5 *(130)*

White must reject the temptation to repeat the queen offer, since after 19 fxg5 exd4 20 ♘e7+ ♔h8 21 ♗xd4 Black can capture at g5 with check.

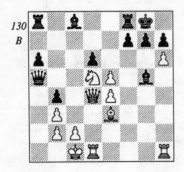

130
B

19 ...   ♗xe3+

Or 19...dxe5 20 ♕xe5! ♗xe3+ 21 ♔b1 and Black must meet the mate threat at g7, whereupon he loses his queen to ♘e7+. It is curious that White's combination has led to a complete reversal of the situation along the fifth rank; in the note to Black's 16th move, it was Black who won White's queen thanks to a discovered attack by a knight, whereas here the tables are turned.

20 ♕xe3   g6

21 ♕g5

Threatening mate in two by 22 ♘e7+.

21 ...   f6

22 ♘e7+   ♔f7

This blunder ends the game immediately, but even after 22...♔h8 23 ♘xg6+ hxg6 24 ♕xg6 ♖a7 (24...♖g8 25 ♕xf6+ ♔h7 26 ♕f7+ ♔h8 27 h7 wins, as does 24...♕c7 25 exf6) 25 ♖dg1 there is no defence to the twin threats of 26 ♕g7+ and 26 h7 followed by 27 ♕g8+ and mate.

23 e6+   1-0

The discovered attack nets Black's queen.

Further evidence of my poor form came in April when, in the final of German Cup, I lost to Christiansen in a mere 20 moves. Clearly something was seriously wrong with my play, but what to do about it was less clear. In June I was due to travel to Rotterdam for my third World Cup tournament and substandard play in such a strong event would be shown no mercy.

I decided that I had still not fully recovered from the overdose of chess at the end of 1988, and that the best cure would be a complete rest from the game. Thus, my 'preparation' for the Rotterdam World Cup was to not look at a chessboard for a month.

The playing conditions and organisation at Rotterdam were excellent, and the tournament attracted a good turn-out of spectators.

As I arrived in Holland, I was extremely nervous about how my plan would turn out, but in fact it succeeded beyond my expectations. I felt enthusiastic about playing chess for the first time in many months and I had plenty of energy for the games. Fortunately, most of my opponents challenged me in openings with which I was very familiar, and after six games I had scored five draws and one win. In the next round I faced Ljubo, who had cost me second place back at the Brussels World Cup in 1988.

Game 24

J.Nunn – L.Ljubojević

Rotterdam World Cup 1989

Sicilian Najdorf

1	e4	c5
2	♘f3	d6
3	d4	cxd4
4	♘xd4	♘f6
5	♘c3	a6
6	♗e3	e5
7	♘f3	♕c7
8	a4	h6

A slightly unusual choice; Black normally delays ...h6 until he is really forced to play it, for example 8...♗e7 9 a5 0-0 10 ♗e2 ♗e6 (10...♘c6 is another possibility) 11 0-0 h6 (now there is no choice as 11...♘bd7 12 ♘g5 is promising for

White) 12 ♘d5 ♘xd5 13 exd5 ♗f5 14 c4 with an edge for White.

9	a5	♗e6
10	♘d5 *(131)*	

One point of Black's move-order is that if White simply develops by 10 ♗e2, then 10...♕c6! awkwardly attacks the e4 pawn. After 11 ♘d2 (11 ♕d3 ♘bd7 12 ♘d2 ♖c8 13 0-0 ♗e7 14 ♖fd1 0-0 15 ♘b3, Sievers-Busch, Bundesliga 1988/9 was also fine for Black since White has lost a lot of time with his king's knight) ♘bd7 12 0-0 ♗e7 Black keeps control of d5, giving him a good game.

Therefore White has to play ♘d5 at once, but as this appears promising there is no reason to hesitate.

131
B

10 ...   ♗xd5

After 10...♘xd5 11 exd5 ♗f5 White has a choice:

1) **12 c4** ♗e7 13 ♗e2 0-0 14 0-0 transposes to the line given in the note to Black's 8th move.

2) **12 ♗b6!?** ♕e7! (12...♕xc2 13 ♕xc2 ♗xc2 14 ♖c1 ♗f5 15 ♖c7 and 12...♕c8 13 ♖a3 ♘d7 14 ♖c3 ♕b8 15 ♘h4 ♗h7 16 ♕g4 are both good for White, with 13...♗xc2 in the latter line failing to 14 ♕c1 ♗f5 15 ♖c3 with a deadly attack down the c-file) 13 c4 ♘d7 14 ♕a4 ♕f6!? and the position is unclear.

3) **12 ♗d3!** e4 (12...♗xd3 13 ♕xd3 is relatively best, although White can still claim a modest positional advantage) 13 ♘d4 exd3 (after 13...♗g6 14 ♗e2 White has a monster knight on d4) 14 ♘xf5 ♕xc2 (14...dxc2 15 ♕e2 followed by 0-0 and ♖fc1 is very bad for Black) 15

♕xc2 dxc2 16 ♖c1 with a promising ending for White.

One gains the impression that losing a further tempo by playing ...♘xd5 is too much for Black's poorly developed position.

11 exd5   ♘bd7
12 ♗e2

Although the theme of the game will be White's queenside majority against Black's kingside counterplay, White should complete his development before pushing his b- and c-pawns, for example 12 c4 ♗e7 (12...♘g4 is also possible) 13 ♗e2 ♘g4 14 ♗d2 ♕c5 15 0-0 e4 16 b4 ♕a7 17 ♘e1 ♘xf2 was unclear in the game Chandler-Hodgson, British Ch 1984.

12 ...   g6

Not 12...e4 13 ♘d4! ♘xd5 14 ♘b5 axb5 15 ♕xd5 ♖xa5 16 ♕xe4+ ♗e7 17 0-0 and after 17...♘f6 18 ♕b4 ♖xa1 19 ♗xb5+ or 17...♘c5 18 ♗xb5+! ♔f8 19 ♕c4 White has an excellent position.

13 0-0   ♗g7
14 c4   0-0?!

If Black plays 14...♘g4 White should continue 15 ♗b6 (15 ♗c1 is possible, since 15...f5 fails to 16 ♘h4, but Black can play 15...0-0 and White must waste time pushing the knight back) ♘xb6 16 axb6 ♕d7 (not 16...♕xb6 17 ♕a4+ ♔f8 18 c5 ♕xb2 19 ♖a2 and the g4 knight is lost) 17 b4 and the queenside pawns are on the move. However, after

17...0-0 it isn't easy to advance them quickly, for example 18 c5 (threat ♗xa6) e4 19 ♘d4 ♘e5 20 ♕b3!? ♘f3+ 21 ♘xf3 ♗xa1 22 ♖xa1 exf3 23 ♗xf3 is unclear. Therefore, White should prefer 18 ♘d2 ♘f6 (18...f5? 19 ♗xg4 fxg4 20 ♘e4) 19 ♕b3, meeting 19...♕d8 by 20 ♕e3, when White may prepare c4-c5 more slowly. However, this line is only slightly better for White, so 14...♘g4 is preferable to the move played.

15   ♘d2

15...♘g4 was a threat, so White takes time out to prevent it. In order to set his pawns in motion, Black needs to free his f-pawn, but unfortunately this involves wasting time by retreating the knight from f6.

15   ...   ♘h7

A very similar position arose in the game A.Ivanov-Kengis, USSR 1984, the only difference being that White had played b4 instead of 0-0. Play continued 15...e4 16 ♖c1 ♘e5 17 0-0 ♕d7 18 h3 (Black's counterplay is at a dead end; he needs to release the f-pawn, but he cannot move his f6 knight without losing the e-pawn) ♖ae8 19 ♕b3 g5 20 c5 with advantage to White.

Ljubojević prepares to generate counterplay by pushing his f-pawn.

16   b4 *(132)*   **e4**

Ljubojević's previous move freed the f-pawn, so now Black can play ...e4 at a moment when he can guarantee supporting the pawn by ...f5.

The alternative is 16...f5 and now:
1) **17 c5!?** f4 18 cxd6 ♕xd6 19 ♘e4! (suggested by Van der Vliet and Den Broeder in the tournament book; after 19 ♗c5 ♘xc5 20 ♘c4 ♕f6! 21 bxc5 e4, threatening both 22...♕xa1 and 22...f3, Black has good counterplay) ♕xb4 20 ♖a4 ♕e7 21 d6 ♕d8 (after 21...♕h4 22 ♘c5! the d-pawn is a serious menace) 22 ♕b3+ ♔h8 23 ♗d2 and in return for the pawn, White has a very dangerous initiative.

2) **17 f3** (the safest reply) f4 (17...e4 18 fxe4 ♗xa1 19 ♕xa1 is also good for White as Black has no reasonable way to prevent ♗xh6) 18 ♗f2 e4 19 ♘xe4 ♗xa1 20 ♕xa1 ♘hf6 (Black must meet the threat of c5) 21 ♗b6! ♕b8 22 ♘xf6+ ♖xf6 (22...♘xf6 23 ♗d3 is also very promising) 23 ♗d4 ♘e5 24 ♗xe5! dxe5 25 c5 and White has a large advantage. There are no open files for Black's rooks and White can steadily improve his position by ♗d3-e4 followed by d6.

17 ♖c1

Certainly not 17 ♘xe4? f5 18 ♘d2 f4 19 ♗b6 ♘xb6 20 axb6 ♕xb6 with advantage for Black.

17 ... f5

Black threatens to develop serious counterplay by the further advance of his f-pawn, so White must block it.

18 f4 exf3

Black is obliged to take on f3, or else his knights will have no decent squares whilst White can play ♘b3 followed by c5 or ♘d4-e6. The exchange of pawns has the defect of bringing White's knight back into the game.

19 ♘xf3 ♖ae8?!

After the game Ljubojević preferred 19...♖fe8 to free f8 for a knight, stopping ♘d4-e6. This may be a slight improvement, but it gives Black fewer prospects for kingside counterplay and White would have some advantage in any case.

20 ♗f2

As so often in chess, time is more important than static advantages. Given the opportunity, Black's counterplay could become dangerous; he has control of the e-file, good squares for his pieces at e5 and e4 and a kingside pawn majority. But none of this matters; he will never have the chance to make use of his assets, because White is already poised for c4-c5.

20 ... ♘g5 *(133)*

Black cannot play slowly because the queenside attack arrives too fast, for example 20...♘hf6 21 c5 ♘e4 22 c6 ♘e5 (22...♘xf2 23 cxd7 ♘xd1 24 dxe8♕ wins a piece) 23 ♗b6 ♕f7 24 cxb7 ♕xb7 25 ♖c7 ♕a8 and now both 26 ♖a7 and 26 b5 are very strong.

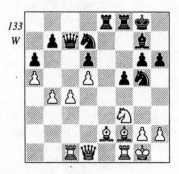

133
W

21 c5

This is better than 21 ♘d4 ♖e4!, when White will never have time to play ♘e6 because 22 h4 fails to 22...♗xd4.

The move played threatens 22 c6 followed by ♗b6. Black cannot move his d7 knight because of cxd6 followed by ♗c5, so he decides to eliminate the immediate danger at the cost of giving White a passed d-pawn.

21 ... dxc5

22 ♘xg5 hxg5

23 d6 ♕c8

The only move, since 23...♕d8 (23...♕c6 24 ♗f3) 24 bxc5 ♕xa5 25 ♗f3 wins the b7 pawn (25...♖b8 26

♗xb7 and ♕d5+), whereupon the two connected passed pawns romp home.

24 bxc5 g4

Not only preventing ♗f3, but also preparing counterplay by ...♘e5 followed by ...f4. In this case White's pawns could become blockaded and Black would seize the initiative.

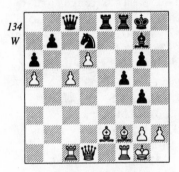

134
W

25 ♗xa6!?

At the time I was very proud of this move. It is easy to see that White can regain his piece, but the important point is that he can do so at a moment of his own choosing.

In fact, the sacrifice should win for White, but it would have been simpler to continue positionally. The key idea is to transfer the e2 bishop to the long diagonal. This could have been achieved by 25 ♗c4+ ♔h8 26 ♗d5; after 26...♘e5 (26...♘f6 27 c6 bxc6 28 ♗xc6 leaves Black in deep trouble, while otherwise White plays 27 ♕b3 attacking b7) 27 ♗d4! (if Black had played 25...♔h7, White

would have an even better line here, namely 27 ♖b1 ♘c6 28 d7!) f4 (what else?) 28 ♖b1 ♘c6 29 ♗xg7+ ♔xg7 30 ♖b6 Black's position collapses.

25 ... bxa6
26 c6 ♗e5

The best defence. White threatened 27 cxd7 ♕xd7 28 ♖c7, so Black's options were limited:

1) 26...♖e6 27 ♕b3 ♖e8 (if the knight moves, White replies 28 d7) 28 ♖fe1 ♔f7 29 ♖xe6 ♖xe6 30 cxd7 ♕xd7 31 ♖c7 wins.

2) 26...♖d8 and now White has several promising lines. Firstly, the simple **27 cxd7** ♕xd7 28 ♗b6 ♕xd6 29 ♗xd8 ♗d4+ 30 ♔h1 ♖xd8 gives White some winning chances. Alternatively, **27 ♗b6** ♘xb6 28 axb6 ♕e6 29 d7 f4 30 b7 f3 31 c7 leads to a messy position, but the main line 31...♖xd7 32 c8♕ appears very good for White. Finally, **27 ♖e1!** is simple and strong; 27...♘f6 is met by 28 ♗b6 while 27...♖fe8 28 ♖e7! wins for White.

3) **26...♖f7** 27 ♕b3! ♘e5 28 ♖fd1 ♖f8 29 d7 followed by ♗b6 and again White wins.

In these lines we can see that it often pays for White to improve his position before regaining the piece.

27 ♖e1

Threatening 28 ♕d5+, followed by 29 cxd7 and 30 ♖xe5. The lines 27...♗d6 28 ♕xd6 ♖xe1+ 29 ♖xe1 ♘f6 30 ♗d4 and 27...♔h8 28 cxd7 ♕xd7 29 ♖c7 ♕xd6 30 ♕xd6 ♗xd6

31 ♗d4+ win for White, so Black must move the bishop, while at the same time preventing ♖e7. Therefore, the reply is forced.

27 ...   ♗f6
28 ♕d5+

With this move White avoids the exchange of rooks, which would weaken his back rank. Once both queen and rook are supporting the d-pawn White will be ready to take on d7.

28 ...   ♔g7 (135)

After 28...♔h8 the line White adopts in the game is less effective, so he should play 29 ♖xe8 ♕xe8 (29...♖xe8 30 ♕f7! ♖d8 31 ♗b6 is also winning for White) 30 cxd7 (but not 30 ♖e1 ♕a8!) ♕xd7 31 ♕c6! ♖d8 (31...♕xc6 32 ♖xc6 wins after 32...♖b8 33 ♗b6, followed by d7 and ♖c8, or 32...♖d8 33 ♗b6 ♖d7 as in the main line) 32 ♗b6 ♕xc6 33 ♖xc6 ♖d7 34 ♖c8+ ♔g7 35 ♖c7 winning.

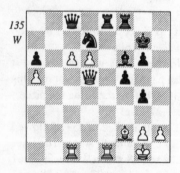

135
W

29 ♖ed1

Not 29 cxd7 ♖xe1+ 30 ♖xe1 ♕xd7 and Black has good defensive chances. The move played threatens cxd7 followed by ♖c7.

29 ...   ♖e5

Or 29...♖d8 30 cxd7 ♕xd7 31 ♖c7 ♕xc7 32 dxc7 ♖xd5 33 ♖xd5, followed by ♗b6 and ♖d8.

30 ♕d3   ♘c5

Equivalent to resignation, but even 30...♕d8 31 ♕xa6 ♖xa5 32 ♕b7! and 30...♖xa5 31 cxd7 ♕b8 (31...♕d8 32 ♖c8) 32 ♖e1 ♖a2 33 ♖e7+ ♔h8 34 ♖f7 are winning for White.

31 ♗xc5   ♕xc6
32 ♗b6

32 ♗d4? ♕xd6 only makes life harder for White.

32 ...   ♕b5

After other moves White simply plays d7.

33 ♕xb5   ♖xb5
34 d7   ♗d8
35 ♗xd8   ♖xd8
36 ♖c8   1-0

A curious game, in which Black slid downhill without making any serious errors.

This win took me up to '+2', but in round 12 I received a setback when I was convincingly beaten by Timman. After 14 rounds, the leading scores were Karpov 9½/12, Timman 8½/13, Vaganian 8/13 and myself on 7/13. Assessing the tournament situation was made harder by the fact that Spassky had withdrawn before the start of the event, while Hübner had departed after the first round. The resulting two byes meant that, at any given moment, the players had completed differing numbers of games. Karpov appeared to be in an unassailable position; not only was he a point ahead of Timman, but he had also played one game less than his principal rivals.

I had invented a scoring system for the World Cup which involved a slightly complicated mixture of points scored and tournament placing. The practical effect of this was that Karpov needed not only to win Rotterdam, but to do so with a big score, if he was to overhaul Kasparov in the final event at Skellefteå. One aim of the system was to prevent a leading player from coasting into first place with a series of draws. Karpov could have won Rotterdam quite easily, but the pressure of having to play for a win in every game eventually proved too much for him, and in round 15 he lost to Salov. Worse was to follow, because in the next round he lost a completely winning position against Ljubojević, who up to that moment had played 14 games without a win. With one round remaining, Karpov and Timman were level with 9½/14. Both were Black in the final round, Timman against Seirawan and Karpov against myself. Seirawan played one

of his worst games of the tournament to lose horribly, which put the pressure firmly on Karpov. In the end the ex-world champion went too far in his winning attempts, fell into time-trouble and allowed my passed pawn to slip through. Although the technical phase of the game lasted until move 81, the result was never in doubt.

This last round win had a dramatic effect on my tournament position. From the point of view of the World Cup (i.e. ignoring the games against 'local player' Van der Wiel), Timman scored 10/14, Karpov 9, and I shared third place with Vaganian and Ehlvest on 8 points. With three good results from my first three tournaments, I was in a promising position with just the final event still to come.

I didn't play a single game during the six weeks between Rotterdam and Skellefteå, having learnt the hard way about the dangers of an overloaded schedule. The World Cup prizes were based on the best three results out of four, so my good results prior to Skellefteå meant that I could only improve my World Cup standing by bettering the worst of my three earlier performances (from Reykjavik). Essentially, that meant making at least '+2' at Skellefteå. At 2575, I was the lowest rated player in the tournament, and the target of '+2' was obviously going to be very hard, given that the average rating was 2633.

The organisation at Skellefteå was excellent, and the tournament was one of the most enjoyable I have ever played in. There were some nice touches; the opening ceremony was one of these. I have seen a wide range of objects being used for the drawing of lots, from urinals (Brussels Ct 1991) to pigeons (Brussels World Cup 1988) to plates at the bottom of a swimming pool (Monaco 1993). At Skellefteå, the players had to choose one of 16 gold bars, each valued at $250,000 (and no, we weren't allowed to keep them). A number was attached underneath each bar. The players were warned that the bars were heavier than they looked. At this point I noticed Garry flexing his muscles, and I knew immediately that he was going to try lifting his bar with one hand. When his turn came, Garry strode purposefully to the gold bars and reached out one hand, but the bar didn't budge. He was eventually forced to use two hands, raising a few chuckles from the other players. To everyone's surprise Portisch went to the gold bars, reached out one hand, effortlessly raised the bar and announced his number.

In fact, I didn't even come close to my '+2' target. The necessity of making a big score proved too heavy a burden. When I played Sax, for example, I turned down a perfectly reasonable draw offer and over-pressed dramatically; within a dozen moves my position had completely collapsed. I also lost to Hübner after the German grandmaster unleashed a stunning opening novelty, and to Andersson who, characteristically, went straight for my little toe. After nine rounds I had a miserable 3/9. In the next round I was facing Kasparov with Black, having just lost my previous two games. It was not an appealing prospect, but by this stage it had become clear that I was not going to reach '+2', so I could just play the rest of the tournament normally, without having any particular target in mind. The result was a dramatic improvement in my play.

It is curious that I have always played best when the result didn't really matter; if there is some additional stress, such as often occurs in the last round of an Olympiad, the result has usually been disastrous. I know some people who operate the reverse way, and achieve their best results when put under pressure. I think the difference is in the level of stress which a normal game of chess engenders in an individual. Some stress is essential for a good performance, and in my case I find a normal game creates just the right level of adrenalin for optimal play. When other factors are added, the balance shifts and my play deteriorates.

Game 25

G.Kasparov – J.Nunn

Skellefteå World Cup 1989

King's Indian

1	d4	♘f6
2	c4	g6
3	♘c3	♗g7
4	e4	d6
5	♘f3	0-0
6	♗e2	e5

Playing the King's Indian against Kasparov might seem to be the height of folly, because he is the world's leading expert on the black side of the opening. Although a 'mirror' strategy involves a certain element of risk, it can be an effective recipe, particularly against a higher-rated opponent.

7	♗e3	h6

This slightly odd move has become one of my specialities. Black would like to play ...♘g4 without allowing the reply ♗g5, but it is surprising that he can afford to spend a tempo achieving this modest aim.

If White prevents ...♘g4 by 8 h3, then Black replies 8...exd4 9 ♘xd4 ♖e8, when the natural 10 f3, normal in the position without h3 and ...h6, would now severely weaken White's kingside dark squares. For a more detailed coverage of 8 h3, see Game 10 (Hort-Nunn) on page 63.

Since 8 dxe5 ♘g4 9 ♗f4 (9 exd6 ♘xe3 10 fxe3 ♗xc3+ 11 bxc3 cxd6 gives Black excellent compensation for the pawn) ♘xe5 is thought to be fine for Black, 8 0-0 has emerged as the critical test of 7...h6.

8	0-0	♘g4
9	♗c1	♘c6
10	d5	♘e7
11	♘e1	

11 h3 ♘f6 leads to a main-line King's Indian with the extra moves h3 and ...h6 added. Quite who benefits from this is not completely clear, but Korchnoi has played like this as White, so it should not be dismissed out of hand. The main alternative is 11 ♘d2, which has also acquired a considerable body of theory. I will only mention that 11 ♘d2 f5 12 ♗xg4 fxg4 13 b4 b6 14 ♘b3 g5 15 a4 ♘g6 16 a5 ♗d7 17 c5 was unclear in Kasparov-Nunn, Reykjavik World Cup 1988.

11	...	f5

According to the most recent (i.e. late-1994) theory, 11...h5 is dubious because of 12 h3 ♘h6 13 f4!, when 13...f5 14 fxe5 dxe5 15 ♘f3 ♘f7 16 c5 f4 17 ♗c4 ♔h8 18 b4 ♘g8 19 d6!

was good for White in Mozetić-
Ligterink, Tilburg 1993.

12 ♗xg4

12 f3 ♘f6 13 ♗e3 leads to a normal King's Indian position in which
Black's knight is on f6 instead of d7,
which should be about half a tempo
better for Black.

12 ...   fxg4 *(136)*

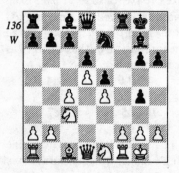

The kingside pawn structure is
unusual. The exchange on g4 has
removed Black's characteristic pressure against e4, and White's unassailable centre gives him extra
freedom to manoeuvre. On the other
hand, White has been forced to part
with his useful light-squared bishop,
and the advanced pawn on g4 might
form part of a dangerous kingside attack if Black's other pieces can find
ways to join in. From Black's point
of view, the danger is that he is taking a big strategic risk. By abandoning the pressure against e4, Black
hands the long-term chances to
White. If his attack on the kingside

fails to materialise, then White will
be able to consolidate and eventually
win on the queenside. The kingside
attack involves moves like ...g5,
...♘g6-f4 and ...♕e8 followed by
...♕g6 or ...♕h5. Black's problem is
that it is hard to take his attack further; there are no obvious pawn
breaks with which he can soften up
the solid pawn phalanx in front of
White's king. In most cases, he will
have to rely on a sacrifice to open up
avenues of attack.

Despite the risk, I believe that this
system is not so bad for Black. In
some situations Black can make use
of White's own queenside attack. If
White pushes his pawns without
adequate piece support, for example
by an early b4 and c5, then his light
squares will be weakened and
Black's c8 bishop may become active via ...b6 followed by ...♗a6.

One interesting plan for White is
to play f3 in order to exchange off
the potentially menacing g4 pawn.
In this case White will play for exchanges along the f-file; his long-
term objective is to liquidate all
Black's pieces except for the g7
bishop. Having exchanged off his
own 'bad' bishop on g4, he will be
very happy to reach a pure minor-
piece ending.

13 ♘c2

Kasparov's novelty. The main alternative is 13 ♗e3 (in Ivanchuk-
Uhlmann, Debrecen 1988 White

gained some advantage after 13 ♘d3
c5 14 ♖b1 a5 15 a3 ♔h7 16 b4, but I
prefer 13...g5, with a likely transposition to the lines given below) and
now:

1) **13...b6** 14 ♘d3 g5 15 b4 (15
f3 gxf3 16 ♖xf3 a6 17 ♖xf8+ ♕xf8
18 ♕d2 ♘g6 19 b4 ♘f4 20 c5 also
gave White some advantage in Be-
lov-Babula, Trebič 1990) ♘g6 16 a4
♘f4 17 a5 ♖b8 18 ♘b5 ♗a6 19
axb6! ♗xb5 20 ♖xa7 ♗xc4 21 bxc7
♕f6 22 cxb8♕ ♖xb8 23 ♗xf4 exf4
and Black doesn't have enough compensation, Korchnoi-Nunn, Wijk aan
Zee 1990.

2) **13...g5** 14 c5 ♘g6 15 ♖c1 (15
♘d3 ♘f4 16 ♖c1 ♕e8 17 a4 a6 18
b4 ♕g6 19 ♘b2 with an edge for
White, Clara-Lau, Bundesliga 1990)
♕e8 16 cxd6 cxd6 17 ♕b3 ♘f4 18
♔h1 ♕g6 was unclear in Marić-
Peng Zhaoqin, Shanghai wom Ct
1992.

The point of ♗e3 is that White
can start his queenside play immediately, waiting until later before deciding whether the knight on e1 is
best moved to c2 or d3, or perhaps
left just where it is.

13   ...   g5

Black has to decide how he is going to meet the threat to his g4 pawn
after White's intended ♘e3. The
most obvious way is to play ...h5, but
the pawn structure g6-h5-g4 is in-
flexible and affords no chance to
bring the e7 knight to a good square.

I therefore decided on a provocative
method of defending g4.

14   ♘e3

14 ♘e2 (far too slow) ♕e8 15
♘g3 ♕g6 (pinning White down to
the defence of e4, and threatening
...h5-h4) 16 ♗e3 h5 17 ♖e1 h4 18
♘f1 h3 19 ♘g3 hxg2 20 ♕d2 ♖f4!
is clearly better for Black, Gross-
Nunn, Bundesliga 1989, played a
couple of months after the Kasparov
game. Black's 20...♖f4 is a direct
echo of the current game.

14   ...   ♖f4!? *(137)*

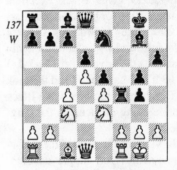

Black is committed since 14...h5
15 h3! (even 15 f3 is slightly better
for White) gxh3 16 ♕xh5 hxg2 17
♔xg2 ♖f6 (17...♕e8 18 ♕xe8 ♖xe8
19 ♘b5) 18 ♘g4 ♗xg4 19 ♕xg4 is
excellent for White, and there is no
other reasonable way to defend the
pawn on g4.

When one of Kasparov's opponents plays a totally unexpected
move, he reacts either by curling
his lip at the move, or by peering

incredulously at the audience, as if to say 'Can you believe what he's just played?'. 14...♖f4 was greeted with a force ten lip-curl from 'Gazza', but the World Champion then rather spoilt the effect by thinking hard for twenty minutes.

15   ♗d2 *(138)*

Of course, Black's last move does look odd because the rook is very exposed to attack on f4, but there is no direct way White can exploit it, for example: **15 ♘f5?** ♘xf5 16 ♗xf4 exf4 (16...gxf4 is also not bad) 17 exf5 ♗xf5 gives Black excellent compensation for his small sacrifice; **15 ♘e2?** ♖xe4 16 ♕d3 ♖f4 17 ♘xf4 exf4 followed by ...♗f5 and again Black has the advantage; **15 g3 ♖f3** 16 h3 h5 17 hxg4 hxg4 and the rook on f3 is hard to remove, while Black has attacking chances on the kingside.

In view of the above lines, Kasparov settles for simple development. There are two other playable lines; these also make no attempt to exploit the rook's position directly . The first is **15 b4!?**. The reason Kasparov preferred the preparatory 15 ♗d2 is that 15 b4 may be met by 15...a5, but after 16 bxa5 ♖xa5 17 ♗d2 the time gained by White may be more important than the damage to his queenside pawn structure.

The most dangerous alternative to the move played is **15 f3**, which simply ignores the rook on f4 for the

moment. The critical position arises after 15...gxf3 16 ♖xf3 (not 16 g3?! g4! 17 gxf4 exf4 18 ♘f5 ♘xf5 19 exf5 ♗e5! and after 20 ♕c2 ♕f8, for example, Black takes the f5 pawn, gaining three pawns and a very strong attack for the rook) ♕f8 (in Li-Rabelo, Havana 1991, Black continued 16...g4!? 17 ♖f1 ♗d7 18 a4 ♕e8 19 g3 ♖xf1+ 20 ♘xf1 ♕g6 21 ♕b3 b6 22 a5 ♖f8 with an unclear position; accepting the pawn by 17 ♖xf4 exf4 18 ♘xg4 is more critical, although Black has some compensation after 18...♘g6 followed by ...♕g5 or ...♕h4) 17 ♘b5 (White's aim was to play g3, forcing Black to exchange rooks, but Black's ...♕f8 has prevented this) ♕d8. When I originally annotated this game, I wrote here that 'White has nothing better than to return to c3'. I continued to believe this for five years, until the game Mephisto Berlin-Nunn, AEGON Man-Machine Tournament 1994. The Mephisto came up with a strong innovation: 18 g3!. After 18...♖xe4 19 ♕d3, Black loses the exchange for inadequate compensation, for example 19...♖d4 20 ♘xd4 exd4 21 ♘c2 c5 22 dxc6 ♘xc6 23 ♕e4 or 19...♖g4 20 ♘xg4 ♗xg4 21 ♖f2 ♗h5 22 ♘c3. Thus I had no choice but to play 18...♖xf3 19 ♕xf3 c6 20 ♘c3 ♕b6. Curiously, I had seen this position before in the game Gschnitzer-Nunn, Bundesliga 1990, but on that occasion the move-order had been 18 ♘c3 c6 19 g3 ♖xf3 20 ♕xf3 ♕b6. My choice of 18...c6 rather than 18...♕f8 was based on my reluctance to draw with a lower-rated opponent. At the time I felt that 18...c6 was dubious, and that Black should be satisfied with a draw. The Mephisto's innovation proves that Black cannot force a draw in any case. The position after 20...♕b6 illustrates the dangers of the line. White has the better long-term prospects, because all his minor pieces are potentially effective, while Black will have permanent problems with his passive g7 bishop. Black's hopes are pinned on his light-squared bishop, which has no enemy counterpart. If the position becomes open, then this bishop would suddenly be very active, especially as White has weakened his kingside by playing g3. White has to solve the immediate problem of completing his development, and Gschnitzer did this is a very effective way: **21 ♔g2 ♗d7 22 ♕e2 ♖f8 23 ♘ed1!**, followed by ♗e3 and ♘f2, when the a1 rook was free to enter the game. This plan solves the development problem, while the knight on f2 covers the sensitive light squares on the kingside. The Mephisto demonstrated that computers still have trouble formulating plans; it played **21 ♕d1?**, threatening 22 dxc6, but after the obvious reply 21...♕d4 Black was already slightly better. I

won rather quickly against the Mephisto, but in the Gschnitzer game I only notched up the full point after a grotesque swindle.

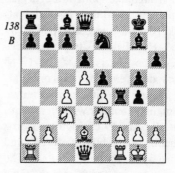

138
B

15 ... ♗d7

Black must bring his remaining pieces into play.

16 b4

With the intention of playing c5, ♖c1 and ♕c2; a timely exchange on d6 will open the door to penetration at c7.

16 ... ♕f8?!

Black's idea is to triple on the f-file, but it turns out that this plan isn't very effective because the eventual capture on f2 doesn't create any serious threats. Another doubtful idea is 16...♕e8 17 c5 ♕g6, when 18 ♘c4! ♖xe4 19 ♘xe4 ♕xe4 20 cxd6 ♘xd5 21 ♕b3 is good for White after 21...c6 22 ♖ae1 ♕f5 23 b5. The best move is 16...♘g6!, aiming for a direct kingside attack, as in Portisch-Nunn (Game 26 on page 192).

17 ♕c2?!

Nikitin analysed this game in *New in Chess*. His comments were generally quite interesting. He criticises this move on the grounds that it deviates from the obvious strategic plan of playing c5, aiming instead to attack Black's queenside pawns by ♘b5. He advocates two alternative lines. The first is 17 ♕e2 ♕f7 18 ♖ac1, defending the pawn on f2, after which 'White can continue mounting his attack without a hitch'. But 18...♖f8 19 c5 ♘g6 leads to a situation in which White doesn't find it so easy to continue his attack. The reason is that the c3 knight must move in order to allow the rook to reach c7, but the knight is needed where it is to defend the e4 pawn. The reason Garry put his queen on c2 was precisely in order to free the c3 knight. Nikitin's other idea is 17 ♖c1 ♘g6 18 a4, intending c5, but so far as I can see it is even better to play 18 c5! immediately, because 18...dxc5 19 bxc5 ♕xc5 is met by 20 ♘e2, and here winning the exchange is effective because Black's pawns on g4 and c7 are very weak. Therefore White has the advantage. In this line White does not commit his queen until he is sure of the best square.

After the move played, it is no longer possible to demonstrate an advantage for White.

17 ...   ♕f7 *(139)*

17...♕f6 is more natural, because then Black can always meet ♘b5 by

...c6. Unfortunately after 17...♕f6 18 c5 ♖f8 19 ♘ed1 White can gradually improve his position, for example by ♖c1 and ♘e2, and take the trapped rook on f4 at an appropriate moment.

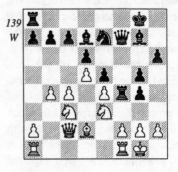

139
W

18 ♖ac1   ♖f8
19 ♘b5!?

Now 19 ♘ed1 has less impact, since Black can reply 19...♖f6, followed by ...♘g6 and either ...♘h4 or ...♘f4. Garry's move appears risky, because it involves abandoning the pawn on f2, but Black's tripled major pieces are much less dangerous than they appear. In the meantime, White captures the pawn on c7, which is the cornerstone of Black's position. Moreover, White's knight gains access to e6, always a sensitive square in the King's Indian.

19 ...   ♖xf2

There is no choice, because after 19...♗xb5 20 cxb5 ♖xf2 21 ♕xc7 ♘c8 (21...♘g6 22 ♕xd6) 22 ♕xf7+ ♖2xf7 23 ♖xf7 ♔xf7 24 ♖c7+ the endgame is completely hopeless for Black.

20 ♘xc7

Now Black is committed, because the disappearance of the vital c7 pawn leaves him positionally lost. Not only is e6 weak, but in an ending the advance c5-c6 will produce a queen very quickly. Therefore he must go for tactics.

20 ... ♕f4! *(140)*

The only way to create a threat (21...g3), but not surprisingly the line-up with the d2 bishop creates some tactical ideas.

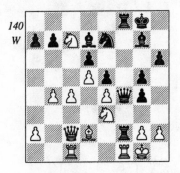

140
W

21 ♘f5

Although this is tempting, White gains no advantage from the complications. The alternative line is 21 ♘e6 ♗xe6 22 dxe6 and now:

1) **22...♘c6** 23 ♕d3 ♘d4 (for 23...g3!, see line 3b) 24 e7! ♘e2+ 25 ♕xe2 ♖xe2 26 exf8♕+ ♗xf8 27 ♖xf4 gxf4 28 ♘f1 ♖xe4 29 ♔f2 (Nikitin), and Black has insufficient compensation for the piece.

2) **22...♕f6** 23 ♖xf2 ♕xf2+ 24 ♔h1 ♕f6 (after 24...g3 25 ♕d3 gxh2 26 ♖f1 ♕h4 27 ♘f5! White's king is safe, and the advanced e-pawn is the dominant feature of the position) 25 ♕a4 (25 ♘xg4? ♕f1+) ♕xe6 (25...a6 26 ♕d7 ♕f2 27 ♕xd6 ♘c6 – Nikitin – and now 28 ♘f5! is crushing) 26 ♕xa7 ♕d7 (so far Nikitin; 26...♖f2 27 ♖d1 doesn't help Black) 27 ♘d5 (Nikitin's 27 ♔g1 is perhaps less clear after 27...♖f4) and the bishop on g7 gives White a clear positional advantage.

3) **22...g3** (the most obvious move) 23 ♕d3 (White abandons the h-pawn to its fate in order to further his own initiative) and now:

3a) **23...gxh2+?** 24 ♔h1 (threatening both 25 ♖xf2 ♕xf2 26 ♖f1 and 25 ♕xd6) ♘c6 (24...♖xf1+ 25 ♖xf1 ♕h4 26 ♘f5 transposes to line 2 above, while 24...♕f6 25 ♕xd6 ♘c6 26 ♘f5! ♖xf1+ 27 ♖xf1 ♖d8 28 ♘xh6+! wins after 28...♕xh6 29 ♕xd8+! ♘xd8 30 e7 or 28...♗xh6 29 ♖xf6 ♖xd6 30 e7 – Nikitin) 25 ♖xf2 ♕xf2 26 ♘f5, with advantage for White.

3b) **23...♘c6!** (it is more important to bring up the reserves than to grab the unimportant h-pawn) 24 ♖xf2 (not 24 ♕xd6? ♘d4 and White's position collapses; the capture on f2 looks ridiculous, but Black cannot maintain his newly acquired passed pawn – in any case White has little else) gxf2+ (after 24...♕xf2+

25 ♔h1 ♖f3! 26 ♖f1 ♕xf1+ 27 ♕xf1 ♖xf1+ 28 ♘xf1 gxh2 29 ♘e3 ♘d4 30 ♘f5 ♘xe6 31 ♘xd6 White will win back the pawn on h2 with an advantage, thanks to his superior bishop) 25 ♔h1 ♘xb4! (25...♕f6 26 ♖f1 ♕xe6 27 ♘f5 picks up the f2 pawn, again with a positional plus for White) 26 ♗xb4 ♕xe3 27 ♕xe3 f1♕+ 28 ♕g1 (28 ♖xf1 ♖xf1+ 29 ♕g1 ♖xg1+ 30 ♔xg1 ♗f8, followed by ...♔g7-f6, also leads to a draw) ♕xg1+ 29 ♔xg1 ♖e8 30 ♗xd6 ♖xe6 31 ♖d1 ♗f8 32 c5 b6 results in a draw.

21 ...   ♗xf5

Or:

1) 21...♖xd2? 22 ♖xf4 ♖xc2 23 ♘xe7+ ♔h7 24 ♖xf8 ♖xc1+ 25 ♖f1 ♖xc4 (or 25...♖xf1+ 26 ♔xf1 and White is effectively a pawn up because the two g-pawns are no better than one) 26 ♘e6 ♖xe4 (there is nothing better) 27 ♖f7 ♗xe6 28 dxe6 followed by ♘f5 and White wins.

2) 21...♘xf5 (this is just as good as the move played) 22 ♖xf2 (not 22 ♗xf4 ♖xc2 23 ♖xc2 ♘d4) ♕xf2+ 23 ♔xf2 ♘d4+ 24 ♔e3 ♘xc2+ 25 ♖xc2 ♖c8 26 ♘e6 ♗xe6 27 dxe6 ♔f8 and Black will soon win the e-pawn, for example 28 ♔f2 ♗f6! (not 28...♔e7 29 ♔g3 ♔xe6 30 ♔xg4, and the threat of penetration by White's king gives him a perceptible advantage) 29 ♔g3 h5, followed by ...♔e7. However, Black's sickly

bishop reduces his winning chances to near zero.

22 ♖xf2

Not 22 ♗xf4? ♖xc2 23 ♖xc2 ♗xe4 24 ♖e2 ♗d3 and wins.

22 ...   ♕xf2+
23 ♔xf2   ♗xe4+
24 ♔e2   ♗xc2
25 ♖xc2 (141)

Even though Black is a pawn up, he is fighting for the draw because of his g7 bishop and the threat posed by c5.

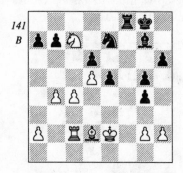

141
B

25 ...   ♖c8?

Black misses a chance to make use of his otherwise valueless front g-pawn. He should have played 25...g3! 26 hxg3 ♘f5 (he could even play his moves in the other order, 25...♘f5 26 ♘e6 g3, whereupon White has nothing better than 27 hxg3), when White cannot improve over 27 ♘e6 ♘xg3+ 28 ♔e3 (28 ♔d1 ♖f1+ 29 ♗e1 e4! is good for Black) ♘f1+ (28...♖f1? 29 c5 is too risky) 29 ♔e2 with a draw.

26 c5? *(142)*

Lured by a tempting combination, White throws away his advantage. 26 ♘b5! would have left Black in difficulties, e.g. 26...♘f5 (26...♘xd5 27 ♘xd6 is also very good for White after 27...♖c7 28 ♘b5 and 29 ♘xa7, or 27...♖c6 28 ♘xb7 ♘xb4 29 ♗xb4 ♖b6 30 c5 when the passed c-pawn becomes very dangerous) 27 ♔d3 a6 28 ♘c3 ♘d4 29 ♖c1 (intending ♘e4, with c5 to follow) b5 30 cxb5 ♘xb5 31 ♘e4 and White's queenside majority is very dangerous. The wretched bishop on g7 plays absolutely no part in the game, while Black's extra g-pawn contributes precisely nothing.

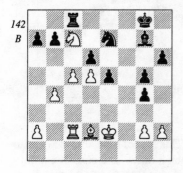

26 ...   e4!

I had completely overlooked White's last move, but after regaining my composure I realised that the move carries no major threat, and so I could afford to spend a tempo improving my own position. There are various reasonable alternatives, but

26...e4 is certainly the most thematic. Black's problems stem from the King's Indian player's perennial affliction, the g7 bishop hemmed in by a pawn on e5. The e-pawn's advance immediately transforms this bishop into the best minor piece on the board. It is true that the e-pawn is weakened by the push to e4, and may eventually be lost, but in this position piece activity is the primary consideration. The tactical justification is that White can do nothing while his knight is *en prise*, and 27 cxd6 ♘f5 (not 27...♘xd5? 28 ♘xd5 ♖xc2 29 d7) 28 ♗e3 (28 d7 ♖d8 is also bad for White) ♘xd6 29 ♗xa7 ♘b5 30 ♗b6 ♗e5 (Nikitin) wins for Black, so there is nothing better for White than to retreat his knight.

Black may also try:

1) **26...♖xc7** 27 cxd6 ♖d7 (certainly not 27...♖xc2? 28 d7 and White wins after 28...♖c8 29 d6 or 28...♘c6 29 dxc6 ♗f6 30 cxb7) 28 dxe7 ♖xe7 (28...♔f7 29 d6! ♖xd6 30 ♖c7 ♗f6 31 b5 is somewhat better for White) 29 ♔e3 e4! 30 ♖c8+ (30 ♖c4 is just a draw) ♔f7 31 ♖d8 ♗e5! 32 d6 (32 g3 ♗c7) ♖e6 and Black forces a draw.

2) **26...dxc5** 27 ♖xc5 ♖d8, with ...b6 to follow, is at least equal for Black.

27 ♘b5   dxc5
28 d6?

After this White is in danger of losing. 28 ♘d6 was correct, and after

28...♖d8 (28...♖c7 29 ♘xe4 ♘xd5 30 ♖xc5 should also be a draw) 29 ♘xb7 ♖xd5 30 ♖xc5 ♖d7 31 ♘a5 ♗d4 Black's extra pawn has little significance.

28   ...   ♘c6
29   ♖xc5 (143)
Not 29 bxc5? a6.

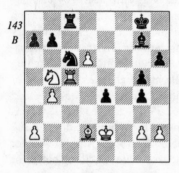

143
B

29   ...   ♖d8
During the game, I rejected 29...a6 because of 30 ♘a7 ♘xa7?? 31 ♖xc8+ ♘xc8 32 d7 and White wins. In fact, 29...a6 would have given Black good winning chances after 30 ♘a7 ♘d4+! 31 ♔e3 ♖d8 32 ♖c8 (32 ♔xe4 ♖xd6 is also unpleasant for White, because the knight on a7 is temporarily out of play) ♘f5+ 33 ♔e2 ♗f6! and White's d-pawn is in danger of being rounded up the black king. The move played is very tempting, but although it eventually leads to the d-pawn's capture, the time spent allows White's pieces to become very active.

30   ♖d5

With this move Kasparov optimistically offered a draw, which I turned down. Black has real winning chances, but accurate play is required.

30   ...   a6
Knocking away one of the passed pawn's props.

31   ♘c7   ♗e5
32   b5
Forced, because otherwise the d-pawn falls.

32   ...   axb5
33   ♘xb5 (144)

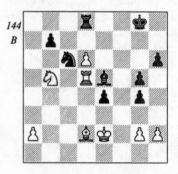

144
B

33   ...   ♔f7?
This loss of time allows White to reach a draw. The correct continuation was 33...♗xh2! 34 ♔e3 ♖e8! 35 d7 ♗f4+ 36 ♔e2 ♖d8. Now Nikitin continues with **37 ♘c3** and 'the balance is preserved', but Black may reply 37...♘e7 38 ♖d4 ♘f5 39 ♖d5 ♘g3+ 40 ♔e1 e3 41 ♗c1 ♔f7 42 ♘a4 (in order to meet 42...♔e6 by 43 ♖d4, when Black cannot take on d7; after other moves White loses his

d-pawn) ♘e4 (heading for f6) 43
♖d3 (43 ♘b6? ♗g3+ wins the rook)
♔e6 44 ♖d4 ♘f6 45 ♘c5+ ♔f5, followed by ...b6, and Black will be two
pawns up for very little. 37 ♘d4 is a
better chance, and now:

1) 37...♘xd4+ 38 ♖xd4 ♗xd2 39
♔xd2 ♔f7 40 ♔e3 ♔e6 41 ♖xe4+
♔xd7 42 ♖xg4, but the extra pawn is
probably not enough to win.

2) 37...♗xd2 38 ♘xc6 bxc6 39
♖xd2 ♔f7 40 ♖d6 h5 41 ♔e3 and
again White has survived the worst.

3) 37...♘b8! 38 ♘e6! ♖xd7 39
♖xd7 ♘xd7 40 ♘xf4 gxf4 41 ♗xf4
♔g7 42 ♔e3 ♘f6 43 ♗e5 ♔g6 44
♔f4 with a tricky ending. Black is
two pawns up, but he will only be
able to make progress by giving up
his e-pawn. One possible line runs
44...h5 45 g3 (or else ...h4-h3) b5 46
♗d4 e3! 47 ♔xe3 ♔f5 48 ♗a7 (to
meet 48...♘e4 by 49 ♗b8) ♘d5+,
with ideas of ...♘b4 or ...♔e4.

Black has good winning chances
in line 3, whereas the move played
allows a relatively simple draw.

34 ♔e3

True to his style, Kasparov offers
his h-pawn in order to gain time.
White could also have drawn by
playing in a more mundane fashion:
34 g3 ♔e6 35 ♘c7+ ♔d7 36 ♔e3
♗xd6 37 ♘b5 ♔e6 38 ♖xd6+ ♖xd6
39 ♘xd6 ♔xd6 40 ♔xe4 ♔e6 41
♗c3. This ending cannot be won;
White plays ♗g7 to force ...h5, then
returns his bishop to d2, attacking

the weak g5 pawn, when Black cannot make progress.

34 ...   ♗xh2

Too late, because White can capture the important e-pawn immediately.

35 ♔xe4   ♔e6
36 ♗c3!

This is the key idea. Black must
be induced to take the d6 pawn,
when the white king can move up to
f5. Black has nothing better than the
immediate capture.

36 ...   ♗xd6
37 ♖xd6+   ♖xd6
38 ♘xd6   ♔xd6
39 ♔f5

Black has no winning chances because his cluster of kingside pawns
is too weak. In comparison with line
3 in the note to Black's 33rd move,
here Black is much worse off because of White's very active king.

39 ...   g3

The knight dreams of reaching e3
or f4. For example, 40 ♔g6? ♔e6 41
♔xh6 ♔f5, intending ...♘e7-d5-f4,
would not be a good idea.

40 ♗g7

Although this leads to a draw, 40
♗e1 would have been considerably
simpler. White could simply remove
the pawn on g3, while maintaining
his excellent king position.

40 ...   ♘e7+ (145)
41 ♔g4!

The right choice. After 41 ♔f6?
♘d5+, the knight homes in on g2.

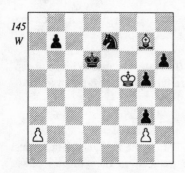

145
W

41 ...   ♘g8

Black has saved the pawn on h6, but at the cost of playing his knight to one of the worst squares on the board.

42 ♔f5

After 42 ♔xg3? ♔e6, followed by ...h5 and ...♘f6, Black would consolidate one extra pawn.

42 ...   ♘e7+

½-½

Lengthy thought convinced me that the position offered no chance to win. After 43 ♔g4 ♘g8 44 ♔f5

Black may try a range of plans, but none of them lead anywhere:

1) **44...♔e7** 45 ♗e5 ♔f7 46 ♗xg3 ♘e7+, but after 47 ♔e5 h5 48 ♗f2 h4 49 a4 White draws easily. Black cannot play 49...g4 because of 50 ♔f4 g3 51 ♗c5 ♘g6+ 52 ♔g4 with total paralysis, while there is now a danger that White's king will head towards the b7 pawn, securing a passed a-pawn against which Black's knight will be ineffective.

2) **44...♔d5** 45 ♗f8 ♔d4 46 ♗d6! and Black cannot hope to win, since his g3 pawn is doomed and his knight is trapped.

3) **44...b5** 45 a3 does not significantly alter the situation.

In the following round I scraped a draw against Salov, and then I had to face Lajos Portisch. Obviously both sides had done their homework on the Kasparov game, and were eager to demonstrate the fruits of their research.

Game 26

L.Portisch – J.Nunn

Skellefteå World Cup 1989

King's Indian

1	d4	♘f6		6	♗e2	e5
2	♘f3	g6		7	♗e3	h6
3	c4	♗g7		8	0-0	♘g4
4	♘c3	0-0		9	♗c1	♘c6
5	e4	d6		10	d5	♘e7

11	♘e1	f5
12	♗xg4	fxg4
13	♘c2	g5
14	♘e3	♖f4
15	♗d2	♗d7
16	b4	♘g6 *(146)*

Black gets his improvement in first! There was a free day immediately before the Portisch game, and some brief analysis had convinced me that this direct plan is better than 16...♕f8. Since I expected Portisch to play a completely different variation, I had spent most of the free day preparing for other lines and had only looked at the general ideas in the position, rather than any specific variations. The plan is simple and rather crude; Black will play ...♘h4 and ...♕e8-h5, when White will be hard pressed to stop a sacrificial breakthrough by ...♘f3+ or ...♖f3-h3. The risk is obvious; if Black is unable to break through, his pieces will be left completely stranded on the kingside and White's queenside attack will cruise home effortlessly.

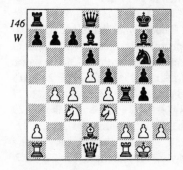

17 ♖c1

The reason I rejected 16...♘g6 against Kasparov was that White has two different ways to win the exchange, and I wasn't sure about Black's compensation. However, by the time this game was played I had concluded that Black has sufficient counterchances in these lines:

1) 17 ♘f5 ♖xf5 18 exf5 ♗xf5 19 ♖e1 (19 g3 allows 19...e4 followed by ...♘e5, while 19 f3 ♕d7 20 fxg4 ♗d3! 21 ♖f2 e4!, with ...♘e5 to come, gives Black a strong initiative for the exchange – note that 19 f3 ♗d3? fails to 20 ♗xg5!) ♘f4 20 ♘e4 ♕e8 (intending ...♕g6) 21 ♘g3 ♗d7 22 ♕c2 ♕f7, intending ...♖f8 followed by ...h5-h4, and Black has fair attacking chances for his relatively small sacrifice.

2) 17 ♘e2 is more dangerous. The obvious sacrifice is 17...♖xe4 18 ♕c2 ♘f4 19 ♕xe4 ♘xe2+ 20 ♔h1, but now 20...♘f4 loses the g-pawn after 21 g3, so Black must play 20...♘d4, when 21 ♘xg4? fails to 21...♗f5. Although White's queen is well placed on e4, Black can eventually drive it away by bringing his queen or rook to f4, while in a position with no open files White's material advantage is not so important. A plausible continuation is 21 ♗c3 ♕f8 22 ♖ae1 (22 ♗xd4 exd4 23 ♘xg4? fails to 23...♖e8 24 ♕f3 ♕xf3 25 gxf3 h5) ♕f4 with an unclear position.

17 ...   ♘h4 *(147)*

Black would prefer to play 17...♛e8, so as to cut out the line of the next note, but I was worried about the reply 18 f3 gxf3 19 g3 f2+ 20 ♖xf2 ♖xf2 21 ♚xf2 ♛f7+ 22 ♛f3 ♛e7 23 ♚g1 ♖f8 24 ♛h5. After a subsequent ♖f1, exchanging the second pair of rooks, White can aim for an ending in which Black suffers from a permanently bad bishop on g7. Moreover, the f5 square is weak and a white knight might land there quite soon.

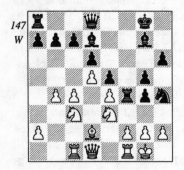

147
W

18 ♚h1?

The critical phase of this game lasts just four moves, after which White is lost. One element of risk in Black's plan is that White can win a piece at any moment by playing f3 gxf3 g3, and then it is a question of whether Black can gain enough compensation for his inevitable loss of material. Portisch decides to tuck his king away before grabbing the piece, but it turns out that the king is

no better placed on h1 than on g1, while the extra tempo is very beneficial for Black. The critical test is the immediate 18 f3! gxf3 19 g3 and now:

1) **19...g4** (19...f2+ immediately is bad, because after 20 ♚h1 the square e2 is clear for the c3 knight, and the capture of the rook is more favourable for White) 20 gxh4! (not 20 gxf4? exf4 21 ♘f5 ♗xf5 22 exf5 ♗d4+ 23 ♚h1 g3 24 hxg3 fxg3 25 ♖xf3 ♘xf3 26 ♛xf3 ♛h4+ 27 ♚g2 ♛h2+ 28 ♚f1 ♛xd2 29 ♛xg3+ ♚h8 30 ♘e2 ♖g8 and Black has a decisive attack) ♛xh4 and now:

1a) **21 ♗e1 ♛g5 22 ♗g3 ♖f7!** (after 22...♖xe4 23 ♘xe4 ♛xe3+ 24 ♘f2 Black has some compensation for the rook, but I doubt if it is really enough) offers good long-term compensation for the piece since Black can aim for ...h5-h4. It is hard for White to blockade the pawns because 23 ♛e1, for example, simply encourages Black to play 23...♗f6, opening up the possibility of a rook switch to g7 or h7.

1b) **21 ♛e1 ♛h5** (not 21...♛f6 22 ♘ed1!, when more material disappears) is critical. White cannot force matters with **22 ♘f5**, because 22...♗xf5 23 ♗xf4 exf4 24 exf5 ♗d4+ 25 ♚h1 g3 26 ♖c2 g2+ 27 ♖xg2+ fxg2+ 28 ♚xg2 ♛g4+ 29 ♚h1 f3 is winning for Black. Instead, White should play more slowly, for example by **22 ♛f2**.

Compared to line 1a, Black will have greater difficulty pushing his h-pawn, so he should adopt a plan based on piece play instead. The most accurate move is 22...♔h8, preventing the natural reply 23 ♘f5 because of 23...♗xf5 24 ♗xf4 exf4 25 exf5 g3 26 hxg3 fxg3 27 ♕xg3 (27 ♕d2 ♖e8!, intending 28...♖e2, is no better) ♗d4+, followed by 28...♖g8. After other moves, Black intends ...♗f6, ...♖g8 and ...♗h4, with an eventual breakthrough by ...g3. Again Black has sufficient compensation for the piece.

2) **19...♕f6** (a playable alternative to 19...g4) and now *(148)*:

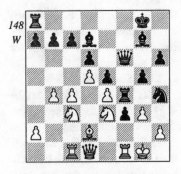

148
W

2a) **20 gxf4?** exf4 21 ♘f5 ♗xf5 22 exf5 ♕xf5 is certainly winning for Black.

2b) **20 gxh4?!** f2+ 21 ♔h1 (21 ♔g2 ♖af8! 22 ♘f5 ♖xf5 23 exf5 ♕xf5 gives Black a decisive attack, for example 24 ♔h1 ♕h3 25 ♘e4 ♕xh4, followed by ...♗g4-f3) ♖xh4 and now:

2b1) **22 ♘g2** (certainly not 22 ♘e2? ♕f3+ 23 ♘g2 ♖xh2+, nor 22 ♘f5 ♗xf5 23 ♖xf2 ♗g4 and Black wins in both cases) ♗g4 23 ♕b3 (and not 23 ♕c2? ♕f3, threatening 24...♖xh2+; White must reply 24 ♗f4, but then 24...♖h5! 25 ♖xf2 ♕h3 regains the piece with a crushing attack) ♖h3 24 ♖c2 (24 ♗e3? ♖xe3 25 ♘xe3 ♕f3+ 26 ♘g2 ♗h3) ♕f3 25 ♘b5 (or else ...♖xh2+) ♕xe4 with a decisive advantage for Black.

2b2) **22 ♕e2** ♖f8 leaves White with few constructive moves. **23 ♘ed1** fails to 23...♗g4 24 ♕xf2 ♕g6 25 ♕g2 ♖xf1+ 26 ♕xf1 ♕h5 27 ♕f2 ♗f3+ 28 ♔g1 ♖g4+ 29 ♔f1 ♕h3+ 30 ♔e1 ♖g2 31 ♕f1 ♕h4+ 32 ♘f2 ♖xh2, with 33...♖h1 to follow, while **23 ♘cd1** allows mate in five by 23...♖xh2+ 24 ♔xh2 ♕f4+ 25 ♔g2 ♕xe4+ 26 ♔h2 ♕h4+ 27 ♔g2 ♕h3. Finally, White can play **23 ♘g2**, when Black is committed to a further sacrifice, because 23...♖h3 is met by 24 ♗e3, surrounding the f2 pawn. The correct reply is 23...g4!, when 24 ♘xh4 ♕xh4 25 ♕d3 ♖f3 is very good for Black, while otherwise ...g3 follows in any case.

2c) **20 ♖f2!** ♖f8. There is a kind of equilibrium in this position. Black would like White to take one of the pieces voluntarily, giving the green light to his attack. White, on the other hand, would prefer to improve his position as much as possible before cashing in on f4 or h4. Black is not in a position to force White to capture by moving one of the attacked pieces away, because the rook and knight have nowhere sensible to go. One can only evaluate this position as totally unclear.

In the above analysis, we frequently met positions in which Black had two advanced pawns against White's extra piece, but Black had no immediate threats. Such positions are very hard to judge. The result often depends on the level of disturbance caused by the pawns. If they control vital squares, and severely disrupt the flow of pieces in the defender's camp, then good compensation is virtually guaranteed. On the other hand, if the defender can manoeuvre around the pawns and firmly control the squares not covered by the pawns, they may become blockaded and the compensation could well prove inadequate. In the present case the pawns are far advanced and substantially interfere with White's piece coordination, so Black certainly has sufficient compensation.

18 ...   ♕e8

In line 2 above, the queen had to settle for the f6 square, but by using the free tempo she can head for h5, an even more appealing destination.

19 f3

Not 19 g3? ♘f3 followed by ...♕h5, nor 19 ♘f5? ♘xf5 20 ♗xf4

gxf4 21 exf5 ♗xf5 followed by ...♕g6, with excellent play for the exchange.

19 ...   gxf3
20 g3   ♕h5 *(149)*

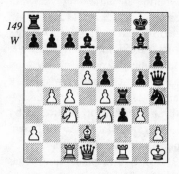

21 gxh4?

This is the second critical moment. The key point of Black's sacrifice is that **21 gxf4?** fails after 21...exf4 and now:

1) **22 ♘f5 ♗xf5 23 exf5 ♕g4!** 24 ♖g1 (or ♖f2) **♕g2+!** 25 ♖xg2 fxg2+ 26 ♔g1 ♗d4+ 27 ♗e3 ♗xe3 mate. An attractive combination.

2) **22 ♘c2 ♗h3 23 ♖f2 ♖f8** (better than the obvious 23...♕g4 which, surprisingly, doesn't threaten anything) defends f4, and so prepares ...g4-g3, against which it is hard to see any defence.

However, it was not necessary for White to take either piece immediately. Instead, he could have improved his position by **21 ♖f2!**. After 21...♖af8! Black's queen is more actively placed than in the note to

White's 18th move, and this should give him some advantage. In particular, 22 gxf4 is bad after 22...exf4 23 ♘f5 (23 ♘c2 g4) ♗xf5 24 exf5 ♗d4 (24...♖xf5 is also dangerous) 25 ♗e1 ♗e3 26 ♖c2 g4 27 ♘e4 ♕xf5 and White's position collapses.

21 ...   ♖xh4

22 ♖f2

After 22 ♕xf3 ♖xh2+ the d2 bishop is lost.

22 ...   g4 *(150)*

Compared to the lines above Black has some extra tempi, and this gives him time to reinforce his attack by the rapid advance of the h-pawn. From this point on, I have been unable to find any defence for White.

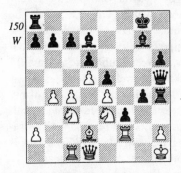

150
W

23 ♘f1

The other main defence runs 23 ♕g1 ♖h3 24 ♘f1 ♕g6 25 ♘g3 ♖f8! (White defends after 25...h5 26 ♘d1 h4 27 ♘f5 ♗xf5 28 exf5 ♕h5 29 ♘e3 g3 30 ♕f1!) 26 ♘d1 (if White ever plays ♘f5 then Black takes with his rook, for example 26 ♘f5 ♖xf5

27 exf5 ♗xf5, with the deadly threat of ...g3) h5 27 ♘e3 (fighting to occupy f5; 27 ♖f1 loses to 27...h4 28 ♘f5 ♖xf5 29 exf5 ♗xf5 30 ♘f2 g3!) h4 28 ♘gf5 ♖xf5! (not 28...♗xf5 29 exf5 ♖xf5, when 30 ♕xg4 saves White) 29 exf5 ♗xf5 and White is strangely helpless despite his extra rook. After 30 ♖cf1 Black can simply reinforce the f3 pawn by playing 30...e4, when ...g3 cannot be prevented; for example, after 31 ♘xf5 ♕xf5 32 ♗e3 g3 33 ♖d2 ♕g4 heavy material loss is inevitable.

23 ...   ♖h3

Threatening 24...g3.

24 ♔g1

Admitting that 18 ♔h1 was a mistake.

24 ...   ♕g6

Now Black intends 25...g3 26 hxg3 ♖xg3+ 27 ♘xg3 ♕xg3+ 28 ♔f1 ♗h3+.

25 ♘g3

White intends to blockade the kingside pawns by 26 ♘f5 ♗xf5 27 exf5 ♕xf5 28 ♕c2 followed by ♘e4, but Black can counter this plan by reinforcing his control of f5.

25 ...   ♖f8!

26 ♘f5 *(151)*

This loses straight away, but in any case there was no defence to the advance of the h-pawn.

26 ...   ♖xf5

In this particular position, Black can even win with the straightforward 26...♗xf5 27 exf5 ♕xf5, with

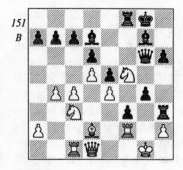

151
B

the decisive threat of 28...g3, because now that his queen is defended, Black can meet 28 ♕c2 by
28...g3. However, I preferred to
leave the queen on the g-file to enhance the strength of ...g3.

27 exf5   ♗xf5

Black keeps control of e4, and
...g3 cannot be prevented for long.

28 ♘e2

Desperation, but 28 ♕f1 was no
better after 28...♗d3! 29 ♕e1 g3
30 ♖xf3 gxh2++ 31 ♔f2 ♖xf3+ 32
♔xf3 e4+ 33 ♔f2 (33 ♘xe4 h1♕)
♗d4+ 34 ♗e3 ♕f6+ 35 ♔g2 ♕f3+
36 ♔xh2 ♗e5+ 37 ♔g1 ♕g4+ and
mates in two more moves.

28 ...   fxe2
29 ♕xe2   ♗d3

Forcing the queen off the second
rank, whereupon the long-awaited
blow falls.

30 ♕d1   g3
31 hxg3   ♗e4

0-1

This game was awarded a prize
for the best game of the round, which

turned out to be a sophisticated
Hewlett-Packard calculator, complete with a thick instruction manual
entirely in Swedish.

I also won my last two games of
the tournament, against Ehlvest and
Vaganian, so I eventually recovered
from my bad start to score 50%, an
entirely satisfactory result. The big
prize at stake in Skellefteå was free
qualification to the second World
Cup cycle, and for this one had to
finish in the top six in the World Cup.
As I did not improve my total at
Skellefteå, my qualification depended entirely on the results of the
other players. In the end I finished in
exactly sixth place. Karpov and Kasparov tied for first place at Skellefteå, which left Kasparov the
overall winner of the World Cup.
Karpov was second, followed by Salov, Ehlvest, Ljubojević and myself.
Taking the cycle as a whole, this was
undoubtedly the best result of my
career. I had achieved isolated excellent results before, as at the Thessaloniki Olympiad in 1984, but there is
a big difference between playing 11
games, only a few against top-class
opposition, and playing 60 games
against all the top players in the
world. I had scored at least 50% in
all four events, and proved that I
could compete on equal terms with
other leading grandmasters.

This was the high point of my
career, and it is unfortunate that

changes in the chess world meant that I would (at least, up to end-1994) never again get the chance to test myself against the leading players. Of course, as everybody now knows, the second World Cup cycle collapsed after only one tournament (held in Reykjavik). I did not participate at Reykjavik, so Skellefteå was my last World Cup event.

I have said before that this book is about chess, and not about chess politics, but perhaps a few words might be appropriate about the demise of the second World Cup cycle and the eventual collapse of the GMA. Chess players are great individualists, usually with sizable egos, so to get them to cooperate together for any period of time is indeed a tricky business. Bessel Kok managed to do this with the GMA. The eventual FIDE-GMA agreement gave the GMA virtually everything that it wanted, but it could not give Garry the one thing he desired most of all – to see Campomanes humiliated. When the GMA, voting democratically, approved the FIDE-GMA agreement, Garry couldn't really accept the turn of events and thereafter he took less and less part in the GMA. Indeed, at times he seemed to be acting against the GMA's interests.

Over the years the GMA was functioning, I put in an enormous amount of work on behalf of the GMA, all of it totally unpaid. I was not alone in this; many people were working behind the scenes to make sure that the organisation could function. I was happy to take part, because I saw a new future for chess in which the players would cooperate with FIDE to find new sponsors and develop novel ways to popularise chess. It was clear that this would require changes in the way FIDE operated, but there were many positive signs that FIDE was moving in the right direction.

Problems arose because an event such as the World Cup would only be attractive to sponsors if the world champion was participating. This gave one person an effective veto over the arrangements. For a long time, Garry maintained that he had a Japanese company which was interested in sponsoring the entire cycle. Months dragged by and nothing happened. Garry repeated that, given a few more months, everything might be confirmed, but eventually he was given a deadline to produce his sponsor or the organisation would be handed over to someone else. The deadline passed and Lubosh Kavalek, who had done a very good job organising the first cycle, was asked to take on the job again. But by now more than a year had been lost, and then a new problem arose: Garry wasn't clear about whether he would take part in the second cycle. He demanded a 'special' payment;

ironically, this was against the principle he had supported for the first cycle, that all the money would go into prizes and there would be no appearance fees. Karpov hinted that if Garry got a 'special' payment, then he deserved one too. At this stage the whole cycle was on the verge of breakdown, and it is amazing that even one tournament actually took place.

The eventual collapse of the GMA was virtually a repeat performance of the collapse of the second World Cup. Without the World Cup, its main *raison d'être* had disappeared, but some of the gains made by the GMA, such as representation on important FIDE committees, would have been worth maintaining in their own right. But the disintegration did not stop with Kasparov. Timman, who had been one of the hardest workers behind the scenes, became unhappy with the GMA's reduced status and resigned. The final blow fell when Nigel Short, who had only been President of the GMA for a few months, suddenly resigned in order to break with FIDE and set up the PCA with Kasparov. He was quite open about the motivation for his move: money. Later, others sought to cloak the move in a thin veil of altruism, but whatever else one may say about the decision, at least Nigel was perfectly honest about his motivation. Another

problem is that chess players are not natural diplomats. A smart move in diplomacy is to find a way for the other guy to climb out of the hole he is in gracefully, preferably without loss of face. The chess player's natural instinct is to stamp on his hands.

It was impossible for the GMA to function when individuals put their own interests above those of the sport as a whole; indeed, no players' organisation, no matter how it is constituted, can function under these conditions. The last two years of the GMA proved an eye-opening and disillusioning experience for me. Garry likes to refer to the example of tennis, but in tennis there are many retired players who have the sport's interests at heart and are no longer personally involved in competition. They can be the players' representatives. This is not so in chess; if there is a body in which the players are powerful, be it the GMA, PCA or whatever, there will inevitably be conflicts of interests. The GMA handled these problems relatively well; there was a sizable board, which prevented one person from exercising too much power, and by being democratically based, board members could be voted off if necessary. Relatively well, perhaps, but in the end not well enough.

My two remaining events from 1989 were both team tournaments. First of all, there was the second

World Team Championship in Lucerne. In the first Championship, held during 1985, England had finished third. This time our team was much stronger on paper (Short, Speelman, Nunn, Chandler, Adams and Hodgson) and it was felt that second place would be a par result. During the period of England's successes in the mid-1980s, the team had been entirely harmonious, with everybody helping each other to ensure the best possible result. The first discords appeared at Lucerne.

One problem was that Dominic Lawson accompanied the team in order to write about the English team from the inside. A sporting team is a closely-knit entity, and having an outsider present during team discussions and analysis sessions proved disconcerting for some members of the team, especially Jon Speelman. This probably wouldn't have mattered if another problem hadn't blown up. Before the match against the Soviet Union in round 5, a couple of players called a team meeting. In the thirteen years I had been playing for England, there had never been a team meeting. In my view such meetings more often lead to dissent and argument than agreement, but the meeting went ahead anyway. I attended with serious misgivings.

The crux of the matter was that Nigel, supported by Murray Chandler, wanted us to make a determined effort to win against the Soviet Union and so challenge for first place. Of course, one is always trying to make the best possible result; to win if possible, or if not to draw. But the argument was that we should try to win even if it meant taking risks which would normally be regarded as unjustified. At this stage of the competition the Soviet Union had 12½ points and England had 10. A 3-1 win would bring us to within half a point of the Soviets, with everything to play for. But, as I pointed out, we had never, in many Olympiads and other team tournaments, beaten the Soviet Union. Why should we take excessive risks now, when we were on course for second place, a creditable achievement? At this stage things turned a bit nasty. It seemed that one of the purposes behind calling the meeting was to launch a public attack on Jon Speelman. He was criticised for his attitude to the event; it was true that he had been out of form and had scored just 1/3, but putting pressure on Jon Speelman is almost always counterproductive. The only thing you are likely to get out of pressurising him is a draw offer. In any case, censuring players who are out of form isn't helpful; everybody wants to win, and equally everybody suffers from bouts of poor form. Making the suffering player feel even worse doesn't help anybody. I left the meeting very unhappy, and walked around Lake Lucerne for an hour to calm down.

The result was that Jon didn't play in the match against the Soviet Union, and England lost 3-1. Only Murray Chandler won; I lost and Nigel lost. This put first place out of our reach, but it was still possible to finish second. Had we won convincingly against China in the last round, we could have taken second place, but Nigel and I were again the losers, and the 2-2 draw was only enough for third place behind Yugoslavia. Curiously enough, Jon Speelman had perked up near the end, and by winning his last two games he finished on '+1', the same as Nigel. I was less than happy with my 50%.

The next event, just three weeks later, was the European Team Championship in Haifa. For various reasons the English team, consisting of Nunn, Adams, Hodgson, King, Hebden, Suba, Kosten and Watson, was missing some of the top players. Nevertheless, the team could reasonably hope for a good result; it was by no means weak, and a number of other countries were also below full strength. But once again there was some disagreement about what the team's objectives should be. In the third round, we were set back by a 3-3 draw against Poland, but then began to pick up with wins against West Germany and Hungary. The fateful clash with the Soviet Union came in round 7 (out of 9). Once again there was a huge amount of talking up expectations. This time I decided to absent myself from any such discussions and simply play my normal game. The result was a devastating 5-1 loss for England, with the only half-points being salvaged by Suba and myself. Unfortunately, the problems did not end with the Soviet match. The next day we had to play Yugoslavia, who were in very good form at Haifa. Now there was talk of 'making up for the Soviet match', rather than simply aiming for a modest win, say 3½-2½, which would have left us with fair chances for medals. The result was another crushing defeat, this time by 4½-1½. A win against Austria in the last round could not make up for losses in the key matches, and England finished in joint eighth position, our worst team result for seven years.

I was happy with my individual result of 5/8 on board one, especially as I had gone through the event without loss, but it was disappointing to be going home without our customary medals.

1990

My first chess event of the new year was the traditional journey to Wijk aan Zee. On my first visit to Wijk, in 1982, I shared first place with Balashov, but although my performances there had always been quite respectable, I had never repeated this success – until 1990.

In the first round I scraped a draw against Petursson, and then I found myself facing Anand with Black. As everybody knows, the Indian grandmaster doesn't hesitate long over his moves. In the first round he had demolished Kuijf using only ten minutes on his clock, refuting a line in *ECO* along the way.

Fortunately, Anand chose to take on my Marshall Attack, so I was able to play the first 15 moves quickly.

Game 27

V.Anand – J.Nunn

Wijk aan Zee 1990

Spanish

1	e4	e5
2	♘f3	♘c6
3	♗b5	a6
4	♗a4	♘f6
5	0-0	♗e7
6	♖e1	b5
7	♗b3	0-0
8	c3	d5

The Marshall Attack has formed part of my repertoire for several years. When I first adopted it, most grandmasters regarded it with some suspicion. Despite this, the Marshall turned out to be not so easy to refute, and gradually other top players, such as Short, Adams and Ivanchuk, started to adopt it. In the 1993 Kasparov-Short match, Garry avoided the gambit entirely, and stuck (successfully, it must be said) to the Anti-Marshall 8 a4, which can be construed as a mark of respect for the Marshall.

These days I do not play the Marshall Attack so often. One reason is that, thanks to its improved reputation, many players simply avoid it. Another is that it is unsuitable for use against lower-rated opponents due to the many forced drawing lines.

9	exd5	♘xd5
10	♘xe5	♘xe5
11	♖xe5	c6
12	♗xd5	

This is the so-called Kevitz Variation. In the normal lines of the Marshall, which arise after 12 d3 or 12 d4, the rook has to retreat to e1 or e2 in reply to Black's ...♗d6. The idea of taking on d5 is to allow the rook to retreat to e3 instead, where it can perform a useful defensive function along the third rank. The defect is that Black immediately acquires the two bishops, and there is no danger that he will fall into an awkward pin along the b3-g8 diagonal, as happens in some of the main lines.

12	...	cxd5
13	d4	♗d6
14	♖e3	♕h4
15	h3 *(152)*	

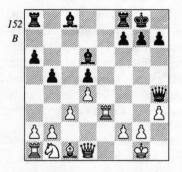

152
B

The first fruits of White's plan. In the Marshall, White is normally forced to meet ...♕h4 by g3, because h3 would allow a devastating piece

sacrifice on h3. With the rook on e3, however, White can avoid the positionally undesirable g3, which severely weakens the kingside light squares. This is particularly relevant when, as here, White's light-squared bishop has been exchanged for the knight on d5.

15	...	g5

Theory considers three possible moves for Black; the other two are 15...f5 and 15...♕f4. 15...f5 is now considered dubious because of the innovation Hübner played against me at Skellefteå 1989. Three months later, at Haifa 1989, I had to face Hübner again; this time I chose 15...g5 and drew comfortably, so I decided to repeat the move against Anand. Five months afterwards, I was put off 15...g5 by M.Hennigan-Nunn, Bayswater Open 1990, which continued 15...g5 16 ♕f3 ♗e6 17 ♕f6 ♖fe8 18 ♘d2 (18 ♘a3 ♕h5 19 ♗d2 ♗e7 20 ♕f3 ♕g6 21 ♖ae1 g4! 22 ♕g3 gxh3 23 gxh3 ♗d6 was equal in Hübner-Nunn, Haifa 1989) ♕f4 19 ♕xf4 ♗xf4 20 ♖e1 ♗xh3 21 ♖xe8+ ♖xe8 22 ♘f3 ♗xc1 23 ♖xc1 ♗f5 24 ♘xg5 a5 (24...♖e2 25 b4 fixes the queenside pawns and reduces Black's winning chances to zero) and now, instead of 25 a4?, White could have played 25 ♘f3 (threat ♖e1) ♖e2 26 ♘e5 ♖xb2 27 ♘c6 ♔g7 28 ♘xa5 ♖xa2 29 ♘c6 and Black has no winning chances in view of his four isolated pawns.

The soundest move is probably 15...♕f4, which is also theory's preference. Perhaps the main defect of this move is that it allows White to force an immediate draw by 16 ♖e5 ♕f6 17 ♖e3 ♕f4, and indeed many games have ended this way, including some of my own!

16 b3!?

A prepared innovation. Suddenly I was worried that I might follow Kuijf into the history books as another victim of Anand's *blitzkrieg* style. The idea behind the move is apparent; the bishop on d6 is an important attacking piece and White wants to swap it off by ♗a3. This would also overcome one of the main defects of the Kevitz Variation – that the rook on e3 blocks in the c1 bishop. White is even prepared to return the pawn in order to realise his plan, for example 16...g4 17 ♗a3 ♗xa3 18 ♘xa3 gxh3 19 g3 ♕f6 20 ♕h5 with a clear advantage to White thanks to Black's many weak pawns.

16 ... f5 *(153)*

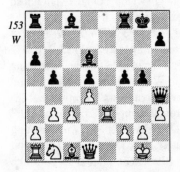

153
W

A natural response. Black doesn't try to prevent ♗a3 directly, but makes use of the extra time afforded by White's rather slow plan to develop his own kingside attack.

17 ♕f3

There is a second critical continuation: 17 ♗a3 f4 18 ♖e5!? (after 18 ♖d3 ♗xa3 19 ♘xa3 ♗f5 20 ♖d2 ♖ac8 21 ♖c1 ♖f6 Black has a strong initiative in return for the pawn, for example he already threatens 22...g4 23 hxg4 ♖h6) and now:

1) **18...♗xa3** 19 ♘xa3 f3 20 g3! and despite the obvious danger of mate on g2, White seems to have the advantage, for example 20...♕xh3 21 ♖xg5+ ♔h8 22 ♕f1 ♕h6 23 ♖xd5 ♗h3 24 ♕c1!, and Black's queen cannot stay on the h-file, or 20...♕h6 21 ♕c1! ♕xh3 (21...♗f5 22 h4, or 21...♗xh3? 22 ♖xg5+ ♔f7 23 ♕f4+ and White wins) 22 ♖xg5+ ♔h8 23 ♕f1 transposing to the first line.

2) **18...♗xe5** and now:

2a) **19 dxe5 ♖e8** (not 19...♖d8 20 ♗e7 ♖d7 21 ♘d2!, when 21...♖xe7 loses to 22 ♘f3 followed by ♕xd5+, so Black has to face the awkward threat of 22 ♘f3 attacking g5) 20 ♗d6 (after 20 ♕xd5+ ♗e6 Black gains time for his attack, for example 21 ♕e4 ♖ad8 is troublesome, since 22 ♗d6 runs into 22...♗xh3!) g4 21 hxg4 ♕xg4 with an unclear position.

2b) **19 ♗xf8 ♗c7!** 20 ♗c5 (20 ♗e7 ♔f7 21 ♗c5 is worse because

Black's rook has access to g8, for example 21...g4 22 hxg4 ♗xg4 23 f3 ♗h3! is very unpleasant for White; 20 ♕f3 ♗e6 21 ♗c5 h5 22 ♘d2 g4 23 ♕d3 ♔g7 gives Black good attacking chances in return for the pawn) g4 21 hxg4 ♗xg4 22 f3 ♗xf3! 23 ♕xf3 (not 23 gxf3 ♔h8!, when both 24 ♘d2 ♖g8+ 25 ♔f1 ♕h3+ 26 ♔e2 ♖g2+ and 24 ♔f1 ♖e8 25 ♘d2 ♕h1+ 26 ♔f2 ♕h2+ 27 ♔f1 ♖g8 28 ♔e1 ♖g2 win for Black) ♕e1+ 24 ♕f1 (24 ♔h2 ♕h4+ 25 ♕h3?? f3+ wins for Black) ♕e3+ 25 ♕f2 (25 ♔h1 f3! is better for Black) ♕c1+ 26 ♔h2 f3+ 27 g3 (27 ♔h3? ♕h1+ 28 ♔g4 fxg2 wins) ♕h6+ (27...♖e8 28 ♕xf3 may be good for White) 28 ♔g1 ♕c1+ 29 ♕f1 ♕e3+ and it's about time for White to acquiesce to the perpetual check, since 30 ♔h2? f2! is winning for Black.

Anand prefers to force Black to play his bishop to b7. The advantage of this is that the bishop is inactive on b7, but the disadvantage is that ...g4 may come with gain of tempo.

17   ...   ♗b7
18   ♖e6

This was the move Anand had prepared in his pre-game analysis, but he had overlooked Black's reply. The safest move was 18 ♗a3, whereupon the forcing continuation 18...g4 19 ♕e2 f4 20 ♗xd6 fxe3 21 ♗xf8 ♕xf2+ 22 ♕xf2 exf2+ 23 ♔xf2 (after 23 ♔f1 ♖xf8 24 hxg4 ♗c8 Black recovers the pawn with a

slight endgame advantage) ♖xf8+ 24 ♔g1 gxh3 25 gxh3 ♗c8 26 ♘d2 (26 ♔g2 ♖e8 27 ♘a3 ♖e3 is good for Black) ♗xh3 leads to a draw.

18   ...   ♖ae8! (154)

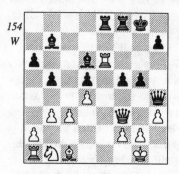

154
W

Black must react actively if he wants to counter White's plan.

19   ♖xe8?!

White would certainly have preferred not to exchange a rook which has moved four times for a rook which has only moved once, but he probably judged that the line 19 ♖xd6 ♖e1+ 20 ♔h2 ♖xc1 was favourable for Black. During the game I thought so too, but now I am not so sure. White may try:

1) **21 ♕e3 ♕f4+** 22 ♕xf4 gxf4 (threatening ...♖e8-e1) 23 ♖e6 ♔f7 (23...f3!? 24 gxf3 f4 is an interesting idea; White's king is sealed in, and Black intends to play either ...♗c8-f5 rounding up the knight, or ...♔h8 followed by ...♖g8-g1, with a mating attack) 24 ♖e5 ♔f6 is probably good for Black. His plan is to continue

...♖f7-e7, exchanging off White's only mobile piece, whereupon White will be practically in zugzwang.

2) **21 ♖d7!** (avoiding the loss of time inherent in line 1) ♗a8 (after 21...♗c6 22 ♖d6, Black has nothing better than 22...♗b7; note that Black cannot play directly for mate, since after 21...♖e8 22 ♖xb7 ♖ee1 23 ♕xd5+ it is Black who gets mated) 22 ♖e7 ♖f1 (22...g4 23 ♕e3) 23 ♕e3 (threat ♕e6+) ♕f4+ 24 ♕xf4 gxf4 25 a4! bxa4 26 ♖xa4 ♖xb1 27 ♖xa6 ♖xb3 28 ♖aa7 and Black certainly has no advantage.

It seems that Black's best course of action is to take the draw by 21...♗c6 22 ♖d6 ♗b7, and therefore 19 ♖xd6 would have maintained the balance.

> **19 ... ♖xe8** *(155)*

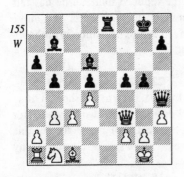

155
W

20 ♔f1?
Only this ugly move definitely tips the balance in Black's favour. White's dilemma is that all the plausible moves look rather unattractive,

but on the other hand it is hard for Black to break through. In my view the resolute 20 ♗d2 would have offered good defensive chances. Black has no better way to save the f5 pawn than by 20...f4 (20...♗f4 threatens nothing, so White can start his counterplay by 21 a4!). After 21 a4! (better than 21 ♕g4 ♕xg4 22 hxg4 a5! and White is practically paralysed; 23 ♔f1 is met by 23...♗a6, while 23 a4 b4 24 c4 dxc4 25 bxc4 ♖e4 just leads to loss of material) bxa4 (21...h5 is met by 22 axb5 axb5 23 ♕d3) 22 ♖xa4 ♕h6! (22...h5 23 ♖xa6! is certainly not better for Black) 23 ♕d3 (preventing ...♕g6) Black has adequate compensation for the pawn, but cannot claim any obvious advantage.

> **20 ... g4!**

I thought for a long time over this move, because the idea of heading for an ending where Black is (temporarily) two pawns down is not the most obvious plan. The point behind White's last move was that 20...f4 can now be met by 21 ♗a3 ♗c7 22 ♘d2, followed by ♖e1, and White develops his queenside pieces.

The next few moves are more or less forced for both sides.

> **21 ♕xf5 gxh3**
> **22 ♕xh3**

Not 22 gxh3 ♗c8 23 ♕xd5+ ♔h8 (much clearer than 23...♖e6 24 ♕g2+ ♔h8 25 ♗g5 ♕xg5! 26 ♕xg5 ♗xh3+ 27 ♕g2 ♗xg2+ 28 ♔xg2

♖e1, when the severely reduced material may make the win hard for Black, even if he does eventually round up the knight on b1) 24 ♗e3 ♕xh3+ 25 ♔e2 (25 ♔g2 ♕h5 26 ♔e1 ♖g8 27 ♕f1 ♕h2 28 ♕d3 ♖g1+ 29 ♔d2 ♕h5 30 ♕e2 ♗g4 wins for Black) ♖xe3+! 26 fxe3 ♗g4+ 27 ♔d2 ♕h2+ 28 ♔c1 ♕g1+ 29 ♔b2 ♕f2+ 30 ♔c1 ♗f5! and White must give up his queen.

22	...	♕xh3
23	gxh3	♗c8
24	♗e3	

After 24 ♔g2 ♖e1 25 ♗b2 ♖d1 White cannot move his knight, and Black threatens to win a piece by 26...♗f5. 26 c4 is the only move, but then Black can either play for the win of a piece by 26...b4 27 c5 ♗c7, followed by ...♗f5 and ...♖xb1, or regain his pawns by 26...dxc4 27 bxc4 bxc4 28 ♘c3 ♖xd4, when the two active bishops give him a clear advantage.

24	...	♗xh3+
25	♔e2	♗g4+ (156)

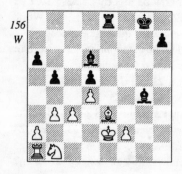

26 ♔d3?!

White does not want to put his king on d2, which would imprison the knight, but 26 f3 is critical. Black continues 26...♗f4 (26...♗h3 27 ♘d2 ♗f4 28 ♘e4! is fine for White) 27 fxg4 ♖xe3+ 28 ♔f2 ♖h3 (other moves are ineffective because White will free himself by b4, followed by a4 and axb5, activating the rook) 29 a4 (29 b4 ♖h1 is too slow, as 30 a4 runs into 30...bxa4, while 29 ♔g2 ♖h2+ 30 ♔f3 ♗g5 is no help) b4! 30 cxb4 ♖xb3 31 b5 (after 31 ♘a3, Black should play 31...♖xb4 32 ♘c2 ♖b2 33 ♔f3 ♗d2! with a clear advantage, rather than 31...♗e3+ 32 ♔f1 ♗xd4 33 ♖d1, which is drawish) ♗e3+ 32 ♔g2 axb5 (32...♗xd4 33 bxa6!) 33 axb5 ♗xd4 34 ♖a8+ ♔g7 and White is worse, but thanks to the reduced material he has fair drawing chances. After the move played White's position is probably lost.

26	...	♗f5+
27	♔e2	♗g4+?!

I was starting to run short of time, so I decided to get two moves nearer the sanctuary of move 40, but this gives White a second chance to play f3.

28	♔d3?!	♗f5+
29	♔e2	♖c8!

The key move. By attacking the weak pawn on c3, Black ties down White's knight and obstructs the development of his queenside pieces.

Playing ♗d2 to defend the pawn doesn't help, because the knight still cannot move. Nor can White play a4, because Black just replies ...bxa4. If White does nothing, Black will be only too happy to send his passed h-pawn racing down the board. On the other hand, if White simply jettisons his c-pawn, for example by playing 30 ♘d2, the two bishops and outside passed pawn should be enough to win.

30 f3

If now 30...h5, then 31 ♘d2! ♖xc3 32 ♖g1+ ♔f7 33 ♖g5 creates some counterplay because of the exposed pawns on the fifth rank. Therefore, Black makes a precautionary king move.

30 ... ♔f7

Threatening to start the pawn rolling with ...h5.

31 ♗d2

White decides to return the pawn by playing c3-c4, but there is no point to this unless White can follow up with ♘c3. Thus the immediate 31 c4 dxc4 32 bxc4 ♖xc4 33 ♘d2 ♖c2 is useless, because White fails to activate his knight. The preparatory ♗d2 is designed to support ♘c3 after c3-c4.

31 ... h5
32 c4 ♖e8+

This is the most convincing way of taking the pawn, because it forces White to waste a further tempo blocking the e-file.

33 ♔f2 ♗d3
34 ♗e3

Forced, as 34 ♘c3 loses a piece after 34...b4.

34 ... h4 *(157)*

There is no doubt that Black should win, and the route to victory is largely a matter of taste. Although this gains a tempo by forcing f3-f4, it does allow White's knight to reach an active square by ♘d2-f3-e5. The immediate 34...dxc4 35 bxc4 bxc4 might have been simpler.

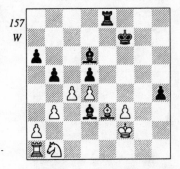

157
W

35 f4 dxc4
36 bxc4 bxc4

36...♗xc4 37 ♘d2 ♗d5 38 ♘f3 ♖c8 39 ♘xh4 ♖c2+ 40 ♔g3 ♗xa2 was another method, when the two connected passed pawns will prove decisive.

37 ♘d2

After 37 ♘c3 ♗b4 38 ♘d5 ♗a5! (threatening to trap the knight on d5) 39 a3 ♗e4 40 ♘b4 ♖g8 41 ♖g1 ♖h8! Black forces the h-pawn home.

37 ... ♖b8?

This makes the win more complicated. After the natural 37...h3 38 ♖h1 c3 39 ♘f3 ♗f5, Black's two passed pawns would prove too much for White, for example 40 ♘g5+ (40 ♘e5+ ♔e6 and ...♔d5) ♔e7 41 ♘xh3 ♖h8 42 ♔g3 ♗a3 and Black wins the bishop for the c-pawn. He will be left with his dark-squared bishop, which is the right colour for the a-pawn.

38   ♔f3

After 38 ♘f3 ♖b2+ 39 ♔g1 c3 40 ♖c1 ♖e2! 41 ♗f2 c2 White's position collapses.

38   ...   c3
39   ♘e4   ♗b4 (158)

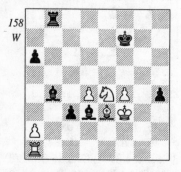

158
W

40   ♖d1?

A mistake allowing Black to win the game immediately. When Anand was younger, he sometimes did not put his full energy into defending lost positions; it was almost as if he considered it undignified to swindle his opponent. These days, as befits one of the world's leading players,

he is more pragmatic. Other moves would have forced Black to work harder:

1) **40 ♘c5** ♗xc5 41 dxc5 c2 (threat ...♖b1) 42 ♖c1 ♗f5 followed by ...h3 is sufficient to win in the long run. Black first of all neutralises the c-pawn by playing his king to d5; then he plays his rook to g2, followed by ...♗e4+ and ...h2.

2) **40 a3** ♗a5 41 ♘c5 ♗c4 42 ♖c1. Black should still win after 42...♖g8, but he would have to play accurately.

40   ...   ♗xe4+
41   ♔xe4   c2

0-1

The two passed pawns are too much for White: 42 ♖c1 (42 ♖h1 ♖e8+ 43 ♔d3 ♖xe3+ 44 ♔xe3 ♗a3) ♖c8 43 ♔d3 (43 ♖h1 ♖e8+ as before) ♖c3+ 44 ♔d2 ♖a3+ 45 ♔e2 ♖xa2 (threat 46...♗a3) 46 ♔f3 (46 ♔d3 ♖a3+ wins after 47 ♔e4 ♖c3 48 ♗d2 ♖a3 or 47 ♔e2 ♖c3 48 ♔d2 h3 49 ♗g1 h2 50 ♗xh2 ♖h3+) ♗a3 47 ♖h1 ♖b2 48 ♖c1 (48 ♖xh4 ♖b3) h3 and Black wins.

After seven rounds, I had scored four points, the other decisive games being a loss to Korchnoi and a win against Short. My game in round 8 proved to be one of the most eventful of the tournament; indeed, it won the brilliancy prize although I must admit that much of the brilliance was accidental.

Game 28

J.Piket – J.Nunn

Wijk aan Zee 1990

King's Indian

1 d4	♘f6
2 ♘f3	g6
3 c4	♗g7
4 ♘c3	0-0
5 e4	d6
6 h3	

Although rather unusual, this line has been played by both Korchnoi and Larsen. The idea is to avoid committing White's king and king's bishop. In some lines White plays g4 and castles queenside, leaving the f1 bishop at home until the best square for it becomes clear.

6 ...	e5
7 d5	♘bd7

Black has many possible lines; this one intends ...♘c5 and ...a5, possibly followed by ...♘e8 or ...♘fd7 in order to prepare ...f5. It is perhaps the most straightforward plan, but on the other hand it makes no direct attempt to exploit White's slow build-up.

8 ♗e3

White will defend the e4 pawn with ♘d2, so the bishop moves to avoid being blocked in.

8 ...	♘c5
9 ♘d2	a5

10 g4

The other important option is 10 a3, which aims simply to dislodge the knight from c5 by playing b4. Whilst this is strategically desirable, it does further delay White's kingside development.

10 ...	♘e8 *(159)*

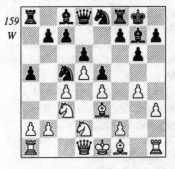

White's g4 reveals that he doesn't intend to castle kingside. If Black plays ...f5, White will gain attacking chances by opening the g-file with gxf5. In this game Black aims for ...f5 in any case, even though this involves falling in with White's plan. The current (i.e., 1994) trend is to delay committing the f6 knight, aiming instead to develop queenside counterplay, for example by 10...c6 11 ♗e2 a4 (or 11...♗d7).

11 ♕c2 *(160)*

The main alternative is 11 h4 (recommended by *ECO*; 11 ♕e2 f5 12 gxf5 gxf5 13 0-0-0 ♘e6? 14 dxe6 f4 15 ♗c5 dxc5 16 ♘f3 ♘d6 17 ♖g1 ♗xe6 18 ♘xe5 ♕e7 19 ♕h5 ♗f7 20 ♘xf7 ♘xf7 21 ♘d5 led to a quick White win in Piket-Dam, Amsterdam OHRA 1990) f5 (11...♗d7 12 ♕e2 c6 13 f3 f5 14 exf5 gxf5 15 gxf5 cxd5 16 cxd5 ♗xf5 17 ♘de4 b6 18 ♕d2?! ♖c8 19 h5 ♔h8 20 ♘g3 ♗d7 21 ♗e2 ♗f6 22 0-0-0 ♘g7 23 ♔b1 ♘f5 was at least equal for Black in Knaak-Nunn, Dortmund 1991; however, Black's plan is an odd mixture of the old ...♘e8 plan and the recent ...c6 idea, and I probably wouldn't repeat it) 12 gxf5 gxf5 13 ♕e2 and now:

1) **13...♘a6** (threat ...f4) 14 ♗g5 was good for White in Bagirov-Sigurjonsson, Tbilisi 1974.

2) **13...♘f6** 14 ♗xc5 dxc5 15 ♗h3 fxe4 16 ♘dxe4 ♘xe4 17 ♘xe4 ♖f4 18 0-0-0 ♕f8 19 ♖dg1 ♔h8 20 ♗xc8 ♖xc8, Kaiser-Autenrieth, Bundesliga 1985, is a perfect example of what Black should avoid in this line. He has been left with his worst minor piece, all the others having been exchanged, while White has an all-powerful knight sitting on e4.

3) **13...f4** 14 ♗xc5 dxc5 15 ♗h3 ♗xh3 16 ♖xh3 ♕d7 17 ♖h1 ♖a6 18 ♘f3 ♖g6 19 0-0-0 ♔h8 20 ♖dg1

♖xg1+ 21 ♖xg1 ♕h3 was claimed to be unclear in Vilela-Moreno, Havana 1991, but it is worth noting that White won the game. In this example Black was again left with a permanently bad bishop on g7.

4) **13...♘e6!?** 14 dxe6 f4 is risky but may be playable.

In these lines, as so often in the King's Indian, Black can easily fall into a position in which all the long-term chances lie with White. Moreover, the fact that White's king is on the queenside means that there is no obvious source of counterplay for Black. My own view is that the current trend of delaying ...♘e8 must be the way for Black to proceed; by making progress on the queenside he will make White's 0-0-0 more of a risk, while if White castles kingside he cannot adopt the dangerous g4 plan.

160
B

11 ...   f5

Not the only possible move. 11...♗f6 12 ♘f3 ♘g7 13 0-0-0 b6 14

♗e2 ♗e7 15 ♖dg1 ♘d7 16 ♖g2 ♘f6 17 ♗d3 h5 led to equality in Larsen-Mestel, Las Palmas 1982, while Larsen-Piket, Lugano 1989 continued **11...♔h8** 12 ♗e2 (12 0-0-0 may be better) f5 13 exf5 gxf5 14 0-0-0 a4! with unclear complications.

12 gxf5

ECO gives 12 exf5 gxf5 13 0-0-0 ♘a6, but I would prefer to follow Piket's lead with 13...a4!?, when 14 ♗xc5 dxc5 15 ♘xa4 ♘d6 gives Black good compensation for the pawn.

12 ... gxf5

13 ♖g1 *(161)*

This plan is a logical consequence of the earlier g4. The only negative point is that White may want to play h4 and ♗h3 to exchange his bad bishop, as in some of the examples given above, and moving the rook away from h1 makes this harder.

161
B

13 ... f4

I considered 13...♘e6, but the pin on the bishop enables White to gain the advantage by 14 dxe6 f4 and now:

1) **15 ♘d5** ♗xe6 (after 15...fxe3 White should not play 16 e7? exf2+ 17 ♔d1 fxg1♕ 18 exd8♕ ♗g4+ and Black wins, but 16 ♖xg7+! ♘xg7 17 e7 exd2+ 18 ♕xd2 ♕d7 19 exf8♕+ ♔xf8 20 ♕h6, with advantage for White) 16 ♘xf4 exf4 17 ♗d4 is the same as in line 2 below, except that Black has the extra tempo ...♗e6. Even this situation is slightly better for White.

2) **15 e7!** ♕xe7 16 ♘d5 ♕d8 17 ♘xf4! exf4 18 ♗d4 with equal material and good attacking chances for White.

14 ♗xc5 dxc5

The blocked pawn structure severely restricts the bishops on f1 and g7, but if the position opens up later the g7 bishop could become extremely powerful because it has no white counterpart. In many of the lines given in the analysis of the alternative 11 h4, White managed to play ♗h3 very quickly, and this normally gives White the advantage. Here it is not so easy for White to play ♗h3, first of all because he has not yet played h4, but also because he has moved his rook away from h1.

15 ♘f3

This prevents ...f3, which might be a good move even if it loses a pawn because it secures the powerful h6-c1 diagonal for the g7 bishop.

With f3 blocked, Black's only constructive plan is to attack White's single weakness, the h-pawn.

15 ...   ♔h8
16 0-0-0   ♖a6

The a8 rook is Black's least active piece; fortunately, it can swing into a good position without loss of time.

17 ♘b5   ♕e7

A useful safety move, defending the weak pawns on c5 and e5, and cutting out any possible sacrifice on g7.

18 ♕c3

If White could play both ♕c3 and ♔b1, Black would be in trouble because the attack on a5 would prevent the queen's rook swinging into the game. As it is, Black is just in time.

18 ...   ♖h6 (162)

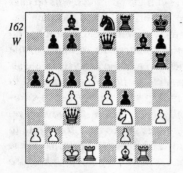

162
W

19 h4

After the game Piket thought that he should have taken on a5 in any case, which would have allowed Black's rook to set a record for hard work after 19 ♕xa5 ♖a6 20 ♕c3

♖xa2 21 ♔b1 (21 ♘a3 ♖a1+) ♖a6. Here, Black has been forced to abandon his attack on the h-pawn, but the open a-file gives him an alternative source of counterplay after ...♘d6, followed by an eventual ...♗d7 and ...♖fa8.

19 ...   b6

Black's queenside is now secure and he has a clear-cut plan of attacking the weak h4 pawn by ...♗f6; after defending e5 by ...♘d6-f7 he can simply take it off. It is up to White to find countermeasures against this plan.

20 ♗d3?!

This move was accompanied by a draw offer. It very often happens that such moves are designed simply to pass the time, and in a critical situation the loss of a tempo can be serious. White could have played more actively by 20 ♖h1!, intending ♗h3. Even if the h-pawn is eventually lost White's grip on the light squares should provide him with ample compensation.

20 ...   ♗f6
21 ♗c2

Another idea was to try for immediate counterplay on the g-file by 21 ♘a7 ♗d7 22 ♖g2.

21 ...   ♘d6
22 ♘a7

After 22 ♘xd6 cxd6 23 ♕b3 ♕d8 all Black's pawns are defended and White's h-pawn is about to disappear. White plays ♘a7 before ♖g2 because the immediate 22 ♖g2 allows an awkward 22...♗h3.

22	...	♗d7 *(163)*

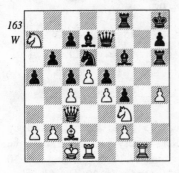

163
W

23 ♖g2?

At some stage White has to commit himself to a positive plan, because if he just continues with routine moves he is in danger of losing the h-pawn. Here White should have played 23 ♘c6!?. During the game, I intended to meet it by 23...♕e8, when 24 ♘cxe5 puts White in a permanent self-pin. Unfortunately, there seems to be no way to exploit this pin, for example 24...b5 25 cxb5 ♘xb5 allows 26 ♕xc5 and the f8 rook is hanging, 24...♕e7 (intending ...♖e8) runs into 25 ♘c6! ♗xc6 26 e5 and finally 24...♖h5 25 ♖g5 ♖xg5 26 hxg5 ♗g7 (with the idea of ...♔g8 followed by ...♘f7 winning the pinned knight) allows 27 g6!. Therefore, Black should reply 23...♗xc6 24 dxc6 ♕e8, but 25 ♖d5!? leads to a completely unclear position.

After the move played Black can think about an advantage for the first time in the game.

23 ... ♖g8!

Now 23...♗h3 is met by 24 ♘c6.

24 ♖xg8+ ♔xg8

Exchanging one pair of rooks reduces the chances that Black's king will get into trouble while he is rounding up the pawn on h4. Moreover, the king moves off the potentially dangerous c3-h8 diagonal.

25 a3

Probably White's best practical chance. Black would be happy to see the last rooks vanish after 25 ♖g1+ ♖g6 26 ♖xg6+ hxg6 followed by ...♘f7 or ...♗g4, when the h-pawn is doomed. Now, on the other hand, 25...♘f7 26 ♘c6 ♕e8 27 ♗a4 is unclear. I therefore decided to switch plans and take control of the g-file, aiming to attack f2.

25 ... ♖g6

The position has been transformed over the past few moves. Black has seized control of the open g-file, White has weak pawns on h4 and f2, and Black's king is secure.

26 ♖h1

White intends to expel the rook from g2 by bringing his queen to f1, but the immediate 26 ♕d3 is impossible because Black simply takes on h4. 26 b4 would have been ineffective after 26...axb4 27 axb4 cxb4 28 ♕xb4 ♘f7 29 ♕xe7 ♗xe7, when ...♗c5 and ...♖g2 will create more problems for White. As mentioned earlier, a general opening of the position can turn Black's dark-squared bishop into a monster.

26 ...   Rg2?!

Black has a large advantage, but this move lets White back into the game. It would have been more accurate to play 26...Wg7! because then 27 We1 is impossible. The critical line runs 27 Wd3 Rg2 28 Wf1 Wg4 29 Bd1 (29 Ne1 f3 attacks e4) Nxe4 30 Ne1 (30 Nxe5 Wg7! 31 Nxd7 Bxb2+ wins) Rxf2 31 Bxg4 Rxf1 32 Rxf1 Bxg4 and the two connected passed pawns coupled with the stranded knight on a7 give Black a winning position.

27 We1   Wg7

Certainly not 27...Nxc4??, when 28 Wf1 picks up a piece.

28 Bd3   Wg4? *(164)*

This leads to a 'brilliant' combination, but I must admit that I had simply overlooked White's reply. The best line was 28...Bg4 29 Nd2 Bh5, meeting 30 Bf1 by 30...Rg1. If White does nothing Black will continue with ...Wg4, and sooner or later White will have to play f3 to save the h-pawn. Then the weak pawns on h4 and f3 give Black a clear and permanent advantage, although this is by no means a forced win. After the move played the game should be a draw.

29 Bf1

Curiously enough, White had a second satisfactory move. After 29

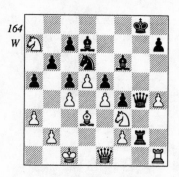

164
W

Be2 (29 We2 Be8 followed by ...Bh5 is very good for Black), the obvious 29...Nxe4 is met by 30 Nd2! (and not 30 Nxe5? Wg7, which wins for Black after 31 Bf3 Bxe5 32 Bxg2 Bxb2+ 33 Kc2 Ba4+, 31 Nxd7 Bxb2+ 32 Kc2 Bc3! 33 Wd1 Nxf2 or 31 Nd3 Nxf2! 32 Nxf2 Bxb2+ followed by 33...Bxa3) Nxf2 (30...Wf5 31 Bd3 Nxf2 32 Bxf5 Bxf5 33 Wf1 Nd3+ 34 Kc2! is good for White) 31 Bxg4 Nd3+ 32 Kb1 Bxg4 (32...Nxe1 33 Bxd7 Rxd2 34 Rxe1 f3 is unclear) 33 We4 Rxd2 34 Rg1 Nf2 35 Wf5 (35 Wf3 Rxb2+! is good for Black) Rd1+ 36 Ka2 Rxg1 37 Wxf6 Nd3 and a draw by perpetual check is by far the most likely outcome. Black can, of course, meet 29 Be2 by 29...Wg7, but after 30 Bf1 the rook has to retreat and White has repelled Black's initiative.

29 ...   Wxf3

More or less forced. 29...Rg3 30 fxg3! (30 Nh2 Wxh4 31 fxg3 fxg3 is less strong, since 32 Rg1 fails to

32...♗g5+ followed by ...gxh2, and 32 ♔b1 ♘xe4 is unclear) ♕xf3 31 ♖g1 is good for White because 31...♘xe4 is met by 32 ♗g2.

30 ♗xg2   ♕xg2!

At this point both sides were drifting into time-trouble and I am satisfied that I had the courage to sacrifice my queen. The alternative was 30...♕b3, but after 31 ♕e2 ♘xc4 32 ♕c2! ♕a2 33 ♘c6 only White has winning chances. After the move played, Black gets only two bishops for the queen, but the tremendous passed pawn on g2 and wayward knight on a7 combine to give Black adequate compensation.

31 ♖g1   f3 *(165)*

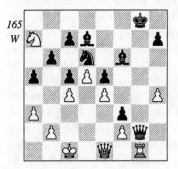

32 ♘b5

The alternatives are:

1) **32 ♖xg2+?!** (simplest, but not best) fxg2 33 ♕g1 ♗h3 34 ♘c6 ♗xh4 35 ♘xe5 ♘xe4 36 ♘d3 b5! 37 b3 (37 cxb5 c4) a4 38 cxb5 axb3 39 d6 (trying to create a passed pawn is the only chance; otherwise ...c4 will

win for Black) ♘xd6 40 ♘xc5 ♘b5 41 ♘xb3 ♘c3 (threat 42...♘e2+) 42 ♘d4 (42 ♔d2 ♗xf2) c5 and Black wins material. The bishops control enough squares to frustrate any attempts by White to deliver perpetual check.

2) **32 ♕f1 ♗h3** doesn't help, since sooner or later White will have to take on g2, and then he will lose a tempo with his queen.

3) **32 ♘c6** (just as good as the move played) and now:

3a) **32...♗g4** 33 ♖xg2 fxg2 34 ♕g1 (not 34 f3 ♗xh4 35 ♕g1 ♗xf3 36 ♘xe5 ♗g5+ 37 ♔c2 ♗xe4+ 38 ♔b3 ♘f5, followed by ...♘d4+ and ...♘e2, when Black wins) ♗f3 35 ♔d2! (or else ...♘xe4, and White's king is blocked out) ♘xc4+ 36 ♔d3 ♘d6 37 ♔e3 ♗xe4 38 f3 ♗xd5 39 ♕xg2+ ♔f7 40 ♘b8 ♘f5+ 41 ♔f2 ♗xh4+ and Black will probably win the f3 pawn as well, when he will have the unusual material balance of 2♗+4♙ v ♕. However, the power of the queen in an open position is such that White cannot be worse.

3b) **32...♘xe4** 33 ♖xg2 fxg2 34 ♕g1 ♗h3 35 f3 is unclear – this position could also arise from line 1 if Black plays 34...♘xe4.

3c) **32...♗h3** 33 ♖xg2+ fxg2 34 ♔c2! (to prevent Black promoting with check; 34 ♕g1 transposes into line 1, while 34 f4 exf4 35 e5 ♗xh4 wins for Black) ♘xc4 (34...♘xe4 35 f3 ♗xh4 36 ♕xh4 g1♕ 37 ♕xe4 is probably better for White) with a completely unclear position.

32 ...   ♘xb5

This natural move doesn't win, but neither do the alternatives, e.g. 32...♘xe4 33 ♖xg2+ fxg2 34 f3! (not 34 ♘xc7? ♗xh4 35 ♕g1 ♗h3 36 d6 ♘g5, followed by ...♘f3, and Black wins) ♗xh4 35 ♕g1 and the g-pawn falls, or 32...♗g4 33 ♖xg2 fxg2 34 ♕g1 ♗f3 35 ♘xd6 cxd6 36 ♔d2!, followed by ♔e3, and Black cannot maintain his advanced pawn.

33 ♖xg2+

Not 33 cxb5? ♗xb5 34 ♖xg2+ fxg2 transposing into the game.

33 ...   fxg2

34 cxb5?

In time trouble White makes a mistake which loses outright. The correct continuation was 34 ♕g1! (166), but the analysis of this move is exceptionally difficult.

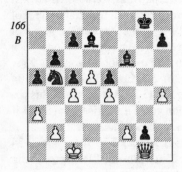

166
B

Black has two main possibilities; he can either give up the g2 pawn and keep the knight, or *vice versa*.

Suppose firstly that Black keeps the knight. He can try 34...♘d6 or 34...♘d4. The main problem with **34...♘d6** is that Black does not control f4, so that after 35 ♕xg2+ ♔f7 36 f4! exf4 37 ♕f3 White can activate his queen (37...♗e5 38 ♕h5+), when a draw is inevitable. **34...♘d4** 35 ♕xg2+ ♔f7 is more dangerous; after the moves 36 h5! (the position would be very good for Black if he could consolidate by ...h5, ...♗g4 and ...♘f3, rounding up the h-pawn) ♘e2+ 37 ♔c2 ♘f4 38 ♕f3 Black has prevented f2-f4, but the question arises as to how he can make progress. The only real prospect is to attack the h5 pawn by means of ...♗e8, but the direct ...♔e7 followed by ...♗e8 is met by ♕g4, and the queen threatens to penetrate to c8. Black can improve his position before playing ...♗e8, for example by 38...a4 (prevents later counterplay by b4) 39 ♔d2 h6 40 ♔c2 ♔e7 41 ♔b1 ♘d6 (41...♔d8 42 ♕g3! threatens 43 ♕g8, and after 42...♗g5 White replies 43 ♕c3 and the bishop has to return to f6) 42 ♔c2 ♗g5 43 ♔b1 ♗e8 44 ♕g4, but even here the capture on h5 is met by ♕c8, gaining sufficient counterplay to draw. Thus Black is not able to strengthen his position sufficiently to make progress.

The other possibility is to play **34...♗h3** 35 cxb5 (167), reaching a peculiar endgame position.

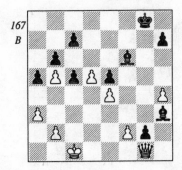

167
B

The pawn on g2 ties White down and it soon becomes clear that White cannot undertake anything active; he can only wait to see if Black can improve his position. The position of the bishop on h3 is Black's main problem, since after he captures the pawn on h4 it blocks the advance of Black's own h-pawn. If White allows Black to transfer the bishop to f3, for example, the h-pawn runs through. For this reason White usually cannot move his queen along the first rank. Even after lengthy analysis, I am not sure that I have discovered all the secrets in this position, since there are many possible defensive plans for White. For example, he may leave his queenside pawns as they are, or push them up to a4 and b3; he may leave the pawn on f2, or move it to f3. However, I believe that the correct result should be a draw. The safest plan is to play a4 and b3, but to keep the pawn on f2. Any other defensive plan risks losing. In view of this, it is natural to ask if Black can

fix the pawns on b2 and a3 by playing **35...a4**, but it turns out that after 36 h5 &g5+ 37 &c2 &f4 38 b3 axb3+ 39 &xb3 White gains counterplay by threatening a breakthrough with a4-a5 followed by d6, and this prevents Black taking the h-pawn with his king, which is necessary for any progress.

Therefore Black must start with **35...&xh4**. The first step in proving the above assertions is to show that Black wins if White plays f3. Firstly we consider the possibility that White plays a4 and b3, as follows: **36 a4 &g5+ 37 &c2 &f4** (now any queen move loses to ...&h2) 38 b3 h5 **39 f3** h4 40 &c3 &f7 41 &d3 &e7 42 &c3 &d8 (the king hides on the queenside to reduce White's chances of giving perpetual check) 43 &d3 &c8 **44 &c3** &b7 45 &d3 &g5 *(168)*:

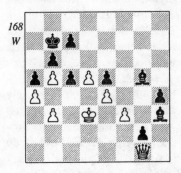

168
W

White cannot do anything to avoid arriving at such a position. Even if he plays his king to f2 he still cannot move his queen, and having the king on f2 only makes it easier for Black to execute his intention of ...♗g5-e7, ...c4 and ...♗c5. After 45...♗g5 there is a choice for White:

1) **46 ♕h2 ♗c1!** wins, e.g. 47 d6 (note that d6 is always impossible when White's king is on c4, because of ...♗e6+ followed by ...h3) ♗f4 48 ♕g1 cxd6, 47 ♔e2 ♗b2 48 d6 cxd6 49 ♕xh3 g1♘+, 47 ♔c4 ♗e3 or 47 ♕g1 ♗b2 followed by ...♗d4.

2) **46 ♕f2** c4+ followed by the manoeuvre ...♗e7-c5.

3) **46 ♔c4 ♗d2!** 47 ♕f2 (47 ♔d3 ♗b4 threatens ...c4+, so 48 ♔c4 is forced, transposing) ♗b4 48 ♕g1 (48 ♕e3 ♗d7) ♗a3 (threat ...♗b2-d4) 49 ♔c3 c4 and ...♗c5.

4) **46 ♔c3** (the best try, keeping the bishop out) ♗h6! (46...c4 47 d6! is less clear, while 46...♗e7 47 ♔c4 achieves nothing) and now White is in zugzwang, e.g. 47 ♔d3 c4+ or 47 ♕f2 ♗c1 48 ♕g1 ♗a3 etc.

The situation is slightly different if White keeps his king near to f2; suppose, for example, that White plays **44 ♔e2 ♔b7 45 ♔f2** *(169)*.

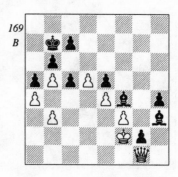

Now 45...♗g5 can be adequately met by 46 ♕h2, so Black has to pass by 45...♔b8 46 ♔e2 and only now 46...♗g5. After 47 ♕h2 c4! 48 d6 (48 bxc4 ♗e7) ♗f4 49 dxc7+ ♔xc7 50 ♕g1 cxb3 51 ♔d3 b2 52 ♔c2 ♗c1 53 ♕f2 b1♕+! 54 ♔xb1 ♗a3 Black's bishop reaches c5 and he wins. White can always jettison a

pawn by 47 d6 cxd6 48 ♔f2, but with an extra pawn Black shouldn't have much trouble winning; for example he can put his king on d7 followed by ...d5, ...e4 and ...♗e5-d4.

A crucial element in the above analysis was the possibility of Black's dark-squared bishop infiltrating round the back of White's queenside pawns, so if White plays f3 but leaves his pawns on b2 and a3 Black must adopt a different plan: **36 f3 ♗g5+ 37 ♔c2 ♗f4 38 ♔c3 h5 39 ♔d3 h4 40 ♔c3 ♔f7 41 ♔d3 ♔e7 42 ♔c3 ♔d8 43 ♔d3 ♔c8 44 ♔c3 ♔b7 45 ♔d3 a4 46 ♔c3 ♗g5** (once again Black intends ...c4 and ...♗e7-c5) **47 ♔c4** (the problem is that Black no longer has the ...♗d2-b4 idea) **♗h6!** (zugzwang) and now *(170)*:

1) **48 ♔c3** (48 ♔d3 c4+ followed by ...♗f8) c4 49 d6 cxd6 50 ♕f2 (50 ♔xc4 ♗e6+ or 50 ♔c2 d5 51 exd5 ♗f5+) ♗f8 followed by ...d5 and ...♗c5 wins.

2) **48 ♕f2 ♗c1** (threat ...♗xb2) 49 ♔c3 c4 50 ♕e1 (50 d6 cxd6 51

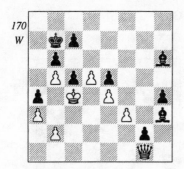

170
W

43 ♔d3 ♚c8 44 ♔c3 ♚b7 45 ♔d3 ♗g5 46 ♔c3 (Black can always play ...c4 and ...♗c5 using the same ideas as in the lines above) c4 47 ♔xc4 ♗e7 48 ♔c3 ♗c5 49 ♔d3 ♚c8 50 ♔c3 ♚d8 51 ♔d3 ♚e7 52 ♔c3 ♚f7 (after 52...♚f6, White might be able to play 53 ♕c1) 53 ♔c2 ♚g6 54 ♔d3 ♗d4 (*171*).

♕e1 ♗f4 52 ♕d1 ♚c7 wins) ♗f4 51 ♕g1 ♗h6 as in line 1.

From this analysis we can conclude that opening the c5-g1 diagonal gives Black too many chances to play ...c4 and ...♗c5, so White should avoid f3. In this case Black cannot make progress by simply advancing his king on the kingside, because with his bishop at f4 the move ...♚g4 may be met by ♕d1+ and the king has to retreat. The only possibility to penetrate on the kingside is again to sacrifice the c5 pawn to put the bishop on the c5-g1 diagonal. Then Black can bring his king to g4. It turns out that this plan is dangerous with the pawns fixed on a3 and b2, but if White has played a4 and b3 then he can defend. We consider both these possibilities together, because they differ only in the queenside pawn structure: **36 a4** ♗g5+ 37 ♔c2 ♗f4 38 ♔d3 h5 **39 b3** (White must avoid ♔e2, which allows Black to force f3 by playing ...♗g4+) h4 40 ♔c2 ♚f7 41 ♔d3 ♚e7 42 ♔c3 ♚d8

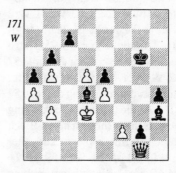

171
W

When I originally analysed this position, I concluded that 55 ♔c2 and 55 ♔c4 lose, but 55 ♔d2 draws. In fact all three moves draw.

First of all, consider **55 ♔d2** ♚g5 56 ♕h2. Now taking on f2 allows perpetual check (56...♗xf2 57 ♕xe5+ ♚g4 58 ♕f5+ ♚g3 59 ♕e5+ ♚f3 60 ♕f6+), while 56...♚g4 is met by 57 ♔e2 and Black has nothing better than to retreat his king. Finally Black may try 56...♚h5, but after 57 ♔d3 Black has achieved nothing since ...♗xf2 is still a draw. If Black retreats his king to the third rank, then White replies ♕g1, and Black hasn't achieved anything. Clear enough.

Now suppose that White continues **55 ♔c2** (55 ♔c4 is the same, but not 55 ♔e2? ♗g4+ and the h-pawn marches) ♔g5. In this case, the 56 ♕h2 defence doesn't work, because after 56...♗xf2 57 ♕xe5+ ♔g4 58 ♕f5+ ♔g3 59 ♕e5+ ♔f3 60 ♕f6+ (60 ♕h5+ ♔g4 61 ♕f7+ ♔e2) ♔e2 Black escapes the checks and wins, for example 61 ♕c3 (threatening mate in two) ♗e3! 62 ♕d3+ ♔f2 and now the result is clear. Originally, I thought that 56 ♔d3 also loses after 56...♔g4, for example 57 ♔e2 ♔f4 or 57 ♕d1+ ♔f4. But White has the surprising defence 57 ♕e1!!. At the moment Black's king obstructs the bishop on h3, so Black cannot free his h-pawn, and after 57...♔f3 58 ♕e2+ ♔f4 59 ♕d2+ ♔g4 60 ♕e1! Black is not making progress.

It is worth noting that White should not leave his queenside pawns on b2 and a3, when Black could fix them by playing ...a4 at some stage. The reason is that he would have to worry about the possibility of ...♗d4xb2 in the above diagram, and this might be enough to cost the game. However, we will not analyse this possibility in depth, because we have already found that the correct plan for White (pawns on f2, b3 and a4) leads to a clear-cut draw.

34   ...   ♗xb5
35   ♕g1

Or 35 f3 ♗xh4.

35   ...   ♗f1 *(172)*

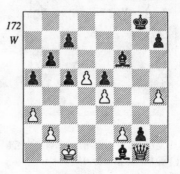

172
W

Now that Black is supporting his pawn from f1 instead of h3, there is no defence to the advance of the h-pawn.

36   ♕h2

Desperation, but after 36 h5 ♗g5+ 37 ♔d1 ♗f4 White can never move his queen (f3 followed by ♕f2 allows ...♗h2) so Black can simply take the h-pawn with his king and then play ...h5-h4-h3-h2.

36   ...   ♗xh4
37   ♕xh4   g1♕
38   ♕d8+

There is no perpetual check.

38   ...   ♔g7
39   ♕xc7+   ♔h6
40   ♕xb6+

Or 40 ♕d6+ ♔h5 41 ♕xe5+ ♕g5+, and Black forces the exchange of queens.

40   ...   ♔h5

Threatening mate in three by 41...♗e2+ 42 ♔d2 ♕d1+ followed

by 43...♕d3, so White has no time to take on c5.

| 41 | b4 | ♗d3+ |
| 42 | ♔d2 | ♕xf2+ |

0-1

In fact 42...♕f1 would have mated in five, but winning the queen by 43 ♔xd3 c4+ is also sufficient!

In the next round I lost to Dokhoian, but regained my position by beating Kuijf in round 10. The crucial game came in the penultimate round, when I faced Max Dlugy. After totally mishandling the early middlegame, I fell into a lost ending, but Dlugy ran short of time and allowed the position to become double-edged. A final blunder in time-trouble let my passed pawns slip through, and I found myself in the sole lead, half-a-point ahead of Andersson and Portisch. That night a terrible storm damaged the roof of the tournament hall so badly that the hall couldn't be used for the final round; instead the grandmasters were banished to the basement of the hotel. The last round was hard-fought, but all the leading games ended in draws, so I preserved my position and won the tournament outright.

My next event, in March, was an unusual team tournament, the VISA Summit in Reykjavik. This was a one-off event consisting of a double-round competition between four teams representing USA, USSR, England and the Nordic countries. Unlike the four and six-board FIDE team tournaments, this was fought over ten boards, so strength in depth was more important than a couple of star players. The USSR were without some of their top men, including the two K's, which was just as well because otherwise the event probably wouldn't have been very interesting from a competitive viewpoint. Despite this, the USSR were hot favourites to win, although the USA, who were fielding a more or less full side, were also formidable. In fact the whole tournament was very closely fought, with England doing unexpectedly well. It had always been assumed that England did better in team events with relatively few boards, but this theory received a setback at Reykjavik.

One curiosity was the way reserves were used. Each team was allowed two reserves, but normally (in Olympiads, for example) dropping a player means that all the lower boards move up by one, with the reserve slipping in on bottom board. In Reykjavik, however, the reserve simply substituted for the resting player, so a reserve could suddenly pop up on any board. The USSR's number one reserve was Eingorn; in the first four rounds he had been used three times, drawing with H.Olafsson on board 2, beating Short on board 1 and beating J.Benjamin on board 7.

This was certainly an excellent performance, which immediately earned Eingorn the nickname 'super-sub'.

After four rounds, the scores were USSR 22½, USA 21, England 20 and the Nordic team 16. In round 5 we were due to meet the USSR; a win would give us fair chances of taking first place in the tournament, since we faced the relatively weak Nordic team in the last round.

I was quietly preparing for Vaganian, the Soviet board three, when the team lists were posted. I wasn't playing Vaganian – instead I had to face 'super-sub' himself.

Game 29
J.Nunn – V.Eingorn
VISA Summit, Reykjavik 1990
French Defence

1	e4	e6
2	d4	d5
3	♘c3	♗b4
4	e5	c5
5	a3	cxd4

This unusual variation has a dubious reputation, but Eingorn is a specialist in obscure French lines; for example after 5...♗xc3+ 6 bxc3 ♘e7 7 ♕g4 he likes to play 7...♔f8.

6	axb4	dxc3 *(173)*

173
W

7 ♘f3

Theory recommends this pawn sacrifice. The alternatives are:

1) **7 bxc3 ♕c7 8 ♘f3 ♘e7!** (8...♕xc3+ 9 ♗d2 ♕c7 10 ♗d3 gives White compensation for the pawn, while 8...♘d7? 9 ♕d4! ♘e7 10 ♗f4 ♘b6 11 ♗d3 ♗d7 12 0-0 a6 13 ♗g5 was good for White in Chandler-Rogers, Wellington match (1) 1986) 9 ♗d3 ♘g6 (or 9...♘d7 10 0-0 ♘xe5 11 ♘xe5 ♕xe5 12 ♖e1 ♕xc3 13 ♖b1 ♕c7 14 ♕h5 ♘g6 15 ♕xd5 0-0 with only slight compensation for the pawn, Kaminski-Rausch, 2nd Bundesliga 1991) 10 0-0 ♘d7 11 ♖e1 ♕xc3 12 ♗d2 ♕c7 with advantage to Black, Em.Lasker-Maroczy, New York 1924, although this didn't stop Lasker from swindling a win.

2) **7 ♕g4 ♔f8** (*ECO* mentions the line 7...♕b6!? 8 ♕xg7 cxb2 9

♗xb2 ♕xb4+ 10 ♔d1 ♕xb2 11 ♖c1 ♘c6 12 ♕xh8 ♔f8 13 ♘f3 ♘b4, which is attributed to Veresov; the final position is quite good for Black, but there are a number of improvements at move 8, for example 8 bxc3, 8 ♘f3 or 8 b3) 8 ♘f3 ♕c7 9 ♗d3 ♘c6 10 0-0 f5 with an unclear position according to Keres. In view of Eingorn's fondness for ...♔f8, he would probably have been quite happy with this line!

7 ...   ♘e7

This was Eingorn's new idea. Previous experience had been highly discouraging for Black, e.g. **7...cxb2** 8 ♗xb2 ♘c6 9 b5 ♘ce7 10 ♗d3 ♘h6 11 ♕d2 ♗d7 12 h4!? ♘c8 13 ♖h3 ♘b6 14 ♖g3 ♘c4 15 ♗xc4 dxc4 16 ♘d4 ♕xh4 17 0-0-0 with an enormous attack for the two pawns in the game Bannik-Tolush, USSR 1963, or **7...♕c7** 8 ♕d4 (8 ♖a3!? cxb2 9 ♗xb2 ♘c6 10 ♕d2 ♘ge7 11 b5 ♘d8 12 ♗d3 b6 is dangerous, I.Zaitsev-Muchnik, USSR 1966, but the text is even stronger) ♘e7 9 ♗d3 ♘d7 10 0-0 cxb2 11 ♗xb2 ♘b6 12 b5 with a clear plus for White.

Eingorn's move is much better than these two alternatives. His idea is that 8 ♕d4 allows 8...cxb2 9 ♗xb2 ♘bc6 10 ♕d2 0-0, when Black is safely castled and White still has to justify his pawn sacrifice. I decided to develop rather than waste time with my queen.

8 ♗d3 *(174)*

8 ...   ♘d7

After **8...♕c7** 9 ♖a3! cxb2 10 ♗xb2 0-0 (after 10...♘bc6 the position is similar to I.Zaitsev-Muchnik above) 11 ♖c3! (the preparatory 11 0-0 is also not bad, but the immediate 11 ♗xh7+ ♔xh7 12 ♘g5+ ♔g8! 13 ♕h5 ♕xc2 14 ♖h3 ♕b1+ is only a draw) ♘bc6 (11...♕b6 12 ♗xh7+ ♔xh7 13 ♘g5+ ♔g6 14 ♖h3 ♕xb4+ 15 c3 ♕f4 16 ♕h5+ ♔f5 17 ♘xf7+ g5 18 ♖f3 is winning for White) 12 ♗xh7+ ♔xh7 13 ♘g5+ ♔g8 (White also wins after 13...♔g6 14 ♖h3) 14 ♕h5 ♕xe5+ 15 ♔f1 Black must give up his queen for the knight on g5, when White has a clear material advantage.

8...♘bc6 9 b5 cxb2 (9...♘b4 10 bxc3 ♘xd3+ 11 cxd3 is also bad for Black) 10 ♗xb2 ♘b4 11 ♗e2 carries the awkward threat of 12 c3, and virtually forces the horrible 11...d4.

9 0-0

It is far more important to maintain the key pawn on e5 than to worry about taking on c3. 9 bxc3 transposes to line 1 in the note to White's 7th move.

9 ...   ♘c6 (175)

Black must play for the win of a pawn, or else he has no compensation for his weak dark squares, but 9...cxb2 10 ♗xb2 leaves White with a huge lead in development and two powerful bishops. Therefore Black plays either to eliminate the important e-pawn, or to take on b4 and then exchange the d3 bishop.

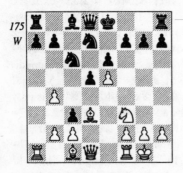

175
W

10 ♖e1

The central e-pawn is much more important than the one on b4. If Black now goes for material by 10...cxb2 11 ♗xb2 ♘xb4 12 ♗a3 ♘xd3 13 cxd3 f5 (or else ♘d4 increases the pressure) 14 exf6 (14 ♘d4 ♔f7) ♘xf6 15 ♘e5, then his king is permanently trapped in the centre. The continuation might be 15...♗d7 16 ♕d2 ♖c8 17 ♕b4 b6 18 ♕d6 and by now White has a winning attack.

10 ...   ♘xb4

Wisely settling for just one pawn. At least Black gets castled in this line.

11 bxc3   ♘xd3

12 cxd3

Better than 12 ♕xd3 b6 (not 12...0-0? 13 ♘g5, nor 12...♘c5? 13 ♕b5+, but 12...♘b6 is playable, since after 13 ♗a3 ♘c4 White cannot keep his bishop on the a3-f8 diagonal) 13 ♗a3 ♘c5 14 ♗xc5 bxc5 15 ♕b5+ ♗d7 16 ♕xc5 ♕e7 with no problems for Black. After 12 cxd3 Black must castle at once, or else ♗a3 is very strong.

12 ...   0-0

White has a substantial lead in development and good attacking chances against the poorly defended kingside, but he must act quickly before Black completes his development and starts pushing his a-pawn.

13 ♖a4   f6

Black must move his f-pawn sooner or later, because otherwise he cannot transfer his pieces to the endangered kingside, so 13...f6 and 13...f5 must be the main candidate moves. Had Black played 13...f5, White would have had the difficult decision as to whether to take on f6. After 14 exf6 ♕xf6 (14...♘xf6 15 ♘e5 ♗d7 16 ♖h4 gives White good attacking chances for the pawn) I do not see a straightforward continuation of White's attack. Indeed, Black may very well grab the c3 pawn, if he is given the chance.

White does better to avoid exf6 and instead build up the attack more slowly, for example **14 罝h4** (14 ♘g5 ♘c5 15 罝h4 h6 defends as 16 ♕h5 is met by 16...♕e8) ♕e7 (14...♘c5 15 ♗a3) 15 ♗g5 ♕f7 16 ♗e3 with sufficient play for the pawn. Another idea is **14 ♗a3 罝e8** 15 h4 ♘f8 16 h5 ♗d7 17 罝b4, when White's grip on the dark squares and kingside attacking chances offer enough compensation for the pawn.

14 罝g4 *(176)*

Now White need not take on f6; instead he can use the tempo to strengthen his attack. It would also have been possible to continue in a more positional vein by 14 ♗a3 罝f7 15 ♗d6, simply maintaining control of e5.

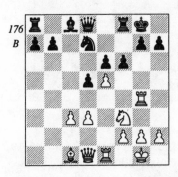

14 ... ♘xe5?

An error tipping the balance in White's favour. The alternatives are:

1) **14...fxe5?** 15 ♗h6 罝f7 16 ♘g5 罝e7 17 ♗xg7! 罝xg7 18 ♘xe6 wins for White.

2) **14...f5** 15 罝g3 leaves Black paralysed, e.g. **15...♕e7** 16 ♗h6 罝f7 17 ♘g5 gxh6 (or 17...f4 18 罝g4 gxh6 19 ♘xf7+ ♔xf7 20 罝xf4+ with an enormous attack after 20...♔e8 21 ♕h5+ ♔d8 22 ♕xh6 or 20...♔g7 21 罝e3) 18 ♘xf7+ ♔xf7 19 ♕h5+ ♔f8 20 ♕xh6+ ♔e8 21 罝g7, or **15...♘b6** 16 ♗h6 罝f7 17 ♘g5 罝c7 18 ♕h5, or finally **15...♔h8** 16 ♘g5 ♕e7 17 ♕h5 h6 (17...g6 18 ♗a3!) 18 ♘h3, followed by either ♘f4-g6+ or 罝g6 followed by ♗xh6.

3) **14...♕c7!?**. This is the logical follow-up to Black's previous move. Black would like White to take on f6, because then the knight enters the game with gain of tempo. Likewise, White would prefer Black to exchange on e5, and to this extent the move in the game plays into White's hands. By playing ...♕c7, Black not only steps up the pressure on e5, aiming to induce exf6, but he also attacks the loose pawn on c3 and indirectly defends g7. The critical continuation is 15 d4! (control of e5 is more important than the c3 pawn) ♕xc3 (perhaps this is just too greedy) 16 罝g3! (so that exf6 ♘xf6 doesn't gain a tempo on the rook) and now:

3a) **16...♔h8?** 17 ♘h4 ♕a5 18 ♗d2 ♕b6 19 ♕h5 with an enormous attack, for example 19...♔g8 20 ♗h6 罝f7 21 ♗xg7 罝xg7 22 ♕e8+ ♘f8 23 罝xg7+ ♔xg7 24 ♕e7+ ♔g8 25 exf6 wins for White.

3b) **16...♕b4** 17 exf6 ♘xf6 (or 17...♖xf6 18 ♗g5 ♖f7 19 ♖xe6 ♘f8 20 ♖e8 with strong pressure for the pawn) 18 ♘e5 (threat ♗a3) ♖e8 19 ♗h6 ♖e7 20 ♗g5! ♔h8 21 ♖f3! ♖c7 22 ♖xf6 gxf6 23 ♗xf6+ ♔g8 24 ♖e3 with a decisive attack for White, who only needs to play h3 to release all his pieces for the onslaught.

3c) **16...♕c7** 17 ♗h6 ♖f7 18 exf6 ♘xf6 19 ♘e5 ♖e7 20 ♕f3! (20 ♗g5 ♘e4! defends) ♘e4 21 ♖c1 ♕d8 22 ♖xg7+! ♖xg7 23 ♗xg7 ♔xg7 24 ♕f7+ ♔h8 25 ♖c7 ♕g8 26 ♕f4 and White wins.

Although these sample lines are favourable for White, after 14...♕c7 White would have had to continue very accurately to justify his attack, whereas after 14...♘xe5? White's attack plays itself.

15   ♘xe5

After 15 ♖xe5 fxe5 16 ♗h6 ♖f7 (16...g6 17 ♗xf8 ♕xf8 18 ♘xe5 is dangerous for Black) 17 ♘xe5 ♖c7 White has nothing better than a draw by 18 ♗xg7 ♖xg7 19 ♖xg7+ ♔xg7 20 ♕g4+ ♔f8 21 ♕f4+ ♔g7! (21...♔e7 22 ♕g5+ ♔e8 23 ♕g8+ ♔e7 24 ♕xh7+ wins) 22 ♕g4+.

15   ...   fxe5
16   ♖xe5   ♖f5

Black attempts to exchange one of White's attacking rooks, but the result is a further weakening of his dark squares. The alternative was 16...♖f7, based on the idea that the obvious attacking plan of ♗e3-d4 and ♖eg5 is not decisive. The reason is that White has to waste a tempo by ♖g4-g3, or else ♖eg5 may be met by ...e5; this gives Black time to defend g7 by ...a5, ...b6 and ...♖a7. Then White has no immediate way to break through, while Black's a-pawn will become a major menace in just two moves. Therefore, White should play 17 ♗e3 a5 18 h4 b6 (a4 is covered, so the passed pawn cannot advance for the moment) 19 h5 ♖a7 20 ♕a4, with a strong attack and no black counterplay.

17   ♕e2 *(177)*

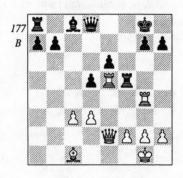

177
B

17   ...   g6

The threat was 18 ♗h6 g6 19 ♖xf5 exf5 20 ♕e5, and most other moves lose immediately:

1) **17...♕f6** 18 ♖xf5 exf5 (or 18...♕xf5 19 ♗h6 g6 20 ♖f4) 19 ♕e8+ ♕f8 20 ♖xg7+ ♔xg7 21 ♗h6+ winning.

2) **17...♔h8** 18 ♗h6! ♖f7 (or 18...gxh6 19 ♖xf5 exf5 20 ♕e5+) 19

≣eg5 g6 20 ≣xg6! hxg6 21 ≣xg6
≣f5 (21...♕h4 22 ♕e5+ ♔h7 23
≣g7+ ♔xh6 24 ≣xf7 wins) 22 ♕g4
and there is no defence to the threat
of 23 ♗g7+.

3) **17...♗d7** 18 ♗h6 ≣f7 19
≣eg5 g6 20 ≣xg6+ hxg6 21 ≣xg6+
♔h7 22 ♕h5 ♕h4 (the only move)
23 ♕xh4 ♔xg6 24 g4! ♔h7 (24...e5
25 ♕h5+ ♔f6 26 ♗g5+ ♔g7 27
♕h6+ ♔g8 28 ♗f6 wins) 25 ♕h5
with a winning position for White.

4) **17...♕d7** 18 ♗h6 g6 19 h4 (19
≣xf5 exf5 20 ♕e5 fxg4 21 ♕f6
wins, but 20...♕f7! is a reasonable
defence) does not lead to an immediate disaster, but White has a stronger
attack than in the game.

18 ♗h6   ♔f7

If Black wants to avoid the lines
in the last note, then this is his only
choice. The idea is that 19 ≣xf5+
exf5 20 ♕e5 doesn't threaten mate,
so Black can simply take the rook on
g4.

After 18...♔f7, White can't break
through directly because the rook on
f5 blocks all the attacking paths, but
this rook is the linchpin of Black's
defence and if it had to move his position would collapse. It follows that
White would like to play his rook
away from g4 to permit g2-g4, but at
the moment there is no good square
for the g4 rook.

19 h4 *(178)*

A useful multi-purpose move,
which removes any worries about

the back rank, prepares a possible
switch to the h-file by h5, hxg6+,
♗g5 and ≣h4, and waits to see
Black's intention.

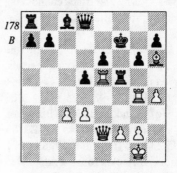

19 ...   ♗d7?

By leaving b7 undefended Black
allows White to shift his g4 rook
with gain of tempo. 19...a5 would
have been a tougher defence, but after 20 ≣g5! all the chances lie with
White, for example:

1) **20...a4** 21 ≣gxf5+ exf5 (after
21...gxf5, White wins by 22 ♕h5+
♔g8 23 ≣e3) 22 ♗g5 ♕d6 23 ≣xd5!
♕e6 (23...♕xd5 24 ♕e7+ ♔g8 25
♗h6 mates) 24 ≣e5 ♕d6 25 ≣e7+
♔g8 26 ♕a2+ (revealing why White
needed to remove the d-pawn) and
wins.

2) **20...♕d6** 21 ≣gxf5+ exf5
(21...gxf5 22 ♕h5+ ♔e7 23 ♕xf5)
22 ≣e8 a4 23 ≣h8 (needless to say,
White can't be satisfied with winning the queen by 23 ≣f8+ when
Black's a-pawn is charging down the
board) ♕e6 24 ♕d2! and White has

dangerous threats. Note that the obvious 24...a3? fails to 25 ♖f8+ ♔e7 26 ♕g5+ ♔d6 27 ♕d8+ ♔c5 28 ♗e3+ ♔b5 29 ♖f6 a2 30 ♖xe6 a1♕+ 31 ♔h2 and Black cannot take the rook, so White has a decisive attack.

3) 20...♖f6 21 ♖g3 ♖f5 (the line 21...♕c7 22 ♖f3 is very dangerous, for example 22...♕xc3 23 ♖xf6+ ♔xf6 24 ♕f3+ ♔e7 25 ♕f8+ ♔d7 26 ♕g7+! and Black loses his queen to a discovered attack) 22 ♖xf5+ exf5 23 ♕e5 (now that White's rook is not *en prise*) ♕f6 24 ♕xd5+ ♕e6 25 ♕b5, with ♖e3 to come.

20   ♖b4! (*179*)

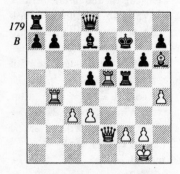

179
B

20   ...   a5

Black has no good move. After 20...♕c7 (on 20...♗c6 White need not bother with the e-pawn, because 21 g4 is extremely strong) 21 ♗f4 ♕c6 22 g4 ♖xe5 23 ♕xe5 the removal of the defensive rook gives White a decisive attack, for example 23...♖c8 24 ♗h6 ♕xc3 25 ♕d6 and

Black cannot meet the threats of 26 ♕xd7+ and 26 ♖f4+.

21   ♖xb7   ♕c8

21...♖b8 loses to 22 ♖xf5+ exf5 23 ♕e5 ♖xb7 24 ♕xd5+ ♔e8 25 ♕g8+, winning the queen.

22   ♖xf5+   exf5
23   ♕b2!

There is no defence to the many threats, including 24 ♕b5 and 24 c4 opening the line b2-g7.

23   ...   a4
24   ♕b5   ♔e6
25   ♖b6+   1-0

Adams, King and Suba also won, with the result that England took the match by 6-4, the first ever victory over the Soviet Union at the senior level (there had been earlier wins in student events). The Soviets cunningly prevented a repetition by splitting their country up.

Before the last round the scores were USSR 26½, England 26, USA 25 and the Nordic team 22½. Unfortunately, disappointment lay in store since we only managed a 5-5 draw against the Nordic team. Curiously, we could still have won the event if the USA had beaten the USSR by 6-4, and for a time this appeared possible, but finally the other match also ended in a 5-5 tie so, just as at Dubai 1986, the USSR scraped home by half a point.

Nevertheless, this was a good result for England. My personal score of 3½/6 was satisfactory, but I was disappointed to have lost in the critical last-round match (see the comments on pages 180 and 241!).

I was inactive over the next few months, playing just a few Bundesliga games and, in June, winning the Bayswater Open with 5/5. My next major tournament was the traditional OHRA event in Amsterdam. This turned out to be the last such tournament, and as no new sponsor could be found it disappeared from the chess calendar. Just as in 1985, it was a six-player double-round tournament. I didn't play especially badly, but at a few critical moments I threw away very promising positions and ended with a mediocre 4½/10, which was only sufficient to tie for fourth and fifth places. Beliavsky was the convincing winner with 6½ points.

A couple of weeks later I took part in the Lloyds Bank tournament in London. My performance here was very up-and-down, with excellent play interspersed with miserable blunders. I was a little lucky in round 3, when the following position arose in Y.Hellwing-J.Nunn (with White to play) *(180)*.

Black's pawn is further advanced, but with White to move the position should be drawn. The game continued with the natural moves **58 a6 ♕e4+**, but what should White play now?

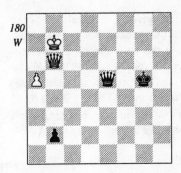

180
W

Hellwing concluded that his position was lost in any case, and the game finished **59 ♔c7? ♕c2+!** (of course, 59...b1♕ 60 ♕xb1 ♕xb1 61 a7 is a draw) **60 ♔d7** (there is no good square, e.g. 60 ♔b7 b1♕ 61 a7 ♕xb6+ 62 ♔xb6 ♕c8) **b1♕ 61 ♕e3+ ♔g4 62 ♕d4+ ♕e4 63 ♕g7+ ♔f3 0-1.**

White could have drawn with the surprising move **59 ♔a7!** *(181)*, setting up various stalemate possibilities.

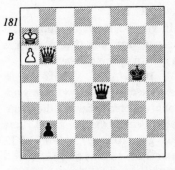

181
B

Then 59...b1♕ (or ♖) allows a draw by 60 ♕f6+ (or ♕h6+) and

White gives perpetual check or forces stalemate. Nor can Black improve the situation by the preliminary 59...♕h7+ 60 ♔a8 (60...♕h1+ 61 ♔a7! restores the stalemate) b1♕, for then 61 ♕xb1 ♕xb1 62 a7 draws. The idea of blocking one's own pawn is not so easy to see.

After nine of the ten rounds I had scored 6½/9, and I needed a win to gain a worthwhile prize. Fortunately, my opponent in the last round, James Howell, needed a win in order to achieve a grandmaster norm, so an uncompromising game was guaranteed.

Game 30

J.Nunn – J.Howell

London (Lloyds Bank) 1990

Sicilian

1	e4	c5
2	♘f3	e6
3	d4	cxd4
4	♘xd4	♘f6
5	♘c3	d6
6	g4	♘c6
7	g5	♘d7
8	h4	a6
9	♗e3	♕c7
10	♕e2	

In view of Howell's situation, it was not surprising that he chose a very sharp opening system.

10 ...   b5!?

An interesting idea, which my opponent adopted because it didn't appear in *Beating the Sicilian 2*! There I only gave 10...♗e7 11 0-0-0 b5 12 ♘xc6 ♕xc6 13 ♗d4 b4 14 ♘d5, following Karpov-Dorfman, USSR Ch 1976. After the game, my opponent said that 10...b5 had been played a

couple of times before, but I have only been able to trace one example. The idea is to exploit an obvious weakness of playing ♕e2, namely that the c3 knight has nowhere to go after ...b5-b4.

The only real answer to the advance of Black's b-pawn is to meet ...b4 by ♘d5, but, provided Black avoids ...♗e7, the knight move creates no immediate threats and Black is not forced to capture it. Despite Black's loss in this game, 10...b5 is playable and it is surprising that it has not been seriously tested in the past four years.

11 ♘xc6

This is the most ambitious continuation. By playing his bishop to d4 White attacks g7 and prevents the development of Black's kingside pieces. Other moves are possible, but the obvious 11 0-0-0 b4 12 ♘d5 appears bad after 12...exd5 13 ♘xc6 ♕xc6 14 exd5 ♕a4 and White doesn't really have enough for the piece.

11   ...   ♕xc6
12   ♗d4 *(182)*

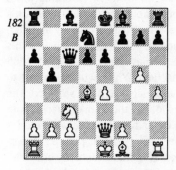

Black cannot relieve the pressure on g7 easily, since ...e5 creates a horrible weakness at d5, and ...♘e5 is usually met by f4. The bishop move also clears the e-file, making ready for ♘d5.

12   ...   ♗b7?

Despite its natural appearance, this move is a mistake; as I have remarked before, in sharp Sicilian positions a single error can have far-reaching consequences. At some stage the moves ...b4 and ♘d5 will be played. If White can maintain the knight on d5, then Black will have serious problems completing his development, because the combination of a knight on d5 and a bishop on d4 will exercise a powerful restraining

influence on Black's kingside. Conversely, if Black can threaten to take the knight in safety then White will be in dire trouble. If the knight retreats, for example to e3, then not only is the e4 pawn hanging, but Black will play ...e5 and trap the bishop on d4. Retreating the knight to f4 is no better, because White would again run into ...e5. In other words, the result of the game depends critically on White's ability to maintain his knight on d5. Whether or not White succeeds will depend primarily on tactical factors, which aren't easy to assess at this early stage.

It turns out that the bishop doesn't achieve anything concrete on b7, and in particular it doesn't help Black to dislodge the knight from d5.

Black should have played 12...b4! 13 ♘d5 a5, with the idea of playing the bishop to a6. After **14 0-0-0?**, for example, 14...♗a6 15 ♕e1 (15 ♕e3 ♖c8 16 ♖d2 ♗xf1 17 ♖xf1 ♕c4 is even worse, since f1, a2 and d5 are all attacked) ♖c8 16 ♖d2 ♗xf1 17 ♖xf1 ♕b5 puts the d5 knight in precisely the dilemma described above. It is better to reply **14 ♕b5!** ♕xb5 (14...♕xc2? 15 ♗d3 and 14...♖a6 15 ♕xc6 ♖xc6 16 ♗b5 ♖xc2 17 ♔d1 are bad for Black) 15 ♘c7+ ♔d8 16 ♘xb5 ♗b7 17 ♗g2 with just an edge for White. If Black continues 17...♘c5, then 18 0-0-0! is good because 18...♘xe4 (18...♗xe4 19

♗xe4 ♘xe4 20 ♖he1 d5 21 ♖xe4) 19 ♖he1 ♘c5 20 ♘xd6! gives White a clear plus.

13   0-0-0 *(183)*

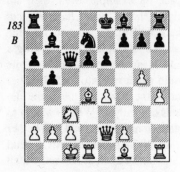

183
B

13   ...   ♖c8

After **13...b4** 14 ♘d5 a5 (upon 14...♘e5 the simple 15 f4 exd5 16 fxe5 dxe4 17 exd6 ♕xd6 18 ♗g2 should give White some advantage because the exposed black king is more important than the temporary extra pawn, but the complicated 15 ♘e3 intending f4 is also possible, since 15...♕xe4 16 ♗g2 ♘f3 17 ♖h3 ♘xd4 18 ♕f1! is very good for White), the continuation 15 h5 ♖g8 16 g6 hxg6 17 hxg6 f5 18 ♗g2 ♗a6 19 ♕e3 ♖c8 20 ♖d2 ♗c4 21 b3 e5 22 ♗b2 ♗xd5 23 exd5 ♕b6 24 ♕xb6 ♘xb6 25 ♖h5 gave White a winning position in Dueball-Rahls, Bundesliga 1989/90. Alternatively, Black can remove his king from the centre by **13...0-0-0** but after 14 a3, followed by ♖h3, it is still not very safe and Black has not solved the

problem of developing his kingside. Nevertheless, this might have been relatively best.

14   ♖h3

If White can complete his development in peace, then the centralised black king will be the dominant feature of the position. Accordingly, it is more important to nullify Black's threats than to play actively by 14 h5, when in contrast to Dueball-Rahls Black may reply 14...b4 15 ♘d5 ♕a4, and White will be forced to make an unclear piece sacrifice. The rook on the third rank is useful both for defending the queenside and for later activity on f3, e3 or d3. Moreover, if White eventually plays h5 and g6 the rook needs to be defended in order to meet ...hxg6 with hxg6.

14   ...   b4

Black has run out of constructive developing moves, so there is little choice.

15   ♘d5   a5

Not 15...♕a4 16 ♘xb4 a5 (16...d5 17 ♖a3! is similar) 17 ♖a3! ♕xb4 18 ♖b3 ♗xe4 19 ♕xe4 and White has an enormous initiative for no material investment.

After 15...a5 Black threatens to play 16...♗a6, when White's queen cannot simultaneously stay on the e-file and defend c2.

16   c4!

Slightly surprising, but very effective. The one defect of White's position is that so long as there is a mate threat on c2, he will always have a piece tied down to its defence. Transferring the pawn to c4, where it can be easily defended by b3, completely nullifies Black's c-file pressure. At the same time White erects a barrier against the b7 bishop and supports the knight on d5.

16 c3 is less accurate; Black replies 16...♔d8! and now he is genuinely threatening to take on d5.

16 ...   ♔d8

Other moves are worse, for example 16...♗a6 17 b3 and Black has achieved nothing, 16...♘e5 17 b3 (intending f4) exd5 18 exd5 ♕xd5 (or else f4) 19 ♗xe5 ♕xe5 20 ♖e3 or 16...bxc3 17 ♖xc3 ♘c5 18 ♗xc5! dxc5 19 ♖b3, followed by ♖b6, and Black's position collapses.

17 ♔b1 *(184)*

Best, or else Black might take twice on d5, and after ♗b6+ (or ♗f6+) Black would get a rook and two pieces for his queen.

17 ...   ♘c5?!

If White can maintain his knight on d5 safely then in the long run Black is doomed, so the key question is whether or not Black can take the knight at some stage. In fact, the present position is the best chance Black will get, because once the h3 rook comes to the centre Black cannot contemplate ...exd5. The critical position arises after 17...exd5 (or 17...♗a6 18 b3 exd5 19 exd5, and now the line 19...♕xd5 20 cxd5 ♗xe2 21 ♗xe2 leads to an excellent ending for White, while 19...♕b7 20 ♖f3 f6 21 gxf6 gxf6 22 ♖xf6 ♗g7 23 ♖xd6 ♗xd4 24 ♖xd4 gives White three pawns and a very dangerous attack for the piece) 18 exd5 ♕a6 (18...♕c7 19 ♖e3 is very good for White after 19...♘e5 20 f4 or 19...♕b8 20 ♕h5) 19 ♖f3 (19 ♖e3 ♔c7 permits Black's king to slip away) ♘e5 (19...♔c7 20 ♖xf7 followed by ♗h3 is crushing) *(185)*

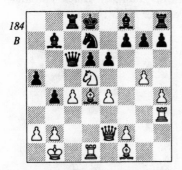

184
B

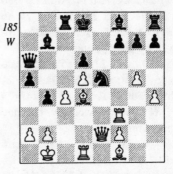

185
W

Now **20 ♗xe5** dxe5 is bad because 21 ♖xf7 loses to 21...♕g6+, while 21 ♕xe5 ♕d6 defends. Therefore, White must proceed more slowly. To begin with, I felt that **20 ♖f5** was the key, and then:

1) **20...g6** 21 ♖xe5! (in my original notes, I recommended 21 ♗xe5 dxe5 22 ♖xf7 ♗d6 23 c5, but the defence 23...♕xe2 24 ♗xe2 ♖c7! holds the balance) dxe5 22 ♕xe5 ♖g8 23 c5 ♕a7 24 c6 and Black is crushed.

2) **20...♘xc4** 21 ♖c1 ♘a3+ (however Black plays, he ends up with a miserable ending) 22 bxa3 ♖xc1+ 23 ♔xc1 ♕xe2 24 ♗xe2 with a large endgame advantage for White.

3) **20...♕xc4** 21 ♗b6+ ♔d7 (or 21...♔e8 22 ♖xe5+ dxe5 23 ♕xe5+) 22 ♗h3 ♔e8 (22...♕xe2 23 ♖xe5+) 23 ♖xe5+ dxe5 24 ♕xe5+ ♗e7 25 ♗xc8 ♗xc8 26 ♖e1 and again White has a massive plus (remember Black can't castle).

4) **20...♔c7** 21 f4 g6 (21...♘g6 22 ♖xf7+ ♔b8 23 h5 ♘e7 24 h6 wins) 22 ♗xe5 dxe5 23 ♖f6, followed by ♕xe5+, and wins.

5) **20...♗e7** 21 ♗xe5 dxe5 22 d6 ♗xd6 23 ♕xe5 ♖c6 (23...♔c7 24 ♖xd6 ♕xd6 25 ♖xf7+) 24 ♕xg7 (24 c5? ♕xf1) followed by c5, and White wins.

6) **20...f6** 21 gxf6 g6 (21...gxf6 22 f4 ♘d7 23 ♖xf6 is very good for White) 22 ♗xe5 gxf5 23 ♗d4! h5 24 f7 ♖h7 25 ♕e8+ ♔c7 26 c5 ♕a8 27 cxd6+ ♗xd6 28 ♖c1+ ♔b8 29 ♗e5! and White wins.

Unfortunately, there is a seventh move, which more or less refutes the attack:

7) 20...♖c7!. This defends the weak f7 pawn, and threatens simply 21...♖e7, so White must take on e5, but after 21 ♗xe5 (21 ♖xe5 dxe5 defends after 22 ♗xe5 ♗d6 or 22 ♕xe5 ♕d6) dxe5 White's attack founders because of Black's dark-squared grip. In particular, 22 d6 is met by 22...♖d7.

Happily, White has two alternative 20th moves which offer much better attacking chances. The first is **20 ♖e1!?.** The point of this move is that ♖f5 is a bit of a waste of time if White is simply going to play ♗xe5 afterwards; it would be much more useful to use the tempo to build up on the e-file. Of course, ♖e1 gives Black the chance to grab more material, but it turns out that taking on f3 is too risky. Black's alternatives after 20 ♖e1 are *(186)*:

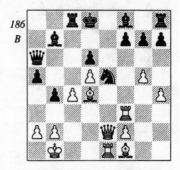

186
B

1) **20...♗e7** 21 **♕e3!** (White has ideas of ♗b6+ or c5) f6 (21...♖e8 22 ♗b6+ ♖c7 23 c5 is crushing) 22 ♖g3! (intending f4; this is clearer than 22 c5 ♕a8 23 c6 ♗xc6 24 dxc6 ♕xc6 25 ♖g3! which is probably also good for White) ♖c7 23 ♗b6 followed by some combination of f4 and c5, with a large advantage for White.

2) **20...♖xc4** (20...♘xc4 21 ♖xf7 is very good for White) 21 ♗xe5 ♗xd5 22 ♗d4! ♕c6 23 ♖f4, followed by b3, with a decisive attack.

3) **20...♕xc4** 21 ♗b6+ ♔d7 22 ♕xc4 ♖xc4 23 ♗xc4 ♘xc4 24 ♖xf7+ wins.

4) **20...♘xf3** 21 ♕xf3 ♔c7 (after 21...♖c7 22 c5 ♗e7 23 ♖d1 ♕a8 24 cxd6 ♖d7 25 ♗b6+ ♔c8 26 ♗h3! Black is crushed) 22 c5 ♕a8 23 ♕xf7+ ♔b8 24 c6 ♗a6 25 ♖e8 ♖xe8 26 ♕xe8+ ♗c8 27 ♗b6! and Black has no defence to the threat of 28 c7+ ♔b7 29 ♕c6 mate.

5) **20...♔c7** 21 ♗xe5 dxe5 22 ♕xe5+ ♗d6 (after 22...♕d6 23 ♖xf7+ Black cannot play 23...♔b8 because of 24 ♖xf8, and 23...♔b6 24 ♕xd6+ ♗xd6 25 ♖e6 ♖hd8 26 ♖xg7 will give White at least four pawns for the piece) 23 ♕xg7 ♕b6 (23...♔b8 24 c5 will leave Black with insufficient compensation for the minus pawns) 24 c5! ♗xc5 25 ♖e6! ♕xe6 (25...♗d6 26 ♖xf7+ ♔b8 27 ♖xd6) 26 dxe6 ♗xf3 27 ♕xf7+ and White wins.

6) **20...♖c7** (once again this is the best defence) 21 ♖e3! (intending f4; 21 ♗xe5 dxe5 22 ♕xe5 is refuted by 22...♕g6+ 23 ♗d3 ♗d6! 24 ♕d4 ♗c5! and Black is at least equal) and now *(187)*:

6a) **21...♖d7** 22 f4 ♘g6 23 ♖e8+ ♔c7 24 ♕f2, followed by c5, and White wins.

6b) **21...♕xc4** (relatively best) 22 ♕xc4 ♖xc4 23 ♗xe5 ♖xh4 (23...♖c5 24 ♗d4 ♖xd5 25 ♗b6+ ♔d7 26 ♖c1 wins the exchange) 24 ♗g3 ♖h1 (24...♖d4 25 ♖e8+ ♔c7 26 ♖c1+ ♔b6 27 f3! with advantage to White) 25 ♖e8+ ♔c7 26 ♖c1+ ♔b6 27 ♗f4 ♗xd5 28 ♗e3+ ♔b7 29 ♖ec8 ♖xf1 30 ♖c7+ ♔a6 (30...♔b8 31 ♗a7+ ♔a8 32 ♖xf1 is worse because Black's king is trapped on the back rank) 31 ♖xf1 and White's more active pieces give him some endgame advantage.

The other possibility for White at move 20 is **20 ♖e3!**, which is similar to variation 6 just above. It might seem odd to play ♖f3 and then ♖e3, but if White can continue with f4 and force Black to retreat his knight, then it will be White and not Black who gains time. Two sample lines are 20...♖c7 21 f4 f6 (aiming to trap the bishop if White takes on e5 immediately) 22 ♕e1! with the unpleasant threat of c5, and 20...f6 21 f4 ♘d7 22 ♕g4 (threat c5) ♕a8 23 ♗h3 ♖c7 24 ♕e6 winning for White.

It is not easy to see a good line for Black after 20 ♖e3!, and in a practical game this would certainly be the best option as there is little for White to calculate. It would be up to Black to find a concrete answer to the threat of f4.

Despite this gloomy assessment, I think Black should have taken the knight, because this would at least have given White the chance to go wrong. After 17...♘c5?! White's initiative grows from move to move, while Black can only make marginal improvements to his position.

18 ♖f3

White immediately homes in on the weakness created by the move ...♔d8.

18 ...   ♖c7

Or 18...♕e8 (18...exd5 19 exd5 wins for White after 19...♕d7 20 ♗h3, 19...♕e8 20 ♖e3, 19...♕c7 20 ♖e1 or 19...♕b6 20 ♖xf7 ♖c7 21 ♖e1) 19 ♖e3 e5 (19...♕d7 20 ♗h3) 20 ♗xc5 ♖xc5 21 a3 ♕a4 22 ♕f3!, followed by ♖b3, and White opens

up the queenside before Black's kingside pieces can come into play.

19 ♖e3

Defending e4 and thereby attacking c7.

19 ...   ♖d7

Once again 19...exd5 is impossible, this time because after 20 exd5 the queen cannot stay on the a4-e8 diagonal (20...♕a4 21 b3 or 20...♕d7 21 ♗h3 f5 22 gxf6 ♕f7 23 ♖e1).

20 ♗h3 *(188)*

Increasing the pressure is much better than 20 ♘f6 ♖c7 21 e5, which allows 21...♔c8 and Black's pieces have suddenly been activated.

188
B

20 ...   h6

This move practically forces White to undermine e6, but even the passive 20...♖g8 (20...exd5 21 exd5 ♕b6 22 ♖e8+ ♔c7 23 ♗xd7 ♔xd7 24 ♖e1 wins) offers no real hope after the positional continuation 21 h5 ♗e7 22 g6 hxg6 23 hxg6 fxg6 24 ♘xe7 ♖xe7 (24...♔xe7 25 ♕g4) 25 e5 and Black's position falls apart.

| 21 | g6 | fxg6 |
| 22 | Rg1? | |

An inaccuracy. The simple 22 Bxc5! (22 Nf4 e5 is less clear) dxc5 23 Nf4 would have been very strong. This thematic continuation increases the pressure on e6, and after 23...Rxd1+ 24 Qxd1+ Ke8 25 Qg4 Black's position disintegrates, for example 25...Bc8 26 Nxg6 Rg8 27 Ne5, followed by Qg6+.

22 ... g5!

The only move. Black must prevent the rook arriving on g6, which would cause the e6 square to collapse. 22...exd5 loses to 23 exd5 Qb6 24 Re8+ Kc7 25 Bxd7 Kxd7 26 Bxg7, while after 22...Rf7 23 Rxg6 exd5 24 exd5 Qb6 25 Re8+ Kc7 26 Qg4 Black cannot meet the threat of 27 Rc8+.

23 hxg5 hxg5

Now White has to be a bit careful, because Black's rook on h8 has entered the game. This is the flaw in 22 Rg1?.

24 Rxg5 *(189)*

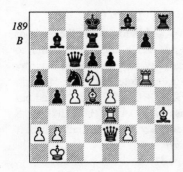

189
B

24 ... Nxe4?

Initiating tactics when you have a serious positional disadvantage usually results in an early train home. The alternatives are:

1) **24...Rxh3** 25 Rxh3 exd5 26 exd5 Qc7 27 Rh8 Rf7 28 Rxg7 Qe7 29 Qxe7+ Kxe7 30 Rxf7+ Kxf7 31 Rh7+ Kg8 32 Rc7 Ba6 33 Bxc5 dxc5 34 d6 (or 34 Rc6+ if Black had played 31...Kg6) is winning for White.

2) **24...exd5!** (the only chance, but Black was too short of time to find it) 25 exd5 Qa6 26 Re8+ (26 Bxc5 Rxh3!) Kc7 27 Bxd7 Nxd7 28 Bxg7 Bxg7 29 Rxg7 Rxe8 (not 29...Rh1+? 30 Kc2 Bc8 31 Kd2!, threatening Qe7, and winning after 31...Rb1 32 Qe7 Rxb2+ 33 Kd3) 30 Qxe8 Bc8 and although White has an indisputable advantage, the win is not straightforward. After 31 b3, for example, Black can introduce counterplay by 31...a4.

| 25 | Bb6+ | Kc8 |
| 26 | Rh5! | |

In the midst of the tactics, a very calm and logical move. The rook on h8 is Black's only active piece, so White swaps it off, at the same time exposing Black's weak back rank.

26 ... Rxh5

There is no escape, because after 26...Nd2+ 27 Kc2 Rxh5 28 Qxh5 Kb8 (28...Qxc4+ 29 Rc3) 29 Kxd2 exd5 30 Qe8+ Bc8 31 Bxd7 Qxd7 32 Qxf8 White wins on material.

27 ♕xh5   ♔b8

The depressing alternative is 27...♘f6 (27...♘d2+ transposes to the previous note) 28 ♖xe6! (threat ♖e8+) ♔b8 29 ♘xf6 ♕h1+ (29...gxf6 30 ♖e8+ ♗c8 31 ♗xd7) 30 ♔c2 gxf6 31 ♖e8+ ♗c8 32 ♖xc8+ ♔b7 33 ♕f5 and wins.

28 ♖xe4   exd5

Black finally takes the knight which has been *en prise* for 13 moves!

29 ♖e8+   ♗c8
30 ♗xd7   ♕xd7
31 ♖xf8   ♕e7
32 ♕e8   1-0

The tournament ended in a tie between Conquest, Adams and Sturua on 8/10. My score of 7½/10 was sufficient for joint 4th-8th places.

I played only a few Bundesliga games between Lloyds Bank and the Novi Sad Olympiad, which took place in November. One of these had an unusual finish. White was to play in J.Nunn-O.Gschnitzer *(190):*

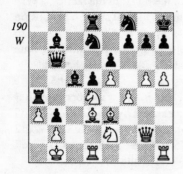

In this fairly typical Sicilian position Black has tried to counter White's kingside attack by exerting pressure on d4. In this case, however, the attack is already too strong.

29 g6!   fxg6

Or 29...♖xd4 (the alternative capture 29...♗xd4 30 ♘xd4 ♖xd4 loses to 31 ♕f2) 30 ♗xd4 ♗xd4 31 gxf7 ♗e3 (the threat was ♘xd4 followed by ♖hg1) 32 ♖dg1 ♗xg1 33 ♖xg1 g6 34 hxg6 with a mating attack.

30 hxg6   ♖xd4 *(191)*

30...h6 31 ♖xh6+! gxh6 32 g7+ ♔g8 33 gxf8♕++ ♔xf8 34 ♖g1 forces mate in a further four moves.

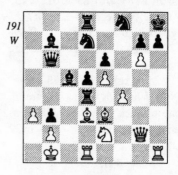

31 ♖xh7+!

White has to destroy the chain of knights defending h7, in order to make way for an eventual mate by the queen. Note that 31 ♗xd4 ♗xd4 32 ♖xh7+ ♘xh7 33 ♖h1 is bad because of 33...♘f6! 34 ♖xh7+ ♔g8 35 exf6 ♗xf6 and suddenly Black is better!

31 ...   ♘xh7

32 罝h1   ᙏf8

Now 32...ᙏf6 fails to 33 罝xh7+ ♔g8 34 exf6 gxf6 35 ♕h2, followed by mate, while 32...罝xd3 33 罝xh7+ ♔g8 34 罝h8+ ♔xh8 35 ♕h3+ leads to mate on f7.

33 罝xh7+   ♔g8

Once again 33...ᙏxh7 34 ♕h3 forces mate.

34 ♕h3   ᙏxg6
35 ♗xg6   罝d1+
36 ᙏc1   1-0

After 36...♔f8 White seals off the escape route by 37 ♕h4, when Black cannot prevent 罝h8 mate.

The main event of the year was, of course, the Olympiad. Having finished in second place in three successive Olympiads, anything less would be regarded as disappointing. However, the signs of fragility had already become apparent in the team competitions at the end of 1989 so, in my view, the inevitable comments about whether 1990 was to be England's year were somewhat misplaced. The USSR were without the K's, but a team with Ivanchuk, Gelfand, Beliavsky, Yusupov, Yudasin and Bareev certainly deserved respect, and in fact the Soviets retained their crown with some ease. A 3-1 win against Sweden in round 12 left us in an excellent position to gain second place, with just two rounds to go. Up to this point I had scored an excellent 5½/7, but unfortunately I suddenly became ill. This, coupled with my usual last-round nerves, caused an even more spectacular collapse than usual. Instead of just losing the last game, I went one better and lost my last two games. The result was that England drew 2-2 against Iceland in round 13, which still left us a point ahead of the USA. In the final round I lost to Arencibia, and England could only manage 2-2 against Cuba. The USA caught us up by winning 3-1 against Bulgaria, leaving us to the mercy of the tie-break. Perhaps it was too much to hope that we would scrape into second place in two successive Olympiads on tie-break, and this time Lady Luck favoured the Americans, who took the silver medals home with them. In a sense we were rather unlucky not to finish second in Novi Sad, but in fact our third place was due almost entirely to Chandler's 9/11. Speelman also played well, but Short and Adams could only score 50%. My final score of 5½/9 was not at all bad, but I was disappointed by my collapse in the last two rounds.

I ended the year by taking part in the traditional pre-Christmas 'Islington' weekend tournament, which was in fact held in the Barbican. I won outright with 5½/6, which at least let me face 1991 in a better frame of mind.

1991

In mid-January, I set off for Wijk aan Zee hoping to repeat my success of the previous year. The early signs were certainly good, since in the first round I won with Black against Kožul. After this, I felt optimistic about my second round game against Fedorowicz; not only was I White, but I have an excellent personal score against 'Fed'. But there was a small problem with my opening preparation...

Game 31

J.Nunn – J.Fedorowicz

Wijk aan Zee 1991

Sicilian Richter-Rauzer

1	e4	c5
2	♘f3	d6
3	d4	cxd4
4	♘xd4	♘f6
5	♘c3	♘c6
6	♗g5	e6
7	♕d2	a6
8	0-0-0	h6
9	♗e3	♘xd4
10	♗xd4	b5
11	f4	♗b7 *(192)*

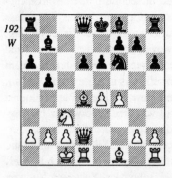

In 1991, I was more or less following the repertoire recommended in *Beating the Sicilian 2*. During my preparation for this game, I noticed that 11...♗b7 had become more popular since the book was published. The point behind 11...♗b7 is that one of the most dangerous ideas against the more common 11...♗e7 is the pawn sacrifice 12 ♗e2; by playing 11...♗b7 Black hopes to force 12 ♗d3, when 12...♗e7 transposes into the normal line without allowing the ♗e2 sacrifice.

I had given the single reference '11...♗b7 12 ♗xf6 gxf6 13 ♗d3

♕b6 14 ♔b1 ♗e7 15 f5 e5 16 ♗e2 followed by ♗f3, Jansa-Spassov, Sochi 1980', which I had assessed as slightly better for White. Searching through my database revealed that the more recent game Rachels-Dlugy, USA Ch 1989 had deviated by 13...b4 14 ♘e2 ♕b6 15 ♔b1 a5 16 f5 e5 17 ♘g3 h5 18 ♕e2 h4 19 ♘f1 ♗h6 20 ♘d2 ♔e7 21 ♘f3 ♕e3 22 ♖he1 ♕xe2 23 ♖xe2 ♗f4 and Black had achieved a roughly equal position. Theory doesn't stand still, and Dlugy's plan of immediate queenside expansion was certainly better than Spassov's passive play. In particular, Dlugy managed to send White's knight on a route which kept it far away from the sensitive d5 square.

This was an alarming discovery. There isn't time for detailed analysis during the morning before a game especially when, as at Wijk aan Zee, the rounds start at half-past-one. Moreover, this was just one of the variations which Fedorowicz might play. In this situation, the important thing is not to attempt the impossible and try to develop a brilliant new innovation in half-an-hour, but just to have some idea of what you will play if the position actually arises on the board. On checking my database, I found that White had only tried a very limited range of moves against 11...♗b7, namely 12 ♗xf6 and the transpositional 12 ♗d3. Surely it

would be possible to think up another idea? I suddenly remembered that White could meet 10...b5 by 11 ♕e3. I had never played this line, but it had been popular during the 1980s. Checking the database showed that Black had never played 10...b5 11 ♕e3 ♗b7 and had preferred to develop the bishop on d7 in order to block the d-file. Transferring this idea to the position after 10...b5 11 f4 ♗b7 produced the 'innovation' 12 ♕e3, which can be 'explained' by claiming that ♕e3 is better now that Black's bishop has been committed to b7. A quick check showed no obvious flaws with the move, and *Fritz* couldn't find anything wrong either, so I moved on to the next line in Fedorowicz's repertoire.

12 ♕e3!?

When the position actually arose on the board, I thought for a couple of minutes to check that I had not overlooked some elementary refutation, and then played 12 ♕e3 with a confident air, while looking directly into my opponent's eyes. This was intended to give the impression that the move was the result of weeks of careful and detailed analysis, rather than having been cooked up in ten minutes the same morning.

12 ... ♕c7?! *(193)*

In view of the obvious danger along the d-file, Black simply moves his queen, but this may already be an inaccuracy. Other ideas are:

1) **12...♗e7** 13 ♗xf6 (now we have transposed into the line 9...♗e7 10 f4 ♘xd4 11 ♗xd4 b5 12 ♕e3 ♗b7 13 ♗xf6) gxf6 (13...♗xf6 14 e5 ♗e7 15 exd6 ♗xd6 16 ♘e4 ♗xe4 17 ♕xe4 0-0 18 ♗d3 g6 19 h4 gives White good attacking chances) 14 f5 ♕a5 15 a3 ♖c8 16 ♖d3 when both 16...♕c7 17 ♔b1 ♕c5 18 fxe6 fxe6 19 ♕h3 ♕e5 20 ♗e2 h5 21 ♖hd1 ♔f7, Balashov-Lerner, USSR Ch 1984, and 16...♖c5 17 ♗e2 ♖e5 18 ♖f1 ♕c7 19 ♕g3 ♗xe4 20 ♘xe4 ♖xe4 21 ♖c3, Tal-Tukmakov, USSR Ch 1983, were highly unclear.

2) **12...b4** 13 ♗xf6 gxf6 (the sacrifice 13...♕xf6 14 ♘b5!? cannot be accepted, since 14...axb5 15 ♗xb5+ followed by e5 is winning, but even 14...♕d8 15 ♘xd6+ ♗xd6 16 e5 ♗d5 17 ♖xd5 exd5 18 exd6+ ♔f8 19 ♕c5 appears promising for White) and now:

2a) **14 ♘a4** (risky) ♕a5 15 ♘b6 (15 b3 is very undesirable because it weakens White's dark squares) ♖d8! 16 ♗c4 d5! (White had the positional threat of ♗b3 followed by ♘c4 or f5, while after 16...♗xe4 17 ♕xe4 ♕xb6 18 f5 White has a very strong attack for the pawn) 17 ♘xd5 (17 exd5 ♗c5) exd5 18 exd5+ ♔d7 and I doubt if White has enough compensation for the piece.

2b) **14 ♘e2** (safer) ♕a5 15 ♔b1 ♕c5 16 ♕d3 h5 17 ♘d4 ♖d8 18 ♗e2 ♗h6 19 ♖hf1 ♔e7, Hellers-Grønn, Oslo Cup 1991, with an edge

for White, although Black later won the game.

This analysis shows that 12 ♕e3 may be no better than other lines, but a new idea always increases the chance of inducing an error.

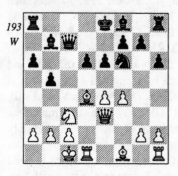

193
W

13   ♗b6!

This was virtually the only significant point I had noticed during my morning preparation. Black's queen has to move, but there are no really tempting squares.

13   ...   ♕c8?

This further error leaves Black in desperate trouble. After **13...♕b8** 14 e5 (14 ♘xb5 axb5 15 ♗xb5+ ♘d7 is tempting, but not really correct) ♘d7 15 ♗d4 White is slightly better, but in the game matters are far worse for Black. The other alternative is **13...♕c6**, and this was played in Nunn-Lobron, Munich 1991, which took place four months after the current game. Nunn-Lobron continued 14 ♘d5 ♖c8 15 ♘xf6+ gxf6 16 ♗d3 (White has a small but permanent advantage because he has doubled Black's f-pawns without the usual price of giving up the two bishops) ♖g8 17 g3 d5 18 ♖he1 ♗e7? (18...dxe4 19 ♗xe4 ♕xe4 20 ♕xe4 ♗xe4 21 ♖xe4 h5 would have restricted White to a small plus) 19 ♕f2! with a clear advantage for White. I won the game quickly, so 12 ♕e3!? earned me an unexpected two points. Lobron's play surprised me because he followed my published annotations of the Fedorowicz game up to move 16, at which point I assessed the position as slightly better for White!

14 e5   **♘d5**

Or 14...dxe5 (14...♘d7 15 exd6) 15 ♖d8+ ♕xd8 16 ♗xd8 ♖xd8 17 ♕b6 (better than 17 fxe5 ♘d7 and Black has survival chances) and White should win, while 14...b4 15 exf6 bxc3 16 b3 gxf6 17 ♗d4 ♗e7 18 ♗xc3 gives White the better pawn structure and leaves Black with no safe place for his king.

15 ♘xd5   **♗xd5**
16 exd6

Stronger than the unclear sacrifice 16 ♖xd5 exd5 17 exd6+ ♕e6.

16 ...   **♕c6 (194)**

Again Black has no choice because he must cover the undefended bishop on d5.

17 ♖xd5!

White's attack plays itself. Black survives after 17 ♗e2 ♖c8 18 d7+ ♕xd7 19 ♗f3 ♕c6, threatening mate

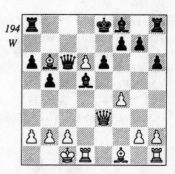

194
W

on c2, but this move eliminates Black's only active piece.

17 ...   **♕xd5**
18 ♗e2   **♕xa2**

There is no real answer to the threats of ♖d1 and ♗f3, for example 18...♕xd6 (18...♖xd6 19 ♗f3) 19 ♖d1 ♕b8 (19...♕e7 20 ♕c3 and 19...♕b4 20 ♕f3 ♖c8 21 ♕b7 also win) 20 ♗f3 ♗e7 21 ♗c6+ ♔f8 22 ♖d7! ♖c8 (22...♗f6 23 ♖b7 ♕c8 24 ♖c7 ♕b8 25 ♗xa8 ♕xa8 26 ♕c5+ wins) 23 ♖c7 ♕b8 24 ♖xe7! (here, surprisingly, 24 ♗xa8 ♗d6! isn't completely clear) ♔xe7 25 ♗c5+ (likewise, there is no immediate win after 25 ♕a3+ b4! 26 ♕xb4+ ♔f6) ♔f6 (25...♔d8 26 ♕d3+) 26 ♗d4+ ♔e7 27 ♗e5 ♕a7 (or else ♕c5+) 28 ♕a3+ ♔d8 29 ♕d6+ ♔c8 30 ♗xa8 and White wins.

19 ♕f3

The most accurate move, avoiding the need to win an ending after 19 ♕c5 ♕d5 20 ♖d1 ♗xd6 21 ♕xd6 ♕xd6 22 ♖xd6.

19 ...   **♗xd6**

The main line runs 19...♕d5 (or 19...♖c8 20 d7+ ♔xd7 21 ♕b7+) 20 d7+! ♔e7 21 ♖d1 ♕xf3 22 d8♕+ winning a piece.

20 ♕xa8+   ♔e7
21 ♕b7+   ♔f8 *(195)*

21...♔e8 22 ♕c6+ ♔e7 23 ♗c5 leads to the same conclusion.

195
W

22 ♗c5!

This move extinguishes any counterplay, since after 22...♗xc5 23 ♕c8+ White takes the bishop with check.

22 ...   ♕a1+

Or 22...♔g8 23 ♗xd6 ♕a1+ 24 ♔d2 ♕xh1 25 ♗d3 f5 (25...g6 26 ♗e5) 26 ♗e5 ♖h7 27 ♕c8+ with a quick mate.

23 ♔d2   ♕xh1
24 ♕b8+   1-0

It is mate in six more moves: 24...♔e7 25 ♕xd6+ ♔f6 26 ♕e5+ ♔g6 27 ♗d3+ f5 28 ♕xe6+ ♔h7 29 ♗xf5+ g6 30 ♕xg6.

I drew my next two games, but in round five I lost with Black to Salov. This was the point in the tournament at which I had two Blacks in a row, and I was nervous about the prospect of facing another strong grandmaster with Black the following day. As it turned out, I had little time to think about the tournament situation because Curt Hansen, who normally plays in a solid positional style, untypically decided to go straight for my throat.

Game 32

C.Hansen – J.Nunn

Wijk aan Zee 1991

King's Indian

1	c4	g6
2	♘c3	♗g7
3	d4	♘f6
4	e4	d6
5	♘f3	0-0

6	♗e2	e5
7	0-0	♘c6
8	d5	♘e7
9	b4	

This immediate queenside push

has retained a certain degree of popularity, even though 9 ♘e1 and 9 ♘d2 have always been the main continuations. 9 b4 is very logical. White makes progress on the queen-side while keeping the knight on f3 so as to meet an early ...f5 by ♘g5, aiming to exploit the weak e6 square. One defect is that Black may prepare ...f5 by the active move ...♘h5, heading for f4, whereas in the normal lines Black must play the relatively passive ...♘d7 (or ...♘e8).

9 ...   ♘h5

10 g3

Preventing ...♘f4. The other possibility is 10 c5, but discussion of the various alternatives would take us too far afield.

10 ...   f5

11 ♘g5   ♘f6

12 f3   f4 *(196)*

A slightly unusual choice, 12...c6 and 12...♔h8 being more common alternatives.

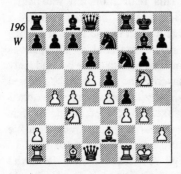

196
W

13 c5 *(197)*

After this game, interest in 13 c5 rapidly waned and **13 ♔g2** became the new fashion. In Van Wely-Nunn, Wijk aan Zee 1992, I replied **13...♔h8**, when established theory gave the continuation 14 ♖b1 ♘e8 15 ♘h3 ♗f6 16 ♘f2 h5 17 gxf4 exf4 18 ♘b5 g5 as slightly better for Black, G.Garcia-Marjanović, Banja Luka 1979. Unfortunately, Van Wely produced the powerful innovation 14 c5!, and after 14...h6 15 cxd6 ♕xd6 16 ♘b5 ♕b6 17 a4! (I had over-looked this move) ♘fxd5 18 exd5 hxg5 19 a5 ♕f6 20 ♘xc7 ♖b8 21 g4! I was already lost.

Then the search was on for Black improvements, and they were not long in coming. The first idea was to play 13 ♔g2 **a5**, the main line continuing 14 bxa5 (Grimm-R.Mainka, Porz 1993 continued amusingly with 14 ♗a3? h6 15 ♘e6?? ♗xe6 16 dxe6 axb4 17 ♗xb4 c5 0-1) ♖xa5 15 ♕b3 with a double-edged position, Lobron-Gelfand, Munich 1992. Later on, Black found another reasonable continuation, namely **13...h6** 14 ♘e6 ♗xe6 15 dxe6 c6 16 b5 ♕c7 17 bxc6 bxc6 18 ♗a3 ♖fd8 19 ♕a4 ♕c8 20 ♖ab1 ♔h8 21 ♖fd1 ♕xe6 22 ♕a6 h5 with unclear play, Van Wely-Ye Jiangchuan, Biel IZ 1993.

If White is satisfied with a draw he can try **13 b5**; after 13...h6 (and not 13...♘e8?! 14 ♘e6 ♗xe6 15 dxe6 ♕c8 16 ♘d5 ♕xe6 17 ♘xe7+ ♕xe7 18 ♕d5+ ♔h8 19 ♕xb7 with an advantage for White, Ghitescu-Uhlmann, Berlin 1982) 14 ♘e6 ♗xe6 15 dxe6 fxg3 16 hxg3 ♕c8 17 ♘d5 ♕xe6 18 ♘xc7 ♕h3 Black forces perpetual check.

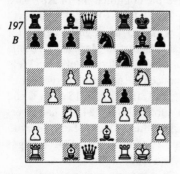

197
B

13 ...   dxc5!?

According to *ECO*, the normal line is 13...fxg3 14 hxg3 h6 15 ♘e6 ♗xe6 16 dxe6 d5 17 exd5 ♘fxd5 18 ♘xd5 ♘xd5 19 ♗c4 c6 20 ♖b1 ♔h7 21 ♖b3 ♕e7 22 ♗xd5 cxd5 23 ♕xd5 ♖ad8 24 ♕c4 ♖d4 25 ♕e2 ♕xe6, Taimanov-Bilek, match Leningrad-Budapest 1957, with an equal position.

However, this is not the only possibility for Black. The game Sieglen-Düster, Bundesliga 1988/9 continued 13...dxc5 14 bxc5 h6 15 ♘e6 ♗xe6 16 dxe6 ♕d4+ 17 ♕xd4 exd4 18 ♘b5 fxg3 19 ♖b1 gxh2+ 20 ♔xh2 ♘h5 21 ♔g2 c6 22 ♘d6 b5 23 f4 with a complicated position which is probably better for White. During 1988, it occurred to me that this variation would be much improved by a preliminary exchange on g3, so as to avoid the possibility that White will not recapture after ...fxg3. Therefore, in my 1990 book *The Classical King's Indian*, I suggested 13...fxg3 14 hxg3 dxc5 15 bxc5 h6 16 ♘e6 ♗xe6 17 dxe6 ♕d4+ 18 ♕xd4 exd4 19 ♘b5 ♘xe4! 20 fxe4 d3 with at least equality for Black. At the board I suddenly realised that this line doesn't work, because after 15...h6 White replies 16 d6! hxg5 17 ♗c4+ ♔h7 (or 17...♔h8) 18 dxe7 with a strong initiative for the pawn. I included this correction in my analysis of C.Hansen-Nunn published during 1991, and the assessment was vindicated by the game Meyer-Schlemermeyer, Bundesliga 1991 (played near the end of the year), which continued 17...♔h7 18 dxe7 ♕xe7 19 ♗e3 c6 20 ♔g2 ♘h5 21 ♕e2 ♗f6 22 ♖b1 ♔g7 23 ♘d1 (heading for g4) with strong pressure for the pawn; White later won the game.

This realisation left me panic-stricken – my intended line had a huge hole in it, and in such a sharp position reasonable alternatives would be hard to come by. Suddenly I saw that the idea could be rescued by using the move-order 13...dxc5 14 bxc5 h6 15 ♘e6 (15 d6 hxg5 is much less dangerous when the h-file is closed) ♗xe6 16 dxe6 fxg3 17 hxg3 (17 ♕xd8 gxh2+ 18 ♔xh2 ♖fxd8 19 ♖b1 b6 is fine for Black) ♕d4+, reaching the target position. I took on c5 with a sense of relief which, however, didn't last very long.

14 ♗c4!?

My heart sank when Curt Hansen played this sharp move very quickly. The position is rather complicated, and such a quick decision implied that either he was following prepared analysis, or the move was so obviously strong that prolonged thought wasn't necessary. Further analysis improved my composure. White's idea is that after 14...♔h8 15 bxc5 h6 16 ♘e6, White's ♗c4 is far more useful than Black's ...♔h8, and in particular the ...♘xe4 and ...d3 trick mentioned on the previous page doesn't work any more. Luckily, Black has playable alternatives and I suddenly saw that I might be able to seize the initiative myself by means of a sacrifice.

14 ... cxb4

Grabbing as much as possible and letting White do his worst along the c4-g8 diagonal.

15 d6+ ♔h8
16 ♘b5

Best. After 16 dxe7 ♕xe7 (threatening both ...bxc3 and ...♕c5+) 17 ♕b3 (17 ♘a4 ♘e8! 18 ♘f7+ ♖xf7 19 ♗xf7 ♕xf7 gives Black three pawns for the exchange) bxc3 18 ♗a3 c5 19 ♘f7+ ♖xf7 20 ♗xf7 ♗h3 21 ♖f2 b5 the pawn army starts to march and Black has the advantage.

16 ... h6

Not 16...cxd6 17 ♘xd6 ♕b6+ 18 ♔g2 ♗h6 (or 18...h6 19 ♘df7+ ♖xf7 20 ♘xf7+ ♔h7 21 ♗b2, and whereas in the game White has a useless bishop on f7, here he has an active knight) 19 ♘gf7+ ♔g7 20 ♘xe5 and White's superbly centralised pieces are worth far more than the miserable extra pawn.

17 ♘f7+

Better than 17 dxe7 (17 ♘xc7 hxg5 18 ♘xa8 ♘c6 19 ♘c7 ♘d4 is very good for Black because 20 ♘b5 ♘xb5 21 ♗xb5 ♕b6+ wins a piece, while 20 ♘d5 ♕xd6 gives Black two pawns and an initiative for the exchange) ♕xe7 18 ♘f7+ ♖xf7 19 ♗xf7 ♕xf7 20 ♕d8+ ♕e8 with a clear plus for Black.

17 ... ♖xf7
18 ♗xf7 cxd6 *(198)*

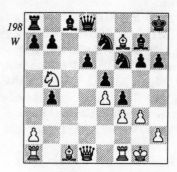

198
W

19 ♘xd6

A very difficult decision as both captures lead to unclear positions. After 19 ♕xd6 ♗h3 20 ♖d1 (20 ♕xd8+ ♖xd8 21 ♖e1 ♘c6 is very awkward for White because 22 ♗xg6 is met by 22...a6 23 ♘c7 ♘d4 heading for f3 or c2) ♕f8! (20...♕a5 21 ♘c7 ♖c8 22 ♗e6! is good for White) 21 ♘c7 (21 ♗b3 is met similarly, except that Black has an extra exchange) ♕xf7 22 ♘xa8 fxg3 23 hxg3 ♘xe4! 24 fxe4 ♕f3 White may play:

1) **25 ♖d2** ♕xg3+ 26 ♔h1 ♗g4 27 ♖g2 (trying to win; 27 ♖d3! ♗f3+ 28 ♖xf3 ♕xf3+ is a draw) ♗f3 (27...♕e1+ draws, but here Black can play for more) 28 ♕d2 ♗xe4 29 ♔g1 ♗xg2 30 ♕xg2 ♕e1+ 31 ♔h2 (after 31 ♕f1 ♕c3 32 ♖b1 ♘f5 Black has five pawns, an attack and chances to trap the knight on a8 in return for the rook) ♕h4+ 32 ♕h3 ♕f2+ 33 ♕g2 (33 ♔h1 ♕d4!) ♕f8 34 ♘c7 e4 with some advantage to Black.

2) **25 ♕d2** ♕xg3+ 26 ♔h1 ♗g4 27 ♖f1 ♗f3+ 28 ♖xf3 ♕xf3+ 29 ♔g1 (29 ♕g2 ♕d1+ 30 ♔h2 ♕d8 is promising for Black) ♕xe4 (and not 29...♕g4+ 30 ♔h2 ♕c8 31 ♕xb4 ♘g8 32 ♖b1, which hands the advantage over to White) and Black is better (30 ♕d8+? ♔h7 31 ♕xe7 fails to 31...♕d4+).

It seems that White can force a draw in line 1, but this doesn't mean that the game continuation is wrong. It is only on his next move that White makes a perceptible error.

19   ...   ♗h3 *(199)*
20   ♗b3?

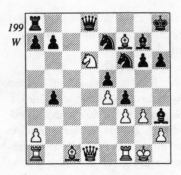

The critical moment passed unnoticed by both players, indeed even in my original annotations I failed to remark on White's missed chance. White cannot play 20 ♖e1 because of 20...♕b6+ 21 ♔h1 ♖d8, so the rook has to go to f2. During the game I believed that the immediate 20 ♖f2 was impossible because of 20...♘c8 21 ♖d2 ♕b6+ 22 ♔h1 ♘xd6 23 ♖xd6 ♕f2 and Black wins. Curt Hansen obviously thought the same, because he decided to defend his queen with gain of tempo.

The hidden flaw in all this is that after 20 ♖f2 ♘c8, White can play 21 ♗e6! avoiding loss of material. Black may continue with 21...♘xd6 22 ♗xh3 ♕b6 23 ♔g2, but his position is much less favourable than in the game. His useful bishop on h3 has gone, to be replaced by its opposite number. Black can play 23...♘b5, aiming for d4 or c3, but he is handicapped by the crippled bishop on g7. White has the advantage.

Therefore, Black should meet 20 ♖f2! by 20...♔h7 (note that 20...♘c6 is impossible while the bishop is on f7), but again 21 ♗b2 gives White an improved version of the game continuation. I would assess this as unclear.

20 ... ♔h7

21 ♖f2

Now White's queen is defended and there is no pin on the d-file, but White has paid a high price for his caution. If the bishop had stayed on f7, then Black would have had to play ...♔h7 in any case, to release the knight to move to c6. Now Black has gained ...♔h7 for free, which gives him practically an extra tempo. In such a sharp position this can swing the whole balance of the position.

21 ... ♘c6 (200)

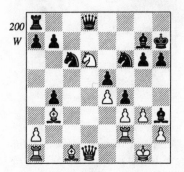

The immediate complications have subsided and we may assess the result. Black has two pawns for the exchange, but at the moment the extra queenside pawns aren't very

important, although they will become more so in an ending. For the moment, the most relevant factor is Black's lead in development and the exposed position of the knight on d6, which may be exploited by ...♘d4 or ...♕e7 followed by ...♖d8. Since White's king is also slightly unsafe, we may assess the position as at least slightly better for Black.

22 ♗b2

It is too dangerous to grab further material, for example 22 ♘xb7? ♕b6 23 ♘d6 ♖d8 or 22 gxf4 ♕e7 23 fxe5 (23 ♗b2 transposes to the following note) ♘xe5! 24 ♗e3 ♖d8 25 ♖d2 ♘fg4! 26 fxg4 (26 ♗xa7 ♕g5 27 fxg4 ♕xd2 wins for Black) ♗xg4 27 ♘f5 (or else 27...♘f3+ and 28...♘xd2) ♗xd1 28 ♘xe7 ♘f3+ 29 ♔h1 ♖xd2 30 ♗g8+ ♔h8 31 ♗xd2 ♗xa1 32 ♗xb4 and Black has a clear extra pawn in the ending.

White sensibly prefers to develop his remaining pieces as quickly as possible. The bishop move not only allows the c1 rook to enter the game, it also inhibits ...♘d4.

22 ... ♕e7

23 ♖c1 (201)

This move was accompanied by a draw offer. The other idea was 23 gxf4, but after 23...♘h5! (23...exf4 is less effective due to 24 ♖c1!, preparing to contest e5 by ♖c5) 24 fxe5 (otherwise ...♘xf4 is clearly good for Black) ♘xe5 (24...♘f4 25 ♕d2 ♗xe5 26 ♗xe5 ♕xe5 27 ♖d1 ♖d8

28 ♔h1 is tempting, because White is virtually paralysed, but equally Black has no obvious way to make progress) 25 ♕d2 (otherwise Black continues with ...♖d8 or ...♘f4) ♖f8 and the pressure on f3 virtually forces White to make the positionally undesirable exchange on e5, when Black's advantage is obvious.

The move played is logical in that Black's plan involves ...♘d4 at some stage, and in the resulting tactics White's rook can sometimes land on c7 to exploit Black's slightly unsafe king. The battle now revolves around the d6 knight. If White is forced to retreat it to c4, then Black will take over the initiative completely by ...♖d8, ...b5 and ...♘d4.

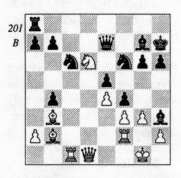

201
B

23   ...   ♘d4!?

23...♖d8 24 ♖d2 ♘d4 is also good, when there are two possibilities:

1) **25 ♗xd4** exd4 26 ♘f7 (26 ♖xd4 loses to 26...♘e8!, a move I failed to notice during the game) ♖f8

27 e5 ♘d7 with an excellent position for Black (28 e6 ♘c5!).

2) **25 ♘c4** fxg3 26 ♗xd4 (not 26 hxg3? b5 27 ♘e3 ♘xf3+) exd4 27 hxg3 ♘h5 28 ♔h2 ♕g5 29 ♕e1 ♗e6 and Black has more than enough compensation for his small material deficit.

24   gxf4

Forced, since 24 ♘c4 (24 ♗xd4 exd4 25 ♕xd4 ♘g4 26 ♕xb4 ♘xf2 27 ♔xf2 ♖d8 wins for Black) is much too passive after 24...♖d8.

24   ...   ♘h5

Black cannot reply 24...♕xd6 because of 25 fxe5.

25   fxe5   ♗xe5 *(202)*

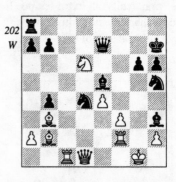

202
W

26   ♘f7

A critical moment, since after this move Black gains a distinct advantage. There are a number of alternatives, but it is doubtful if they are superior to the move played:

1) **26 ♗xd4** (relatively the best) ♗xd4 27 ♕xd4 ♕g5+ 28 ♔h1 ♕xc1+ 29 ♗d1 gives Black an extra

pawn, but White has a certain amount of counterplay. The best idea is probably to return the pawn by 29...♘f4 30 ♘xb7 (30 ♖c2 ♕xc2! 31 ♗xc2 ♗g2+ 32 ♔g1 ♘e2+ wins) ♕c3 (after 30...♖c8 31 ♖d2 ♖c3 32 ♘d6! White is saved by perpetual check) 31 ♖d2 ♕xd4 32 ♖xd4 ♖c8 33 ♔g1 ♗e6 and Black has some advantage in view of his queenside majority, active knight and chances of playing his king to e5. Nevertheless, White has fair drawing chances. It is surprising that Black does not have any better alternative in this line, but I have not been able to find one.

2) **26 ♘c4** (looks risky, but there is no tactical refutation) ♗g7! (after 26...♕g5+ 27 ♔h1 ♗xh2 28 ♕xd4 I don't see how Black can justify his extravagant play) 27 e5 (the threats were 27...♖d8 and 27...♘f4) ♘xb3 28 ♕xb3 (28 axb3 ♘f4 29 ♔h1 ♖d8 followed by ...♘d3 is winning for Black) ♖c8 and Black has a strong initiative in return for a very small material deficit.

3) **26 ♖c5** ♗xd6 (26...♕g5+? 27 ♔h1 ♘f4 28 ♖c7+ wins) 27 ♖xh5 gxh5 28 ♗xd4 ♗e5! (if Black allows White to play e5 his own king will become very exposed) 29 ♗xe5 (the threat was ...♕g7+) ♕xe5 and although the extra pawn is unimportant, Black has the advantage because of White's weak back rank. The threat is ...♖c8, with the ideas of ...♕g5+ and ...♖c1, or simply ...♖c7

followed by ...♖g7(+), and White's poor king position makes it hard to develop any counterplay. Note that 30 ♕d5 is bad after 30...♖c8! 31 ♖d2 (31 ♕f7+ ♔h8) ♕g7+ 32 ♔f2 ♕g2+ 33 ♔e3 ♖c3+ 34 ♖d3 ♕g1+ 35 ♔d2 ♕xh2+ 36 ♔e1 ♕g1+ 37 ♔d2 ♕g5+ and the two extra pawns should be enough to win.

26 ...   ♘xb3
27 ♘xe5

After 27 ♕xb3 ♗f4! White faces the multiple threats of 28...♗e6, 28...♖f8 and 28...♗xc1.

27 ...   ♘xc1

Certainly not 27...♕g5+?? 28 ♘g4 and White's pieces land on Black's weak second rank.

28 ♕xc1   ♖c8 *(203)*

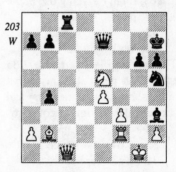

29 ♖c2?

A fatal error in time-trouble. After the correct 29 ♕e3 Black has a pawn more and some threats against White's king, but Black's king is also not totally safe and the opposite-coloured bishops will help White if he can reach an ending. The best reply is probably 29...♕e6, meeting 30 ♖d2 (30 ♕xa7? ♕xe5 wins) by 30...♕xa2 (but not 30...♕xe5? 31 ♖d7+) and 30 f4 by 30...♖d8 31 ♗d4 a5. Black has fair winning chances.

29	...	♖xc2
30	♕xc2	♕g5+
31	♔h1	♕e3

Despite the reduction in material Black has a very strong attack. White must cover e1, and 32 ♕c1 (32 ♕d1 ♘f4 wins) ♕e2 33 ♕g1 ♘f4 is no good.

32	♕c7+	♘g7
33	♕c1	

Perhaps White overlooked when playing his 29th move that 33 ♕xg7+ ♔xg7 34 ♘c4+ loses to 34...♕c3, finally making use of the queenside pawns.

33	...	♕e2
34	♕g1	

The last trap is 34...♕xb2?? 35 ♕xg6+ with perpetual check, but White is hopelessly tied up and Black can take the time to cover g6.

34	...	g5
35	♗d4	♘e6
36	♕g3	

Or 36 ♗e3 ♕xa2 followed by the advance of the b-pawn.

36	...	♘f4

0-1

It is mate in three more moves.

A half-point saved is the same as a half-point gained and in the next

round I had to use pure desperation to save my game against Van der Wiel. I was White and we arrived at this position with Black to play *(204)*.

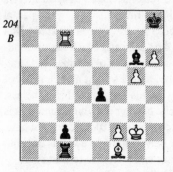

204
B

Earlier on I had been clearly better, but in time-trouble I allowed Black's c-pawn to get out of control and by now it was clear that the most I could hope for was a draw. I expected 44...e3 45 ♖c8+ ♔h7 46 ♗c4! ♗e4+ (46...♖g1+ 47 ♔xg1 c1♕+ 48 ♔h2 is also drawn because Black must move his queen, whereupon White gives perpetual check) 47 ♔g3 ♖g1+ 48 ♔f4 c1♕ 49 ♖c7+ ♔g6 50 ♗f7+ ♔h7 51 ♗c4+! and White delivers perpetual check, but Van der Wiel surprised me with **44...♗f5!**. This cuts out the check on c8, and threatens simply ...e3 followed by a rook move. For a long time I could see no defence whatsoever and I sat there until I had only six minutes left for 16 moves. Suddenly I saw a miracle! Quickly, I flashed out **45 ♗e2! e3** (Black must react quickly, or else White will play ♗h5 followed by g6) **46 ♗h5 exf2** (46...e2 47 ♗xe2 ♖e1 48 ♗g4! ♗e4+ 49 f3 ♗d3 50 ♖c8+ ♔h7 51 ♖c7+** is also drawn since 51...♔g6?? allows mate, while after 51...♔g8 52 ♖c8+ ♔f7?? 53 ♗h5+ White wins) **47 ♔xf2 ♖h1 48 ♗f7!**. This last move is the hidden point; Black can win the rook but his king is bottled up in the corner. For a moment van der Wiel appeared perplexed, but then he saw the idea. After a few minutes he shook his head in disbelief. The game concluded **48...c1♕ 49 ♖xc1 ♖xc1 50 g6 ♗xg6 51 ♗xg6 ♖c6 ½-½**.

Further wins against I.Sokolov and an out-of-form H.Olafsson took me to 8/12, giving me a half-point lead over C.Hansen and Adams going into the last round. Fortunately, Michael Adams was in a cooperative mood and agreed a quick draw with me, which left C.Hansen the only player who could catch me. In the end Piket drew with C.Hansen, so I had won Wijk aan Zee outright for the second consecutive year.

My success at Wijk aan Zee 1991 was a high point in my career, but the next eight months proved a disappointment.

Round about this time the chess world started to change. The borders with the Soviet Union were starting to come down, resulting in a flood of strong but inexpensive chess talent pouring into Western Europe. Unfortunately, this coincided with a decline in the number of high-quality tournaments. The problems were especially severe in Britain, because the level of chess activity had already been on the slide for several years. In the January 1991 issue of the British Chess Magazine, I published a slightly controversial article entitled *The Decline of British Chess*, which showed how the relative position of Britain as a chess nation had suffered during the 1980s. I took a selection of 15 West European countries, including England, as my sample, and ranked the countries according to the number of Elo-rated events taking place in their territory. In 1981, England was in fourth position, but by 1989 it had slid to 10th; even small countries such as Switzerland and Denmark were organising more events.

The article was intended to highlight the problems facing British chess at a time when it might still have been possible to take remedial action. To my surprise, the article provoked a hostile response from chess organisers. The majority of leading players accepted the thesis as being axiomatically true, but a few, including Jon Speelman, rejected the conclusion of the article.

In the March 1991 issue of the *BCM*, Ray Keene responded by pointing out some positive aspects of the British chess scene, including 'the Foreign & Colonial sponsorship' of Hastings, 'the Granada Park Hall tournament in 1989, the Iclicki tournament, the increase in one-day quickplays' and 'the Watson, Farley and Williams series of grandmaster tournaments'. I would have preferred not to have been proved right by events, but regrettably I have. The Foreign & Colonial sponsorship of Hastings departed, and no replacement sponsor was found, the Granada Park Hall and Iclicki tournaments were never repeated and the Watson, Farley & Williams series of events collapsed. One may add the disappearance of the Leeds Quickplay, the ending of the Lloyds Bank sponsorship and the continuing lack of a sponsor for the British Championship. Just as I write (July 1994), the George Goodwin series of one-day quickplay events has been cancelled due to lack of support.

One leading grandmaster remarked to me recently 'John, you realise that your article on the decline of British chess was all wrong?'. When I showed surprise, he continued 'I can't understand how you could have been so over-optimistic.'

The British Chess Federation has presided over all this with sublime indifference.

The practical effect has been that many leading players have either given up playing, or have adopted part-time playing careers. Chandler runs the *British Chess Magazine*, I have moved into the chess publishing world (with a computing sideline), Speelman and King are mainly involved in non-playing activities, Watson is becoming a lawyer, Norwood intermittently tries to become a banker, and so on. Of the top group, only Adams, Hodgson, Miles and Sadler are full-time players. In view of this it is hardly surprising that the team results have declined. The regular cut-and-thrust of tournament play is essential to maintain one's competitive edge, but the almost total lack of worthwhile tournaments has forced the talented players mentioned above to indulge in other activities. When you are twenty years old it is possible to starve for the sake of chess, but when you advance into your thirties this prospect is somewhat less appealing.

Anyhow, back to 1991. During March I took part in the Dortmund Chess Festival for the first time since 1987. The result was a disaster. I was totally unable to concentrate on my games and sometimes my mind would wander far away from chess while my clock was ticking. Out of nine games, I suffered four brutal losses, including three in a row. Even the two games I won were not especially convincing. I had a winning position against Razuvaev when he suddenly played a move which appeared to have no point whatsoever. After thinking for a few seconds, I realised that his move threatened mate in one. Purely by accident, my previous move had prepared a tactical defence against this mate, but I could easily have lost on the spot.

My one good result during this period was at Munich during May. The tournament started well when Anand overpressed against me and lost, but in round 2 I went down to Wahls after playing the opening far too passively. The following game is from round 3.

Game 33

J.Nunn – B.Gelfand

Munich 1991

Pirc

1	e4		d6

It is not often that one receives a big surprise on the very first move. Gelfand is practically married to the Najdorf, so I was shocked to see him stray from it. Surprising your opponent can be effective, but there is a danger. Every player develops a 'feel' for the positions resulting from his regular openings; memorising the theory of a new opening is not the same as having a close familiarity with the resulting positions.

Fortunately, not long before the tournament, I had prepared the ♗e3 system as a new (for me) anti-Pirc weapon. This seemed to be the ideal moment to try it out, because Gelfand had undoubtedly prepared for my usual anti-Pirc lines, and ♗e3 might lead him into relatively unfamiliar territory.

2	d4	♘f6
3	♘c3	g6
4	♗e3	c6
5	♕d2	b5

This is the natural move, but in some lines it gives White the chance to break open the queenside by playing a4. Another possibility is to delay ...b5 by playing 5...♘bd7 6 ♘f3 ♕a5 (6...♕c7 is also possible), for which see game 40, Nunn-Azmaiparashvili (page 311).

6	♗d3

The current fashion is to aim for 0-0. The move ...b5 is bad news for White if he castles queenside, but after 0-0 White can play a4 aiming to open lines on the queenside while Black's king is still in the centre.

6	...	♘bd7

Black should avoid playing the move ...♗g7 for as long as possible.

White will be reluctant to play ♗h6 while the bishop is still on f8, because if Black can play ...♗f8xh6 in one move he will effectively gain a tempo.

7 ♘f3 (205)

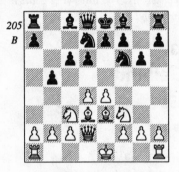

205
B

It is always tricky for White to decide when to include h3. For the moment there is no real reason to play it, because 7...♘g4 can be met by 8 ♗g5. Of course, Black can chase White's bishop, but the fun is likely to be short-lived, for example 8...f6 9 ♗h4 ♗h6 10 ♕e2 and now Black has to go into reverse gear to counter the threat of h3.

7 ...   e5

A year later I again reached the same position, but this time my opponent delayed taking action in the centre: 7...♕c7 8 0-0 e5 9 a4!? (thanks to Black's rather slow play, White can try to save a tempo by missing out h3) b4 10 ♘e2 exd4 11 ♘exd4 c5 12 ♘b5! (the knight cannot retreat from b5, but Black has no

time to win it) ♕c6 13 ♗c4 ♗b7 (13...♘xe4 14 ♕d5) 14 ♗f4 a6 (or 14...♘xe4 15 ♖fe1 ♘e5 16 ♖xe4 ♕xe4 17 ♗xe5 dxe5 18 ♗xf7+ winning) 15 ♗d5 ♘xd5 16 exd5 ♕b6 17 ♖fe1+ ♔d8 18 ♘g5 axb5 19 ♘xf7+ ♔c7 20 ♘xh8 and White went on to win in Nunn-McNab, Walsall Kipping 1992.

8 dxe5

It is certainly safer to stabilise the centre before thinking about probing Black's queenside with a4. In some games White has played the immediate 8 a4, but 8...b4 9 ♘e2 exd4!? 10 ♘exd4 c5 11 ♘e2 is unclear after 11...♗g7 or 11...♗b7!?.

Exchanging on e5 in the Pirc often leads to sterile equality; all the major pieces are exchanged on the d-file, and the players shake hands. Here the situation is far less clearcut, because of White's a4 plan. Black will probably reply ...b4, and after ♘e2 White may continue to annoy Black with c2-c3. Eventually White hopes to open the c-file, place his rooks on the c- and d-files and generate lasting pressure. It is also worth noting that Black's ...b4 will weaken the c4 square, and after ♗d3-c4 the bishop will be activated and may even create threats against f7.

8 ...   dxe5

After 8...♘xe5 9 ♘xe5 dxe5 10 h3 a6 (not 10...♗b7? 11 ♘xb5 cxb5 12 ♗xb5+ ♘d7 13 0-0-0 ♗c8 14

♕d5 and wins, nor 10...♗g7 11 a4 with a clear plus for White) White can gain a slight plus by 11 ♗h6!? or 11 a4.

9 h3 *(206)*

This is a reasonable moment for the prophylactic h3, but it may be possible to play 9 0-0. One critical continuation would be 9...♘g4 10 ♗g5 f6 11 ♗h4 ♗h6 12 ♕e2 ♗g7 13 h3 ♘h6 14 a4, when White has a temporary initiative but there is a danger that the bishop on h4 will be left out of play.

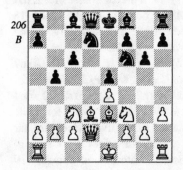

9 ... ♗g7?

This bears out the remark made at the start of the game. Moving the bishop off the f8-b4 diagonal weakens Black's queenside, and White's plan suddenly becomes genuinely menacing.

Other players have preferred to leave the bishop on f8 for the moment:

1) **9...a6** 10 ♗h6 ♗xh6 11 ♕xh6 ♕e7 (better than 11...♘h5 12 0-0 ♕f6 13 a4, when White gains an advantage after 13...♗b7 14 axb5 axb5 15 ♖xa8+ ♗xa8 16 ♖a1 ♔e7?! 17 ♗xb5! cxb5 18 ♖xa8 or 13...b4 14 ♘e2 ♕g7 15 ♕d2) 12 0-0 ♗b7 13 ♖fe1 (13 a4!) ♕f8 14 ♕g5 h6 15 ♕e3 ♕e7 16 a4 ♔f8 17 axb5 axb5 18 ♖xa8+ ♗xa8 19 ♘e2 ♔g7 with equality, Rašik-Pribyl, Czechoslovakia Ch 1992.

2) **9...a5** 10 a4 (10 0-0 is better, waiting for ...♗g7 before playing a4) b4 11 ♘e2 ♕e7 12 0-0 ♘c5 13 ♘g3 ♗g7 14 ♗h6 0-0 15 ♖fe1 ♘xd3 16 cxd3 c5 ½-½, Ye Jiangchuan-Torre, Shenzhen 1992.

3) **9...♕e7** 10 0-0-0 a6 11 ♖he1 ♗g7 12 ♗h6 ♗xh6 13 ♕xh6 ♗b7 14 ♔b1 0-0-0 15 a3 with equality, as in the game Tolnai-Ftačnik, Stara Zagora Z 1990.

10 a4 b4

11 ♘e2

The first fruits of Black's error on move nine; he must waste time defending the pawn on b4.

11 ... a5

12 c3 c5

Black has continuing problems because the b4 pawn needs further defence. White gains the advantage after 12...bxc3 13 ♕xc3, intending ♘d2-c4, or 12...♖b8 13 ♖c1 taking aim at the weak pawn on c6.

The move played may appear to be the safest solution, because it enables Black to avoid serious pawn weaknesses on the queenside, but

...c6-c5 involves making two major concessions. First of all, it allows a second open file. White is in a position to bring both rooks to the open files in just three moves (0-0, ♖fd1 and ♖ac1), but it will take Black at least five moves to accomplish the same objective. If there were only one open file Black could probably bear the pressure, but two will cause serious problems. The second concession is to allow White's bishop to occupy the outpost at b5; combined with the d-file pressure, this will make life interesting for the knight on d7.

13 cxb4   cxb4
14 0-0   0-0

This game contains few tactical elements. Up to a point, White's initiative plays itself; he just develops his pieces to the obvious squares, and waits to see how Black intends to counter the increasing pressure. The hard part comes later, when White has to play precisely to prevent Black freeing himself.

15 ♖fd1   ♗b7

Black uses some clever tactics to unpin the knight on d7 and generate counterthreats against the pawn on e4. After 15...♕e7 16 ♖ac1, intending ♖c7, White also has strong pressure.

16 ♗b5 *(207)*

At first sight this puts Black in dire trouble, because the d7 knight has no moves.

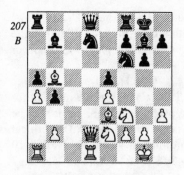

16 ...   ♕b8

The alternative is 16...♕e7 and now:

1) **17 ♕d6** (of course, 17 ♗xd7 ♖fd8 is fine for Black) ♕xd6 18 ♖xd6 ♘b8! and suddenly the e4 pawn is in trouble.

2) **17 ♕xd7!?** ♘xd7 18 ♖xd7 ♕xd7! (18...♕e6 19 ♖xb7 ♕b3 20 ♘d2 ♕xb2 21 ♖b1 ♕a2 22 ♘c1 ♕e6 23 ♘cb3 is very good for White because his active pieces are far more important than Black's insignificant material advantage) 19 ♗xd7 ♖fd8 20 ♗b5 ♗xe4 is not so clear. Black has ♖+♙ v 2♘, but suddenly the two open files favour Black by providing highways for his rooks to enter White's position. After 21 ♘d2 ♗d3! (Black must remove the powerful b5 bishop) 22 ♘b3 e4!, for example, Black's pieces are active and he has good counterplay.

3) **17 ♖ac1!** (simplest is sometimes best; by covering c5, White again stops the d7 knight moving) ♖ac8 (17...♖fd8 18 ♖c7 ♘xe4 19

♕xd7! ♖xd7 20 ♖dxd7 really is crushing, while 17...♗a6 fails to 18 ♗xa6 ♖xa6 19 ♕c7 ♖d8 20 ♗g5 and Black cannot defend d7) 18 ♗xd7 ♖xc1 19 ♕xc1 ♘xd7 20 ♕c7 ♗c8 21 ♕xa5 and White makes off with a pawn.

After the move played, 17 ♗xd7 can be safely met by 17...♖d8.

17 ♘g3 (208)

As a young player, I was puzzled by games in which White played the manoeuvre ♘c3-e2-g3 against the Pirc. It seemed to me that the knight was not very well placed on g3, because Black's g6 pawn prevented the knight advancing. Indeed, its one and only duty seemed to be to defend the pawn on e4. Then, in 1984, I lost a game with Black against Murray Chandler, in which he used precisely this manoeuvre. The crucial distinction is whether White is attacking or defending. If White doesn't hold the initiative then the knight on g3 is truly inactive, but if White holds the initiative and has pressure in the centre then the knight can be very useful. The rooks and queen operating on the open files are so dangerous for Black that he cannot counter them directly; instead, Black must somehow aim for counterplay. The only weakness in White's position is the vulnerable pawn on e4. If this is secure, then White has plenty of time to improve his position. The function of the g3

knight is precisely to support the e4 pawn, and give White the freedom of action he needs to step up the pressure.

In the current position, Black is attacking e4 twice, but at the moment he cannot consider taking the pawn because of the exposed knight on d7.

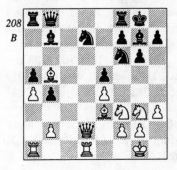

17 .. ♖c8

The alternative is 17...♖d8, in order to attack e4. The reply 18 ♗c4 (targeting the new weakness on f7; 18 ♖ac1 is inferior, as Black can play 18...♘xe4 19 ♘xe4 ♗xe4, when 20 ♗xd7 ♗f5 and 20 ♘g5 ♘f6! are satisfactory for Black) ♕c7 (18...♘f8 19 ♕xd8 ♕xd8 20 ♖xd8 ♖xd8 21 ♘xe5 is good for White) 19 ♕c2 ♖ac8 20 ♖ac1 is surprisingly awkward. White threatens both 21 ♗xf7+ and 21 ♕b3, and after the more or less forced 20...♔f8, he can play 21 ♘g5 ♗a6 22 ♘xf7! ♗xc4 23 ♘d6! with a huge advantage for White.

The move played also prepares ...♘f8, while at the same time preventing ♗c4. 18 ♗xd7 may still be answered by 18...♖d8.

18　♖ac1　　♖xc1

After 18...♘f8, the continuation 19 ♗c4 is similar to the game.

19　♖xc1　　♘f8 (209)

The knight on d7 is no longer indirectly defended, so Black must take action. 19...♕d8 doesn't lose a piece to 20 ♖d1, because Black can repeat his earlier defensive motif by 20...♕c7!, and 21 ♗xd7 ♖d8 defends. However, 19...♕d8 is strongly met by 20 ♗g5! ♘f8 21 ♕xd8 ♖xd8 22 ♖c7 ♖b8 23 ♗c4 ♘e6 24 ♗xe6 fxe6 25 ♖e7 and Black has a lousy ending as 25...♘xe4 loses to 26 ♖xb7.

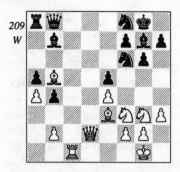

209
W

20　♗c4!

Black has survived so far, but only at the cost of blocking in his queen's rook. This gives White time to latch onto a new target – the f7 pawn.

20　...　　♘e6

Not a very attractive move, but there was hardly any other answer to the threat of ♘g5. 20...♘xe4 (20...♗xe4 21 ♘g5 is similar) 21 ♘xe4 ♗xe4 22 ♘g5 followed by ♘xf7 wins, while 20...♘e8 21 ♘g5 ♘d6 22 ♗d5 (threatening ♗c5 to eliminate the defensive knight) h6 23 ♗c5! ♗xd5 24 ♕xd5 ♕b7 (24...hxg5 25 ♗xd6 ♕d8 26 ♖c7 ♘e6 27 ♖b7 is even worse) 25 ♗xd6 ♕xd5 26 exd5 hxg5 27 ♗e7 leads to a very unpleasant ending for Black.

21　♗xe6　　fxe6
22　♘g5　　♖a6

Forced, as 22...♕e8 23 ♖c7 ♗c6 24 ♕d6 ♗d7 (24...♗xa4 25 ♖e7) 25 b3 virtually paralyses Black.

23　♖d1

Once again, White finds a new avenue of attack. The threat is ♕d8+, exchanging queens and clearing the way for White's rook to penetrate into Black's position.

23　..　　h6?

This error hands White a clear-cut win. Black would have had drawing chances after 23...♗f8 24 ♕d8 ♕xd8 25 ♖xd8 ♖d6 26 ♖xd6 (26 ♖b8 ♗c6 27 ♗c5 is tempting, but there is nothing clear after 27...♖d1+ 28 ♔h2 ♘d7 29 ♖d8 ♗xa4 30 ♘xe6 ♔f7!) ♗xd6 27 ♗b6; although White is quite likely to end up with an extra pawn, the two bishops provide some compensation and often enable Black to seek salvation in an opposite-coloured bishop position.

| 24 | ♕d8+ | ♕xd8 |
| 25 | ♖xd8+ | ♗f8 *(210)* |

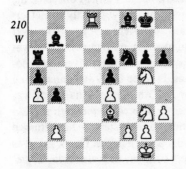

210
W

26 ♖b8!

Black's bishop is trapped, so White forces a winning ending.

| 26 | ... | hxg5 |

26...♗a8 27 ♘xe6 is even worse.

| 27 | ♖xb7 | ♖d6 |

Black's pawn structure is impressively bad and it is not surprising that his pawns start dropping within a few moves.

28	♖b5	♖d1+
29	♔h2	♖b1
30	♖xe5	♗d6

Black cannot even play 30...♖xb2 31 ♖xe6 ♔f7 because of 32 ♖xf6+.

31	♖xe6	♗xg3+
32	♔xg3	♔f7
33	♖a6	♘xe4+
34	♔f3	♘f6
35	♗d4	1-0

White defends b2 and wins the a5 pawn. Two extra pawns and further juicy targets on the kingside are too much for Black.

The rest of the event was equally fluctuating. In the end I scored 7½/13, which was quite a good result for a category 14 tournament. The annual Munich tournament is organised by Dr. Heinrich Jellissen, who has single-handedly done a great deal for German chess, both by finding (and keeping!) sponsors and by devoting a lot of his own time to chess organisation. He also runs the enormously successful Bayern München (Bavaria Munich) club, which has won the Bundesliga on several occasions.

My next few months were a period of inactivity. The only serious chess I played was a four-game training match against the Greek player Grivas, held just outside Athens. After winning the first game I expected to win the match, but Grivas played unexpectedly well, particularly in tactical situations, and he deserved the final 2-2 result. Fortunately, we had agreed beforehand that the match would not be submitted for Elo rating. Curiously enough, when I visited ChessBase some time later, I discovered that someone had entered the result of one of the games incorrectly, and the match was recorded in their database as ending 2½-1½ in favour of Grivas. So far as I know, this error is still there, which perhaps helps to explain the discrepancy between my FIDE and PCA ratings (as at July 1994).

264 J.Nunn – P.Nikolić

I had enjoyed my stay in Athens, and I decided to return to Greece in September to play in a small open tournament held in the northern city of Kavala. Unfortunately, the tournament was less pleasant than I expected. The playing conditions and hotel were not very attractive, and in addition I played very badly. In round 3 I lost to Tsorbatzoglou, rated 2300, who severely mistreated my King's Indian Defence. Although I staged a limited recovery near the end, including a win against Grivas, I couldn't recover from an appalling start, and my final score of 6½/9 against relatively weak opposition represented a significant loss of Elo points.

My Bundesliga season started in October with a crushing loss against Shirov, but this turned out to be the low point. I flew directly from Germany to Vienna for a 10-player round-robin tournament, which was played in very attractive surroundings. I scored 5½/9 at Vienna, tying for 3rd-5th places. This result was exactly in accordance with my Elo rating, so some stability had returned to my performances. This was just as well, since my next event was a category 15 tournament held in Belgrade during November. My start was not too wonderful, since I lost to Kamsky in the second round. The following game, which won the brilliancy prize, was played in round 3.

Game 34

J.Nunn – P.Nikolić
Belgrade 1991
French

1	e4	e6
2	d4	d5
3	♘c3	♝b4
4	e5	c5
5	a3	♝xc3+
6	bxc3	♘e7
7	♘f3	b6
8	♝b5+	♝d7
9	♝d3	♝a4 *(211)*

This move is an interesting attempt to inconvenience White. If

Black wants to put his bishop on a4, then the most familiar line is 9...c4 10 ♝f1 ♝a4 11 g3, when White repositions his bishop at g2 or h3 and then castles. The idea behind 9...♝a4 is to wait for White's 0-0 before playing ...c4. White then has to play ♝e2 and after a later 0-0, ♖e1 and ♝f1 White has wasted a tempo. That's the theory, but in the recent games given in the next note White has tended to play ♗e2 in any case, so I am not sure how useful Black's finesse really is.

It is worth mentioning that 9...h6 is playable, when 10 a4 ♘bc6 11 0-0 ♕c7 transposes to a standard line.

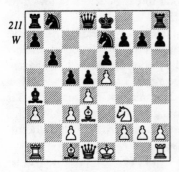

211
W

10 dxc5!?

This is the only real attempt to exploit Black's omission of ...c4. There have been few games with 9...♗a4, but most have continued **10 h4 h6 11 h5** and now 11...c4 (11...♘bc6 12 ♖h4 c4 13 ♗e2 ♔d7 14 ♗e3 ♕g8 15 ♕d2 ♕h7 16 ♖c1 ♔c7 was unclear in A.Sokolov-Yusupov, Riga Ct (1) 1986) 12 ♗e2 (12 ♗f1 ♘bc6 13 g3 ♔d7 14 ♗h3 ♕g8 15 0-0 ♕h7 16 ♖a2, Anand-Quillan, Prestwich 1990 was similar, except that White's bishop went to f1 and h3 instead of e2 and g4) ♔d7 13 ♘h4 ♕g8 14 ♗g4 ♕h7 15 ♖a2 ♘a6 16 ♖h3 was unclear in Kir.Georgiev-Yusupov, Las Palmas 1993.

The general structure arising after Black's ...c4 is very static. A long period of manoeuvring lies ahead, but it is worth mentioning that Black's practical results have been quite good.

Note that **10 ♘g5 h6 11 ♕h5** (11 ♘h3 ♕c7 12 0-0 ♘d7 13 ♗e3 ♕c6 14 ♖b1 a6 15 ♖b2 ♗b5 was fine for Black in Nijboer-Brenninkmeijer, Dutch Ch 1992) g6 12 ♕h3 is bad because of 12...c4 and the c2 pawn falls.

I am not sure whether 10 dxc5!? is any better than the alternatives; it is hard to judge from one game, and for some reason it does not seem to have been repeated.

10 ... bxc5

The pawn exchange on c5 has prevented Black completely blocking the position with ...c4. White hopes to use his bishops to good effect in the more fluid struggle which results. He also wishes to prove that the move ...♗a4 was a waste of time. The defect is that White leaves himself with a weak pawn on e5.

11 0-0 c4

The start of an ambitious plan by Black. He again takes the chance to force White to block the e-file, but this is more double-edged than in the line given above. Admittedly the e5 pawn becomes weak, but Black's dark squares are vulnerable and the d4 square is freed for White's pieces.

12 ♗e2 ♘g6?! *(212)*

This is probably going too far. The idea is that 12...♘bc6 13 ♗f4

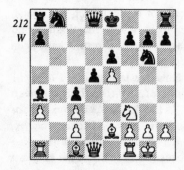

212
W

♘g6 14 ♗g3 allows White to defend
his e5 pawn, so Black seeks to attack
e5 while at the same time preventing
♗f4. Unfortunately, White is able to
exploit Black's poor development to
launch a direct attack. The best line
is probably 12...♘bc6 13 ♗f4 (on 13
♗e3, Black can either play the
greedy 13...♘g6 14 ♗c5 ♘gxe5 15
♘xe5 ♘xe5 16 ♕d4 ♕f6 17 ♗d6
♘d7!, or the simple 13...♕a5) ♘g6
14 ♗g3 0-0 15 ♕d2 f5 16 exf6 ♕xf6
with an unclear position. Black has a
central pawn mass, but White has the
two bishops.

13   ♘g5!

White must play vigorously or he
will be in serious trouble with his e5
pawn. 13 ♘d4 is weaker because
13...♘xe5 14 f4 ♘ec6 15 f5 e5 enables Black to keep the position
closed.

13   ...   ♘xe5

After some thought Black decided to take the pawn, because if he
allows White to play f4 he will be
slightly worse, for example 13...0-0

14 f4 ♘c6 (or 14...h6 15 ♘f3 and
now 15...f6 16 ♗e3 and 15...f5 16
♗e3 are a little better for White) and
now White has a pleasant choice between the positional 15 ♗e3 and the
direct 15 ♗h5!? with the rather
crude threat of ♗xg6 followed by
♕f3-h3.

Objectively speaking, the move
played probably deserves another
'?!' symbol, because White's advantage after 13...0-0 is much less than
in the game, but the capture on e5 is
the logical consequence of Black's
previous move so I cannot really crit-
icise it.

14   f4   ♘d3! *(213)*

The best defence. After 14...♘d7
15 f5 0-0 16 fxe6 fxe6 17 ♗g4! (17
♘xe6 ♕b6+ 18 ♘d4 ♘c6 is less
effective) ♕b6+ 18 ♔h1 Black has
a miserable position, while after
14...♘ec6 15 f5 e5 16 ♗h5 0-0 17 f6
gxf6 (or 17...g6 18 ♘xh7 ♔xh7 19
♕d2 and Black gets mated) 18 ♕g4!
fxg5 19 ♗xg5 ♕d7 20 ♖f5 White's
attack breaks through.

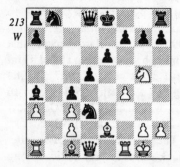

213
W

15 ♗xd3

White exchanges an attacking piece, but gains time because the queen can come into play with tempo. After 15 ♗e3 (15...♕b6+ was a threat) h6 16 ♘xf7 (16 ♘f3 ♘d7 rescues the knight) ♔xf7 17 ♕d2 ♗xc2 18 ♕xc2 ♘d7 19 ♗xd3 cxd3 20 ♕xd3 ♖f8 White might claim a small advantage, but the move played is much stronger.

15 ... cxd3

16 f5 e5

There are few other moves to meet the threat of fxe6:

1) 16...0-0 17 ♕h5 h6 18 f6 gxf6 (18...hxg5 19 ♕xg5) 19 ♕xh6 fxg5 20 ♗xg5 ♕b6+ 21 ♗e3 ♕d8 22 ♖f4 mates in four more moves.

2) 16...exf5 17 ♕h5! (neither 17 ♖e1+ ♔f8 18 ♕xd3 h6 nor 17 ♖e1+ ♕e7 18 ♕h4 ♗d7 19 ♖e1 ♗e6 is really convincing) and now 17...g6 loses to 18 ♖e1+ ♔f8 (18...♔d7 19 ♕f3 wins) 19 ♕h4 (threats ♕xa4 and ♘e6+) ♕d7 20 ♘xh7+, and 17...♕b6+ 18 ♔h1 ♕g6 19 ♖e1+ ♔d7 20 ♕h4 ♗xc2 (after 20...♗c6, simply 21 cxd3 is very good for White) 21 ♕d4 ♔c6 22 ♖e7 gives White a very strong attack. Therefore Black must reply 17...♕e7, but the simple 18 ♗d2 leaves him in a terrible mess, for example 18...g6 19 ♕h4 ♗d7 20 c4! and the threats of ♖ae1, ♗b4 and cxd5 are too much.

Black decided to keep as many lines closed as possible.

17 ♕h5 ♕e7 (214)

This is practically forced. After 17...♕b6+ (or 17...g6 18 fxg6 and now 18...fxg6 19 ♕f3 is very strong while 18...♕b6+ 19 ♔h1 ♕xg6 20 ♕h4 ♗d7 21 ♘xf7 0-0 22 ♘h6+ mates) 18 ♔h1 ♕f6 19 ♘e6 (threats ♗g5 and ♘c7+) g6 20 ♕g4 (if Black had played 17...♕f6 without checking on b6 first, White would be able to play fxg6 here) fxe6 21 ♕xa4+ ♘d7 (21...♔d8 22 ♕a5+ ♔c8 23 ♕c5+ also wins, because if Black's king ever moves to d7, White replies ♖b1) White wins by 22 ♗g5! ♕xg5 (22...♕f7 23 fxe6 ♕xe6 24 ♖f6) 23 fxe6 ♕e7 (or 23...♖d8 24 ♖f7) 24 ♕c6 followed by ♖f7.

18 ♘e6?

Flaw number 1. In my desire to continue with direct threats I missed the strongest continuation. This was the moment for the simple 18 cxd3! when Black is in big trouble:

1) 18...g6 19 ♕h6 ♕f8 when both 20 ♕h4 and 20 ♕xf8+ are crushing.

2) **18...♘d7 19 ♘e6 g6 20 fxg6 fxg6** (20...♕xe6 21 gxf7+ followed by ♕h4+ and ♕xa4) **21 ♕g4** (threatening both 22 ♗g5 and 22 ♘c7+) **♘c5 22 ♘xc5 ♕xc5+ 23 d4** and Black's king is trapped in the centre.

3) **18...♘c6 19 f6 gxf6 20 ♘xh7 0-0-0** (20...♔d8 21 ♕g4) **21 ♕f5+ ♕e6 22 ♘xf6 ♕xf5 23 ♖xf5 ♗c2 25 ♘g4** and White has an extra pawn.

The point is that for the moment the attack on f7 prevents Black fleeing with his king, so he doesn't have any really constructive moves. By restoring the material balance White makes 19 f6 gxf6 20 ♘xh7 and 19 ♘e6 into strong threats.

18   ...   ♔d7!

Black seizes his chance to escape from the danger area. 18...♘d7 is met by 19 ♘c7+, and other moves allow ♗g5, for example 18...dxc2 19 ♗g5 ♕b7 20 ♘xg7+ ♔f8 21 ♘e6+! ♔e8 22 ♗f6 and White wins.

19   ♗g5

By forcing ...f6 White secures e6 for his knight, at least temporarily. The only real alternative was 19 ♘xg7, but then 19...f6 20 ♘e6 (20 ♖b1 ♔c6!) ♗xc2 is better for Black than the game.

19   ...   f6
20   ♗e3   ♘a6?

Flaw number 2, after which the rest of the game does indeed seem to have been played accurately. In a practical game with limited time it is understandable that Black wanted to develop a piece and cover c5, but the best defence was the greedy 20...♗xc2!. The bishop makes it very hard for the white rooks to enter the attack, while it turns out that White's other pieces cannot deliver mate all by themselves. They can only net the exchange, but Black already has two pawns in the bag. The analysis runs 21 ♗c5 (21 c4 d4! 22 ♕f3 ♘c6 and now 23 c5 ♖hc8! and 23 ♗xd4 exd4 24 c5 ♖hc8 25 ♕d5+ ♔e8 26 ♖ae1 ♘e5 appear fine for Black) ♕e8 22 ♕f3 (22 ♕g4 ♔c8 23 ♕xg7 ♘d7 is also murky) ♔c6! (22...♔c8 23 c4! is very dangerous) 23 c4 ♕d7 24 ♗f8 (this looks odd, but otherwise Black plays ...♘a6) ♖xf8! (the threats were 25 cxd5+ ♕xd5 26 ♘d8+ and 25 ♗xg7) 25 ♘xf8 ♕d6 26 ♘e6 ♘a6 and the position has become very unclear. White has a powerful knight and chances to grab some kingside pawns with his queen, but Black has dangerous passed pawns. Perhaps White is still better after 27 ♖ac1, but this is a long way from the clear and safe advantage he could have had after 18 cxd3!.

21   cxd3!

White corrects his previous error and restores material equality. If Black cannot achieve something tactically, then the e6 knight and Black's exposed king will give White a clear advantage.

21   ...   g6

Quick action is essential. Black undermines the e6 knight, which is cut off without any retreat. At first sight it isn't clear how White is going to rescue this piece.

22 ♕g4

The alternative was 22 ♕f3 ♗c6 23 ♕f2, preparing to extract the knight via c5, although this will not give White any advantage.

22 ... ♗c6 *(215)*

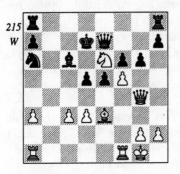

215
W

23 ♘d4!!

The solution is this surprising piece sacrifice. *Mephisto Genius 2* finds this positional sacrifice, one of the best moves I have ever played, in only 16 seconds (on a 486/66), and after 50 seconds evaluates it as 0.48 pawns better for White. *Fritz 3* takes just two seconds to converge on ♘d4, and after 36 seconds evaluates it as 0.31 pawns better for White; after 127 seconds White's advantage is evaluated as 0.66 pawns. It is not especially impressive that the programs find ♘d4, because there aren't

any reasonable alternatives (if the sacrifice were bad for White, then I would have had to play a different move earlier). What is impressive is that they so quickly assess the resulting position as favourable for White.

Black can decline the offer by 23...h5 24 ♕h3 (24 ♘xc6 hxg4 25 ♘xe7 ♔xe7 26 fxg6 ♖hg8 27 ♖ab1 is also good for White) g5, but then White returns by 25 ♘e6 having persuaded Black's g-pawn to abandon the attack on f5.

23 ... exd4
24 ♗xd4 *(216)*

This was a difficult choice because White had a second very strong continuation: 24 fxg6+ ♕e6 25 ♕xe6+ ♔xe6 26 ♗xd4 hxg6 (26...♖hf8 27 g7 ♖f7 28 ♖ae1+ ♔d7 29 ♖xf6 ♖xf6 30 ♗xf6 looks good for White) 27 ♖xf6+ ♔d7 28 ♖f7+ ♔e8 (not 28...♔e6? 29 ♖af1 and mates) 29 ♖g7! (29 ♖af1 ♖g8 is not so clear; White should take the g6 pawn while it is still available) and Black has to give White the g-pawn too because 29...♖h6 30 ♖e1+ ♔f8 31 ♖f1+ ♔e8 32 ♖f6 wins for White. Thus White secures three pawns for the piece, while retaining a strong initiative and a dominant bishop on d4.

After the move played, the threats along the h3-c8 diagonal, the possibilities for penetrating down the e-file and the monster bishop on d4 also give White more than enough for the piece.

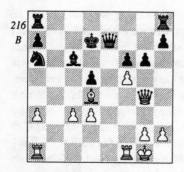

216
B

24   ...   h5

Black cannot both block the di-agonal and hold the e-file, so he de-cides to abandon the file. 24...gxf5 (after 24...♖ae8 25 fxg6+ ♕e6 26 ♕g3 the threat of ♖xf6 is too strong) 25 ♕xf5+ (25 ♖xf5 ♖ag8! is awk-ward because 26 ♖g5+ is met by 26...♕e6) ♕e6 26 ♕xe6+ ♔xe6 27 ♖xf6+ ♔d7 28 ♖f7+ ♔e8 (28...♔e6 29 ♖af1) 29 ♖af1 ♖g8 30 ♖xh7 is excellent for White. In comparison to the line given in the previous note, White has already taken the third pawn, while keeping his rook on the seventh rank.

25   ♕h3   g5

Now 25...gxf5 is met by 26 ♖ae1 (26 ♕xf5+ is no good because White doesn't take the h-pawn this time) ♕h7 27 ♖xf5 ♔c7 28 ♖xf6 with a crushing attack. After 25...♖ae8 26 fxg6+ ♕e6 27 ♕h4 ♕g4 28 ♕xf6 White has three pawns and a strong attack for the piece (28...♖e2 loses to 29 ♕g7+).

26   ♖fe1

More accurate than 26 ♖ae1 which in some lines gives Black the option of taking on a3.

26   ...   ♕f8

Better than 26...♕g7 27 ♖e6 ♖hf8 28 ♕g3 with an immediate collapse. The move played retains control of d6.

27   ♖e6   ♖h6

Not the most brilliant square for the rook, but after 27...♖e8 28 ♖xf6 Black has no sensible square for the queen (a3 is covered!). The only alternative was 27...♘c5 28 ♖xf6 ♕e7, but after 29 ♖g6 g4 30 ♕g3, threatening both 31 ♖g7 and 31 ♖e1, Black's position collapses.

28   ♕e3

This prevents Black's threat of ...♘c7 (because of the reply ♗c5) and envisages tripling on the e-file followed by ♖e7+.

28   ...   ♖e8

Black must contest the file or he will simply be mated.

29   ♖e1   ♘c7

29...♖h8 fails to 30 ♗xf6 with ♕xa7+ to come.

30   ♗c5 (217)   ♕f7

Or 30...♕g8, when White wins by a totally different method: 31 ♖xe8 ♘xe8 (31...♕xe8 32 ♕g3 wins) 32 ♕e7+ ♔c8 33 ♗xa7 (threat ♕c5) and now either 33...♘c7 34 ♕c5 ♗d7 (or else ♖e7 followed by ♗b6) 35 ♕b6 and White wins, or 33...♖h7 (33...♕h7 34 ♕c5 followed by ♖e6 or ♖e7 wins) 34 ♕c5 ♔d7 (34...♖c7

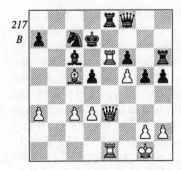

217
B

35 ♗b6 and 34...♔c7 35 ♖e6 win)
35 ♖e6 ♗b7 (35...♗a8 36 ♕b5+ and
♕b8+) 36 ♗b6 with a decisive
check to come on b5. After the move
played, White has no check on e7, so
♖xe8 doesn't work, but White can
exploit the position of the queen on
f7 by a different continuation.

31 ♗e7!

The tower of white pieces on the
e-file cuts off Black's queen and
rook from the defence of the king.
Black cannot capture any white
piece (31...♕xe6 32 fxe6+ ♔xe7 33
♕c5+) and there is no answer to the
threats of ♕c5 and ♕xa7.

31 ...   ♖h7

After most moves White wins by
♕xa7, e.g. 31...♗b5 32 ♕xa7, so
Black prevents this by attacking the
e7 bishop a fourth time.

32 ♕c5   ♗b7

After 32...♗a8 (32...♖xe7 33
♕d6+ ♔e8 34 ♖xe7+ wins) White
wins by 33 ♗d6! ♘xe6 (33...♘a6 34
♕xa7+) 34 fxe6+ ♖xe6 35 ♕c7+
♔e8 36 ♕c8 mate. The move played

prevents this win by covering c8, but
White can exploit the undefended
bishop.

33 ♕xa7   ♔c8

Or 33...♗c6 (33...♗a8 is the
same, while 33...♘xe6 34 fxe6+
♕xe6 35 ♕xb7 is mate) 34 ♖d6+
♔c8 35 ♖b1 mating.

34 ♖b1   ♖xe7
35 ♖xb7   1-0

There is no defence to 36 ♕b8+.
White mates in a further four moves.

I did not lose another game at
Belgrade and further wins against
Ljubojević, Yusupov and Beliavsky
took me to joint second place with
Kamsky on 7/11, half-a-point be-
hind the outright winner Gelfand.

Later on UN sanctions were im-
posed against Serbia, and I regret-
fully declined a second invitation to
participate in Belgrade.

I mentioned my poor start to the
Bundesliga season on page 264, but
by December my results had improved and I won an interesting ending against Christiansen:

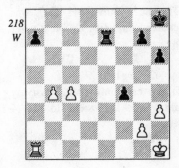

218
W

Playing White, it was my turn to move. The passed c-pawn confers some advantage on White, but I doubt if this would be sufficient to win without a second factor: Black's protruding f-pawn is weak and exposed to attack. The game continued

37 c5   ♚g8

The main alternatives involve an immediate attack on the queenside pawns:

1) **37...♖e4** (37...♖c7 38 ♔g1 resembles line 2) 38 b5 ♖e5 (38...♖b4 39 ♖a5 ♖b1+ 40 ♔h2 ♖b2 41 ♔g1 ♖b1+ 42 ♔f2 and the king escapes, whereupon c6-c7 is decisive) 39 ♖c1 ♔g8 40 c6 ♖e8 41 ♖a1 ♖e7 42 ♖xa7! ♖xa7 43 b6 and Black cannot stop the pawns.

2) **37...♖b7** 38 ♖a4 ♖c7 (the line 38...♔g8 39 c6 ♖c7 40 b5 ♔f7 41 ♖xa7! wins as before) 39 ♔g1 ♔g8 40 ♔f2 ♔f7 41 ♔f3 g5 42 ♔g4, preparing to attack the h-pawn by ♔h5 and ♖a6, and White should win.

38 b5   ♚f7
39 b6   axb6
40 cxb6   ♚f6

The only move; 41 ♖a7 was threatened, and 40...♔e8 lost to 41 ♖a8+.

41 ♖b1   ♖b7
42 ♚g1

Black can only wait passively while White lays siege to the f4 pawn.

42 ...   g5
43 ♚f2   ♚e7

This allows White's king to penetrate to h5. The main line runs 43...♔g6 44 ♔f3 ♔h5 (hoping for some counterplay after 45 ♔e4 ♔h4) 45 h4! gxh4 (or 45...♔g6 46 hxg5 hxg5 47 ♔g4 ♔f6 48 ♖b5, and Black is in zugzwang) 46 ♔xf4 ♔g6 47 ♔g4 ♔f6 48 ♔xh4 ♔g6 49 ♖b5 ♔f6 50 ♔h5 ♔g7 51 ♖b2 ♔h7 52 ♖b3 (zugzwang) ♔g7 53 ♖g3+ ♔h7 (53...♔f7 54 ♖g6 is the same) 54 ♖g6 winning the h-pawn.

44 ♚f3   ♚d8

The game concluded **45 ♚g4 ♚c8 46 ♖c1+!** (heading for c6) **♚b8** (46...♔d7 47 ♖c7+) **47 ♖c6 ♖d7 48 ♖xh6 ♖d2 49 ♔xg5 ♖xg2+ 50 ♔xf4 ♖f2+ 51 ♔g3 ♖b2 52 ♖f6 ♖b3+ 53 ♔g4 ♖b4+ 54 ♔g5 ♖b5+ 55 ♖f5 ♖xb6** (at the time this game was played, I had just started writing the ♖+a♙ v ♖ section of *Secrets of Rook Endings*, but White's next too moves wouldn't have been too hard in any case!) **56 h4 ♚c7 57 h5 1-0.**

The year ended with the English Championship, a one-off event with a knock-out format based on two game mini-matches. This is certainly not my favourite form of competition, and I lost 1½-½ to Hodgson in the first round. Conditions for this event were reminiscent of the Hastings tournaments of old, even to the sight of leading grandmasters playing in overcoats when the heating broke down. I was not too concerned about my early departure.

1992

The year started with a truly disastrous result at Wijk aan Zee. After having won outright in 1990 and 1991, I had high hopes of making it three in a row, but I was brought down to earth very quickly. In the first round I achieved a winning position against Seirawan, only to blunder horribly in time-trouble and lose. In round 2, Van Wely destroyed my King's Indian with an important opening novelty (see page 247). Further losses followed in rounds 4 and 7; indeed, after 11 of the 13 rounds I had just 3½ points. I have always been proud of the fact that I have never gone through a tournament without a win, but with just two rounds to go this record seemed to be in serious danger. I pulled my act together just in time, and by beating Nikolić and Van der Wiel in the last two rounds I managed to avoid the ignominy of the wooden spoon.

This disaster led me to think about the nature of chess results. Everybody has good and bad results, but why is there such variability? Chess players themselves tend to ascribe bad performances to outside effects. Of course, this can easily happen, for example if one is physically ill during a tournament, or is suffering from a personal crisis which prevents full concentration on the games. Nevertheless, while occasional events can be affected in this way, it doesn't seem enough to explain the regular ups and down of play throughout the year. My own feeling is that statistical factors play a much larger part than is normally believed. For example, the result at Wijk aan Zee 1992, which was clearly my worst result in the three years 1992-1994, depended on just two serious mistakes.

A more cynical view would be that my errors were largely the result of getting into time-trouble too often. Under normal circumstances, I very rarely get into time-trouble because I handle time shortage poorly. At Wijk aan Zee, the problem was that, thanks to my errors in the earlier rounds, I had lost confidence in my own moves and spent far too long checking my analysis over and over again, whereas normally I would just play a move at once.

Chess players usually regard good results as 'normal' and poor results as 'abnormal', but I suspect that most of the time the results depend on the operation of the laws of chance. A couple of errors can turn an average performance into one which is either excellent or disastrous, depending on which side of the board you happen to be sitting.

After Wijk aan Zee, I travelled to Cannes for an unusual team event. Four teams took part, from France, USA, England and Holland, in a double-round competition using a 'one hour for all your moves' time-limit. I played on board one in what turned out to be an exceptionally pleasant event. Not only were the weather, food and playing conditions excellent, but there was even free champagne after the game. England won the event convincingly, and I was happy with my personal score of 4/6.

The next significant event was the Olympiad in Manila. Olympiads normally take place in November, but this time the tradition was broken and it took place in June. In case you hadn't already guessed, it is hot and humid in Manila during June. Despite this, I enjoyed the event. We were staying in the excellent Manila Hotel, and everything was very efficiently organised, including a regular schedule of buses between the hotel and the tournament hall. The playing conditions were not so wonderful, and there was the additional problem of an erratic electricity supply which led to the windowless hall being plunged into total darkness on several occasions. The English team

was, on paper, one of the strongest ever, consisting of Short, Speelman, Adams, Nunn, Chandler and Hodgson. But there were a few problems. First of all, the team had to operate with a new captain, since Michael Stean had replaced David Anderton, who had been the captain for the previous 20 years. Being team captain is certainly no sinecure, and involves a great deal of hard work. David had done a fantastic job and nobody could expect that Michael would learn all the subtleties of the job straight away. However, I think the change of captain proved more disturbing than most people expected. After a time, the players become used to the way the captain operates, and know that they will be told by a certain time whether they have to play the following day, and on which board. Now everyone had to get used to a new approach.

I have already remarked on the weakening of the team spirit, starting in 1989, and this process continued at Manila. The team preparation sessions, which had been such an important event at previous Olympiads, were more or less absent at Manila. Nigel, in particular, preferred to work by himself.

The other main problem was that the character of the Olympiad had changed. At one time there was the match against the Soviet Union, and then there were the other 13 matches. Now the USSR had fissioned into the separate republics, several of which were almost as strong as the English team. This meant that we faced very close matches virtually every day. Of course, other teams encountered the same problem, but the real point is that in previous Olympiads there were maybe half-a-dozen teams who could be described as medal contenders; now there were about 15. This meant that, purely on statistical grounds, our chances of gaining medals were severely diminished. Nevertheless, it is possible to make too much of the problems posed by the Soviet republics. Of course, it didn't help that we lost 2½-1½ against Uzbekistan and Georgia, but the really damaging results were losing 3-1 to Iceland and 2½-1½ to India. These results couldn't have anything to do with the Soviet republics.

Another obstacle was that Chandler was in poor form and scored just 2/5. But again, it is easy to over-emphasise this factor. It is unusual for all six members of the team to be in good form and play a full part. In Dubai 1986, our best result ever, Flear played just three games.

Towards the end of the event it became clear that we weren't going to win any medals, but there was an important secondary prize, since teams finishing in the top five would automatically qualify for the 1993 World Team Championship to be held in Lucerne. This would still have been possible had we won 3-1 in the last round, but unfortunately we had the worst possible pairing – Russia. Normally, we would have played the Russians much earlier in the event, but we had been too low to meet them. This would only have been useful if we had avoided them completely; as everybody knows, in a Swiss event the last round is the worst time to catch a strong opponent. A 3-1 win against Russia would have been a miracle, but even the miracle became out of the question when Speelman agreed a draw in seven moves. The final result was 2-2 and England finished in 10th place, our worst Olympiad result since Lucerne 1982.

This poor result was due to a combination of reasons. Some I have mentioned above, but perhaps the main point is that the chess world has changed and the English team is no longer as outstanding as it once was. Many other countries also have first-rate teams, and their players are often more in practice than the English players.

In the first round I won with an attractive combination, which later gained the Duncan Lawrie prize for the best game by an English player at Manila.

Black is to move in Hsu-Nunn:

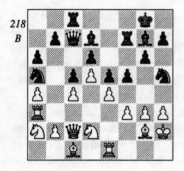

218
B

I played **21...♕d8**. Hsu didn't see the threat and replied **22 ♖c3?** (22 ♘f1 was essential, although Black has a clear advantage in any case). The continuation was **22...♘xg3!!** (at this point Shirov walked up to the board, looked a little confused and wandered away again; of course, I couldn't tell from this whether he had seen the point or not) **23 ♔xg3 ♕h4+**. Unfortunately the game concluded **24 ♔h2 ♕xe1 25 ♘f1 fxe4 26 ♘g3 exf3 27 ♗xf3 ♘xc4 0-1**. Had White played 24 ♔xh4, I intended winning by 24...f4 (threat ...♗f6 mate) 25 ♔g5 h6+ 26 ♔xg6

♖f5! 27 h4 (27 exf5 ♗e8 mate) ♖bf8 28 exf5 ♗e8 mate. My spoilsport computer points out that I could have mated one move more quickly, by 25...♖ff8!, and there is no defence to the threat of 26...h6+ 27 ♔xg6 (or 26 ♔h4 ♗f6 mate) ♗e8 mate.

After Hsu's 24 ♔h2, I understand why Alekhine sometimes 'improved' his games by substituting the brilliant finish he had foreseen for the mundane conclusion which actually occurred.

After six rounds, England had scored 16 points and were already three points behind the Russians. In round seven we faced the formidable Armenian team. My game against Lputian was not a great brilliancy, but it was a good example of a typical tournament game – a confrontation in the opening, followed by a complex middlegame leading to a double-edged endgame. Then, just when the game should have concluded in a draw, time-trouble intervened in my favour.

Game 35

J.Nunn – S.Lputian

Manila OL 1992

French

1	e4	e6	4	e5	♘fd7
2	d4	d5	5	f4	c5
3	♘c3	♘f6	6	♘f3	♘c6

7	♗e3	cxd4
8	♘xd4	♗c5
9	♕d2	0-0
10	0-0-0	a6

This variation started to become popular in 1989. Even though White appears to have a free hand, it isn't so easy to create genuine threats on the kingside, while Black's apparently slow advance on the queenside can be very effective when it finally arrives.

11 h4 *(219)*

This has been my preference ever since Nunn-Timman, Linares 1988, when 11 ♔b1 ♗xd4 12 ♗xd4 b5 13 ♗e2 b4 14 ♘a4 ♘xd4 15 ♕xd4 ♕a5 16 b3 ♗b7 followed by ...♗c6 led to an inferior position for White. The moves ♔b1 and ♗e2 contributed almost nothing to White's position, while Black's moves were all purposeful. These days, with the impatience of middle age, I prefer to get on with the attack straight away.

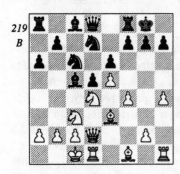

219
B

11	...	♘xd4

Curiously enough, the practical results in this line have been heavily in Black's favour (10/16 for Black in my database), although I doubt if this is due to the opening variation. Black has also tried 11...♕c7 and 11...♗xd4 12 ♗xd4 b5 (this can transpose to Nunn-Lputian after a later exchange on d4). Discussion of these possibilities would take us too far afield.

12	♗xd4	b5
13	h5	

Prior to Nunn-Lputian, White had tried:

1) 13 ♗xc5 ♘xc5 14 ♕d4 ♕c7 15 f5!? ♗b7! 16 f6 gxf6 17 exf6 ♔h8 with a small plus for Black, A.Ivanov-Glek, USSR 1987.

2) 13 ♘e2 a5 14 ♕e3 ♕c7 15 ♗xc5 ♘xc5 16 ♘d4 b4 17 g4 ♗a6 18 f5 ♘e4 19 fxe6 ♕xe5 20 exf7+ ♖xf7 21 ♗g2 ♖c8 22 ♖he1 ♖e7 23 ♘f5 with an edge for White, Kamsky-M.Gurevich, Belgrade 1991.

I don't like the idea of taking on c5 myself, which only serves to accelerate Black's knight towards e4. Therefore, I decided to press ahead on the kingside with 13 h5. Recently, however, White players have tended towards a different plan:

3) **13 ♖h3!?**. This is a multi-purpose move; the obvious idea is that White may reinforce his kingside attack by ♖g3, when the rook may generate threats against g7, for example by f5 and ♕h6. But there is a

more subtle purpose behind the rook move. Very often Black defends by exchanging on d4 and then offering to swap queens, taking the sting out of White's kingside initiative. With the rook on the third rank White's chances in an endgame are much improved, for example if Black has played ...b4 then White may continue with a3 or c3, forcing an exchange of pawns and allowing the rook to swing across to the queenside. After 13 ♖h3, play may continue 13...b4 14 ♘a4 ♗xd4 15 ♕xd4 and now:

3a) **15...f6?** 16 ♕xb4! fxe5 17 ♕d6 ♕f6 18 f5! (very energetic play by Kasparov) ♕h6+ (18...♕xf5 19 ♖f3 ♕g4 20 ♖xf8+ ♘xf8 21 ♘b6 wins material) 19 ♔b1 ♖xf5 20 ♖f3 ♖xf3 21 gxf3 and White has enormous pressure for the pawn, Kasparov-Short, Amsterdam (VSB) 1994.

3b) **15...♕a5** 16 b3 ♗b7 (intending ...♗c6) 17 c3 (17 h5 is also possible – see the note to Black's 15th move in the game) ♖fc8 18 ♔b2 (18 ♔b1 is a somewhat similar idea) bxc3+ 19 ♖xc3 ♖xc3 20 ♕xc3 with an edge for White, Nijboer-Luther, Leeuwarden 1992.

3c) **15...a5** 16 ♗b5! (the position is the same as in Nunn-Lputian, except that White has played ♖h3 instead of h5) ♖b8 17 ♗d3 ♕c7 18 h5 ♗b7 19 g4 ♖fc8 20 ♖h2 ♕c6 21 b3 was played in Fogaraši-Luther, Kecskemet 1993, when *New In Chess*

assesses the position as slightly better for White. I am not sure about this, since White has made no use of the move ♖h3; indeed, his later ♖h2 is a real loss of time. However, 18 ♖g3 ♗b7 19 ♖e1, intending f5, is a genuinely dangerous line, so Black may do better to play the immediate 17...♗b7, when after 18 ♖g3 ♗c6 19 f5 exf5 (19...♗xa4 20 f6 g6 21 ♕f4 does appear dangerous for Black) 20 ♗xf5 ♗xa4 21 ♗xd7 ♗xd7 22 e6 g6 23 exd7 ♕xd7 24 ♕xd5 the position appears more or less equal.

13   ...   b4 (220)

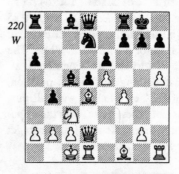

220
W

14   ♘a4

In this line it is always hard to decide whether the knight should go to e2 or a4. On a4 the knight holds up Black's queenside play, but it is in danger of being left offside and can be attacked by ...♗b7-c6. On e2 the knight might end up on the excellent square d4, but Black's queenside pawns are free to advance and the f1 bishop is temporarily blocked in.

In Smirin-Lputian, Rostov 1993 White preferred e2 and won a nice game: 14 ♘e2 a5 15 ♗xc5 ♘xc5 16 ♕e3 ♕b6 17 f5 a4 18 ♔b1 b3 19 cxb3 axb3 20 a3 exf5 21 ♖xd5 ♖a5?! 22 ♘f4 h6 23 ♗d3 ♗e6 24 ♖d6 ♕b7 25 ♖c1 ♖c8 26 ♕d4 ♘xd3? 27 ♖xc8+ ♗xc8 28 ♘g6 ♔h7 29 ♘f8+ ♔g8 30 ♖d8 g5 31 ♕d6 1-0. Smirin mentions the improvement 21...♘a4, when he assesses the position as unclear.

At the board I instinctively preferred 14 ♘a4, but the theoretical jury is still out.

14 ...   ♗xd4
15 ♕xd4   a5

If Black plays 15...♕a5 16 b3 ♗b7 then White has almost two extra tempi compared to Nunn-Timman given above. However, despite this White has no immediate route to the advantage, for example 17 f5 ♗c6 18 f6 is met by 18...gxf6 19 exf6 ♔h8. Probably White should play 17 ♖h3 ♗c6 18 ♘b2, when 18...♕xa2 really is dangerous after 19 f5 a5 20 ♖g3.

Kasparov comments that 15...f6 'would have allowed him (i.e. Black) to seize the initiative.' It is certainly true that White cannot continue as Kasparov did in his game against Short, because he lacks the move ♖h3-f3. On the other hand, White can play 16 exf6 ♕xf6 17 g3 and the main struggle still lies ahead.

16 ♗b5

A useful move. Black intended 16...♗a6, but now 16...♗a6 loses to 17 ♗xd7 ♕xd7 18 ♘b6.

16 ...   ♖b8 *(221)*

There was nothing better, but now Black cannot play ...♗a6.

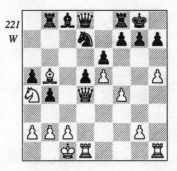

221
W

17 ♗d3

The rather bizarre idea 17 h6 g6 (17...♖xb5 18 hxg7 ♔xg7 19 ♕d3) 18 ♗c6 ♕c7 19 ♗xd5 exd5 20 e6 ♘f6! 21 ♕xf6 fxe6 22 ♕e5 ♖b7 is not very good for White. The position is opening up and White will be left with his stranded knight on a4.

17 ...   ♗b7

The threat is ...♗c6, so White must react vigorously on the kingside. Although my general plan was correct, its implementation left something to be desired.

18 h6?

The wrong move-order. I should have played 18 f5 ♗c6 (for 18...exf5 19 h6 g6 see the next note) 19 h6, when 19...g6 would transpose into the game. Accepting the piece by

19...♕g5+ 20 ♔b1 ♗xa4 is too dangerous because after 21 hxg7 ♖fc8 22 f6 h6 23 ♕h4! White has a crushing attack.

18   ...   g6
19   f5!? (222)

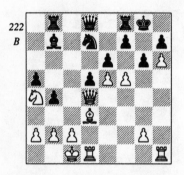

222
B

19   ...   ♗c6?

Lputian selects the safest line, but it is not the best:

1) **19...exf5** 20 ♗b5!? ♗a8 21 ♗xd7 ♕xd7 22 e6 fxe6 23 ♖he1 and now Black must be careful, for example 23...♕c7 24 ♖xe6 ♖fc8 25 ♘c5 ♖b5 fails to 26 ♖de1! ♖xc5 27 ♕h8+!. However, after 23...♖fe8! 24 ♘c5 ♕a7 the position is completely unclear. One possible continuation runs 25 ♕f6 ♕f7 26 ♕d4 ♕a7 (the threat was ♖xe6, and 26...♕f8 27 ♘d7! ♕xh6+ 28 ♔b1 is good for White) with a draw by repetition.

2) **19...♕g5+** 20 ♔b1 gxf5 21 ♗b5 ♖fd8 22 g4! fxg4 23 ♗xd7 ♖xd7 24 ♖dg1 and White's attacking chances are worth more than the sacrificed pawn.

3) **19...gxf5!**. Although this looks like the most dangerous choice, it exposes 19 f5!? as being a bit of a bluff. I intended 20 ♖h5!? with the variations **20...♗c6?** 21 ♗xf5! exf5 22 ♖xf5 f6 23 ♕g4+ ♔f7 24 e6+! ♔e7 (24...♔xe6 25 ♖fxd5+ ♔e7 26 ♕e4+!) 25 exd7 and White has a very dangerous attack, or **20...♔h8?** 21 ♗xf5 exf5 22 e6+ ♘f6 23 e7! ♕xe7 24 ♖xf5 with advantage for White. However, **20...f6!** brings the attack to a halt, for example 21 ♗xf5 exf5 22 ♖xf5 ♘xe5 23 ♖xe5 fxe5 24 ♕g4+ ♔f7 25 ♕g7+ (25 ♖f1+ ♔e7) ♔e8 26 ♕xe5+ ♔d7 27 ♘c5+ ♔c6 and Black escapes. Other 20th moves are no better, for example 20 g4 ♕g5+ 21 ♔b1 fxg4 and e5 is hanging.

20   fxe6

White cannot play 20 fxg6 hxg6, when both a4 and e5 are under threat. 20 ♘c5 ♕b6! is also bad, for example 21 fxg6 ♕xc5! 22 gxh7+ ♔h8 23 ♕g4 ♕e3+ 24 ♔b1 ♕xe5 25 ♖de1 f5! with advantage for Black.

20   ...   ♕g5+

Not 20...fxe6? 21 ♘c5 and the permanent mating threats around Black's king give White the advantage.

21   ♔b1   ♕xe5
22   ♕xe5   ♘xe5
23   ♘c5

The exchange of queens has relieved a lot of the pressure on

Black's position, since he need not worry about a possible mate on g7. Apart from the double mistake above, both sides have played reasonably moves and the result is a roughly equal ending. But now, as so often in over-the-board play, the clock starts to lend a hand.

23 ...   fxe6

After 23...f6 24 ♖hf1 White has a slight advantage.

24 ♖he1   ♘xd3
25 cxd3   d4?!

With one more accurate move Black would have been completely safe, but Lputian's bishop had been blocked in for so long that he couldn't resist the chance to activate it. However, it turns out that this wasn't the best way to employ the spare tempo and Black should have used the time to activate his rooks rather than his bishop. The alternatives are:

1) **25...♖f2** 26 ♖xe6 ♗b5 27 ♖e7 ♖xg2 28 ♖f1 ♖e8! (28...♖c8? 29 ♖g7+ ♔h8 30 ♖b7! ♗c6 31 ♖c7) and White has nothing better than to force a draw by 29 ♖xe8+ ♗xe8 30 ♘e6 ♗f7 31 ♘d8 ♗e8 32 ♘e6.

2) **25...♖be8** 26 ♖xe6 ♖xe6 27 ♘xe6 ♖f2 28 ♘d4 ♗d7 29 ♖c1 ♔f7 (the line 29...♖f4 30 ♖c7 ♖xd4 31 ♖xd7 ♖xd3 is also drawish, but not 29...♖xg2? 30 ♖c7 ♗e8 31 ♖g7+ ♔h8 32 ♖e7 and Black's bishop will be trapped) 30 ♖c5 with a roughly equal position.

26 ♘xe6   ♖fe8

White has some advantage after 26...♖f2 27 g3, as the d4 pawn is still under fire.

27 g3 *(223)*

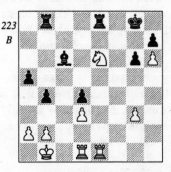

223
B

This position may be assessed as very slightly better for White, because Black's erroneous 25th move has left him with a sickly pawn on d4. Now Black must play actively, because if White is given time he will simply round up the vulnerable d-pawn.

27 ...   ♗b5?

A serious error which leads to the loss of a pawn. The correct defence was 27...♗a4! 28 b3 (28 ♖c1 ♗b5) ♗b5 29 ♔b2 (29 ♔c2 ♖bc8+, followed by ...♖c3) ♗xd3! (29...♖bc8 30 ♘xd4 ♖xe1 31 ♖xe1 ♗xd3 32 ♖e7 is good for White, for example 32...♖f8 33 ♖g7+ ♔h8 34 ♖a7, or 32...♖d8 33 ♖g7+ ♔h8 34 ♖a7 ♗e4 35 ♘e6!) 30 ♖xd3 ♖b6 31 ♖xd4 ♖bxe6 32 ♖xe6 ♖xe6 33 ♖d8+ ♔f7 34 ♖h8 ♖e2+ and Black has safely steered the game into a drawn rook ending.

28 &c2!

Now Black has no square on c3 for his rook, so after this simple move he cannot save the pawn on d4. Moreover, Black still has problems with his king because of the cramping influence of the pawn on h6.

28 ...   Eec8+
29 &d2   &c6

The trick 29...b3 30 axb3 &a4 is possible, but after 31 &xd4 &xb3 32 Ec1 White keeps a safe extra pawn.

30 &xd4   &d5
31 Ee5   Ed8
32 Ec1

Suddenly White's rooks are occupying the open files and threaten to overrun the seventh rank.

32 ...   Eb7
33 &c6

Not the only method, but probably the simplest.

33 ...   &xc6
34 Exc6   Ebd7
35 Ee3   Ed6?!

After a passive move such as 35...Ea7, White replies 36 Ef3 keeping Black's king confined. 35...Ef7 was more resilient, but after 36 Ece6! White will force off a pair of rooks, simplifying the technical task. The move played allows an immediate liquidation to a winning single rook ending.

36 Exd6   Exd6
37 Ee8+   &f7

38 Eh8   g5
39 Exh7+   &g6
40 Ea7   &xh6
41 Exa5   &h5

Heading for g4, but White can bring his rook back to e3, defending both pawns and freeing his own king to advance to c2 and b3.

42 Ee5   &g4
43 &c2

Simpler than 43 Ee3 Ec7.

43 ...   Eg6
44 Ee3   Ed6
45 &b3   Ed4
46 Ee4+   1-0

Kasparov wrote that 'the final outcome of this game had no connection whatsoever with the opening battle.' Quite right, Garry!

I ended the Olympiad with my traditional loss in the crucial last round match, although I must admit that playing Black against Kramnik I might well have lost whatever the situation. Despite this, I was reasonably satisfied with my overall score of 6½/10.

My next event was the Lloyds Bank tournament in London. Here I was unusually solid, and indeed went through the tournament without a loss. Unfortunately, this doesn't guarantee success in an open tournament and my 7/10 was only enough to tie for 8th-18th places. One example illustrates how hard it is to make a living playing chess professionally. At Lloyds Bank 1992

I played ten games over ten days, essentially two weeks' work. My performance rating for these 10 games was 2600. This earned me a prize of £82. Of course, grandmasters normally receive an appearance fee in addition to any prize they might win, but in their early years players have to subsist only on prize money. Note that this calculation doesn't include any time spent preparing for the event.

Game 36

K.Arkell – J.Nunn

London (Lloyds Bank) 1992

King's Indian

1	d4	♘f6
2	♘f3	g6
3	g3	♗g7
4	♗g2	0-0
5	c4	d6

I often play the boring variation with 5...c6 followed by 6...d5. Whilst this is an excellent drawing weapon against strong opponents, there are no winning chances at all for Black, so it is less appropriate against non-grandmasters.

6	0-0	♘bd7
7	♘c3	e5
8	♕c2	♖e8
9	b3	c6
10	e3	

Keith Arkell is a player with excellent positional sense, but he doesn't like tactics, and tends to handle complicated positions using intuition rather than calculation. Therefore, he prefers to prevent any lines involving ...e4 and ...e3, even at the cost of playing a slightly passive move.

10	...	exd4
11	♘xd4	h5!? *(224)*

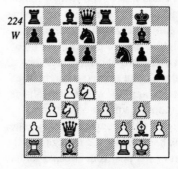

The inspiration for this cheeky move came from the game Timman-Kasparov, Tilburg 1991. If Arkell had continued 12 ♗b2 ♕e7 13 ♖fd1 a5 14 a3 ♘c5, we would have had an exact transposition. I decided to get on with ...h5 straight away, but this is probably inaccurate because it allows White to put his bishop on a3 instead of b2. Therefore 11....♕e7 is better, waiting for 12 ♗b2 before playing 12...h5.

Black's ...h5 might seem to be a beginner's move, since everybody knows that a flank attack cannot work unless it is based on central control. In this position the centre is quite fluid, which is another signal warning against a flank advance. Nevertheless, the move is far from stupid. Admittedly, White can create pressure against d6 by playing ♗a3 and ♖ad1, but Black can shield d6 with ...♘c5 and, hopefully, ...a5. This means that White doesn't have any terrifying threats.

In this line of the King's Indian, Black's main problem is that he has no completely stable squares for his knights. He can put a knight on c5, but eventually it can be ousted by a3 and b4, or he can put a knight on e5, but h3 and f4 will force it back. Without the guarantee that one of his knights will occupy a stable square, it is hard for Black to organise the rest of his position, because he has no idea where his knights will be ten moves from now. If Black can play ...h5-h4 and ...hxg3, forcing hxg3 by White, the whole situation changes because e5 becomes a stable square for a black knight. White could only push it away by f4, but then the knight would occupy another stable square, g4, which is ominously

close to White's king (for example, Black's queen might arrive on the h-file, or something might happen on the b6-g1 diagonal). It is worth Black spending time pushing his h-pawn if, at the end of the day, he will be able to play ...♘e5 knowing that the knight can stay on e5. The real question is whether White can create enough play against d6 to deflect Black from his plan. Here Black's inaccurate move-order has given White unnecessary extra chances.

12   ♗a3   ♕e7
13   ♖ad1 *(225)*

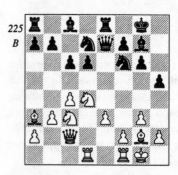

225
B

This is a good idea; the f1 rook is left in place to defend the kingside. However, the fact that Black obtains a reasonable position despite having paid no attention to adopting the best move-order suggests that playing b3 and e3 is too passive to offer White an advantage.

13   ...   ♘c5
It is tempting to play the cautious 13...a5 first, and only then ...♘c5,

but the continuation 14 ♘de2 ♘c5 15 ♕d2 is dangerous for Black, for example 15...♘fe4 16 ♘xe4 ♘xe4 17 ♕d3 ♗f5 18 ♗xe4 ♗xe4 19 ♕xd6 and Black does not have enough for the pawn.

14 b4!?

White continues to play aggressively, so as not to give Black a chance of carrying out his plan of ...a5 and ...h4. It is interesting to note that Keith Arkell reached the same position the following year. The second game continued 14 e4 h4 15 ♖fe1 hxg3 16 hxg3 ♗g4 17 f3 ♗d7 18 b4 ♘e6 19 ♘xe6 ♗xe6 20 b5 c5 21 ♕d3 ♘d7 (heading for e5) and Black had a clear advantage in K.Arkell-Daly, Dublin Z 1993. Despite this, White eventually won the game (readers may find the fascinating conclusion on p.208 of *Secrets of Pawnless Endings*).

14 ...   ♘ce4
15 ♘xe4   ♘xe4
16 b5

Certainly not 16 f3 ♘xg3 17 hxg3 ♕xe3+, but now White threatens to win the d6 pawn by taking twice on e4. Black's reply is forced but ugly.

16 ...   c5
17 ♘e2

This position pits Black's active pieces against White's control of d5. It is easy to see that White intends to play ♘f4-d5 coupled with the exchange of Black's active bishop by ♗b2. The successful execution of

this plan would give White a near-decisive positional advantage. For his part, Black must try to prevent ♗b2 and develop kingside counterplay by ...h4. The long-term advantage lies with White, so Black must waste no time.

17 ...   ♗f5 (226)

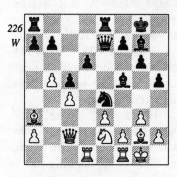

226
W

18 ♕b3

After 18 ♕c1 Black can try:

1) **18...a6?!** 19 b6! (not 19 ♗b2? ♗xb2 20 ♕xb2 axb5 21 cxb5 ♕e5! and Black has a slight advantage because of White's weak queenside pawns – in this line White doesn't get a chance to enjoy his control of d5) ♕d8 (otherwise the interpolation of ...a6 and b6 has just given White the additional square c7 when his knight arrives on d5) 20 f3, followed by ♗xc5, with a large advantage for White.

2) **18...h4**, with play similar to the game.

18 ...   h4
19 ♘f4

This move is tempting because it both prevents ...h3 and aims at d5. White could have played 19 ♗b2, but after 19...hxg3 20 hxg3 ♗g4! 21 f3 (21 ♖fe1 ♘xf2! 22 ♔xf2 ♗xb2 23 ♕xb2 ♕xe3+ 24 ♔f1 ♖e5 25 ♖d5 ♖xd5 26 cxd5 ♖e8 is good for Black) ♗xb2 22 ♕xb2 ♘f6! 23 e4 (23 fxg4 ♕xe3+ 24 ♔h1 ♕h6+ is perpetual check) ♗e6 24 ♕c3 a6 the position is quite unclear. If White plays 25 b6, then 25...♘d7 is awkward, while otherwise Black opens the a-file onto the weak a2 pawn, gaining counterplay.

19 ...   ♕e5!

After long thought I decided that it was impossible to achieve anything directly on the kingside, so the first priority must be to prevent ♗b2. Now White has a badly placed bishop on a3 to balance the outpost on d5.

If White does nothing, Black's next move might be 20...a5!?, since after ...a4 White has no obvious square for his queen.

20 ♖d5

The start of a risky plan. There were two reasonable alternatives.

The first is the obvious 20 ♘d5; after 20...h3 (20...♖ac8 21 gxh4!?) 21 ♗h1 ♖ac8 the position is more or less balanced. One possible continuation is 22 b6 axb6 23 ♘xb6 ♖cd8 24 ♘d5 ♗g4! 25 f3 ♘xg3 26 fxg4 ♘e2+ 27 ♔f2 ♘c3! 28 ♔g1 ♘e2+ with a draw.

The second is **20 gxh4!?**, when 20...♕f6 21 h5! (21 f3 ♘c3 22 ♖de1 ♕xh4 23 ♗b2 g5!? is unclear) g5 22 ♘d5 is good for White, so Black should play 20...a5 in any case.

20 ...   ♕f6

21 g4? (227)

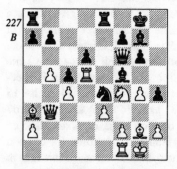

227
B

I was astonished when my opponent played this move with relatively little thought, because it triggers a tactical storm which is not very promising for White. A waiting policy was better, such as 21 ♖dd1, when Black must try to find a plan other than just returning to e5 (...a5 is less attractive when ♘d5 comes with gain of tempo).

21 ...   ♗xg4

22 f3

Not 22 ♗xe4 ♖xe4 23 f3 ♖xf4 24 exf4 ♗h3, followed by ...♕xf4, with two pawns and an attack for the exchange.

22 ...   h3

The impudent pawn, whose advance on move 11 brought smiles to the faces of the other players, starts to become a real danger. After 23 Nxh3 (23 Bxh3 Bxh3 24 Nxh3 Nc3 25 Rd3 Qf5 is also very good for Black) Bxh3 24 Bxh3 (24 fxe4 Qe6) Nc3 25 Rd3 Qg5+ 26 Kh1 (26 Kf2 Qh6) Qh6! (26...Rxe3 27 Bc1) 27 Bg4 Rxe3! 28 Bc1 Be5 29 Qc2 Ne2! the tactics work out in Black's favour, so the bishop has to move to h1, even though this blocks in White's king.

23 Bh1   Nc3!

The choice was between 23...g5 24 fxg4 gxf4 25 Rxf4 Qh4, which is unclear, and the piece sacrifice of the game. Within the time limitations of an over-the-board game, it is practically impossible to make such decisions on any rational basis, and this is where personal style enters the equation. My intuition told me to sacrifice, but another player might well have chosen 23...g5.

24 fxg4 (228)

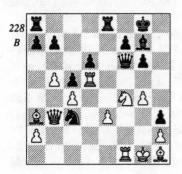

24 ...   Qh4?

But if you're going to sacrifice, you should at least follow it up correctly! My original intention had been 24...Rxe3, but then I became worried about the position after 25 Bc1 (25 g5? Qe7 is very bad because Black has the added threat of 26...Nxd5 followed by 27...Qxg5+) Rae8 (25...Nxd5 26 Nxd5 Rxb3 27 Nxf6+ Bxf6 28 axb3 Bd4+ 29 Rf2 Re8 30 Kf1 Bxf2 31 Kxf2 is very good for White because the rook cannot become active, while h3 and d6 are weak) 26 Bxe3 Rxe3. Black is a rook down for two pawns, and the only real threat is 27...Qh4, which looks rather slow. Nevertheless, White has no satisfactory move:

1) 27 Qc2 Qh4 28 Bf3 Rxf3! 29 Rxf3 Nxd5 30 Qe4 (if White takes the knight on d5, then ...Qe1+ followed by ...Bd4+ mates) Qxg4+ 31 Kf1 Nxf4 32 Rxf4 Qd1+ and Black has a material advantage plus a strong attack.

2) 27 Rd2 Qg5 28 Bxb7 Qxg4+ 29 Kh1 Qxf4 wins for Black.

3) 27 g5 Qe7 (threat 28...Nxd5 followed by 29...Qxg5+) 28 Kf2 Bd4 with a very strong attack.

25 Rd3?

Once again I was surprised by my opponent's lack of thought. The correct defence was 25 Bf3! Rxe3 26 Rd3! (not 26 Bc1? Nxd5 27 Bxe3 Nxe3 with material advantage for Black – it was because of this variation that I decided to play 24...Qh4 rather than 24...♖xe3, since I wanted to deter ♗c1) ♖ae8 27 ♗c1! (now this is possible; 27 ♕c2 is bad after 27...♖xf3! 28 ♖dxf3 ♕xg4+ 29 ♖g3 ♗d4+ 30 ♔h1 ♕xf4 31 ♖xg6+ ♔f8 and there is nothing better than 32 ♕d3 ♕e4+ 33 ♕xe4 ♘xe4 followed by 34...♘f2+ with a winning ending for Black) and Black has no clear attacking continuation; indeed he has to play accurately in order to maintain the balance:

1) 27...♖xf3 28 ♖dxf3 ♕xg4+ 29 ♖g3 ♗d4+ 30 ♔h1 loses for Black because the c1 bishop defends f4 (I overlooked this during the game).

2) 27...♖e1 28 ♗d2 ♗d4+ 29 ♖xd4 ♖xf1+ 30 ♔xf1 cxd4 31 ♕c2 and Black's attack is at an end. Indeed, White will soon take over the initiative.

3) 27...♖xd3 (the best chance) 28 ♘xd3 ♖e2 (28...♘e2+ 29 ♔h1 leads to nothing) with the lines:

3a) 29 ♗xe2? ♘xe2+ 30 ♔h1 ♕xg4 31 ♘f4 ♘xf4 32 ♕g3 ♕xg3 with a promising ending for Black.

3b) 29 ♗f4 (29 ♔h1 ♕e7 is similar) ♕e7! intending ...g5 with dangerous threats, for example both 30 ♔h1 g5 31 ♗c1 ♖xa2 32 ♗b2 ♕e3! and 30 a3 g5 31 ♗c1 ♖e3! are favourable for Black. After other moves, Black has two pawns for the piece, White's king is in danger and the queen on b3 is completely locked out of play, providing ample compensation.

3c) 29 ♕xc3!? ♗xc3 30 ♗xe2 and material is roughly equal, but if White's knight can reach d5 Black will be in trouble. Therefore, Black should try to stir up complications by 30...♕e7 31 ♗f3 ♕e6 attacking c4 and g4, with an unclear position.

Thus Black may just about survive after 25 ♗f3!, but clearly his previous move was incorrect.

25   ...   ♕xg4+
26   ♔f2 (229)

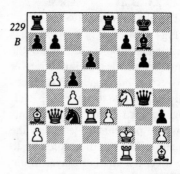

26   ...   ♗d4!

The only good move. The lines 26...g5 27 ♖xc3! (but not 27 ♖g1? ♕h4+, when 28 ♔f3 ♖xe3+ mates and 28 ♔f1 ♖xe3! 29 ♖xe3 ♕xf4+ 30 ♖f3 ♕d2! wins for Black) gxf4 (27...♗xc3 28 ♕xc3 gxf4 29 e4 is also very good for White) 28 ♖g1 ♕h4+ 29 ♔e2, 26...♗f6 27 ♔e1! and 26...♖xe3 27 ♔xe3 ♖e8+ 28 ♔d2 ♕e2+ (28...♖e2+ 29 ♔c1) 29 ♘xe2 ♖xe2+ 30 ♔c1 ♗h6+ 31 ♖d2 ♖xd2 32 ♕xc3 are all excellent for White.

27 ♖xc3

The alternative 27 ♖xd4 (27 ♔e1 ♗xe3 is winning for Black) cxd4 28 ♗c1 g5! 29 ♖g1 ♕h4+ 30 ♖g3 dxe3+ 31 ♗xe3 ♖xe3 32 ♔xe3 ♕xf4+ 33 ♔d3 ♘e2! 34 ♔xe2 ♖e8+ 35 ♔d3 ♕f1+ 36 ♔d4 ♕xh1 37 ♖xg5+ ♔f8 gives Black an extra pawn and a strong attack (38 ♕xh3? loses to 38...♖e4+). The next few moves of the game are forced.

27	...	♕xf4+
28	♔e2	♕xh2+
29	♔d1	♗xc3
30	♕xc3	♖e5

The position is still not completely clear even though Black has a rook and three pawns for two bishops. The long diagonal is weak, b7 is hanging and f7 is exposed. However, the strong h-pawn gives Black the advantage.

31 ♗b2   ♖ae8 *(230)*

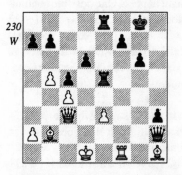

230
W

32 ♗d5?

In time-trouble White misjudges the situation. He had to try taking the b-pawn, when the advance of the a-pawn gives him long-term counter-chances if he can blockade Black's h-pawn. After 32 ♗xb7 ♕g3 33 ♗d5 ♖8e7, followed by ...h2, Black holds an advantage, but it would still be a fight.

32	...	♖8e7
33	♕d2	

There is nothing better because otherwise Black continues with ...♕g3 and ...h2, while White has no obvious way to strengthen his position.

33	...	♕xd2+
34	♔xd2	♖f5!

After 34...♖xe3 35 ♗f6 White has some counterplay, but by forcing the exchange of rooks Black removes any danger.

35 ♖xf5

Otherwise 35...♖f2+ is too strong.

35	...	gxf5
36	♔e2	

Forced, since 36 ♗f6 ♖e4 wins for Black.

36	...	h2
37	♔f2	♖e6

Heading for g6 and g4 to start rounding up White's pawns.

38 ♗c1?!

White could put up more resistance by 38 ♗xb7 (or 38 ♔g2 ♖xe3 39 ♗f6, but after 39...♖e2+ 40 ♔h1 b6 41 ♗g5 ♔f8!, preventing ♗e7, Black's rook is free to attack the queenside pawns) ♖g6 39 ♗g2 (39 a4 ♖g1 40 a5 h1♕ 41 ♗xh1 ♖xh1 and Black can easily stop the queen-side pawns) ♖g4 40 ♗f6 ♔f8 41 a3 ♖xc4 42 ♔g3 ♖a4, but Black's material advantage should be enough to win in the long run.

	38	...	♖g6
	39	♗g2	♖g4
	40	♗d2	♖xc4

0-1

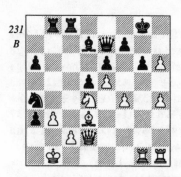

231
B

The Bundesliga season started again in October, and in the very first match I found myself opposite Vladimir Kramnik for the second time in five months. The performance of the relatively unknown Kramnik had been one of the sensations of the Manila Olympiad. When the composition of the Russian team was announced, and the name Kramnik was mentioned, several players said 'Who?'. However, the selectors of the Russian team obviously knew what they were doing because Kramnik, who celebrated his 17th birthday during the Olympiad, made the incredible score of 8½/9 (with a little help from me in the last round).

This time I had White, and the following tense position arose just as the players were starting to run a little short of time. Black is to play (231).

27 ... a2+!?

The alternative is 27...♘c3+ 28 ♔a1. After the game Kramnik evaluated this position as better for White, but I am not so sure. Black may

continue 28...♕c5 29 ♗xa6 (29 ♘f3 is too slow because 29...♘e4 is good for Black, while the sacrifice 29 ♗xg6 fxg6 30 ♖xg6+ ♔h8 31 ♘xe6 ♗xe6 32 ♖xe6 is also very promising for Black after 32...♘e4) ♘e4 30 ♕e3 ♖c6 31 ♗e2 ♖b4 32 h5!? (32 ♖d1 ♘f2! looks good for Black) with a very unclear position, for example 32...♕xd4+ (32...♖xd4 33 hxg6!) 33 ♕xd4 ♖xd4 34 hxg6 fxg6 35 h7+ ♔h8 36 ♗b5 and anything might happen. One possible continuation is 36...♖xc2 37 ♖xg6 ♖d1+! 38 ♖xd1 ♗xb5 (38...♘c5? 39 ♖g3! ♗xb5 40 ♖h1 wins) 39 ♖h1 ♖c8 40 ♖xe6 d4 and the complications continue.

28 ♔a1?!

It was also possible to play 28 ♔xa2, although this does allow an immediate draw by 28...♘c3+ 29 ♔b2 ♘a4+ 30 ♔a2 (30 ♔c1?! ♕a3+ 31 ♔d1 is very risky; 31...♕a1+ 32 ♔e2 ♕xd4 33 bxa4 is unclear, but the improvement 31...♖b4! gives Black a dangerous attack) ♘c3+

with perpetual check. Black can play for a win by 28...♘c3+ 29 ♔b2 ♕b4!?, but after 30 ♕e3! there is nothing clear, e.g. 30...♘a4+ 31 ♔c1 ♘c5 32 ♔d1 ♘xd3 33 ♕xd3 ♖c3 34 ♕d2 and Black's attack has temporarily abated, while White only needs one free move to rip Black's kingside open with h5.

Objectively speaking, taking on a2 is probably best, but in view of the double-edged position I decided to press for the win.

28 ... ♕a3

Black must proceed with immediate threats.

29 ♕c1 ♕b4

Or 29...♕c5 30 ♘e2 ♗b5!? 31 ♗xb5 ♖xb5 32 h5, also with a very murky position.

30 ♘e2 ♘c5 (232)

Probably best; the cautious alternative 30...♘c3 31 ♘xc3 ♕xc3+ 32 ♕b2 ♗b5 is a likely draw.

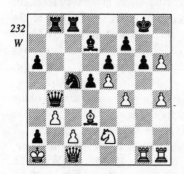

The move played appears very strong because both 31...♘xd3 and

31...♘xb3+ are threatened, while 31 ♕e3 loses to 31...♘xd3 32 ♕xd3 ♗b5 33 ♕d1 ♗xe2 34 ♕xe2 ♕c3+ 35 ♔xa2 ♖b5 and White can resign.

31 ♖xg6+!

Just at the moment when Black appears to have broken through on the queenside, White makes a counterattack on the other wing. I played this move very quickly, because it is clearly White's only chance.

31 ... ♔h8?!

Kramnik chose to decline the sacrifice, but it was also possible to take the rook: 31...fxg6 (31...♔f8? 32 ♕g1 fxg6 33 h7 wins for White) 32 ♕g1 ♔h8 (other moves are bad, for example 32...♗e8 33 ♗xg6 ♔h8 34 ♗f7! ♘xb3+ 35 cxb3 ♕f8 36 ♗xe6 followed by ♘d4 gives White a distinct advantage) 33 ♕xg6 ♘xb3+ 34 cxb3 ♕e7 with a very unclear position in which I believe that White cannot be better. One idea is 35 ♕g5 (35 h7 is met by 35...♗b5!), but then 35...♕f7 (35...♕xg5?! 36 fxg5 ♖xb3 37 ♘f4 is dangerous) 36 ♗g6 ♕f8 37 ♘d4 ♖b4 38 ♖d1 a5! 39 f5 a4 appears to be advantageous for Black. In such a complicated position it is hard to say anything for sure, but Black's extra exchange gives him a head start. In particular, White will not be able to make use of any liquidating options.

After the move played, the complications are enormous, but with best play the game should be a draw.

32 Rg7! *(233)*

The only move because 32 Wg1 loses to 32...Dxb3+ 33 cxb3 Wxb3 34 Wd4 fxg6 when Black has a material advantage and an attack. After 32 Rg7! Black has the choice between taking the bishop and taking the queen; which is correct?

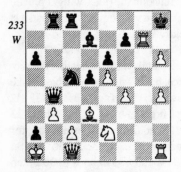

233
W

32 ...   Dxb3+!

Taking the queen is best. The other possibility runs 32...Dxd3 33 Wg1 (threat 34 Rh7+) Rg8 (or 33...We4 34 cxd3 Wxd3 35 Rh3 Wb1+ {35...Wf5 36 Dd4 is no better} 36 Wxb1 axb1W+ 37 Rxb1 and White has a clear plus in the endgame). During the game I intended to continue **34 Wg5** (threats 35 Wf6 and 35 Rg1), thinking that after **34...Wa3** (34...Wf8 and 34...Dxf4 both lose to 35 Rg1 with mate to follow) 35 cxd3 Wxb3 36 Rxg8+ Rxg8 37 Wf6+ Rh7 38 Wxf7+ Rh8 39 Wxd7 White would win, for example 39...Wxd3 40 Rc1 Wxe2 41 Wxe6 and there is no defence to the threat

of 42 Wf6+. However, Black has a very awkward defence in **34...De1!**, and it is time for White to give perpetual check by 35 Rxg8+ Rxg8 36 Wf6+ Rh7 37 Wxf7+ Rh8 (Black should not risk 37...Rxh6 38 Wxg8 Dxc2+ 39 Rxa2 Wa3+ 40 Rb1 Wxb3+ 41 Rc1, when only White can have the advantage) 38 Wf6+.

Home analysis showed that White has a much stronger continuation in **34 Wg3!** with the threats of 35 Rg1 or simply 35 Wxd3. Black is peculiarly helpless, for example 34...Dc5 35 Rg1 Dxb3+ 36 cxb3 Wf8 37 Wd3 or 34...Dxf4 35 Dxf4 We4 36 Rg1 Rgf8 37 Wg5 and White wins in both cases. 34...Wa3 35 Wxd3 Rxg7 36 hxg7+ Rxg7 is relatively best, but even then 37 Dd4 gives White a large advantage.

33 cxb3   Rxc1+
34 Rxc1

After 34 Dxc1 Black can force perpetual check at the very least, for example 34...Wc3+ 35 Rxa2 Wd2+ 36 Ra1 (36 Rb1 Rxb3+ 37 Dxb3 Wxd3+ 38 Rb2 Ra4 is better for Black) Wc3+ and there is no escape.

34 ...   Wxb3

Absolutely forced because of the deadly threat of 35 Rcg1 (34...Rb5? 35 Rh7+ Rg8 36 Rg1+ Rf8 37 Rh8+ and 38 Rxb8 wins for White, as does 34...f5 35 exf6 Wxb3 36 Rh7+ Rg8 37 Rg1+ Rf8 38 Rh8+ Rf7 39 Rxb8 Wxb8 40 h7). The next few moves are also forced.

35	**♖h7+**	**♔g8**
36	**♖g1+**	**♔f8**
37	**♖h8+**	**♔e7**
38	**♖xb8**	**♕xd3** *(234)*

After 38...♕xb8?! 39 h7 ♗a4, White cannot play 40 ♖g8 immediately because Black would save himself by 40...♕b3 41 h8♕ ♕d1+ 42 ♘c1 ♕xc1+ 43 ♔xa2 ♕d2+ 44 ♔a3 ♕xd3+ 45 ♔xa4 ♕b5+ with perpetual check. However, after 39...♗a4, Black is completely tied up and White can try to improve his position and eventually capitalise on his h-pawn. At any rate, Black would be doomed to prolonged defence.

234
W

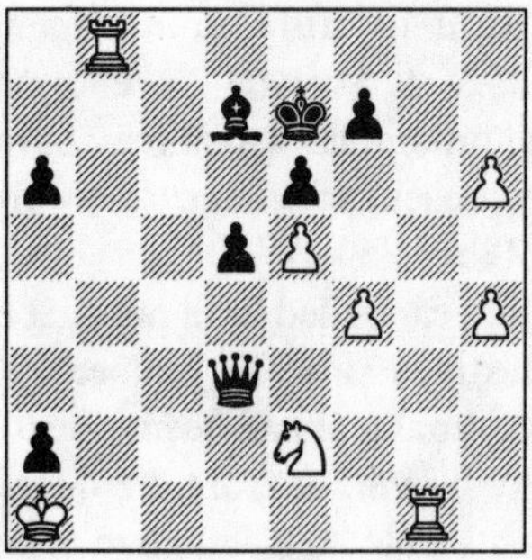

39 ♖c1

This leads to a forced draw. The alternative was 39 ♖b2, and if Black goes for the pawn immediately by **39...♕h7** White can launch a dangerous attack by 40 ♘d4 ♕xh6 41 ♖b7, for example 41...♕xf4 42 ♘c6+ ♔f8 43 ♖xd7 f6 44 ♖g8+! ♔xg8 45 ♘e7+ winning the queen. However, **39...♗b5!** is much better, cutting off the b2 rook, and in this case Black has the advantage because White's exposed king is the most important factor in the position.

39 ... ♕xe2

There is nothing better than to accept the offer.

40 h7 ♕d2

White cannot play for a win from this position, since after 41 ♖c7 the result is also perpetual check by 41...♕d1+ 42 ♔xa2 ♕d2+ 43 ♔a1 (White is taking an unnecessary risk if he allows ...♕d3+) ♕d4+ 44 ♔a2 ♕d2+.

41 h8♕ ½-½

White threatens three different mates in one, so Black has to take the perpetual check.

In November, the English team travelled to Debrecen in Hungary for the European Team Championship. Debrecen was the last possibility to qualify for the 1993 World Team Championship, and for this we needed to finish in the top two places. Russia once again dominated proceedings, with Kasparov (6/8) and Kramnik (6/7) their star performers. The English team did not fare at all badly, but, despite an excellent 3½-½ win against Armenia in the last round, we did not gain the coveted qualification. Nevertheless, third place was a creditable performance; Nigel Short (5½/8) and

Mickey Adams (6½/8) were the best individual scorers amongst the English team. I was not very happy with my 3/6. I won in the first round, drew four games and then lost to Romanishin whereupon I was dropped for the last two rounds. However, merely giving the scores doesn't reveal the unusual feature of the event from my point of view. This was that I had to play all six games with Black. Since my main strength lies with the white pieces, I found the tournament a frustrating experience.

The Elo system doesn't take into account whether you are White or Black. In average international play, White scores 57% and Black 43% (the difference is even larger at higher Elo ratings), so in Debrecen I suffered an automatic rating loss of five points (compared to a 3-3 colour distribution). The PCA rating list, although it has some other defects, at least takes colour into account.

My last chess event of 1992 was the rapid chess event at Oviedo in Spain, played at the rate of '45 minutes for all your moves'. With eleven games packed into four days, there wasn't much time to admire the local scenery, but I enjoyed the event despite the hectic schedule. It took me a few rounds to get used to the 45-minute time-limit, which I had never experienced before, and indeed in round two I blundered away a piece and lost to a 12-year-old Vietnamese girl. In an 11-round event it is possible to come back from a single setback and in the end I finished in a tie for 7th-14th places. As there were roughly 60 grandmasters participating in this giant event, I was quite happy with my final result.

In keeping with the great chess tradition of truly unmanageable trophies, I received an enormous metal ornament, which may or may not represent an orange tree, weighing 10lbs (4.5 kg).

The year ended with my first trip to Hastings since December 1987. The tournament had been transfomred by moving it from the decrepit Queen's Hotel to the modern Cinque Ports Hotel, to the relief of players and spectators alike.

1993

This year Hastings was a double-round eight-player tournament. The highest-rated player was Bareev with 2670, followed by Speelman and Polugaevsky on 2640. Judit Polgar could also be counted amongst the most dangerous competitors, even though her rating was relatively low at 2575.

The tournament started in the best possible way for me with the following game against a leading exponent of the Sicilian Defence. Readers with an eye for detail might protest that this game was actually played in 1992, but I have included it here to avoid splitting the tournament between two chapters.

Game 37
J.Nunn – L.Polugaevsky
Hastings 1992/3
Sicilian Najdorf

1	e4	c5
2	♘f3	d6
3	d4	cxd4
4	♘xd4	♘f6
5	♘c3	a6
6	♗e3	e6
7	f3	b5
8	g4	h6
9	♕d2	♘bd7
10	0-0-0	♗b7
11	h4	b4
12	♘ce2	d5

This position is one of the most important in the whole English Attack. The main line is 13 ♗h3, but 13 exd5 has been played a few times.

13 ♘g3

This is one of my specialities. The move is quite logical in that it defends the rook on h1 and therefore prepares g5, but my results with it have been mixed. I first adopted it against Stohl at Dortmund 1991, but after losing this game I gave up 13 ♘g3 and reverted to 13 ♗h3. Later on, I decided to take another look at 13 ♘g3 and came to the conclusion that it wasn't so bad after all.

13 ... ♕a5

Other moves are:

1) **13...e5** (13...♕c7? is bad because 14 g5 ♕xg3 15 ♗f4 traps the

queen, while Stohl gives 13...g6 14 g5 hxg5 15 hxg5 ♖xh1 16 ♘xh1 ♘h5 17 ♗h3 with the idea of ♗xe6 as good for White) 14 ♘b3! (the sacrifice 14 exd5 exd4 15 ♗xd4 ♕a5 is probably not correct) d4 15 ♗f2 ♕c7 16 ♗h3 g5 17 ♗f1 ♖g8 18 ♔b1 was slightly better for White in Nunn-Stohl, Dortmund 1991.

2) **13...dxe4** 14 g5 hxg5 15 hxg5 ♖xh1 16 ♘xh1 ♘d5 17 g6 ♕a5! (the latest idea in this variation; 17...f5? 18 ♘xe6 ♕c8 19 fxe4 fxe4 20 ♗h3 ♕c6 21 ♕xd5 1-0 was Maahs-Beyer, Baden-Baden 1990) 18 gxf7+ ♔xf7 19 fxe4? ♕xa2 20 ♘b3 ♘7f6! 21 exd5 ♗xd5 22 ♗d3 ♖c8 and Black had an enormous attack for the piece in Nunn-Ivanchuk, Monaco Blindfold 1994.

3) **13...♗d6** is also critical. After 14 ♘gf5, Black may be able to accept the knight sacrifice, but perhaps 14...♗f8 is the simplest reply, when White appears to have nothing better than returning to g3. 14 ♖g1!? was tested in Nunn-Rogers, Hastings 1993/4, but for more on this move readers will have to wait for the next volume of my best games!

14 ♔b1		**dxe4**
15 ♘xe4!? *(235)*		

This is a new idea, but it is logical. In Arnason-H.Olafsson, Reykjavik 1992, White played 15 g5, but after 15...hxg5 16 hxg5 ♖xh1 17 ♘xh1 ♘d5 18 g6 0-0-0 19 fxe4 ♘xe3 20 ♕xe3 ♘c5 21 ♘f2 fxg6 22 ♗h3

♔b8 23 ♕g5 ♔a8 24 ♗xe6 b3 25 axb3 ♖xd4 26 ♖xd4 ♕e1+ 27 ♖d1 ♘xe6 28 ♕xg6 ♕xf2 29 ♕xe6 ♔a7 30 ♖d7 ½-½ the complications had petered out to a draw.

White's main problem in this line is the poor position of his knight on e2, and the move 13 ♘g3 was intended to bring the knight back into play. 15 ♘xe4 is a natural follow-up.

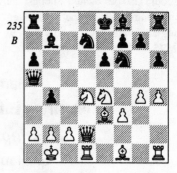

235
B

15 ...		**♘xe4?**

Polugaevsky settled quite quickly on this doubtful move. It is very tempting to break up White's pawns, and it seems that the weaknesses on e4 and g4 must give Black a good game. However, it turns out that Black doesn't have time to exploit his positional advantage because of his backward development, and in fact White's initiative is the most important feature of the position. There was no need to take on e4 immediately, and Black should have kept White guessing about whether or not he would make this exchange.

15...0-0-0 was correct, when 16 ♘b3 ♕c7 17 ♕f2 leads to an unclear position.

16 fxe4 ♘f6

White was threatening 17 ♘xe6, so Black has no time to take on e4. 16...0-0-0 also fails to equalise, for example 17 ♘b3 ♕c7 18 ♕f2 ♘e5 (18...♘f6 19 ♖xd8+ ♕xd8 20 ♗e2 is similar; 20...♘xe4 21 ♕xf7 ♘c3+ 22 bxc3 ♗xh1 23 ♗xa6+ mates, while otherwise White plays ♖d1 with an initiative) 19 ♖xd8+ ♕xd8 20 ♗e2, and White has the advantage because of his pressure along the diagonals leading to Black's exposed king.

17 ♗g2

Forced, or else Black can take one of the pawns. White should avoid playing ♗g2 while Black's knight is on d7, because he wants to meet ...♘e5 by ♗e2 restricting the knight. However, once Black has committed the knight to f6 then White can play ♗g2 because the knight can no longer travel to e5 and c4.

17 ... 0-0-0

Not 17...♘xe4 18 ♗xe4 ♗xe4 19 ♘xe6, nor 17...♗xe4 18 ♘xe6 fxe6 19 ♗xe4.

18 ♕e2 ♕c7

Black thought for a long time before making this move. Alternatives:

1) **18...♘xe4?** (18...♗c5?? loses to 19 ♘b3) 19 ♕c4+! ♕c7 (19...♔b8 20 ♘c6+ wins, while 19...♕c5 is also met by the spectacular 20 ♘xe6!) 20

♘xe6! ♖xd1+ 21 ♖xd1 fxe6 22 ♗b6! winning Black's queen.

2) **18...♗d6** 19 ♘b3 ♕c7 20 ♖d4! ♔b8 21 e5 ♗xe5 22 ♖xb4 ♘d5 23 ♗xd5 ♖xd5 24 ♕xa6 with a clear advantage for White.

19 ♖hf1

This adds to the pressure on Black's position, because it introduces the dangerous new threat of g5 followed by g6, undermining e6. This square is the linchpin of Black's structure; if it falls, his position will disintegrate. The preliminary ♖hf1 is necessary because 19 g5 hxg5 20 hxg5 ♖xh1 21 ♗xh1 ♘xe4 isn't dangerous for Black. White needs to avoid the exchange of rooks on the h-file in order to create major threats.

19 ... ♗d6

This doesn't really help. 19...♗c5 would have been met the same way as in the game, while 19...e5 20 g5! hxg5 21 hxg5 exd4 22 ♗f4 ♗d6 23 e5! is very promising for White, for example 23...♗xg2 24 ♕xg2 ♗xe5 25 ♗xe5 ♕xe5 26 gxf6 gxf6 27 ♕c6+ with a huge advantage.

20 g5! hxg5
21 hxg5 ♘xe4 *(236)*

Or 21...♘h5 22 e5! ♗xe5 23 ♗xb7+ ♔xb7 (23...♕xb7 24 ♕c4+ ♗c7 25 ♖xf7 is crushing) 24 g6! ♘f6 25 gxf7 ♕xf7 26 ♕c4 with an enormous attack for White.

22 g6!

Much stronger than 22 ♗xe4 ♗xe4 23 ♕xa6+ ♗b7, when Black's

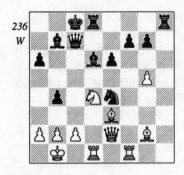

light-squared bishop becomes very active.

22 ...   Rh2

There is no defence to the undermining of e6. After 22...♘g3 23 ♗xb7+ ♕xb7 (23...♔xb7 24 ♕g2+ followed by 25 ♖xf7 wins) 24 ♕c4+ ♕c7 25 ♕xa6+ ♕b7 26 ♕xb7+ ♔xb7 27 ♖xf7+ White takes too many pawns.

23 Rxf7   Rxg2

White wins material after 23...♗e7 (or 23...♖d7 24 ♘xe6) 24 ♗f4 ♖xg2 25 ♗xc7 ♖xe2 (25...♖xd4 26 ♕e1!) 26 ♗xd8.

24 Rxc7+   ♗xc7

25 ♕c4   Rxg6
26 Rf1

Avoiding the last trap 26 ♗f4?? e5 27 ♗xe5 ♘d2+!. After the move played Black is almost equal on material, but he is doomed by the many weaknesses in his position, especially the troublesome e6 square. Perhaps 26...♘d6 was relatively best, but after 27 ♕xb4 White has a material advantage and an initiative.

26 ...   e5?

In severe time-trouble, Black loses at once.

27 ♘e6   Rxe6
28 ♕xe6+   ♔b8
29 ♕e7   a5
30 Rf8   1-0

Hastings was a curious tournament for me, in that I played very well in some games, but embarrassingly badly in others. In round 5 I lost to Bareev and in the following round I was totally crushed by Ilya Gurevich. In round 9 I faced Judit Polgar, who was leading the tournament at the time.

Game 38

J.Nunn – J.Polgar

Hastings 1992/3

Sicilian

1	e4	c5
2	♘f3	e6
3	d4	cxd4

4 ♘xd4   ♕b6

This was the first time in my life anybody had played 4...♕b6 against me. I discovered later that it had been adopted several times by the Lithuanian player Kveinys. About 20 years ago, Basman started to play 4...♗c5, and this new system bears some resemblance to Basman's idea; indeed, they can transpose into each other if White replies 5 ♘c3. Since I was already in unknown territory, I decided to adopt safety-first tactics.

5 ♘b3

After 5 ♘c3 ♗c5 we have transposed to Basman's system, whereupon White may continue with 6 ♘a4 or 6 ♗e3. 5 ♘b5 ♗c5 6 ♕f3 is a recent idea, but this appears artificial to me.

5 ... ♕c7

Black's idea is to play a normal Kan Sicilian, but with White's knight less actively posted on b3. I decided to send the game along different paths by using the chance to play c4.

6 c4

Not only was this a new move at the time, but nobody has repeated it since, at any rate up to July 1994.

The alternatives are:

1) **6 ♘c3** a6 7 ♗d3 b5 8 ♗g5!? (8 a3 ♗b7 9 0-0 ♘f6 10 ♕e2 d6 11 f4 ♘bd7 12 ♗d2 ♗e7 13 ♖ae1 e5 14 g4 exf4 15 g5 f3 16 ♖xf3 ♘g4 was unclear in A.Bach-Kveinys, Bad Wörishofen 1993) ♗b7 9 0-0 ♘f6 10 f4 b4 11 e5 bxc3 12 exf6 cxb2 13 ♖b1 g6 14 ♖xb2 with advantage to White, Hellers-Kveinys, Oslo 1992,

but Black's play can probably be improved.

2) **6 ♗d3** ♘f6 7 ♘c3 (7 0-0 d5 8 ♘c3 dxe4 9 ♘xe4 is completely harmless; both 9...♘xe4 10 ♗xe4 ♘d7 11 ♕d4 ♗d6, Torok-Kveinys, Budapest Spring 1992 and 9...♘bd7 10 ♘xf6+ ♘xf6 11 ♗b5+ ♗d7 12 ♗xd7+ ♘xd7 13 ♘d4 a6, Luther-Kveinys, Bonn 1993, were satisfactory for Black) a6 8 f4 d6 9 0-0 ♘bd7 10 a4 b6 11 ♕e2 ♗b7 12 ♗d2 ♗e7 shows Black's plan in action; he has reached a normal position, but with the knight on b3 instead of d4. This was played in Umanaliyev-Kveinys, Manila OL 1992, with perhaps just an edge for White. Note the similarity to Bach-Kveinys from line 1.

3) **6 g3** ♘c6 7 ♗g2 ♘f6 8 ♗f4 d6 9 ♘a3 a6 10 0-0 ♗e7 11 c4 0-0 with equality, Kir.Georgiev-J.Polgar, Budapest Z 1993.

6 ... ♘f6
7 ♘c3 ♗b4

Black could continue with normal development by 7...a6, intending to adopt a hedgehog set-up. However, the position of the knight on b3 introduces some slight differences, for example White might try to meet ...d6 by ♗f4, ♕d2 and ♖d1 with a quick attack on d6.

8 ♗d2

During the game, I rejected 8 ♗d3 because of 8...d5 9 exd5 exd5 10 cxd5 ♗xc3+ 11 bxc3 ♕xc3+ 12

♕d2 ♕xd2+ 13 ♗xd2 ♘xd5, and while the powerful bishops may provide sufficient compensation for the pawn, it seems unlikely that White has any advantage. However, White can improve by 10 ♕e2+!, when both 10...♗e6 11 ♘d4 and 10...♕e7 11 ♕xe7+ ♔xe7 12 0-0 are good for White. In view of this, Black would do better to meet 8 ♗d3 with the quiet 8...♘c6.

8 ...   ♘c6

This move is playable but slightly risky. After 8...♗xc3 9 ♗xc3 ♘xe4 10 ♗xg7 ♖g8 11 ♕d4 ♘c6 12 ♕xe4 ♖xg7 White has some advantage, but 8...a6 is more solid, intending ...♘c6 next move. One problem is that if White ever plays f4, then Black can reply ...♗xc3 and White must recapture with the pawn to avoid losing the pawn on f4. Therefore, 8...a6 should be met by 9 a3 ♗e7 10 f4 d6 11 ♗d3, followed by 0-0 and ♕e2.

9 ♘b5 (237)

The critical continuation. White aims to exploit the weakness of d6, even at the cost of moving the same piece twice and therefore delaying his development. The knight not only heads for the critical square, but it also provokes the exchange of dark-squared bishops, which weakens Black's defence of d6.

The rest of the game revolves around the battle for d6. The stakes are certainly high, because if White can consolidate his grip, then the backward d7 pawn will give Black a positionally lost game. On the other hand, if Black can frustrate White's plan, then the waste of time inherent in ♘b5 may return to haunt White later. In such a double-edged position, a slight slip can mean the difference between success and failure.

The analysis below shows that White's plan is doubtful against precise play. In the game, however, Black makes an inaccurate move and White's plan succeeds, although he has to be prepared to sacrifice along the way.

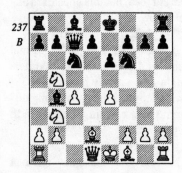

237
B

9 ...   ♕f4?!

It was better to play 9...♕e5 and now:

1) **10 ♗xb4?** ♘xb4 11 ♕d2 ♘xe4! (not 11...♕xe4+ 12 ♔d1 and White wins a piece because of the twin threats of 13 ♕xb4 and 13 ♘d6+, nor 11...♘c6 12 ♘d6+ ♔e7 13 0-0-0 ♘xe4 14 ♘xe4 ♕xe4 15 ♗d3 followed by ♖he1 with a dangerous initiative for the pawn) 12

♕xb4 a6! (12...♘g3+ 13 ♔d1 ♘xh1 14 ♘d6+ ♔f8 15 ♘xc8+ d6 16 ♕xd6+ ♕xd6+ 17 ♘xd6 ♘xf2+ 18 ♔e1 is very good for White) 13 f4 (after 13 ♘5d4, Black can safely take the rook on h1) ♕xf4 14 ♘5d4 ♘f2 15 ♖g1 ♕e3+, followed by 16...♘d3+ winning the queen.

2) **10 f3** (aiming for a position similar to the game) d5! (this is the difference) 11 ♗xb4 ♘xb4 12 ♕d2 ♘c6 13 0-0-0 (13 f4 ♕xe4+ 14 ♔d1 threatens 15 ♗d3, 15 ♘d6+ and 15 ♘c7+, but Black can play 14...♕g6! 15 ♘c7+ ♔e7 16 ♘xa8 dxc4 with good compensation) dxe4 14 ♘d6+ (14 f4 ♕b8 15 ♘d6+ ♔e7 gives White nothing clear) ♔e7 15 ♘xe4 ♖d8 and Black has a very satisfactory position.

After the move played Black is in hazardous territory.

10 ♗xb4   ♘xb4
11 f3 *(238)*

Over the next couple of moves, both sides must take into account the possibility of ♕d2, forcing an exchange of queens. For example, if Black plays 11...0-0, then 12 ♕d2 ♕xd2+ 13 ♔xd2 is good for White, e.g. 13...d5 (after 13...♘e8 14 ♔c3 ♘c6 15 ♖d1 White maintains his grip on d6) 14 cxd5 (14 e5 dxc4!) exd5 15 e5 ♘d7 16 f4 and Black cannot play 16...f6 because of e6-e7 coupled with ♘c7. On the other hand, ♕d2 is wrong if Black hasn't castled, because by playing ...♔e7

and ...♘e8 Black can easily maintain control of d6.

238
B

11 ...   b6

In this position, **11...d5** doesn't work because of 12 cxd5 exd5 13 ♕c1! ♕xc1+ 14 ♖xc1 0-0 15 ♘c7 ♖b8 16 a3 ♘a6 17 e5 ♘xc7 18 ♖xc7 ♖e8 19 f4 ♘e4 20 ♗b5, with a favourable ending for White.

The main alternative is **11...a6** 12 ♘d6+ ♔e7 13 c5 b6 14 a3 ♘c6 and now:

1) **15 ♕d3** (attempting to maintain the knight at d6) bxc5 (not 15...a5 16 g3! ♕h6 17 e5! ♘d5 18 ♕xd5 exd5 19 ♘f5+ inflicting terminal damage on Black's pawn structure) 16 ♖d1 ♖b8! 17 ♘xc5 ♖xb2 18 g3 ♕g5 and White has nothing concrete for the pawn.

2) **15 g3!** ♕e3+ 16 ♗e2 bxc5 17 ♘c4 ♕g5 18 ♕d6+ ♔e8 19 ♘xc5 and White has a massive positional advantage; there is little Black can do about the weakness of d6 and her bad king position.

The move played intends ...a6 next move, when White cannot support his knight on d6 by c5. However, the extra tempo allows White to adopt a different plan.

12 ♗e2

Now that ...♕e3 isn't check, White can meet 12...a6 by 13 g3.

12 ... a6

Again, 12...0-0 is met by 13 ♕d2.

13 g3 ♕e5

Black has little choice, because 13...♕b8 14 ♘d6+ ♔e7 15 e5 ♘e8 16 ♕d2 ♘c6 17 ♘xe8 ♖xe8 18 f4 gives White a clear positional advantage.

14 f4 ♕xb2

15 ♘d6+!

This move came as a shock for Black. Judit had calculated that 15 ♘c7+ ♔d8 16 ♘xa8 ♘c2+ 17 ♔f2 ♘xe4+ 18 ♔g1 (18 ♔f3 ♗b7) ♘xa1 19 ♘xa1 ♘c3 is winning for Black, but White wants to sacrifice material rather than take it!

15 ... ♔e7

16 0-0

The knight on d6 paralyses Black's position and forces immediate action, or else e5 followed by f5 will start a mating attack.

16 ... ♘xa2 *(239)*

The other possibility is 16...♘e8 17 e5 ♕c2 18 ♕e1 ♘c6 (after 18...♘xd6 19 ♕xb4 ♕xe2 20 ♖fe1 ♕f3 21 ♘d4 ♕b7 22 ♕xd6+ ♔e8 23 ♖ab1, 23...♖b8 24 f5 followed by f6 mates, so Black has to play 23...♕b8

24 ♖xb6 ♕xd6 25 exd6, even though this leaves White firmly in control) 19 ♗f3 ♘xd6 20 exd6+ ♔xd6 (after 20...♔d8, the continuation 21 ♕e3 ♖b8 22 ♗xc6 dxc6 23 ♘d4 ♕a4 24 ♕e5 is very strong) 21 ♗xc6 dxc6 22 ♖d1+ ♔e7 (22...♔c7 23 ♕e5+ ♔b7 24 ♘a5+ bxa5 25 ♖b1+ mates) 23 ♘d4 ♕a4 24 ♘f5+ ♔e8 25 ♕e5 and White wins.

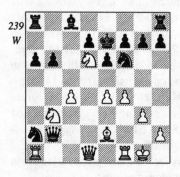

239
W

17 ♖xa2

This move can be criticised for being unnecessarily flashy. Judit correctly pointed out after the game that White could have won without further sacrifices by 17 ♗f3 (threat ♖f2) ♘c3 18 ♕d3 ♕xb3 (after 18...♘e8 19 e5 ♖b8 20 ♘xe8 ♔xe8 21 ♕d6 ♕xb3 22 ♕xb8 ♕xc4 23 ♕xb6 Black has a very poor position because she can't castle and the bishop on c8 is imprisoned) 19 ♖fb1 and there is no reasonable way for Black to give up her queen, for example 19...♕xb1+ 20 ♖xb1 ♘xb1 21 e5 is decisive. However, the move played also wins, albeit in a more complicated way.

17 ... ♕xa2
18 e5

White has made a substantial material investment – an exchange and two pawns – but in return all Black's active pieces have been eliminated and White's lead in development is now extremely dangerous.

18 ... ♕a3

Returning some material only delays the attack slightly. The main line runs 18...♘e8 19 f5 f6 (or 19...♖f8 20 ♗f3 ♖b8 21 fxe6 and now both 21...dxe6 22 ♘xe8 and 22...fxe6 23 ♘xe8 ♔xe8 24 ♕d6, followed by ♗h5+, are winning for White) 20 fxe6 dxe6 21 ♗f3 ♖b8 22 ♘xe8 ♖xe8 (22...♔xe8 23 exf6 gxf6 24 ♕d6 threatens 25 ♕xb8 and 25 ♗h5 mate; after the forced 24...♖b7 25 ♗h5+ ♖f7 26 ♖d1 Black cannot avoid mate) 23 ♕d6+ ♔f7 24 exf6 (threatening both 25 ♗h5+ and 25 ♕c7+) ♖b7 (24...gxf6 25 ♗h5+ ♔g8 26 ♗xe8 wins on material) 25 ♗xb7 ♗xb7 26 ♕d7+ ♔g6 27 ♕xg7+ ♔h5 28 g4+ ♔h4 29 ♕h6+ and mate next move.

19 exf6+ gxf6
20 c5

This move enables White to maintain his knight on d6. After 20...bxc5 21 ♘c4 ♕a4 (21...♕b4 22 ♕d6+ ♔e8 23 ♘xc5 ♕b8 24 ♗f3 ♕xd6

transposes) 22 ♕d6+ ♔e8 23 ♘xc5 ♕c6 24 ♗f3 ♕xd6 25 ♘xd6+ ♔e7 26 ♘f5+ exf5 27 ♗xa8 White wins easily.

20 ... ♕a4
21 ♘c4

With the threat of ♘xb6. Black therefore gives up further material in a desperate bid for counterplay.

21 ... ♗b7
22 ♘xb6 ♕e4
23 ♗f3 ♕e3+
24 ♔g2 ♗e4

The only move, as 24...♗xf3+ loses to 25 ♖xf3 ♕e4 26 ♕xd7+ ♔f8 27 ♘xa8 wins. Now, however, 25 ♕xd7+ ♔f8 26 ♘xa8 fails to 26...♕e2+.

25 ♕d6+ ♔e8
26 ♘xd7

The last finesse. Black has no reasonable way to prevent mate by ♘xf6.

26 ... ♕e2+
27 ♔g1 ♕e3+
28 ♖f2 1-0

After 28...♕e1+ 29 ♔g2 ♗xf3+ 30 ♖xf3 ♕e2+ 31 ♔h3 ♕b2 32 ♘d4 Black cannot delay the inevitable any longer.

The roller-coaster ride continued when, in the very next round, I played very weakly against Sadler and was efficiently annihilated. The round after I won against backmarker Crouch, and then I faced the new leader Bareev.

Game 39
E.Bareev – J.Nunn
Hastings 1992/3
King's Indian

1	d4	♘f6
2	c4	g6
3	♘c3	♗g7
4	e4	d6
5	♗e2	0-0
6	♗g5	♘a6

The old methods of countering the Averbakh Variation, which are based on an immediate ...c5, have fallen out of fashion. These days, Black usually prefers to prepare his central counterplay by ...♘bd7 or ...♘a6.

7 h4 *(240)*

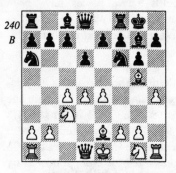

240
B

This move is Bareev's speciality. Although his practical results are rather poor, he has been unlucky in some of these games. The idea is to make immediate use of the bishop on e2 to force through h4-h5, and thereby lay the foundations for a later kingside attack. This is quite a logical idea, because usually White has to prepare his kingside attack laboriously, by f3, g4 and only then h4-h5. The only problem is that while White is realising his strategic ambitions, he is not developing his pieces.

7 ...   c5

This move was first played in Bareev-J.Polgar, from an earlier round at Hastings. When Bareev played 7 h4 for the first time, in Bareev-Kasparov, Linares 1992, the World Champion responded by 7...h6 8 ♗e3 e5 9 d5 ♘c5 10 ♕c2 c6 11 h5 g5 12 f3 a5 with an unclear position. White later missed a definite win, and the game ended in a draw. Since Bareev lost the two games from Hastings, one might have expected that, with ½/3, he would have given up 7 h4. However, he used it again in a critical game against Gelfand from the 1993 Biel Interzonal; this continued 7...e5 8 d5 h6 9 ♗e3 ♘c5 10 ♕c2 c6 11 h5 cxd5 (deviating from the Kasparov game) 12 cxd5 ♗d7! 13 hxg6 fxg6 14 b4 ♘a6 15 a3 h5, which Gelfand evaluates as unclear. Bareev once more achieved a winning position, only to go wrong in time-trouble and lose.

It isn't clear whether 7...c5 or 7...e5 is the most promising response to Bareev's system; both appear playable.

8	d5	♘c7
9	♕d2	e6
10	e5!?	

Bareev also played this pawn sacrifice against Judit Polgar. I was surprised that he decided to repeat it against me, and I awaited his improvement with trepidation. Objectively speaking, it may well be better to continue more quietly, for example with the obvious 10 h5.

10	...	dxe5
11	d6	♘ce8
12	♖d1!?	

At last Bareev deviates from the earlier game. That had continued 12 0-0-0 ♕d7! (both unpinning the knight and blockading the d-pawn; in particular, White can no longer play ♘e4) 13 h5 b5 14 cxb5 (14 ♘xb5 ♘e4) ♗b7 15 ♗h6 ♕xd6! (a neat trick to remove the dangerous pawn) 16 ♕g5 ♗xh6 17 ♕xh6 and now 17...♕e7, as played in the game, is enough to give Black an edge, but 17...♕c7 may well be even stronger.

The move played introduces some slight differences, for example Judit Polgar's ...♕xd6 trick doesn't work

any more, because ...♗xh6 isn't check. On the other hand, White's king, although not in any immediate danger, might eventually suffer from being in the centre.

12	...	♕d7 (241)

12...♕b6 is a reasonable alternative, but I saw no reason why I should deviate from Judit's plan.

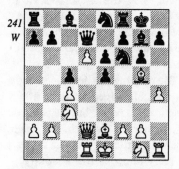

241
W

13 ♕e3

After 13 ♘f3, Black can continue 13...e4 14 ♘e5 ♕xd6! 15 ♕xd6 ♘xd6 16 ♖xd6 ♘e8 and now:

1) 17 ♖d8? ♗xe5 18 ♗e7 (18 ♘xe4 ♘c7) ♗f6 with a solid extra pawn for Black.

2) 17 ♖d2 ♗xe5 (not 17...f6? 18 ♗e3 fxe5 19 ♗xc5 with advantage for White) 18 ♗e7 ♘f6 19 ♗xf8 ♔xf8 and Black has two pawns plus a dominant dark-squared bishop for the exchange.

3) 17 ♘xf7 ♔xf7 18 ♖d2 (18 ♖d8 ♗f6) ♗xc3 19 bxc3 ♘f6, intending ...e5 followed by ...♗e6, is roughly equal. Black is a pawn up,

but his e-pawns are not very attractive and White has the two bishops.

Other moves are possible, for example **13 ♗f3**, when 13...♖b8 prepares ...b6 and ...♗b7, or **13 h5** (by analogy with the Polgar game), when 13...b5 and 13...♕c6 are reasonable replies.

    13 ...   **b6**

Not 13...♘xd6? 14 ♗xf6 ♗xf6 15 ♘e4 ♗e7 16 ♖xd6 and White wins. The move played not only defends the c5 pawn, it also prepares to develop by ...♗b7.

The opening has developed into a very double-edged position. Black has his extra pawn, but the pawn on d6 in a thorn in his flesh. The knight on e8 is a particular problem in that it severely impedes Black's development.

    14 ♘f3

After 14 ♕xe5 (14 ♗f3 ♗b7 frees Black's cramped position) h6 15 ♗xf6 (or else ...♘d5) ♘xf6 16 ♕g3 ♗b7 Black can develop freely and, in view of White's poor development, the d6 pawn is likely to come under fire before White can support it.

    14 ...   **♘h5!**

An excellent move. Black is prepared to offer the exchange in order to maintain his pawn on e5 and activate his pieces.

    15 ♗e7 *(242)*

Not 15 ♘xe5? ♗xe5 16 ♕xe5 f6 17 ♕e4 ♗b7 and Black wins.

242
B

    15 ...   **f6!**

My original idea was to play 15...♘f4?, but I suddenly noticed that White had an incredible combination, namely 16 ♕xe5!! ♗xe5 17 ♘xe5 and now:

1) **17...♕b7** 18 ♗f3 ♕b8 19 ♘c6 ♕b7 and now White can force a draw by 20 ♘e5, but he would be well justified in playing on by 20 0-0! with an advantage.

2) **17...♘xe2** 18 ♘xd7 ♘xc3 19 ♘xf8 ♘xd1 20 ♔xd1 ♘f6 21 ♗xf6 (21 ♘xg6? ♘g4) ♔xf8 22 h5 with a large advantage for White since 22...♔e8 loses to 23 hxg6 hxg6 24 ♖h8+ ♔d7 25 ♖d8+ ♔c6 26 d7.

I checked these lines several times because I simply couldn't believe that White could make a positional sacrifice of his queen for just one minor piece. In the end, I had to accept the results of my concrete analysis, even though it contradicted my intuitive assessment.

The move played is essential to defend the e5 pawn. It also threatens

...♖f7, so White is obliged to take the exchange immediately.

16 ♗xf8   ♗xf8

16...♔xf8? is a blunder on account of 17 ♘xe5! fxe5 18 ♕f3+.

17 ♘e4   ♘f4

The battle now revolves around the pawn on d6. If Black can safely round it up, he will have two solid pawns for the exchange, and therefore the advantage. Just at the moment Black is tactically exposed because of the possible sacrifice on f6, but if Black is careful White cannot save his advanced pawn.

18 0-0   ♗g7!

Safety first. After the immediate 18...♗b7, White can play 19 ♘xf6+! ♘xf6 20 ♘xe5 ♘xe2+ 21 ♕xe2 ♕g7 22 d7 ♖d8 23 ♘c6! ♖xd7 (23...♗xc6 24 ♕xe6+ ♕f7 25 ♕xc6 ♖xd7 26 ♖xd7 ♘xd7 27 ♖e1 is slightly better for White, since the queen and rook make an effective attacking combination, whereas the minor pieces have no targets) 24 ♕xe6+ ♕f7 25 ♕xf7+ ♖xf7 26 ♘d8, exchanging the b7 bishop, and leading to a roughly equal ending. Once again, White's rooks will be quite effective on the open central files, whereas the minor pieces can't easily reach d4.

19 ♖fe1   ♗b7

It is better not to exchange on e2, because the knight serves a useful function in holding up h4-h5. After 19...♘xe2+ 20 ♕xe2 ♗b7 (20...f5?!

21 ♘xc5! bxc5 22 ♘xe5 ♗xe5 23 ♕xe5 ♕c6 24 h5! is promising for White) 21 h5 White has much better chances than in the game.

20 ♗f1   ♗h6 *(243)*

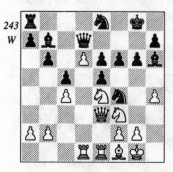

243
W

The end is in sight for the d6 pawn. The immediate capture on e4 is bad, because White gains a tempo by hitting the rook on a8, but now the queen has to move.

21 ♕c3

Or 21 ♕a3 (21 ♔h1 ♘xg2 22 ♕xh6 ♘xe1 23 ♖xe1 ♗xe4 24 ♖xe4 ♘xd6 25 ♖e1 ♘f5 26 ♕c1 ♖d8 is also favourable for Black; in this position the three pawns are worth more than a piece because White's minor pieces have no active squares – note that 21...♔g7?! is met by 22 ♘eg5!) ♗xe4 22 ♖xe4 ♘xd6 23 g3 ♕c6 (23...♘d5!? 24 ♖ee1 ♘b4, heading for c6 and d4, is also promising) 24 ♖xd6 (or 24 ♖ee1 ♘h5) ♕xd6 25 gxf4 ♗xf4 and the avalanche of pawns will start rolling by ...f5 and ...e4.

21	...	♗xe4
22	♖xe4	♘xd6
23	♖ee1	e4!? *(244)*

If White had time to organise his position by g3 and ♗g2, then he would not stand badly, so I decided to act immediately, even though this gives White a chance to initiate complications.

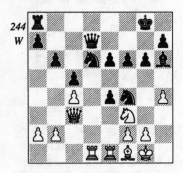

244
W

24 ♘h2?

This passive move gives Black everything he wants. The alternatives are:

1) **24 ♕xf6?** (24 ♘d2? f5 is too passive) exf3 25 g3 ♘e2+ 26 ♗xe2 fxe2 27 ♖xe2 ♗g7 (27...♖e8 is also good) 28 ♕xe6+ ♕xe6 29 ♖xe6 ♘xc4 is sufficient to win.

2) **24 ♖xe4 ♘xe4 25 ♖xd7 ♘xc3 26 bxc3 e5 27 g3 ♘e6** and Black retains his extra pawn, although White has good drawing chances in view of his active rook and the opposite-coloured bishops.

3) **24 g3!? ♘h5 25 g4 (25 ♖xe4 ♘xe4 26 ♖xd7 ♘xc3 27 bxc3 is similar to line 2) ♘f4 26 g5 fxg5 (26...exf3? 27 ♕xf3) 27 ♘xg5 ♗xg5 28 hxg5 e5 29 ♕xe5 (29 ♕g3 ♖f8 is also promising for Black) ♕g4+ 30 ♔h1 ♘f5!? (30...♕h4+ is a draw) 31 ♕xe4 ♖f8 and Black has a dangerous attack in return for the sacrificed exchange. Indeed, White has almost no constructive moves, while Black threatens to play 32...♘d4.

Line 2 may well offer the best drawing chances, but psychologically it isn't easy to accept a depressing ending.

24 ... f5

Advancing the pawns to f5 and e4 has enormously improved Black's position; his bishop has increased scope, White's knight is shut out of play and the pawn chain forms an effective barrier against White's bishop.

| 25 | ♕e5 | ♖d8 |
| 26 | ♖xe4 | |

In view of Black's steadily increasing positional advantage, White decides to return the exchange in order to activate his knight. After 26 g3 ♕e7! (26...♘h5 27 g4 ♗f4 28 ♖xd6 ♗xe5 29 ♖xd7 ♖xd7 30 gxh5 ♗xb2 is less clear) 27 ♕c3 ♗g7, followed by 28...♘h5, White has a thoroughly miserable position.

26 ... ♘h3+

After 26...fxe4 27 ♘g4, Black has nothing better than 27...♘h3+ transposing.

| 27 | gxh3 | fxe4 |

28 ♘g4   ♗g7

This position should be winning for Black. He has an extra pawn, and his weak e-pawns are balanced by White's damaged pawn structure; the only problem is the awkward pin on the d-file.

29 ♕g5

Or 29 ♘f6+ ♗xf6 30 ♕xf6 ♖f8 31 ♕e5 ♘xc4! 32 ♖xd7 ♘xe5 33 ♖xa7 ♘f3+ and Black wins.

29 ...   ♖f8

A necessary precaution. Black wants to block the d-file with ...♗d4, but first he must cover f6 to prevent the reply ♖xd4.

30 b4

White tries his hardest to generate counterplay, even at the cost of more material. The alternatives 30 ♕d2 ♗d4, 30 ♘e5 ♗xe5 31 ♕xe5 ♘xc4 and 30 h5 gxh5 31 ♕xh5 ♗d4 are hopeless.

30 ...   ♗d4

It seemed most sensible to keep the outpost on d4. After 30...cxb4?! 31 c5 bxc5 32 ♕xc5 ♖d8 33 ♕xb4 White's position has improved because there is no way for Black to block the d-file.

31 ♖xd4

After 31 h5 ♕d8 Black has a clear extra pawn.

31 ...   cxd4

32 ♕e5

Better than 32 ♘f6+ ♖xf6 33 ♕xf6 ♘e8 34 ♕f4 d3 and the d-pawn storms forward.

32 ...   h5?

I played this move without much thought, but it makes the win harder. The simplest line was 32...♘f5 33 ♕xe4 (33 ♘f6+ ♖xf6 34 ♕xf6 d3) ♕e7!, intending ...♘xh4, and White has no chance.

33 ♘f6+   ♖xf6

34 ♕xf6 (245)

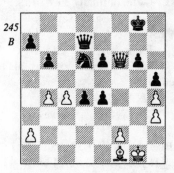

245
B

34 ...   d3

Once again, Black misses an easier variation: 34...♘f5! 35 c5 (35 ♕xg6+ ♕g7 36 ♕xg7+ ♔xg7 37 c5 bxc5 38 bxc5 ♔f6 is winning for Black) ♔h7! and White's counterplay is inadequate, for example 36 ♗c4 d3 37 ♗xe6 d2 38 ♗xd7 d1♕+ and 39...♕xd7.

35 ♕d4

Or 35 c5 (35 ♕xg6+? ♕g7 loses at once) bxc5 36 bxc5 ♘f5 37 ♕xg6+ ♕g7 38 ♕xg7+ ♔xg7 39 c6 ♔f6 40 c7 ♘d6 41 ♔g2 ♔e7 42 ♔g3 e5! and Black wins.

35 ...   ♕c6

36 f3

White is understandably eager to break up Black's central pawns, but it turns out that this move exposes White's king too much. However, Black should also win after **36 c5** bxc5 37 bxc5 ♘f5 38 ♕f6 ♕e8, **36 ♗g2** e5! 37 ♕xe5 (37 ♕xd3 exd3 38 ♗xc6 d2 39 ♗a4 ♘e4 followed by ...♘c3 wins) ♘xc4 38 ♕b8+ ♔g7 39 ♕xa7+ ♔f6, or finally **36 ♕f6** ♘e8! 37 ♕xg6+ ♘g7, followed by ...♕xc4.

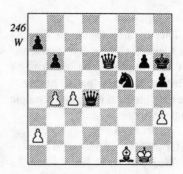

246
W

36 ...   ♘f5

36...d2 37 ♕xd2 exf3 is also good.

37   ♕d8+   ♔h7
38   fxe4   ♕xe4
39   ♕xd3

Black wins after 39 ♗xd3 ♕e1+ 40 ♗f1 (40 ♔g2 ♘xh4+) ♕xb4 41 ♕c7+ ♕e7.

39   ....   ♕xh4
40   ♕d7+

Or 40 c5 ♕xb4 41 ♕d7+ ♔h6 42 c6 ♕c5+ and there is no square for White's king, for example 43 ♔h1 (43 ♔g2 ♘e3+) ♕f2 44 ♗g2 ♘e3.

40   ...   ♔h6
41   ♕xe6   ♕d4+ *(246)*
42   ♔h1?

Losing immediately. **42 ♔h2?** also loses after 42...♕f2+ 43 ♗g2 ♘e3 44 ♕c6 (44 ♕e4 ♘f1+ 45 ♔h1 ♘g3+) ♘f1+ 45 ♔h1 ♘g3+ 46 ♔h2 ♘e2 forcing mate. **42 ♔g2** would have put up the greatest resistance, but even here 42...♘e3+ 43 ♔g1 ♘xc4+ 44 ♔h1 (44 ♔h2 ♕f2+ 45

♗g2 ♘e3 wins) ♘e3 45 ♕g8 (45 ♗e2 ♕d2 and 45 ♕f7 ♕xb4 are even worse) ♘xf1 46 ♕f8+ ♔g5 47 ♕xf1 ♕xb4 leaves Black two pawns up with an eventual win in the queen ending.

42   ...   ♕f2
43   ♗g2   ♘g3+
44   ♔h2   ♘e2

0-1

Incredibly, the ups and downs hadn't ended. In the following (penultimate) round, I obtained a completely winning position against Ilya Gurevich, but then blundered away my queen. A quick draw in the last round meant that I finished with 7/14, which left me in joint 4th-6th positions. This result was a bit of a disappointment for me, but it bears out my theory that pure chance plays a large part in determining whether one makes a good or a bad result. Had I not made the awful blunder against Gurevich, then I would have finished in joint 3rd-4th places, and I would have regarded the tournament as a modest success. In an exciting last round, Judit Polgar beat Bareev to tie with him for first place.

When Hastings finishes, Wijk aan Zee starts. In most years it has been possible to play in both events, although there have been occasions when the two traditional tournaments clashed. Even in the years when it was possible to play in both, I had generally chosen one or the other, thinking that to play two tough tournaments in quick succession would be too much. But by 1993, good tournaments were so hard to come by that when I was invited to play in both events, I decided to take the chance. It didn't work out too badly. Although Hastings ended on a slight sour note, I enjoyed Wijk aan Zee and played reasonably well.

Wijk aan Zee had adopted a new format for the 1993 tournament. Instead of the traditional 14-player round-robin event, the organisers had switched to a knock-out system based on two-game mini-matches. The format was particularly unusual in that a Swiss system event was run in parallel. Players who were knocked out were transferred to the Swiss event. Depending on when you were knocked out, you could join the Swiss tournament at various stages, having been allocated a certain number of points according to the stage of the competition.

This system proved equally confusing for players and journalists alike. After seven rounds, Adams was in sole lead in the Swiss event with 5½ points – only he wasn't, because Salov and Oll, who had just been knocked out by Karpov and Illescas respectively, suddenly parachuted into joint first place with him. Salov promptly beat Adams, Hodgson and Oll in the last three rounds to win the Swiss event outright, so he went home having gained two large prizes!

I had been seeded into the second round of the knock-out, where I was paired against Azmaiparashvili. This was the first game of the two game mini-match.

Game 40
J.Nunn – Z.Azmaiparashvili
Wijk aan Zee 1993
Pirc

| 1 | e4 | d6 | 3 | ♘c3 | g6 |
| 2 | d4 | ♘f6 | 4 | ♗e3 | c6 |

5 ♕d2   ♘bd7

For 5...b5, see Nunn-Gelfand on page 257. The advantage of Azmaiparashvili's move is that it doesn't give White a target to hit with a later a4. The danger is that White will play a4 in any case, preventing queenside expansion by Black and leaving Black with a slightly passive position.

6 ♘f3

Just as in Nunn-Gelfand, White's main decision is when to play h3. It isn't necessary yet, because 6...♘g4 can be met by 7 ♗g5.

6 ...   ♕a5
7 ♗d3   e5 (247)

Once again, 7...♘g4 8 ♗g5 is satisfactory for White, but only because of the important tactical point 8...h6 9 ♗h4 e5 10 0-0 exd4?? 11 ♘d5! winning Black's queen.

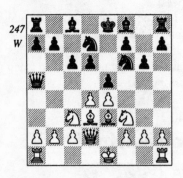

247
W

8 h3

This move appears to be a novelty. 8 0-0-0 was played in Kupreichik-Short, USSR-England (telex) 1982, with White gaining a crushing victory. However, as I explained in the notes to Nunn-Gelfand, the modern tendency is to play the ♗e3 system with 0-0 rather than 0-0-0, directing the game along positional lines. The immediate 8 0-0 is perhaps a little dubious, as Black may reply 8...♘g4 9 ♗g5 (9 ♘e2 ♕b6) f6 (certainly not 9...h6? 10 ♘d5!) 10 ♗h4 exd4 (10...h5 is also interesting) 11 ♘xd4 ♘xh2!? 12 ♔xh2 ♕e5+ 13 f4 ♕xd4 winning a pawn. Of course White has some compensation, but to adopt a solid line and then immediately plunge headlong into complications seems inconsistent.

8 ...   ♗g7
9 0-0   0-0

Black cannot prevent White's a4, because the immediate 9...b5? loses to 10 ♘xb5.

10 a4   ♖e8

This position can also arise from the anti-Pirc system involving ♘c3, ♘f3, h3 and ♗e3 (the system with no name).

The big question is how the central tension is going to be resolved. There are two main possibilities; either White will play dxe5, or Black will play ...exd4 (if Black plays ...♘f8, then White can also contemplate d4-d5, because it keeps the knight out of e6). Black's ...exd4 will be good if he can muster enough pressure against e4 to interfere with White's development. White's dxe5 will be good if he has enough initiative to overcome to natural equalising tendency of the open d-file; being able to play a5 and ♗c4 will help in this respect.

The move played indirectly steps up the pressure on White's e4 pawn, and so helps create the conditions necessary for a favourable ...exd4. Black could also have considered the immediate 10...exd4 11 ♘xd4 (11 ♗xd4 ♘e5, and 12 ♗e2 is impossible because of 12...♘xe4! 13 ♘xe4 ♘xf3+ 14 ♗xf3 ♕xd2 15 ♘xd2 ♗xd4) ♘c5.

11 ♖fd1 *(248)*

White is thinking about the open d-file after dxe5, and this move is useful preparation.

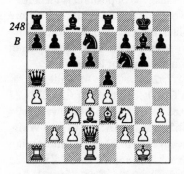

248
B

11 ...   ♕c7

Black is worried about possible ♘d5 tricks, so he withdraws his queen from a5. Other moves:

1) **11...♘f8** 12 d5!? (12 dxe5 dxe5 13 ♘d5 ♕xd2 14 ♘xf6+ ♗xf6 15 ♘xd2 ♘e6 16 ♘c4 ♖d8 17 a5

also gives White an edge because of the nagging pressure against the pawn on a7, which ties down the rook on a8) ♕c7 (12...cxd5 13 ♘xd5 ♕xd2 14 ♘xf6+ ♗xf6 15 ♘xd2 is very good for White) 13 ♗c4! with some advantage for White.

2) **11...exd4** (there are tactical reasons why this would have been better on the previous move) 12 ♗xd4 (sometimes White can take back on d4 with the knight, but it is more usual to capture with the bishop) ♘c5?! (after 12...♘e5 13 ♗e2, Black has no ...♘xe4 tricks because the queen is defended by the rook) 13 b4! ♕xb4 14 ♗xf6 ♗xf6 15 ♘d5 ♕b2 (after 15...♕xd2 16 ♘xf6+ White wins material because of the black rook on e8) 16 c3! with a clear plus for White.

12 a5   exd4

Black has more or less run out of useful preparatory moves, so he decides to resolve the central tension. The only alternative was 12...♘f8, but then 13 ♗f1 (13 dxe5 dxe5 14 ♗c4 ♗e6 15 ♕e2 is also possible, but 13 d5? cxd5 is bad, because Black will end up playing ...e4) exd4 (13...♘e6 14 d5) 14 ♗xd4 ♘xe4 15 ♘xe4 ♖xe4 16 ♗xg7 ♔xg7 17 ♕xd6 gives White an edge.

13 ♗xd4   ♘c5?

This allows White to liquidate into a promising ending. 13...♘f8 14 ♕e3!? or 13...♘e5 14 ♗e2 were more appropriate.

14 e5

The next few moves are practically forced.

14 ...   ♘fd7
15 exd6   ♕xd6
16 ♗f1!

This is the key move, avoiding the exchange of Black's knight on c5. Later on this knight will be attacked by b4, and then it will have to retreat to d7 or e6, blocking in the c8 bishop.

16 ...   ♘f8 *(249)*

After 16...♘f6 17 ♕g5! ♗f5 (not 17...♘e6 18 ♗xf6 winning material) 18 ♘h4! (I gave 18 ♗e5 ♕e6 19 ♖d6 'and wins' in my *Informator* notes, but I overlooked 19...♘fe4!) ♘ce4 (18...♘fe4 19 ♘xf5 ♕xd4 20 ♘xe4 ♘xe4 transposes) 19 ♘xf5 ♕xd4 20 ♘xe4 ♘xe4 (20...♕xe4 21 ♘d6) 21 ♖xd4 ♘xg5 22 ♘xg7 ♔xg7 23 ♖d7 White has a promising ending.

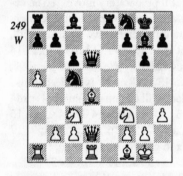

249
W

17 ♗xg7

White fails to make the most of his position. In the game, Black is able to meet b4 by the relatively favourable ...♘e6, but if White had played the immediate 17 b4!, then Black would have to play 17...♘cd7 (17...♗xd4 loses to 18 bxc5, and 17...♘ce6 18 ♘e4 ♕e7 19 ♗xg7 ♔xg7 20 ♕c3+ f6 21 ♖d6! is very unpleasant for Black). Then 18 ♗xg7 ♕xd2 19 ♘xd2 ♔xg7 20 ♘c4 gives White an improved version of the game.

17 ...   ♕xd2
18 ♘xd2

The knight is heading for d6.

18 ...   ♔xg7
19 b4   ♘ce6
20 ♘c4

20 ♘de4 is also slightly better for White.

This type of position is ideal for a two-game match. White can torture Black for a long time, without having to take any risks which might put him in danger of losing.

20 ...   ♖d8

Or 20...c5 21 b5 (21 ♘d6 ♖d8 22 bxc5 ♘xc5 23 ♖ab1, followed by 24 ♖b5, is also sufficient to give White an edge) ♘d4 22 ♘d5! (threatening 23 c3, but not 22 ♘e3? ♖xe3! 23 fxe3 ♘xc2 24 ♖ac1 ♘xe3) ♖b8 (22...♘xb5 23 ♘ce3 is awkward for Black) 23 ♘ce3 ♗e6 24 ♘c7 ♖ed8 25 b6 and White maintains a slight advantage.

21 ♘e4   ♖b8!

After a white knight arrives on d6 Black will be unable to move the c8 bishop unless he has first defended the b7 pawn with his rook.

22 ♘ed6

It is tempting to play a6 at some stage, but the b4 pawn is attacked after the immediate 22 a6 ♖xd1 23 ♖xd1 bxa6.

The move played avoids the exchange of rooks, which would help Black to free his cramped position, and threatens 23 a6! bxa6 24 ♘e5.

22 ... ♘c7 *(250)*

Preventing a6 and intending to play ...♘d5.

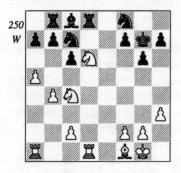

250
W

23 ♘e5?!

Even though this turns out well, it is not the most accurate move. The idea of preparing c4 was correct, but 23 ♘e3 was the way to do it. In this case White would retain his slight advantage.

23 ... ♗e6?!

Perhaps the most obvious move, but curiously enough it doesn't help Black much. His problem is that all his minor pieces would like to be on e6, but as soon as one of them occupies it, the others are blocked.

The best defence was 23...f6! 24 ♘ef7 ♖d7 25 ♘xc8 ♖xf7 (25...♖xc8 26 ♖xd7 ♘xd7 27 ♘d6 ♖b8 28 ♖e1 ♔f8 29 c4 is also minutely better for White) 26 ♘d6 ♖d7 27 c4, with just the faintest edge for White.

24 c4

Thanks to Black's loss of time, White manages to play c4, keeping Black's minor pieces out of d5 and maintaining his queenside pressure.

24 ... ♘e8

Displacing the knight from d6, but now it heads towards the equally dangerous square c5.

25 ♘e4 f6

26 ♘f3 ♗f7

This type of position is very unpleasant to defend. Nothing appears to offer real chances of equalising, but on the other hand nothing is clearly losing, so one cannot even use a process of elimination. Moreover, the opponent has many possible plans to strengthen his position, and you have no idea which one he will actually adopt. Even very strong players can quickly go downhill in such positions, especially when, as here, time-trouble starts to play a part.

27 ♘d4

Once again this knight exerts pressure on c6, and so threatens 28 a6.

27 ... ♖dc8

27...♖bc8 28 a6 b6 29 b5 is similar to the game.

28 a6

The time has come to make a definite move.

28 ...   b6

29 b5!   cxb5

Or 29...c5 30 ♘c6 ♖a8 31 ♖d2, followed by ♖ad1, and White can steadily increase the pressure.

30 ♘xb5

White's position is so strong that he can afford to ignore the weak c-pawn; the pressure against a7 is more important.

30 ...   ♖a8

31 ♖ac1   ♖c6? *(251)*

If Black does nothing, then White will play 32 c5 bxc5 33 ♘xc5, opening up fresh attacking possibilities such as ♗e2-f3 or ♖e1-e7. The move played permits an even stronger continuation.

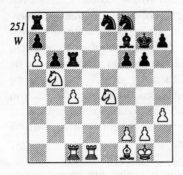

251
W

32 g3!

Black's rooks are temptingly lined up on the long diagonal. Even

if he saves them, the a8 rook will have to move, and once White takes on a7, the pawn on a6 will run through.

32 ...   ♖cc8

An admission of failure.

33 ♗g2

A safety-conscious player might prefer 33 ♘d2 followed by ♗g2, but I had calculated a forced tactical win.

33 ...   ♗xc4

Or 33...♖xc4 34 ♘xf6 and wins.

34 ♘ed6   ♘xd6

35 ♘xd6   ♗xa6

Hoping to net two pawns for the exchange.

36 ♖a1!

This leaves Black with no survival chances. The bishop only has one square, and after 36...♗e2 37 ♖d2! it is completely dominated by White's pieces. Black therefore jettisons the piece immediately, but to no avail.

36 ...   ♖ab8

37 ♖xa6   ♖c7

38 ♘b5   ♖c5

39 ♖xa7+   ♔h6

40 ♘d6   b5

41 ♘f7+   ♔g7

42 ♘e5+

In fact 42 ♘d8+ would have won more quickly, since after 42...♔h6 43 ♖f7 the knight is trapped, but of course anything sensible will win. Azmaiparashvili plays on hoping for a miracle.

42 ...   ♔h8

43 ♘d7   ♖d8

44	♘xc5	♖xd1+
45	♗f1	h5
46	♔g2	b4
47	♖b7	♖d5
48	♘d3	g5
49	♘xb4	♖d6
50	♗c4	h4
51	gxh4	♖d4
52	♗d3	♘e6
53	♗f5	♘f4+
54	♔f3	♖c4
55	hxg5	fxg5
56	♘d3	♔g8
57	♗h7+	1-0

The second game ended in a draw, so I was through to the next round. Unfortunately, the luck of the draw brought me up against Karpov, and after two hard-fought games Anatoly won by 1½-½. This deposited me in the Swiss with 3½/5. Here I started well enough, with a draw against Nikolić and a win against Khuzman, but towards the end I tailed off, losing to Piket and Tukmakov. The solid month of chess had finally caught up with me. I finished in joint 14th-21st places in the Swiss, which may not sound very impressive, but it was an exceptionally strong tournament and I was level with such distinguished players as Adams, Gelfand and Shirov.

After Wijk aan Zee, the general shortage of tournaments meant that I played very little chess in the next five months. I did complete the

Bundesliga season with an excellent score of 5/7, for a performance rating of 2718. My most entertaining combination of the season was played in Dresden during February.

I was Black against V.Bologan, and White is to play *(252)*.

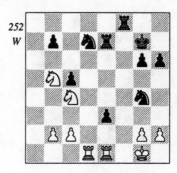

252
W

Black is a pawn up, but White's pieces are active and the advanced pawn on e3 seems likely to fall.

29 h3

The alternative was 29 ♖e2, so as to prepare h3, but then 29...♖f2 30 ♖de1 ♘de5! is good for Black, the main point being that 31 ♘xe3 ♖xe2 32 ♖xe2 ♘c6! (not 32...♘c4?? 33 ♘f5+) wins material.

29 ... e2

30 ♖d2? *(253)*

White should have played 30 ♖xe2 ♖xe2 31 ♖xd7+ ♖f7 32 ♖xf7+ ♔xf7 33 hxg4 ♖xc2 (material is about equal, but Black's rook is active and White's kingside pawns are weak) 34 ♘ba3! (not 34 ♘cd6+? ♔e7! 35 ♘xb7 ♖xb2 36 ♘7d6 c4, when White's knights are paralysed and he cannot stop the pawn) and White frees his king, whereupon the result should be a draw. It may well be that Bologan was playing for a win, and this caused him to reject 30 罝xe2.

253
B

30 ...   ◊b6!!

It was perhaps not surprising that White, who was short of time, had failed to anticipate this move.

I arrived at this surprising combination via an unusually logical chain of thought. My first idea was to play 30...罝f1+ 31 罝xf1 e1豐, but suddenly I saw Bologan's idea – after 32 罝xd7! Black has no reasonable reply. White either gets 罝+2◊ v 豐, or Black plays 32...豐xf1+ 33 會xf1 ◊h2+ 34 會g1 罝xd7 35 會xh2, but this is also very good for White. I cast around for an alternative continuation, but other lines simply lose the e2 pawn, after which White may well be slightly better. For lack of any other option, I returned to the

idea of ...罝f1+, and it suddenly occurred to me that a preliminary knight sacrifice validates the whole idea.

The point is that 30...◊b6 31 ◊xb6 罝f1+ 32 罝xf1 e1豐 is much better because the c4 knight has been deflected, so there are threats of 33...豐xd2 and 33...豐e3+. White would have to play 33 罝d3 (33 ◊c4 豐e6), but then 33...豐a5 34 ◊d5 罝e1! will give Black an ending with 豐 v 罝+◊ in which he has excellent winning chances.

When I played 30...◊b6!!, Bologan had about six minutes left on his clock; he used four of them before playing ...

31 罝dxe2   罝xe2
32 罝xe2   ◊xc4
33 hxg4   ◊xb2

... which is in fact White's best defence. For the moment the knight on b2 isn't very well placed, and White's active pieces partly compensate for the extra pawn. Indeed, were it not for White's weak kingside pawns, he would probably draw without too much trouble. In this position, however, Black has fair winning chances, even against best play by White.

34 ◊d6

After 34 罝e7+ 會f7 35 罝xf7+ 會xf7 36 ◊d6+ 會e6 37 ◊xb7 會d5 38 會f2 ◊c4 it is now White's knight that is poorly placed, and this makes it impossible to avoid the loss of either the c2 pawn or the g4 pawn (after ...♘e5).

34 ... b6 *(254)*

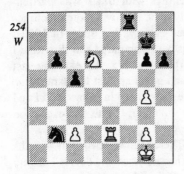

254
W

35 ♖e7+?

Now White is definitely lost. After the game Hübner pointed out that White's pieces are already on good squares, so he should have played 35 g3!, which stops the threat of ...♖f4. Of course, Black can continue to play for a win, but White has drawing chances.

35 ... ♔f6

36 ♖b7

White attacks Black's queenside pawns, but a more important factor is that Black's king can become active.

36 ... ♘a4

37 ♘c4 ♔g5!

38 ♘xb6 ♘xb6

39 ♖xb6 ♖f4!

The pawn on g4 will not run away, so Black should take the chance to force White's rook into a passive position. After ...♖f4-c4, White's rook will be tied down to defending the

weak pawn on c2. Then Black can safely capture the g4 pawn, gaining both a material and a positional advantage.

40 ♖d6 ♖c4

41 ♖d2 ♔xg4 *(255)*

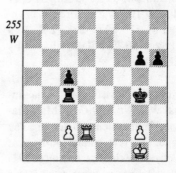

255
W

42 ♔f2 ♖c3

Imprisoning White's king. Now White can only wait to see how Black intends improving his position.

43 ♔g1 h5

44 ♔h2

White's idea is that after ...h4, ...♔f4 and ...g5-g4-g3+, he will be able to reply ♔h3. However, Black puts his king on h4 instead and then White's king is trapped on the back rank after ...g3+.

44 ... g5

45 ♖e2 ♔h4

46 ♖e4+ g4

47 ♖e2 g3+

48 ♔g1 ♔g4

49 ♔f1 ♖c4

0-1

White had seen enough. There are several ways to win; one method is to play the king over to attack the c2 pawn. Another is to play ...h4-h3, for example 50 ♖d2 h4 51 ♖e2 ♖f4+ 52 ♔g1 ♖d4 53 ♖e1 h3 54 gxh3+ ♔xh3 55 ♖c1 c4 56 c3 ♖d2 57 ♔h1 and now Black can force mate in seven by 57...g2+ 58 ♔g1 ♖e2 59 ♖d1 ♔g3 60 ♖a1 ♖e8 followed by ...♖h8-h1.

During May I participated in an unusual event – the AEGON Man-Machine Tournament, held in The Hague. This is an annual tournament which, at the time of writing (1994) is already into its ninth year. It is a Swiss event, with an equal number of human and machine participants; the pairings are made with the additional rule that man-man and machine-machine pairings are not allowed. In effect, every round is a match between men and machines. The average strength of the human participants is more or less constant from year to year, so the event provides a benchmark by which to measure the progress (if any) of the machines. It isn't completely clear whether this is valid, because as the humans become more experienced in playing against the machines, they also learn how the exploit the machines' weaknesses. I had taken part in the 1992 AEGON tournament, but my inexperience let me down and I finished with just 5/6. My choice of openings with Black was particularly poor, and two of the machines came away with a draw. In 1993 I was better prepared and this time I started with 5/5. An exciting last round game against Chessmachine The King ended in a draw, and I tied for first place with Bronstein on 5½/6.

There followed two more months of inactivity, which I devoted mainly to writing. I returned to the chessboard for a category 14 event held just down the road from the Semtex factory at Pardubice in the Czech Republic. I was nervous about my play after five months without a single game against a human being, and when I lost in the first round it appeared that my fears might be justified. I decided to play very cautiously during the rest of the tournament, and I eventually finished on 50%, having won just a single game against Stohl and drawn the other seven games. Not exactly a sparkling performance, but at least I had played myself back into form without too much damage to my Elo rating.

Unfortunately it is just here, at the end of July 1993, that this book comes to an end.